A LEAGUE *of* AIRMEN

U.S. AIR POWER IN THE GULF WAR

James A. Winnefeld ◆ **Preston Niblack** ◆ **Dana J. Johnson**

RAND

Project AIR FORCE

Prepared for the
United States Air Force
Approved for public release; distribution unlimited

The research reported here was sponsored by the United States Air Force under Contract F49620-91-C-0003. Further information may be obtained from the Strategic Planning Division, Directorate of Plans, Hq USAF.

Library of Congress Cataloging in Publication Data

Winnefeld, James A., 1929–
   A league of airmen : U.S. air power in the Gulf War / James
A. Winnefeld, Preston Niblack, Dana J. Johnson.
      p.   cm.
   "Prepared for the United States Air Force."
   "MR-343-AF."
   Bibliography: p.
   ISBN 0-8330-1503-6
   1. Persian Gulf War, 1991—Aerial operations, American.
2. Persian Gulf War, 1991—United States.   3. United States.
Air Force—History—Persian Gulf War, 1991.   I. Niblack,
Preston, 1957– .   II. Johnson, Dana J.   III. United States.
Air Force.   IV. RAND.   V. Title.
DS79.724.U6W56   1994
956.704´4248´0973—dc20   93-48872
                                    CIP

RAND is a nonprofit institution that seeks to improve public policy through research and analysis. RAND's publications do not necessarily reflect the opinions or policies of its research sponsors.

Published 1994 by RAND
1700 Main Street, P.O. Box 2138, Santa Monica, CA 90407-2138
To order RAND documents or to obtain additional information, contact Distribution Services: Telephone: (310) 451-7002; Fax: (310) 451-6915; Internet: order@rand.org.

The 1990–1991 war in the Persian Gulf was one of the most thoroughly reported and commented-on military actions in U.S. history. It etched a series of vivid media images in the public mind: tracer fire over Baghdad on the first night of the war; laser-guided bombs entering air shafts to destroy buildings with pinpoint accuracy; the "highway of death" where allied forces attacked Iraqi ground troops fleeing Kuwait. Most of these images featured air power and associated technology. The impact of these images, in conjunction with the fact that for many months air forces alone waged the campaign's only offensive operations, have helped to shape the widely held perception that air power was decisive in defeating Iraq.

Since the war's end, defense analysts and scholars have vigorously debated the validity of this perception. Some have argued that air power could have won the war alone, without the employment of ground forces, if only given more time to work. Others have disputed the validity and effectiveness of certain aspects of the air war, such as the strategic campaign. Yet others have focused on the shortcomings of some weapon systems to bolster their argument that air power performance was inadequate.

In an era of shrinking budgets and reduced forces, it becomes increasingly important to understand the potential contributions and limitations of various force elements. In this volume the authors have attempted to evaluate the claims and counterclaims of the current air power debate and to provide a comprehensive and objective account of the contributions and limitations of air power in the Gulf War.

RAND's Project AIR FORCE division conducted an extensive program of original research before, during, and after Operations Desert Shield and Desert Storm. This research effort covered many different aspects of operations during the Gulf War, including strategic airlift, munitions and logistics support, command and control, intelligence and bomb damage assessment, and analysis of enemy prisoner of war interviews, among other topics. This book draws on this body of original research, insofar as is possible under classification restrictions, as well as on the authors' interviews with participants and reviews of secondary sources. A significant effort has been expended over the last two years in cleaning, linking, and analyzing a vast quantity of raw data. These data and subsequent analyses were made available to both the Pentagon's Conduct of the Persian Gulf War analysis and the official Air Force study led by Eliot Cohen. Much of the data is still in classified or in draft form. Some of the more interesting unclassified data can be found tabulated in the appendix. Analysis and evaluation of this information and other lessons learned will be continued over the next several years.

RAND is a nonprofit institution that seeks to improve public policy through research and analysis. Project AIR FORCE, a federally funded research and development center, performs studies and analysis for the United States Air Force.

George Donohue
Director, Project AIR FORCE
RAND

CONTENTS

TABLES

ACKNOWLEDGMENTS

This study would not have been possible without the prior efforts of many individuals at RAND, in the services, and elsewhere who have sought to identify and assess the role of air power in the Gulf War. This study builds on the analysis RAND staff members conducted for the Air Force and other Defense Department agencies in 1990–1993 on specific topics such as operations, command and control, battle damage assessment, and logistics. In many respects they are coauthors of this book. These individuals include Lieutenant Colonel Joe Alt (former RAND Air Force Fellow), Lieutenant Colonel Michael Anderson (former RAND Air Force Fellow), Ruth Berg, Glenn Buchan, Major Robert Butler (former RAND Air Force Fellow), Mary Chenoweth, Natalie Crawford, Donald Emerson, John Folkeson, David Frelinger, Fred Frostic, Jean Gebman, Daniel Gonzales, Stephen Hosmer, Leland Joe, David Kassing, John Lund, Major Thomas Marshall (former RAND Air Force Fellow), Rich Mesic, Major David Minster (former RAND Air Force Fellow), Ted Parker, Katherine Poehlmann, Raymond Pyles, Hyman Shulman, Major Stewart Turner (former RAND Air Force Fellow), and Edward Warner. This study also benefits from an earlier RAND work conducted by two of the three authors and published in 1993 by the Naval Institute Press, entitled *Joint Air Operations: Pursuit of Unity in Command and Control, 1942–1991.* Many interviews with officers who directed and participated in the air campaign were conducted for the earlier effort, and they proved invaluable to this study as well.

We also wish to acknowledge our debt to James Coyne, Richard Hallion, and Eliot Cohen, and to the authors of the Pentagon's official *Conduct of the Persian Gulf War*, who preceded us in their analyses of the Gulf air war. To a large degree we have stood on their shoulders in writing this book.

In addition, the authors benefited from discussions with many officers, officials, and analysts in the Air Force, the Marine Corps, and the Navy. Jamil Nakhleh, Christine Fox, and the staff of the Center for Naval Analyses were particularly helpful in providing us with their Desert Storm Reconstruction reports; these reports helped furnish us with the Navy perspective on the air campaign. Discussions with Eliot Cohen, director of the Secretary of the Air Force's Gulf War Air Power Survey, and his staff were also useful. Follow-up discussions with several individuals, including Richard Hallion and Wayne Thompson, served to clarify our thinking on several key issues. Colonel William Mulcahy, USAF, Commander Theresa Dorphinghaus, USN, and others at USSPACECOM were also very helpful.

An early draft of this book was reviewed by RAND's Chris Bowie, Natalie Crawford, Fred Frostic, Jerry Sollinger, and Ken Watman. David Adamson provided a very useful critique at a later stage, and he gave ongoing assistance that helped us clarify our thinking and its expression.

We also benefited greatly from reviews of the manuscript by several key service participants in the air war, including Colonel John Bioty, USMC, Lieutenant Colonel David Deptula, USAF, Lieutenant General Buster C. Glosson, USAF, General Charles Horner, USAF, Lieutenant Colonel Richard Lewis, USAF, Rear Admiral Dan March, USN, and Lieutenant General Royal Moore, USMC (ret.). We are greatly in their debt for sharing with us their insights into the Gulf air war, correcting errors, and working to remove any single service bias. We are grateful to General Michael J. Dugan, USAF (ret.) and RAND's Brent Bradley for their many helpful comments and suggestions.

While none of these individuals agrees with all our judgments (and some would disagree strongly), we have benefited enormously from their counsel and recommended revisions, most of which were happily accepted and incorporated in the text. All the errors that remain, either of fact or interpretation, can only be attributed to the authors.

We also wish to express our thanks to our sponsor, Vice Chief of Staff General Michael P. C. Carns and his predecessor General John Loh, and to James A. Thomson, president of RAND, and George Donohue, vice president for Project AIR FORCE, who provided the impetus for this study and smoothed the way for us from a management perspective. The research for this study was conducted within Project AIR FORCE's Force Structure and Modernization program, headed by Natalie Crawford, and under the guidance of the Associate Director for Force Structure, Fred Frostic. Project AIR FORCE's Laura Zakaras, Emily Rogers, and Jessie Cho helped us make effective use of the extensive RAND research on the Gulf War. Lieutenant Tom Dillaplain, USAF, worked diligently to declassify portions of it for our use. Finally, we would be remiss if we did not mention the valuable help of Shirley Lithgow and Rosalie Fonoroff, who patiently and cheerfully prepared multiple versions of the manuscript.

AAA	Antiaircraft artillery
ABCCC	Airborne Command and Control Center
ACC	Airspace Coordination Center
ACE	Airborne command element
AFAC	Airborne forward air controller
AFB	Air Force Base
AFID	Antifratricide identification device
AFLC	Air Force Logistics Command
AFSPACECOM	Air Force Space Command
AI	Air interdiction
ALCM	Air-launched cruise missile
AMRAAM	Advanced mid-range air-to-air missile
ANGLICO	Air Naval Gunfire Liaison Company
AO	Area of operations
AOR	Area of responsibility
APC	Armored personnel carrier
APOD	Airport of debarkation
ARCENT	U.S. Army Component, Central Command
ASOC	Air Support Operations Center
ATACMS	Army Tactical Advanced Missile System
ATO	Air tasking order

AUTODIN	Automated digital network
AUTOVON	Automated voice network
AWACS	Airborne Warning and Control System
BAI	Battlefield air interdiction
BDA	Battle damage assessment
C^2	Command and control
C^3I	Command, control, communications, and intelligence
C^3IC	Coalition Coordination, Communications, and Integration Center
CAFMS	Computer-Aided Force Management System
CAMS	Communications Area Master Station (Navy)
CAP	Combat air patrol
CAS	Close air support
C-day	7 August 1990, Operation Desert Shield begins
CENTAF	U.S. Air Force component, Central Command
CENTCOM	U.S. Central Command (also USCENTCOM)
CEP	Circular error probable
CIA	Central Intelligence Agency
CINCCENT	Commander in Chief, U.S. Central Command (also USCINCCENT)
CJCS	Chairman, Joint Chiefs of Staff
CJTFME	Commander, Joint Task Force Middle East
CLF	Combat logistics force
CNA	Center for Naval Analyses
COA	Course of action
COCOM	Combatant command
CONOP	Concept of operations
CONOPS	Contingency operations
CONUS	Continental United States

CPGW	*Conduct of the Persian Gulf War* report (Department of Defense, April 1991)
CRAF	Civil Reserve Air Fleet
CRC	Control and Reporting Center
CSAR	Combat search and rescue
CSSA	Combat Supplies Support Activity
CUDIXS	Common User Digital Information Exchange System
DARPA	Defense Advanced Research Projects Agency
DARS	Daily Aerial Reconnaissance and Surveillance
DASC	Direct Air Support Center
DCA	Defense counterair; Defense Communications Agency
D-day	17 January 1991, Operation Desert Storm begins
DDN	Defense Data Network
DIA	Defense Intelligence Agency
DIAC	Defense Intelligence Analysis Center
DMA	Defense Mapping Agency
DMPI	Designated mean point of impact
DMSP	Defense Meteorological Satellite Program
DNA	Defense Nuclear Agency
DoD	Department of Defense
DRB	Division Ready Brigade
DSCS	Defense Satellite Communication System
DSP	Defense Support Program
ECM	Electronic countermeasures
EOSAT	Earth Observation Satellite Corporation
EPW	Enemy prisoners of war
EUCOM	(United States) European Command
EW	Electronic warfare
FAC	Forward air controller
FLIR	Forward-looking imaging infrared

FLTSAT	Fleet Satellite (Navy communications)
FMC	Full mission capable
FSCL	Fire support control line
FSE	Fire support element
Gapfiller	Leased portion of Marisat (maritime communications satellite) (Navy)
GAT	Guidance, apportionment, targeting (cell)
GCC	Gulf Cooperation Council
GCI	Ground control intercept
G-day	24 February 1991, Desert Storm ground campaign begins
GOES	Geostationary Orbiting Environmental Satellite
GPS	Global Positioning System
HARM	High-speed Anti-Radiation Missile
HET	Heavy equipment transporter
H-hour	0300 local time, 17 January 1991, the hour the war began
HIDACZ	High-density air control zone
HUMINT	Human intelligence
IADS	Integrated Air Defense System
IFF	Identification Friend or Foe
IMINT	Imagery intelligence
INMARSAT	International Maritime Satellite Organization
INTELSAT	International Telecommunications Satellite Organization
IOC	Initial operational capability
IR	Infrared
ITC	Intelligence Task Force
I&W	Indications and warning
JAIC	Joint Air Intelligence Center
JCS	Joint Chiefs of Staff
JFACC	Joint Force Air Component Commander
JFTS	Jet fuel, thermally stable

JIC	Joint Intelligence Center
JSTARS	Joint Surveillance Target Attack Radar System
JTCB	Joint Target Coordination Board
JTF	Joint task force
JTF-PF	Joint Task Force Proven Force
KTO	Kuwaiti theater of operations
LAAR	Low-altitude air refueling
LANTIRN	Low-altitude navigation and targeting infrared system for night
LEASAT	Leased Satellite (communications)
LGB	Laser-guided bomb
LOC	Lines of communication
LOROP	Long-range oblique photograph (camera)
MAC	Military Airlift Command
MACSAT	Multiple Access Communications Satellite
MAGTF	Marine Air-Ground Task Force
MAP	Master attack plan
MARCENT	U.S. Marine Corps component, Central Command
MARG	Mediterranean amphibious ready group
MAW	Marine Air Wing
MC	Mission capable
MC&G	Mapping, charting, and geodesy
MDS	Mission design series
MEB	Marine Expeditionary Brigade
MEF	Middle East Force (Navy); Marine Expeditionary Force (USMC)
MEU	Marine Expeditionary Unit
MIB	Military Intelligence Board
MILSATCOM	Military Satellite Communications
MLRS	Multiple launch rocket system

MTBF	Mean time between failure
MTL	Master target list
MV	Mobilization value
NATO	North Atlantic Treaty Organization; also name of satellite
NAVCENT	U.S. Navy component, Central Command
NBC	Nuclear, biological, chemical (weapons)
NCA	National Command Authority
NCTR	Noncooperative target recognition
NESDIS	National Environmental Data and Information Service
NMIC	National Military Intelligence Center
NMIST	National Military Intelligence Support Team
NOAA	National Oceanic and Atmospheric Administration; also name of satellite
NSA	National Security Agency
OB	Order of battle
OCA	Offensive counterair
ODS	Operation Desert Shield; Operation Desert Storm
OICC	Operational Intelligence Crisis Center
OPCON	Operational control
OPEC	Organization of Petroleum Exporting Countries
OPLAN	Operations plan
PAX	Passengers
PGM	Precision-guided munitions
POES	Polar Orbiting Environmental Satellite
POL	Petroleum, oil, lubricants
QRP	Quick reaction packet
RAF	Royal Air Force (U.K.)
RAS	Replenishment at sea
ROE	Rules of engagement
RSAF	Royal Saudi Air Force

SA	Selective Availability (GPS)
SAC	Strategic Air Command
SAM	Surface-to-air missile
SAR	Search and rescue
SEAD	Suppression of enemy air defenses
SHF	Super high frequency
SIGINT	Signals intelligence
SITREP	Situation report
SLAM	Standoff land attack missile
SLGR	Small, lightweight GPS receiver (unit)
SOC	Sector operations center
SOCCENT	Special Operations Command, Central Command
SOF	Special operations forces
SPEAR	Strike Projection Evaluation and Antiair Research (organization, USN)
SPG	Special planning group ("Black Hole")
SPINs	Special instructions
SPOT	Satellite Probatoire d'Observation de la Terre
SRBM	Short-range ballistic missile
STU	Secure telephone unit
TAC	Tactical Air Command
TACC	Tactical Air Control Center
TACON	Tactical control
TALD	Tactical air-launched decoy
TARPS	Tactical Aerial Reconnaissance Pod System
TBM	Tactical ballistic missile
TEL	Transporter-erector-launcher
TERCOM	Terrain contour mapping (Tomahawk guidance system)
TFS	Tactical fighter squadron
TFU	Tactical Forecast Unit

TFW	Tactical fighter wing
TLAM	Tomahawk Land Attack Missile
TPFDL	Time-phased force deployment list
TSS	Tactical shelter system
UAV	Unmanned aerial vehicle
UHF	Ultra high frequency
USA	United States Army
USAF	United States Air Force
USAFE	United States Air Forces Europe
USARSPACE	United States Army Space Command
USCENTCOM	U.S. Central Command (also CENTCOM)
USCINCCENT	Commander in Chief, U.S. Central Command (also CINCCENT)
USMC	United States Marine Corps
USN	United States Navy
USSPACECOM	United States Space Command
USTRANSCOM	United States Transportation Command
UTE	Utilization
VHF	Very high frequency
VTR	Video television recorder
WRSK	War Readiness Spares Kit

To the "League of Airmen"—

the men and women of the Gulf air war

Chapter One

INTRODUCTION

Although the air campaign was probably the most publicized element of the 1990–1991 Gulf War, little solid analysis to date has objectively evaluated its performance and its role in contributing to the Coalition victory against Saddam Hussein. The present volume is intended to fill that gap.

It may seem surprising that there is any gap to be filled. The Gulf War has certainly not lacked for articles, books, reports, and other commentary. It undoubtedly had the most reportorial coverage of any war in history. In spite of media complaints about restrictions placed on their activities, reporters were at headquarters and on the battlefield in unprecedented numbers.[1] Television coverage, picking up where it left off in Vietnam, was present at the scene of combat during the first minutes of the war and seldom left it thereafter. The war has also provided a fertile field for official fact gathering, "white papers," surveys, "reconstructions," and other documents that describe the contributions of one service, weapon system, or command. Outside analysts have not been slow off the mark. Many "instant histories" written by professional commentators have appeared on the book market.[2] Serious scholars are now engaged in describing the war and its implications for the future.[3]

The reporting of the war has been criticized from two points of view: it was unduly hampered by DoD-imposed restrictions, and it was conducted for the most part by amateurs in military matters, albeit amateurs with high-quality

---

[1] See comparative data in Winant G. Sidle, "Battle Behind the Scenes," *Military Review*, September 1991, p. 58.

[2] For one review of some of these histories, see Mackubin Thomas Owens, "Lessons of the Gulf War," *Strategic Review*, Winter 1992, pp. 50–54.

[3] In particular, the Gulf War Air Power Survey, commissioned by the Secretary of the Air Force to conduct a comprehensive evaluation of air power in the Gulf War, has produced a multivolume classified study covering all aspects of air operations in Operations Desert Shield and Desert Storm—focusing, as noted below, on the Air Force contribution. We had access to and drew on a preliminary draft of the unclassified summary report; the final report was released in January 1994: Thomas A. Keaney and Eliot A. Cohen, *Gulf War Air Power Survey Summary Report*, Washington, D.C.: U.S. Government Printing Office, 1993 (hereafter cited as *GWAPS*.)

reporting skills.[4] Both criticisms, if valid, work to limit the utility of much of the media coverage of the war. The postwar analyses conducted by the Department of Defense have suffered from different maladies: a mixture of pride and defensiveness, a masking of important doctrinal and organizational differences among the services, and an attempt to use the Gulf War experience to support specific force capabilities and weapons programs. Biases and selective reporting have crept into service-sponsored analysis and after-action reports.[5] Many have cited the "unique" nature of the war to defend service capabilities not fully utilized during the war. Others, both within and outside DoD, have enshrined the 1986 Defense Reorganization Act (Goldwater-Nichols) as the architect of victory.

Uninformed (or constrained) reporting and special-interest commentary, then, are the principal shortcomings to be observed in much of the analysis published to date. These shortcomings apply particularly to the air war. Except in rare instances, reporters and analysts were not aloft during the war. And differences among the services are nowhere as acute as in their views on the role, control, and performance of air power. Few books have been devoted to the air campaign in the Gulf War. Their number include Richard P. Hallion's *Storm Over Iraq* and James P. Coyne's *Airpower in the Gulf.* The Air Force's *Gulf War Air Power Survey* is the most exhaustive official DoD document devoted to the air war. All are sponsored by the Air Force or written by historians affiliated with the Air Force. There have been no books to date that focus on the air campaign from the point of view of the other services. The book now before the reader is also sponsored by the Air Force, but our objective has been to take a broader "total force" air power view. We carry no Air Force brief, and some of our observations will go against that service's grain. We have been careful to portray the contributions of the other air services and their views on the Gulf air war. Almost as many Navy and Marine officers as Air Force officers were interviewed as we undertook the research that forms the basis for this book. We

---

[4]The former point of view is set out in the following: Everett E. Dennis et al., *The Media at War: The Persian Gulf Conflict: The Press and the Persian Gulf Conflict. A Report of the Gannett Foundation,* New York: Columbia University Press, 1991; and John J. Fialka, *Hotel Warriors: Covering the Gulf War,* Washington, D.C.: Woodrow Wilson Center Press, 1991. Fialka and Peter Braestrup (who wrote the foreword to the Fialka book) are sympathetic to the latter point of view, one widely held by military officers who served in the Gulf. For a somewhat contemptuous view of the alleged amateurish reporting of the Gulf War, see James F. Dunnigan and Austin Bay, *From Shield to Storm: High-Tech Weapons, Military Strategy, and Coalition Warfare in the Persian Gulf,* New York: William Morrow, 1992, pp. 446–464. Richard Hallion in his book *Storm over Iraq: Air Power and the Gulf War,* Washington, D.C.: Smithsonian Press, 1992, p. 2, notes that even the military commentators employed by the news media were generally specialists in ground or naval warfare who "consistently ignored or (at least) underestimated air power and its potentialities." An exception was Major General Perry Smith, USAF (ret.), who commented for CNN.

[5]For one commentary on how the Gulf air war experience is being exploited to advocate new service-specific programs, see Barton Gelman, "Disputes Delay Gulf War History," *The Washington Post,* January 28, 1992, p. A14.

eschew any brief for a particular service, a particular weapon system, a particular theory for the application of air power, or a particular model for the future role of air power in conflict. In preparing this study, we have drawn on original research conducted at RAND and elsewhere, on interviews conducted for this and an earlier study, and on secondary sources where necessary to complete the story or provide a range of views on potentially controversial points.

Our purpose is to provide an independent evaluation of the role and performance of air power in the Persian Gulf War. We have sought to be inclusive, focusing on all aspects of air operations in Desert Shield and Desert Storm, not just on one period or aspect of the air campaign or on the performance of certain weapon systems (although necessarily some topics have received less than their due). We have devoted chapters to what we consider some of the unheralded but crucial contributors to the success of air power and to areas where air power made a crucial contribution to success, namely strategic mobility, logistics and sustainment, and information management. And we have sought to address some of the important and often controversial issues, sometimes bucking the conventional wisdom and sometimes confirming it on such issues as unity of command and control of joint air operations, the importance of high-technology weaponry in the Coalition victory, and the role played by air power in achieving victory against Iraq.

We begin in Chapter Two with an overview of developments in U.S. security policy in the Gulf region and trends in military developments in the years preceding the Gulf War. In many respects, the war occurred at the moment that numerous trend lines intersected—the end of the Cold War, a new focus on regional security issues, the culmination of the defense buildup of the 1980s and of developments in service doctrines and organization—all of which combined to the advantage of the United States and its allies during the confrontation with Iraq.

In Chapter Three, we review in some detail the initial deployment of air power to the Gulf, with emphasis on the role of airlift and the buildup of combat air power. The deployment was one of the war's extraordinary successes, revealing how capable operators were in overcoming the major obstacles posed by the lack of detailed planning. Chapter Four discusses planning for the air campaign. That campaign began with a plan, code-named Instant Thunder, developed by the Air Staff (rather than at U.S. Central Command, or USCENTCOM, headed by General Schwarzkopf), that reflected a particular Air Force doctrinal view on the strategic role of air power. This plan was then expanded by the theater commander's planners into a broader campaign including both strategic targets and a much larger battlefield-preparation phase against the Iraqi army in Kuwait and southern Iraq. Only the first three days of the war were scripted in advance in the Master Attack Plan. We also describe the process of *daily* planning of the air war that followed the opening, scripted phase.

Command, control, communications, and organization in the air war are the subject of Chapter Five. How command relations were organized and interacted, and how control of air operations was exercised, provide important insights into the progress in achieving unity in command and control of joint air operations following the 1986 Goldwater-Nichols legislation and successive interservice agreements.

Chapter Six describes the execution of the air campaign, beginning on the night of 17 January 1991. The Coalition delivered a stunning blow on the first night from which the Iraqis never fully recovered, and the allies continued to pound Iraq unrelentingly for the next 42 days. The day-to-day conduct of operations is described, as well as the course of the campaign. The weight of effort shifted after the first two weeks from strategic targets to bombing Iraqi positions in Kuwait in preparation for the ground campaign, the final phase of air operations being support of the ground war. We assess the effects of each phase of the campaign on the final outcome.

Chapter Seven discusses tactics, including Scud hunting, strike tactics, defense suppression, and close air support. There were a few noteworthy innovations in tactics developed during the war, such as "tank plinking," but for the most part the Gulf War was not notable for revolutionary tactics. Rather, the services built on the successful tactics of earlier operations, and exploited changes in technology to improve upon them.

Chapters Eight and Nine cover two other topics that are unglamorous but contributed mightily to the Coalition success: information management and logistics. The former received its share of (mostly negative) publicity, including from General Schwarzkopf himself. The intelligence system that was cobbled together virtually from scratch for Desert Storm revealed deficiencies in the organization of intelligence capabilities in support of a theater commander, but it also revealed just how big a player information management can be. Desert Storm was truly the first "information war." It was also a showcase for developments in service and joint logistics doctrine. The highly successful logistics operation in Desert Shield and Desert Storm was the key to sustaining the intensive, round-the-clock tempo of operations that ultimately drove the Iraqi army to collapse once the ground war began.

Chapter Ten reviews the performance of several key air war systems. While some of the newer and more spectacular systems garnered much of the media attention—notably the F-117A stealth fighter—much of the work was still done by systems that had seen service in Vietnam. Much of what appeared "revolutionary" in air warfare on television reveals itself to have been the product of a continual evolution in military technology, captured after two decades of quiet and steady work in the sudden glare of publicity that surrounded the Gulf War. Such revolution as there was lay more in integrating air operations into a single campaign format than in new aviation hardware.

Finally, in Chapters Eleven and Twelve, we offer some concluding thoughts on the performance and role, respectively, of air power in the Gulf War. Where did air power perform particularly well, and where did it fall short of expectations? As mentioned before, it was in the largely unseen (by the press and public) and unglamorous functions of mobility, logistics, and information management that air power excelled, as well as in the combat functions. We also examine the *joint* performance of air power, that is, the integration of air forces from all three services (and other nations) into an effectively applied whole.

Was Desert Storm so "unique" that no valid lessons can be drawn from it? What role did air power really play in winning the Gulf War? Was it "decisive"? Certainly, the war highlighted air power's role in ways that future operations may not, and it highlighted the contributions of land-based air power especially. Mass, overwhelming technological superiority, and lack of determined opposition may not characterize future wars as they did this one. As a whole, air power was a decisive instrument of military power *in this war*. It played the critical "enabling" function that allowed Coalition ground forces to win a quick and nearly bloodless victory and eject Iraq's army from Kuwait.

Air power's advocates will certainly be tempted to oversell air power, to overlook both the advantages the Coalition enjoyed in the Gulf and the deficiencies in the performance of air power in their eagerness to capture as large a share as possible of a shrinking resource pie. Air power's detractors, on the other hand, predictably will focus on its shortcomings and overlook its undeniable achievements in helping achieve the Coalition's objectives with historically low casualties. We hope that this volume, without overselling either air power in general or any one service's contributions or shortcomings, will provide a fair and evenhanded evaluation that will contribute to making air power even more effective in the future.

Chapter Two

THE SETTING FOR THE GULF AIR WAR

Wars frequently begin ten years before the first shot is fired.
—K. K. V. Casey

The brief desert war in early 1991 provided a test of the importance and effectiveness of air power. In one sense, the air campaign was a controlled experiment on the modern application of force—with most of the variables under the tight control of the United States. After a series of post–World War II conflicts and contingency operations in which the contribution of air power was masked in part by its interaction with other combat arms and in part by the constraints of the conflict scenario, Operation Desert Storm proved a demonstration of air command and control, weapons, and sustainability. The Gulf campaign had three distinct phases:

- A diplomatic and maritime phase extending from early August 1990, elements of which continue as these words are written, a period during which Iraq was isolated strategically and an unopposed Coalition force buildup was conducted.

- An air combat phase (while the first phase continued) from 17 January 1991 through the end of the war on 28 February 1991, a period during which the enemy's "centers of gravity" and his field army in and around Kuwait were systematically neutralized.

- A ground phase (while the first two phases continued) from 24 February 1991 through the end of the war, a period during which the Iraqi army was rolled up and ejected from Kuwait.

Without downplaying the importance of the first phase, our focus in this book is principally on air power planning for, and operations in, the second and third phases. Although Coalition helicopters played their own distinctive role in the air campaign, in this book they are considered as adjuncts to land and naval forces. We recognize the artificiality of this assumption: Does it matter whether air-delivered ordnance is launched from a rotary or fixed-wing platform? Our answer is, of course not—particularly if you are on the receiving end. But from the point of view of the "sender" or "owner," helicopter forces were subject to different control and support systems and were used with few exceptions by and in direct support of surface field commanders.[1]

DEFINING DESERT STORM AS AN INTERSECTION OF TREND LINES

The Desert Storm air campaign has been cited as unique in many dimensions: terrain, weather, access to the theater, existing base structures, maladroitness of the opponent, etc.[2] In Chapter Twelve, we will discuss this matter in some detail. But in a larger sense, Desert Storm was unique as an intersection of trend lines. There was a brief time at the end of the Cold War—perhaps over a period of 12–24 months—when the time was ripe for the effective employment of U.S. military power against a regional opponent in an operation enjoying broad international and U.S. domestic support.[3] That opponent emerged in the form of Saddam Hussein, who went on to oblige an international coalition by playing to its strengths and misunderstanding his own weakness. The trends that defined that short period included the following:

- A greater U.S. willingness, as the Vietnam experience faded, to use deployable forces to protect vital interests, e.g., Grenada 1983, Libya 1986, and Panama 1989.[4]

- An increasing U.S. sensitivity to events in the Gulf and potential threats to the national interest in that region, e.g., the fall of the Shah and the U.S. response to the Soviet invasion of Afghanistan in 1979, the Iran-Iraq war in 1980–1988, and the Persian Gulf tanker war in 1987–1988.[5]

---

[1]Two of the authors used this somewhat artificial division in an earlier work (James A. Winnefeld and Dana J. Johnson, *Joint Air Operations: Pursuit of Unity in Command and Control, 1942–1991*, Annapolis: Naval Institute Press, 1993). If one opens the field of inquiry to helicopters, there is little rationale for not opening it up to artillery and naval gunfire, and thence to direct-fire weapons. We have chosen to focus on fixed-wing aircraft because they delivered the largest tonnage of ordnance during the campaign, and because they are the usual focus of differences of opinion on doctrine, tactics, and systems.

[2]A literature is developing on the "unique" features of the Gulf War. One of the best catalogs is contained in James A. Blackwell, Michael J. Mazarr, and Don M. Snider, *The Gulf War: Military Lessons Learned*, Washington, D.C.: Center for Strategic and International Studies, July 1991.

[3]Michael A. Palmer reaches a similar conclusion. See his article "The Storm in the Air: One Plan, Two Air Wars," *Air Power History*, Winter 1992, p. 25.

[4]Harry G. Summers, Jr., *On Strategy II: A Critical Analysis of the Gulf War*, New York: Dell Press, 1992, pp. 7–19.

[5]See Christopher J. Bowie, *Concepts of Operations and USAF Planning for Southwest Asia*, RAND, R-3125, 1984. See also OSD (PA&E), *Capabilities for Limited Contingencies in the Persian Gulf*, a 1979

- The rise of Iraqi military power and their propensity to use it when regional and global powers were apparently distracted by other events.[6]

- The technological evolution in warfare, e.g., increasing reliance on space-based communications and surveillance systems, the fielding of accurate precision-guided munitions in large numbers, and the improved maintainability of combat systems.

- The improved professionalism of the U.S. military that resulted from institution of the all-volunteer force in the 1970s, improved training, and the defense buildup of the 1980s.[7]

- A movement towards better commanded, organized, and supported joint operations and associated training. This movement started before the passage of the Goldwater-Nichols legislation and reflected a gradual cultural change in the services based on a realization that no one service could go it alone.[8]

As these trends moved to their convergence point in the summer of 1990, Iraq invaded Kuwait. The invasion led to the establishment of a U.S.-led coalition that was based heavily on the demonstrated U.S. will to not "let the Iraqi aggression stand" and on major relevant U.S. military capabilities. Before examining the events of that summer, we will discuss each of the trends that defined the moment and the events that were to follow over the next seven months. Those trends had particular relevance for the role of air power in the ensuing Gulf War.

The End of the Post-Vietnam Era

The wounds that the Vietnam experience inflicted on the American national psyche have been slow to heal. But even at the height of the Vietnam-induced malaise and the beginning of the recovery from it, there was evidence that a reaction would set in. The American public's attention span is short and its outlook fundamentally forward rather than backward looking. The trauma of the Iranian hostage experience in 1979–1980 worked to produce a nadir in public confidence in the ability of the United States to influence events overseas and in

---

work authored principally by RAND colleague Paul Davis working with Paul D. Wolfowitz. The Davis-Wolfowitz study (originally classified) examined a broad range of possible Persian Gulf contingencies, including notably an Iraqi invasion of Kuwait, and proposed a variety of force-building and presence-enhancing measures that were subsequently realized.

[6]Hallion (1992), pp. 124–132.

[7]The buildup commenced during the last year of the Carter administration (with the FY80 DoD budget), but the major force increases and system modernization occurred as a result of initiatives taken during the Reagan administration.

[8]This development was not uniform nor always accepted, particularly in the Navy and the Air Force.

the competence of the U.S. military. But that feeling of powerlessness carried the seeds of a more activist role in foreign affairs, a determination to improve the U.S. military establishment, and a much-reduced reluctance to use America's improved military power. The election of Ronald Reagan in November 1980 served to underline the new direction in U.S. security policy and the acquisition of capabilities to carry it out.

Even during the Iranian hostage crisis, the Carter administration with no good options attempted the ill-fated Desert One operation—an obvious demonstration of an increased willingness to use force when the stakes were high enough. The Reagan administration, though still sensitive to the dangers of open-ended military involvement on the Vietnam model, initiated a more activist foreign policy (including armed intervention) against a backdrop of the largest peacetime force buildup in American history. Intervention in Grenada and Lebanon in the early 1980s was followed by strikes against Libya in the mid-1980s and the Gulf tanker war later in the decade.

There were still some echoes of Vietnam in such official statements as the Weinberger doctrine that laid out very stringent conditions that must be met before U.S. forces were committed to combat.[9] But for the most part the Reagan administration emphasized national self-confidence and strong military capabilities while carefully picking its targets—the ill-fated Lebanon intervention in 1983 being the only major exception.

This trend toward lowering the barriers to intervention when major interests were at stake was continued in the Bush administration, as best illustrated by force deployments in the Philippines and to Panama in 1989. U.S. air power played a key role in all these post-Vietnam interventions. In some it played the only military role, as in the cases of the December 1983 strike into Lebanon and the April 1986 strikes into Libya. In other cases, air power performed an "enabling" function for the other forms of U.S. military power. Air power was becoming an equal partner with naval power in providing rapid response to protect U.S. interests. Moreover, increasingly it was being wielded in a joint environment that put a premium on operating with other arms and across the air forces of all services.

In retrospect, it is clear that there was a renewed U.S. readiness to use force to achieve its security objectives when the Soviet Union was not directly involved. Saddam Hussein in the summer of 1990 was to provide a test of this readiness: a tyrant and aggressor in defiance of the UN Charter, a threat to U.S. access to

---

[9]For a reprise of the tests that armed intervention must meet and their applicability to the 1990 Gulf crisis, see Caspar W. Weinberger, "An Ideal Case for Military Intervention," *Los Angeles Times*, August 9, 1990, p. B7.

Middle East oil, an opponent who could be isolated diplomatically and militarily, and a theater well suited to the strengths of U.S. military power. The contrast with Korea and Vietnam could not have been more stark. The air weapon available to the United States had been improved, tested, and made ready.

THE GULF AS THE NEW COCKPIT OF U.S. SECURITY INTERESTS[10]

The perceptible decline of the Soviet Union in the mid-to-late 1980s greatly reduced the threat to U.S. interests in the Middle East, provided scope for anti-U.S. actors to pursue their interests outside a Cold War context, and focused U.S. attention as never before on the Gulf region. The establishment and buildup of the Rapid Deployment Joint Task Force (RDJTF) and its ultimate successor, U.S. Central Command (USCENTCOM), was a tangible response to these developments and was supported by large increases in U.S. military capabilities in the region. The United States expanded the base at Diego Garcia, procured maritime prepositioning ships (to be based at Diego Garcia and at Guam) and Marine equipment, sold a great deal of equipment and munitions to regional states, and developed a series of base-access agreements. In addition, presence was increased by maintaining a deployed carrier battle group in the region and conducting short-duration Air Force deployments in discretely conducted exercises with Gulf security partners.[11] Naval power in or near the region and deployable air power from outside the region were the only forces available to respond quickly to defend U.S. interests.

These factors provided the backdrop for the two major contingency operations in the Gulf region occurring during the 1980s: Desert One in 1980 and the tanker reflagging and escorting (Operation Earnest Will) in 1987–1988. The latter operation resulted in the activation of a largely standby U.S. regional command structure. When the focus of U.S. planning began to shift from Soviet and Iranian threats to an Iraqi threat in late 1989, the tempo of U.S. force deployments and exercises in the region increased as well.[12]

During this period of increased planning intensity, the question of the availability of Gulf bases—whether or when under conditions of ambiguous warning—

---

[10]See Michael A. Palmer, *Guardians of the Gulf,* New York: The Free Press, 1992, pp. 85–127, for an excellent discussion of the events summarized here.

[11]OSD (PA&E) (1979).

[12]United States Department of Defense, *Conduct of the Persian Gulf War; Final Report to Congress Pursuant to Title V of the Persian Gulf Conflict Supplemental Authorization and Personnel Benefits Act of 1991 (Public Law 102-25),* Washington D.C.: Department of Defense, April 1992 (hereafter cited as *CPGW*), p. 42.

moved to the fore. Curiously, most of the focus of contingency planning was on the maritime and ground dimensions as OPLAN 1002-90, the principal plan for the defense of Saudi Arabia, was developed. Although a major air deployment was envisioned and many suitable airfields in the region were potentially available, planning for offensive air operations in the theater had received less attention.

The Rise of Iraqi Military Power

The rise of Iraqi military power was clearer after the fact than before. The long war with Iran served to build up Iraq's military machine—a machine that benefited from subsidies from other oil-rich Arab states. Less obvious was the surreptitious accumulation of the necessary capabilities to manufacture chemical, biological, and nuclear weapons and the means to deliver them. Iraq had created an army on the Soviet model with the means to conduct a heavy-firepower defense of vital areas and with sufficient mobility to move quickly and in mass over desert terrain. Its air force was provided with impressive air-defense and missile equipment, even though it was seriously hampered by inadequate crew training and an overly rigid Soviet-style control system. A crude short-range tactical ballistic missile capability had been put in place and tried out against the cities of Iran. Only the Iraqi navy was comparatively neglected, though equipped with a mining capability that was to pose problems to Coalition naval force movement in the upper reaches of the Gulf.

Since the Gulf War, some have assessed this military as a Third World force that looked better on paper than in the field.[13] Those who now hold this opinion were not much in evidence before the war started, when news and expert accounts commented on a battle-hardened Iraqi army entrenched behind multi-layered defenses built by some of the best combat engineers in the world. Some have commented that the Iraqi forces were more war-weary than battle-hardened. Whatever the fact and fiction of these various observations, it is clear that the Iraqi forces were the best-equipped forces the United States had faced since World War II. To be second rate is not quite as much a disadvantage when one is fighting on one's own turf and one's enemy must deploy from bases halfway around the world. In our view, the Iraqis were a worthy opponent but their forces were fragile. They weren't beaten so much by better weapons as by more professional and better-trained Coalition forces. We will return to this subject in Chapter Eleven.

---

[13]U.S. News & World Report, *Triumph Without Victory: The Unreported History of the Persian Gulf War*, New York: Random House, 1992, pp. 404–409 (hereafter cited as *Triumph Without Victory*).

The Technological Evolution in Warfare

Revolution is too strong a word to describe what happened to the tools of warfare during the 1970s and 1980s.[14] Many of the weapons used in the Gulf War were updated versions of systems used in Vietnam. These veteran systems included the A-6, F-4, F-111, B-52, A-7, KC-135, OV-10, SH-3, UH-1 (Huey), C-130, and CH-46 aircraft and such ordnance as laser-guided bombs, antiradiation missiles, and most rapid-fire gun systems. Most of the iron bombs used would have been old friends to the weapons-loading sergeants of 25 years earlier.

There were some important new players: the F-117A stealth fighter, the Tomahawk missile, all the first-line tactical fighters deployed by the United States, most of the tanks and fighting vehicles, and the JSTARS and AWACS aircraft. But some of the highest-leverage systems were unseen to all but the practiced eye: space support to battlefield commanders, enormous and very flexible communications and computer systems, and logistics support systems that undergirded very high equipment reliability and in-service rates. *If there was a "revolution," it involved placing all these systems—old and new—into high-intensity combat together for the first time and demonstrating prowess in using and maintaining them.* While it is true that many problems were encountered, most were either manageable or did not prove to be critical. This excellent performance clearly discomfited the military reform analysts and their spokesmen who were more focused on waste, overlapping functions, and operational incompetence than on the improvements made since the Vietnam era.[15]

The real contribution of technology was to enable the Coalition to win efficiently with few casualties on either side. An apocryphal quote attributed to U.S. veterans of the war is "We could have won with their weapons." Whether or not that is true, the professionalism of the U.S. military was carefully noted by friend and foe alike.

Revived Professionalism[16]

Perhaps nothing so surprised—and delighted—the American public and overturned preconceptions built up since the Vietnam experience as the profes-

---

[14]Hallion (1992), pp. 275–312, contains an excellent summary of the advances of combat air technology between the Vietnam War and Operation Desert Storm. Hallion does believe that a technology revolution occurred between these wars (pp. 279, 293, 295). See also Michael J. Mazarr, Don M. Snider, and James A. Blackwell, Jr., *Desert Storm: The Gulf War and What We Learned*, Boulder, Colorado: Westview Press, 1993, pp. 97–101. For a more skeptical view (and one more in line with our own), see *GWAPS*, chap. 10.

[15]Owens (1992), p. 50.

[16]Hallion (1992), pp. 83–120, contains a particularly useful account of the renewal of military confidence and professionalism between the Vietnam War and the Gulf War.

sional performance of their military establishment during the Gulf War. While it is true that the U.S. war machine was fighting a Third World enemy and not the Soviets, there were many before the Coalition victory who cited the combat experience of the Iraqi forces, their expertise at defense, their strong positions, their tenacity, their Soviet advisers, and so forth as providing the basis for a true test of American military mettle.[17]

The fact of the matter is that the quality of the U.S. armed forces had improved. A deliberate effort to overcome the mistakes of the Vietnam era, the movement to an all-volunteer force starting in 1972–1973 with the attendant increases in military compensation, the motivational effects of new hardware, and a deliberate focus on quality in both hardware and training (at the expense of quantity if need be) all combined to produce a very competent, well-trained, professional force. At the colonel (and Navy equivalent) level and above, this force was commanded by veterans of the Vietnam conflict. It had trained with a very capable prospective opponent—the Cold War Soviet Union—in mind. The Gulf War was the final exam of the force buildup of the 1980s: U.S. forces passed with high grades.

The air services in particular were beneficiaries of this wealth of experience and professionalism. Major fighter and strike weapons schools had been established during and after the Vietnam era, and flight crews benefited enormously from the training they delivered. These crews had the *routine* of combat operations down pat and were left free to deal with *what was different* or demanded the most attention in Gulf air operations.

Maintenance personnel had received training of equal quality and were superbly supported by the necessary support equipment and spares, as we will see in Chapter Nine. Often forgotten is the fact that the all-volunteer force placed a premium on an older and more experienced and costly force. Trained personnel were retained and improved, whereas during the draft era the high personnel turnover required continuous training on the more basic levels. Instead of the death spiral of talent and readiness that characterized the draft-driven force of the Vietnam era, there was an updraft of synergy as well-trained officers and NCOs transitioned to modern systems that were serviced by trained ground crews who could keep systems flying.[18] Personnel economists on congressional staffs and in the Department of Defense complained of an ex-

---

[17]See Dunnigan and Bay (1992), pp. 346–402 (a chapter with the title "Myths, Misconceptions, and Revelations"), for a systematic debunking of poorly informed judgments about Iraqi and Coalition force performance during the war.

[18]Rear Admiral Daniel March reminds us that these benefits were enhanced by the improvements in maintainability incorporated in the newer aircraft systems such as the F-15, F-16, and F/A-18.

pensive (personnel) force, but their defeats in the budget battles were translated into victory in the air over Iraq and Kuwait.

A hallmark of this renewed professionalism was the post-Vietnam revival of interest in service and joint doctrine. After Vietnam, the services returned to the study of war and the exercise of military power. As Mackubin Thomas Owens points out:

> Although the doctrines of such services may have differed among themselves, they shared an emphasis on maintaining the initiative, integrating logistics, and pitting strength against weakness. . . .
>
> Many of the commentators who were predicting heavy losses . . . had been in the forefront in calling for doctrinal change in the U.S. military. Ironically, however, most of them had apparently missed the significance of the doctrinal revolution of the past decade.[19]

Saddam's forces were not to be confronted with the caricature of the Vietnam-era GI—on drugs, full of self-doubt, unable to shoot straight, and led by officers who did not understand the nature of the fight. Rather, they were to meet steely-eyed professionals who knew exactly what to do and how to do it. These professionals were to wield the air weapons with deft precision and decisive effect.

The Arrival of (Almost) True "Jointness"

Not only did Saddam face a band of professional soldiers, sailors, marines, and airmen, he faced a force that had made enormous strides in exercising, operating, and fighting together. While the media have given a large share of the credit for this improvement in joint war fighting to the 1986 Department of Defense Reorganization Act (Goldwater-Nichols), it is unfair to overlook the importance of the many steps the services and unified commands within DoD had taken before August 1990 to achieve unity of effort and effective combined-arms operations.[20] Goldwater-Nichols was an important milestone, but even the law of the land is not omnipotent when it comes to overcoming long and strongly held views. The services (by themselves) had reached a series of agreements that boded well for the success of the 1986 legislation. Starting with the Johnson-McConnell agreement of 1966 (sorting out who "owned" theater fixed-wing and helicopter assets), proceeding to the 1982 Navy–Air Force agreement (further defining the Air Force role in maritime warfare), then to the

---

[19]Owens (1992), p. 53. For a similar assessment, see Stephen S. Rosenfeld, "Military Doctrine Today," *The Washington Post*, March 22, 1991, p. 23.

[20]Summers (1992), pp. 110, 243–245.

Army–Air Force agreement of 1984 (the "34 initiatives" that inter alia enhanced the AirLand Battle doctrine), and finally to the 1986 "omnibus agreement" (clarifying the control of Marine air operations), major steps were taken to close ranks among the air services.[21]   At the same time, many important steps were taken in improving and expanding joint system acquisition programs such as in missiles and bombs.

In the doctrinal realm and in operational practice, important complementary steps took place. A series of significant joint publications centering on air operations were tested and accepted—step by step putting in place the procedures that would be used so effectively in Desert Storm. In operational practice, more use of joint task forces became the norm, and their use was demonstrated in operations against Libya, in Grenada, and in Panama. More attention was paid to joint exercises—with CINCPAC (particularly Seventh Fleet and Fifth Air Force) and CINCLANT (JTF 120) leading the way, but with CENTCOM not far behind.[22] Indeed, in the month before the Iraqi invasion of Kuwait, U.S. Central Command held a major command post exercise, "Internal Look 90," that was to become in effect a rehearsal for Operation Desert Shield.

Goldwater-Nichols had the important effect of "empowering the CINC" by letting him organize his command as he saw fit, without fear (unlike the Vietnam experience) of being sandbagged in Washington by a service chief who saw service-specific doctrine or other interests violated. A CINC could now set up a functional component commander to coordinate and task the air forces of all services in theater. But all this good news can be overemphasized. There remained important unresolved differences among the services as well as service practices and states of mind that did not enhance joint operations. We will discuss this point at greater length in Chapter Five. Suffice it to say that in spite of these difficulties, the nation's fighting organizations were never better prepared to conduct a joint campaign from the outset than they were for Desert Storm.

Looking back over these intersecting trends, we see a United States that had largely thrown off the shackles of the Vietnam syndrome, confronting an enemy in a region of vital interest, and fielding forces equipped with technologically advanced systems and manned by professionals who were trained to conduct effective joint and combined operations. The contrast with Korea in 1950 and Vietnam in 1965 could hardly be clearer. But this comparison has not discussed a theory, doctrine, and plan for wielding the air weapon. Would the mind and

---

[21]Winnefeld and Johnson (1993), pp. 100–103.

[22]CINCPAC and CINCLANT are Commander in Chief, Pacific and Atlantic, respectively.

the hand guiding the air weapon be better prepared for the Gulf conflict than they were in earlier wars?

THE STATE OF AIR DOCTRINE ON THE EVE OF THE GULF WAR

To understand how matters stood in early August 1990, one must go back to the Vietnam experience. There is a school of thought that holds that the Air Force mislearned the lessons of air power employment in Vietnam and held the (purportedly mistaken) belief that air power, particularly Linebacker II operations in December 1972, finally brought the North Vietnamese to the bargaining table.[23] There were echoes of the Korean War experience, in which the Air Force interpretation of the importance of air power in that conflict after the winter of 1950–1951 was at variance with opinions held by many other observers. Regardless, the central tenets of the Air Force view as expressed in its doctrinal publications remained unchanged: that air power (properly employed) could be the decisive weapon, and that unity of air command was the sine qua non of proper employment.

The three leading theorists of air power to emerge during the post-Vietnam period were Colonel John Boyd on tactics, Colonel Thomas Cardwell on command and organization, and Colonel John Warden on the linkage between strategy and the operational art.[24] Their views were to be put to the test of combat in the Gulf War, since they provided much of the intellectual underpinnings for both the Joint Force Air Component Commander (JFACC) organization of General Charles Horner and the master strike plan for the first few days of the war. All owed much to the experience and writings of Generals George Kenney and William Momyer.[25]

---

[23]See Mark Clodfelter's *The Limits of Air Power: The American Bombing of North Vietnam,* New York: The Free Press, 1989; also his "Of Demons, Storms, and Thunder," *Airpower Journal,* Winter 1991, pp. 17–32; Caroline F. Ziemke, "Promises Fulfilled? The Prophets of Airpower and Desert Storm," paper presented before the Washington Strategy Seminar series on Airpower and the New Security Environment, January 1992, pp. 14–15; and Earl H. Tilford, Jr. "Setup: Why and How the U.S. Air Force Lost in Vietnam," *Armed Forces and Society,* Spring 1991, pp. 327–342. For contrary views, see William W. Momyer, *Air Power in Three Wars,* Washington, D.C.: Office of Air Force History, 1978; and Charles A. Horner, "The Air Campaign," *Military Review,* September 1991, p. 17.

[24]See, in particular, Warden's *The Air Campaign: Planning for Combat,* Washington, D.C.: National Defense University Press, 1988, and Cardwell's *Command Structure for Theater Warfare: The Quest for Unity of Command,* Maxwell AFB, Alabama: Air University Press, September 1984. In addition to these theorists, there were many perceptive historians and analysts of the Air Force experience, including Price Bingham, Carl Builder, Mark Clodfelter, Dennis Drew, Alan Gropman, Richard Hallion, I. B. Holley, Jr., Lieutenant General Brad Hosmer, General William W. Momyer, John J. Sbrega, John Schlight, Earl H. Tilford, Barry Watts, John Werrell, and Carolyn Ziemke, among many others.

[25]Momyer (1978) and George C. Kenney, *General Kenney Reports,* Washington, D.C.: Office of Air Force History, 1987.

The official Air Force doctrinal publication, Air Force Manual 1–1, *Basic Aerospace Doctrine*, had been in revision for the better part of a decade prior to the Gulf War. The revised manual was not published until March 1992, but early drafts had been circulated throughout the Air Force before the war. Alone among the services, the Air Force had a theory and doctrine of air power. Moreover, in the Air Force's view this doctrine applied to all air forces regardless of service or nationality. The details of the doctrine, as they applied to Desert Storm, are discussed in Chapters Four and Five.

The Navy had no air power doctrine separate from naval doctrine and its maritime strategy. The latter was more a policy, and a rationale for forces, than it was a strategy.[26] Navy doctrine rested on the primacy of gaining sea control and on striking littoral areas that jeopardized that control. There was no center of gravity theory such as Warden's and no unity of theater air command theory such as Cardwell's.[27] The Navy was optimized by theory and doctrine more for the extremes—not the middle—of the combat spectrum. Its maritime strategy postured it conceptually to strike at the flanks of the Soviet Union at one extreme, and to conduct short-duration contingency operations against Third World adversaries at the other. Left out was dealing with a sustained air campaign against enemy strategic targets and providing air support to a large ground force in battle.[28]

The Marine air doctrine was tailored to the support of Marine ground forces, and it scarcely addressed other possible uses of Marine air units. Marine Corps doctrine for that role was fully developed and was consistent with Navy views on the employment of air power in theater conflict. The Navy and Marine Corps doctrines did not encompass a *sustained* air campaign against potential enemy targets.[29] Navy and Marine neglect in considering an air *campaign* conducted jointly by all the air services resulted in the Air Force view's dominating discussion of joint air doctrinal issues. However, both services (particularly the Marines) had strong views on the subordination of their air forces

---

[26]See Summers (1992), pp. 84–86, for an outside but evenhanded discussion of the maritime strategy. For a critical view of the maritime strategy, see Robert Komer, "Maritime Strategy vs. Coalition Defense," *Foreign Affairs*, Summer 1982, pp. 1124–1144.

[27]It is ironic that the Navy, with perhaps the best professional publication among the four services (the U.S. Naval Institute *Proceedings*) providing a lively forum for the discussion of professional issues, has developed few theorists of air power or naval air power.

[28]Winnefeld and Johnson (1993), pp. 100–101, 111–113; see also Admiral Robert J. Kelly in *Navy Times*, January 13, 1992, p. 8 ("Kelly: Unfamiliar Enemy is New Navy Challenge"); also William J. Toti, "Sea-Air-Land Battle Doctrine," U.S. Naval Institute *Proceedings*, September 1992, pp. 70–74.

[29]An exception was Navy (Seventh Fleet) and Air Force (Fifth Air Force) planning for targets on the Pacific Rim. This joint planning, however, focused on the first phase of war, with a series of strikes on littoral targets (or targets of naval interest) over a short period of time. (From conversations with former commanders of the Third and Seventh Fleets and their staffs.) Also see Stuart Ramsdell, "Trip Report," letter to the Director, Navy Historical Center, 14 May 1991.

to a future joint air commander. In the 1986 "omnibus agreement," the Marines were able to keep control of the sorties necessary to support their ground forces, releasing "excess" sorties to the joint force air component commander.[30] The agreement recognized the power of the CINC to set priorities and overturn this understanding if circumstances warranted. Nevertheless, to the observer not burdened with the baggage of practice in previous wars, it was becoming clearer that an era of centrally controlled or coordinated joint air operations was closer at hand than at any time since World War II.

PREWAR DEVELOPMENTS[31]

Having examined the trends that led to the Iraqi invasion of Kuwait and the Coalition response to it, as well as the different service views on the employment of air power in regional wars, we now turn to the scenario setting for the war itself. Because we assume the reader is already familiar with the political backdrop, we concentrate on prewar military developments, including plans, exercises, force readiness, and the prewar movements and status of forces.

Starting in late 1989, U.S. planning increasingly focused on the Iraqi threat to the Gulf oilfields.

> In the fall of 1989, in the course of the Department of Defense's (DoD) regular planning process, the Under Secretary of Defense for Policy (USD(P)) recommended a shift of focus in the Persian Gulf. During most of the 1980s security concerns in the Persian Gulf focused mainly on the Soviet Union as the primary threat. Now, however, the USD(P) and the Commander in Chief, Central Command (CINCCENT) judged that this was no longer the primary threat. Instead, the disruption of the regional balance of power caused by Iraq's decisive defeat of Iran, the growing ambitions of Iraq, and the sharp disparity between its forces and those of the wealthy oil-producing nations of the Arabian Peninsula pointed to the growing possibility of regional, vice Soviet, threats to US interests in this vital region.... Accordingly ... the Chairman, Joint Chiefs of Staff directed CINCCENT to develop the necessary war plans.[32]

---

[30]This agreement is set out in JCS Pub. 2–01.1 (*Joint Doctrine for Theater Counter Air Operations*), 1 April 1986, pp. III-4/5, and was put into practice during Operation Desert Storm.

[31]This discussion of the events leading up to Operation Desert Shield draws heavily on the following RAND reports authored by Project AIR FORCE, Desert Shield Assessment Team: *Project AIR FORCE Assessment of Operation Desert Shield: Volume I, The Buildup of Combat Power*, MR-356-AF, 1994; *Project AIR FORCE Assessment of Operation Desert Shield: Volume I, The Buildup of Combat Power* (U), R-4147-AF, 1992; and *Project AIR FORCE Assessment of Operation Desert Shield: Volume II, The Buildup of Combat Power—Technical Appendices* (U), N-3427-AF, 1992. (The assessment was conducted by a RAND team led by Fred Frostic. Hereafter cited as *PAF Assessment*.)

[32]*CPGW*, p. 42. This view omits consideration of Washington's genuine fears of an Iranian victory in its war with Iraq in the early and middle 1980s.

The following spring, CENTCOM developed a new concept plan for the defense of the Gulf states. The plan identified force requirements and was used to develop a draft operations plan (OPLAN 1002–90). This plan was tested in July 1990 during the exercise Internal Look 90. Somewhat coincidentally, the annual GLOBAL war game, sponsored by the Office of the Secretary of Defense, at the Naval War College dealt with an Iraqi invasion of Kuwait and Saudi Arabia as one of its principal scenarios. Senior representatives of the services, the Joint Staff, and the unified commands participated in the game.[33]

It is important to understand what OPLAN 1002–90 and the various war games were and were not. The OPLAN was a draft. It was principally defensive in nature, as are all U.S. war plans; nevertheless, they do envision offensive operations to restore the status quo ante.[34] Supporting plans and the all-important time-phased force deployment list (TPFDL) were to be developed *after* the Internal Look exercise was completed.[35] That exercise focused on procedures and force needs, and not on the deployment except in a very aggregated way. The GLOBAL game was intended to sensitize top-level policymakers to the range of decisions they might face. In short, these exercise preparations framed the problem—but the devil remained in the details, details that had not been identified sufficiently to provide a basis for moving and sustaining forces. We will return to this subject in the next chapter when we examine the force deployment.

The massing of Iraqi forces near the Kuwait border in July foreshadowed subsequent events. But the course of those events was uncertain before the fact, and the indications available painted an ambiguous picture that was interpreted by different observers in different ways. Even if U.S. leaders had had perfect knowledge of what was to occur, it is doubtful that U.S. forces would have been granted access to bases in the Gulf states before the Iraqi invasion.[36]

Movement to Crisis

On 16 July 1990, Iraq sent a letter to the Arab League protesting Kuwaiti oil production and pricing policies. The next day, Saddam Hussein threatened the use of force to resolve these grievances. Increased air activity and the possible

---

[33]RAND's Project AIR FORCE conducted a similar parallel analysis during the summer of 1990 that further sensitized Air Force leadership to the relevant requirements and capabilities associated with the defense of the Gulf.

[34]*GWAPS*, p. 2.

[35]The TPFDL will be discussed in more detail in Chapter Three. It is the key tool in setting and communicating lift requirements.

[36]See *Triumph Without Victory*, pp. 13–39, for an excellent unclassified discussion of these events in July 1990.

movement of two Iraqi divisions were noted. Increasing tensions in the region prompted the United Arab Emirates (UAE) on 21 July to request that Washington provide aerial tanker support for their Mirage fighters. The UAE request was approved in Washington the next day.

In late July, Kuwaiti and Saudi forces maintained increased alert status, raising or lowering it in reaction to events and attempting to balance the opposing objectives of combat readiness and avoiding provocation. The representatives of the Organization of Petroleum Exporting Countries (OPEC) met on 26 July to consider the Iraqi complaints. This action was seen by many Arab states as defusing the crisis. But shortly thereafter, additional Iraqi divisions were reported adjacent to Kuwait. In the ensuing week there were talks between Iraq and Kuwait as well as other diplomatic efforts by Arab leaders to head off Iraqi military action. These efforts were to no avail, and on 2 August the invasion began.

The Initial U.S. Response

Until the actual initiation of Operation Desert Shield on 6–7 August, political factors set severe limits on military preparations and available options. These factors played a major role in invalidating peacetime planning assumptions of available warning and deployment time. The types of political constraints faced were rooted in the complexity of events and could not be considered exceptional or, in many respects, preventable. In the weeks preceding Iraq's invasion, there was a pervasive perception both within much of the U.S. policymaking community and among Gulf state leaders that Iraq's hostile rhetoric and military activities were posturing designed to politically intimidate Kuwait and the UAE. Direct military action by Iraq was viewed as unlikely or was expected to be of a very limited, punitive nature, short of a major invasion.[37]

This perception prevailed virtually up to the 2 August invasion. Consequently, military preparations and actions by both the United States and the Gulf states were very limited in scope. Although Commander in Chief U.S. Central Command (USCINCCENT) expectations of an Iraqi attack were high by the end of July, views among the leaders of the Gulf states made it doubtful that major deployments could have been made prior to the invasion, regardless of the expectations of U.S. policymakers.

The one visible military activity undertaken by the United States during the month of July in response to the building crisis, exercise Ivory Justice (the de-

---

[37]See Paul K. Davis and John Arquilla, *Deterring or Coercing Opponents in Crisis: Lessons from the War With Saddam Hussein,* Santa Monica, California: RAND, R-4111-JS, 1991, which describes the many problems that led to the failure of deterrence and proposes procedural improvements in crisis planning.

ployment of two USAF tankers to the UAE), was very limited in scope. Even so, the UAE expressed its desire to involve no combat aircraft and to keep the activity very low profile and "secret," even though it considered an air attack by Iraq likely. The Saudis for their part expressed concern over even this limited level of U.S. military activity. Regional fears of further antagonizing Saddam or giving credence to his claims of Gulf-state collaboration with the United States curbed what could be done on a cooperative basis. Consequently, the political concerns of the regional leadership again were key factors in determining the range of available U.S. options and the extent to which U.S. forces could "lean forward" even if greater expectations of an invasion existed.

Although CINCCENT had conducted some preliminary contingency planning before 2 August 1990, formal Joint Chiefs of Staff–initiated course of action (COA) development did not begin until the actual invasion of Kuwait. This delay set severe limits on the extent of preinvasion planning and preparation by the commands that would ultimately provide the forces for Operation Desert Shield. But given the sensitivity of ongoing negotiations, regional resistance to U.S. involvement, and fears of further escalation, delays were probably unavoidable. However, one knowledgeable journalist observes that "the [ensuing] airlift/sealift was made all the harder . . . because the Joint Chiefs of Staff and Lieutenant General Thomas W. Kelly, the Joint Staff's Director of Operations, adamantly refused time and again, to issue any warning orders . . . until after Saddam Hussein had seized Kuwait."[38]

When the JCS warning order was sent on 2 August, planning uncertainties were compounded by the limited distribution given to the message. The evidence indicates that a very limited U.S. reaction was expected up until 5 August, when it became clearer that the U.S. deployment of forces would be both rapid and massive. This story will be continued in Chapter Three when we examine the force deployment. But before leaving our scenario setting for Operation Desert Shield, we sketch out the location of forces in the region at the onset of hostilities.

2 August 1990

As the morning sun climbed over the Zagros Mountains on 2 August 1990, an observer with the ability to monitor all military operations in the Gulf and its vicinity would have noted the following activities in the region.

---

[38]From Benjamin F. Schemmer's review of the book *Triumph Without Victory* in *Strategic Review*, Spring 1992, p. 52.

Kuwait was in the process of being overrun by three Iraqi divisions.   The Kuwaiti air force had been neutralized early, and parts of it were en route to bases in other Gulf states to avoid capture.   No U.S. military units were present in Kuwait or Saudi Arabia except for two KC-135 tankers in Saudi Arabia.[39]   As shown in Figure 2.1, the *Independence* battle group was in the Indian Ocean, about 250 miles north of Diego Garcia.   At Diego Garcia, a dozen prepositioning ships swung to their buoys in the anchorage.   To the west in the Mediterranean were the *Eisenhower* battle group and the Mediterranean amphibious ready group (MARG).   Saudi forces were being brought up again to high alert levels. In the Gulf region, eight U.S. ships of the Middle East task force, including a cruiser, a destroyer, and five frigates led by the flagship *La Salle*, were on normal peacetime patrol.

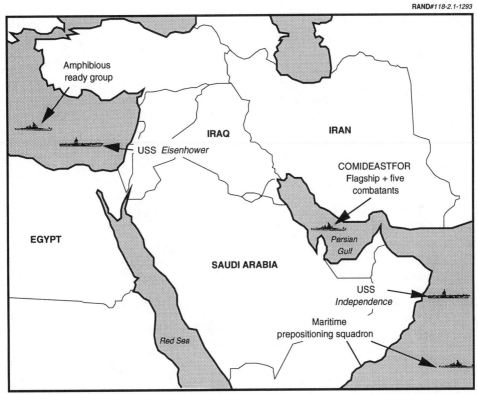

SOURCE: U.S. Navy briefing slide.

Figure 2.1—Snapshot of USN/USMC Forces in Southwest Asia, 2 August 1990

_____

[39]*Triumph Without Victory*, p. 50.   These tankers had been in the UAE for exercise Ivory Justice.

Back in the United States, almost all military units were at normal peacetime levels of readiness, since no warning orders had been issued or increased alert conditions established except at a few headquarters. At USCENTCOM head-quarters at MacDill Air Force Base in Tampa, the lights had been burning most of the night as news of the Iraqi invasion filtered in and the responses by the GCC states were monitored. Major political decisions were to be announced later that day in Aspen, Colorado, by President Bush. Military decisions were to follow as details of the U.S. response were worked out. Those early decisions centered on readiness, deployment, and planning, and they are the subject of the next two chapters.

Chapter Three

THE DEPLOYMENT

Operation Desert Shield was the fastest buildup and movement of combat power across greater distances in less time than at any other time in history.[1]

My [initial] job was to receive forces. Then, figure out where to put them and how we would use them if Saddam attacked.[2]

This chapter covers two topics: airlift of forces and support, and the buildup of aerial combat power. First we address strategic airlift operations, followed by Civil Reserve Air Fleet (CRAF) participation and aerial refueling operations. Next, we describe the deployment of Air Force, Navy, and Marine air combat units. Intratheater airlift is discussed in Chapter Nine. Although sealift and prepositioned equipment and supplies were to be key to the Coalition's success in the Gulf War, this chapter focuses on the contribution of air power to the rapid and massive movement of forces to the Gulf.

The deployment was a magnificent achievement. It is unique in the annals of warfare: a field army, a large combined and joint air force, and a major combat fleet were deployed to a distant theater over a period of some five months and provided the wherewithal to conduct a major campaign. It will remain a testimonial to the wisdom of the expansion and modernization of the U.S. armed forces in the 1980s. More specifically, the rapidity of the deployment and the assemblage of usable combat power in the Gulf are generally considered to

---

This chapter leans heavily on *PAF Assessment*, and on John Lund, Ruth Berg, and Corinne Replogle, *Project AIR FORCE Analysis of the Air War in the Gulf: An Assessment of Strategic Airlift Operational Efficiency*, Santa Monica, California: RAND, R-4269/4-AF, 1993 (hereafter cited as Lund and Berg). Navy and Marine deployment information is taken from the *CPGW* report (particularly app. E); from the Navy's *The United States Navy in "Desert Shield," "Desert Storm,"* Office of the Chief of Naval Operations, 1991; and from Center for Naval Analyses, *Desert Storm Reconstruction Report, Volume I: Summary* (U), 1991, and *Volume IV: Third Marine Air Wing Operations* (U), 1992.

[1]Attributed to General H. Norman Schwarzkopf in *CPGW*, p. E-1.

[2]Lieutenant General Charles Horner, as quoted in James P. Coyne, *Airpower in the Gulf,* Arlington, Virginia: Air Force Association, 1992, p. 153.

have deterred Iraq from invading Saudi Arabia during the critical days of August and September 1990.[3] Most of our examination in this chapter centers on the first two months of the deployment.

As great as this achievement was, the deployment was not without problems caused by incomplete planning, incorrect assumptions, shortages of material, and less-than-expected hardware performance. Our intent in this chapter is to provide a balance between describing the achievements and the problems. In addition to achievements and problems, there is the matter of luck. Except for its remoteness from existing U.S. bases and forces based in the continental United States and Europe, the Gulf was a near-ideal theater for deploying a large expeditionary force. Saudi Arabia, the principal host for the incoming forces, had over the years developed a robust infrastructure of ports, airfields, highways, and communications facilities—perhaps the best of any state in the Third World.[4] Petroleum supplies were available. The Saudi hinterland, though afflicted with the heat of the desert, did not pose major obstacles to force movement and the building of additional bases.

In many respects, the United States was able to "plug" its expeditionary force into a host state infrastructure and geography that were well configured to receive it.[5] That said, it was still necessary to get the forces and their support to a potential combat theater some 8,000 miles away from the United States. Moreover, much work was needed to convert "bare bases" into full-up wartime operating bases. Strategic airlift was to play the critical role in the early force deployments, and it is to that subject we now turn.

OVERVIEW OF STRATEGIC AIRLIFT OPERATIONS[6]

The deployment that began on 7 August 1990 was just the beginning of a large, complex operation involving all aspects of the strategic deployment system.

---

[3]Palmer (1992a), p. 165. *Triumph Without Victory* (p. 98) sees no hard evidence of Iraqi interest in invading Saudi Arabia. But it is difficult to envisage what "hard evidence" would have looked like and how it would have been obtained in view of the uncertainty about Iraqi plans and intentions. Schwarzkopf (p. 58), however, states: "Not until mid-September did we see a clear indication that Iraq was abandoning the idea of invading Saudi Arabia and assuming a defensive posture."

[4]See the summary of remarks by Major General Jasper Welch, USAF (ret.) before the Washington Strategy Seminar, 14 November 1991, p. 1.

[5]While many observers have cited the availability and utility of the base structure in the Gulf, others have pointed out its "uniqueness." We should add that most areas where the United States might have to deploy a Desert Storm–size expeditionary force also have excellent base structures. The argument usually turns on problematic conflict locations and the timing of base access. Some argue that we will probably not get involved in conflicts where our security partners do not provide base access. Assumptions about the locations of future contingencies and the timing of base availability are important, and the conventional wisdom has frequently proved wrong.

[6]This overview is taken almost verbatim from Chapter II of Lund and Berg (1993).

Prepositioned stocks, both ashore and afloat, provided a massive, early supply of munitions and combat and support equipment. Sealift would ultimately move 85 percent of all the dry cargo going to the Gulf, but it would be several weeks before the first ship arrived. Strategic airlift provided the means of moving critical assets rapidly, especially in the first weeks of Desert Shield and in the period leading up to and into the war. It carried over 75 percent of the people deployed to and from the Gulf.[7] It also transported a higher-than-expected proportion of dry cargo (15 percent versus the expected 5 percent) and sustainment cargo (30 percent versus the expected 10 percent).[8]

The operation can be usefully divided into four periods:

• Phase I: 7 August to 9 November 1990. Deploying and sustaining forces to defend Saudi Arabia and the Gulf Cooperation Council states.

• Phase II: 10 November 1990 to 16 January 1991. Deploying offensive forces intended to evict Iraq from Kuwait, and sustaining deployed forces.

• Phase III: 17 January to 28 February 1991. Supporting and sustaining wartime operations.

• Phase IV: March to August 1991. Redeploying forces, sustaining remaining in-place forces, and supporting humanitarian operations.

HISTORICAL SUMMARY

From the start of Operation Desert Shield (ODS) until the end of the war, Military Airlift Command (MAC) controlled just under 15,000 airlift missions. Of these, 77 percent were flown by organic MAC airlifters (C-5s and C-141s), 3 percent by KC-10s of the Strategic Air Command,[9] and the remainder by civil aircraft (both CRAF and volunteers).[10] Table 3.1 summarizes the missions flown by aircraft type and by month.[11] The level of effort varied significantly over

---

[7]Most naval and many air units deployed their assigned personnel in unit aircraft and ships. For example, most of the some 98,000 naval personnel in theater traveled there in their assigned warships, as did the some 17,000 Marines in assault shipping. We estimate that 75 percent of the uniformed personnel in theater got there as passengers on a lift aircraft. For a service-by-service breakdown of personnel in the Gulf, see Coyne (1992a), p. 37.

[8]Attributed to General H. T. Johnson, "MAC Faces Widening Gap in Peacetime, Crisis Needs," *Aviation Week & Space Technology,* September 9, 1991, p. 49.

[9]The KC-10 is a combined tanker and airlifter, based on the civilian DC-10. At the time of ODS, the KC-10s were assigned to SAC.

[10]We shall use "CRAF" as a shorthand for both CRAF-activated aircraft and aircraft volunteered by carriers. CRAF is a voluntary contract arrangement between the U.S. government and U.S. commercial airlines. Its role and performance during ODS will be discussed later in this chapter.

[11]Many data tables provided to us by MAC used 30-day periods to normalize comparisons between months. The "months" correspond to these periods:

Table 3.1

Missions Flown: August 1990–February 1991

Type	Aug 90	Sep 90	Oct 90	Nov 90	Dec 90	Jan 91	Feb 91	Total
Organic								
C-5	397	510	437	416	570	680	552	3,562
C-141	967	998	682	710	1,399	1,639	1,457	7,852
KC-10	17	88	55	50	115	48	0	373
Organic subtotal	1,381	1,596	1,174	1,176	2,084	2,367	2,009	11,787
CRAF								
Narrow-body: cargo	60	86	45	91	154	289	346	1,071
Narrow-body: PAX	3	9	8	9	11	40	47	127
Wide-body: cargo	21	93	51	71	112	200	279	827
Wide-body: PAX	88	121	145	44	281	246	109	1,034
CRAF subtotal	172	309	249	215	558	775	781	3,059
Total	1,553	1,905	1,423	1,391	2,642	3,142	2,790	14,846

SOURCE: Lund and Berg (1993), p. 9.
NOTES: Totals are for 30-day periods. PAX = passenger.

time. In August and September, MAC surged to deploy the initial forces. In October and early November, the pace slackened slightly as the initial units finished deploying but picked up dramatically in December as the second set of deployments began and the United States prepared for war. Each period has its own story.

Precrisis Preparations

The initial CENTCOM planning for the defense of the Arabian peninsula in the event of Iraq's aggression had begun some months before the invasion, as part of the normal planning process. As Iraqi forces massed on the border of Kuwait in July 1990, planning efforts accelerated. Unfortunately, on 2 August 1990, the relevant CINCCENT plan existed only as a "Concept Outline Plan," and as such lacked a transportation plan.[12]

August:	8/7/90–9/5/90
September:	9/6/90–10/5/90
October:	10/6/90–11/4/90
November:	11/5/90–12/4/90
December:	12/5/90–1/3/91
January:	1/4/91–2/2/91
February:	2/3/91–3/4/91

[12]*CPGW*, p. 3-1.

After the invasion on 2 August, planning became more intensive, and specific courses of action were considered. However, all of this planning was "close-hold." To the best of our knowledge, based on numerous interviews with Air Force and Army planners, no experienced transport planners were involved in this process until the deployment order was issued on 7 August. Expectations of transportation capability appeared to have been based on older operational plans whose assumptions were invalid in this case. As a consequence, the initial requirements passed down by CENTCOM and JCS planners were infeasible in many cases.

On 2 August, MAC activated its Crisis Action Team (CAT). Although the team did not have any specific orders, it queried units about their status, estimated the available capacity under various assumptions, and developed its initial concepts of operations. Unfortunately, it could not plan a flow without explicit requirements, and none were being passed down from JCS or CENTCOM. MAC even closed the CAT on 6 August because it had nothing more to do, only to reactivate it several hours later after getting informal notification from the MAC liaison officer at CENTCOM that the President was about to announce a major deployment. MAC put its primary numbered air forces—the 21st at McGuire AFB and the 22nd at Travis AFB—on alert.

Phase I: 7 August–6 November 1990

Early in any deployment, the airlift system tends to generate aircraft faster than deploying units can generate cargo; since airlift operations continue around the clock in peacetime, the initial shift for a contingency is relatively minor. This pattern held true in ODS. The first airlift sorties left with an advance team from CENTAF (the Air Force component of Central Command) on 7 August. The first Division Ready Brigade (DRB) of the 82nd Airborne Division began to load onto airlifters in the early morning hours of 8 August. The F-15Cs of the 1st Tactical Fighter Wing, along with some AWACS, began to move a few hours later. In the first few days, MAC sent airlift aircraft to these units as fast as they became available. Unfortunately, the units to be moved had trouble handling these initial high flow rates, as will be discussed later.

As more units prepared to move and the requirements continued to grow, demand for airlift quickly outstripped available capacity. Although MAC had access to all its aircraft, airlift capacity was limited. Almost half of MAC's crews are in the reserves, which limits the length of time that MAC can continue at surge sortie rates absent a reserve call-up. Many reserve crews volunteered, but not enough to continue operations for a sustained period. Also, to move large numbers of passengers, MAC usually plans to use civil aircraft such as the Boeing 747. Although some civil aircraft were made available, MAC needed a more complete and reliable solution. On 17 August (C+10), General H. T. Johnson, Commander in Chief of MAC (CINCMAC) and of the U.S. Transportation Command (CINCTRANSCOM), ordered the activation of the first stage of the Civil Reserve Air Fleet (CRAF). CRAF Stage I added 17 passenger and 21 cargo aircraft. This event marked the first time since the inception of the program in 1952 that CRAF had been activated. CINCMAC has the authority to declare a transportation emergency and to call up CRAF Stage I. Unfortunately, he does not have similar authority to activate MAC reservists; this authority rests with the President. Not until 23 August (C+16) was a limited call-up of reserves initiated, allowing MAC to gain sufficient crews to fully utilize the airlift fleet.

Despite the problems encountered, MAC transported an impressive combat force to the Gulf in that first month. By 10 August (C+3), over 100 combat aircraft were in theater; the first ready brigade of the 82nd Airborne deployed within a week. The first maritime prepositioning ship for the Marines would arrive on 16 August (C+8), carrying equipment for a Marine Air-Ground Task Force (MAGTF); with MAC providing the airlift for the personnel, a moderately heavy ground force would be deployed in less than two weeks. By the time the first ships were arriving from the continental United States (CONUS), on 27 August MAC had deployed the equipment and personnel for several hundred combat aircraft, an airborne division, personnel for the MAGTF, and elements of an air assault division.[13] By 6 September (C+30), MAC had transported almost 50,000 short tons of cargo and over 70,000 passengers to the Gulf (see Tables 3.2 and 3.3 for the monthly totals of cargo and passengers, respectively).

By late September, most high-priority units and cargo had been deployed. As requirements slackened, MAC began to reduce the pace of its operations. It flew fewer missions and conducted much deferred maintenance. However, this proved to be merely the lull before the storm.

Phase II: 9 November 1990–16 January 1991

On 9 November, President Bush ordered the deployment of large numbers of additional combat troops to the Gulf. Counting the support personnel, this additional complement would ultimately grow to 250,000 troops beyond those deployed in Phase I. These forces were intended to permit the United Nations coalition to take offensive actions to expel Iraqi forces from Kuwait if necessary. For MAC, Phase II deployments were dominated by (a) passenger moves in support of the deployment of VII Corps stationed in Germany, a third armored

---

[13]*CPGW*, pp. 3-1 to 3-2.

Table 3.2

Short Tons Transported

Type	Aug 90	Sep 90	Oct 90	Nov 90	Dec 90	Jan 91	Feb 91	Total
Organic								
C-5	23,145	32,385	26,133	26,250	34,314	42,568	33,562	218,356
C-141	18,470	19,261	12,071	12,922	26,161	31,469	28,703	149,058
KC-10	546	3,450	1,848	1,660	3,439	1,344	0	12,286
Organic subtotal	42,161	55,096	40,052	40,832	63,914	75,381	62,265	379,700
CRAF								
Narrow-body: cargo	1,764	2,331	1,256	2,020	3,203	6,445	8,235	25,253
Narrow-body: PAX	59	181	96	135	155	448	437	1,511
Wide-body: cargo	1,464	7,031	3,947	5,829	8,042	14,560	19,837	60,710
Wide-body: PAX	4,523	5,881	5,423	1,901	14,612	11,783	5,287	49,410
CRAF subtotal	7,810	15,424	10,722	9,885	26,012	33,236	33,796	136,884
Total	49,971	70,519	50,774	50,717	89,926	108,617	96,060	516,582

SOURCE: Lund and Berg (1993), p. 13.
NOTE: Totals are for 30-day periods.

Table 3.3

Passengers Carried

Type	Aug 90	Sep 90	Oct 90	Nov 90	Dec 90	Jan 91	Feb 91	Total
Organic								
C-5	20,207	13,362	5,943	5,034	12,768	16,320	7,231	80,865
C-141	18,566	8,184	3,342	4,828	19,166	28,683	5,828	88,597
KC-10	102	114	94	135	529	125	0	1,099
Organic subtotal	38,875	21,660	9,379	9,997	32,463	45,128	13,059	170,561
CRAF								
Narrow-body: cargo	6	0	0	18	92	434	208	758
Narrow-body: PAX	415	1,143	353	624	728	2,672	2,712	8,647
Wide-body: cargo	27	37	0	0	0	20	28	112
Wide-body: PAX	31,293	37,437	40,281	12,047	77,809	67,970	27,675	294,512
CRAF subtotal	31,741	38,617	40,634	12,689	78,629	71,096	30,623	304,029
Total	70,617	60,278	50,012	22,686	111,093	116,223	43,682	474,589

SOURCE: Lund and Berg (1993), p. 14.
NOTE: Totals are for 30-day periods.

division from CONUS, a second Marine division, and various support units; and (b) a growing sustainment cargo requirement. The VII Corps would form the main armored attack force in the Coalition. While its equipment would go primarily by sea, its personnel would be flown to the Gulf. Moving these additional forces to the Gulf required, in turn, an increase in the transport of sustainment cargo.

The movement of passengers posed the greatest challenge to MAC in this second phase. CENTCOM established a deadline of 15 January 1991 for the deployment of all combat troops. During the months of December and January, MAC carried over 225,000 passengers (see Table 3.3), or an average of 3,750 per day. Clearly, the CRAF wide-body passenger aircraft dominated in this mission, carrying 62 percent of all the troops deployed to the Gulf. Yet, while civil aircraft carried most of the passengers, not enough capability was available with the civil aircraft at hand (CRAF Stage I and contracted aircraft) to meet the requirement. Therefore, MAC converted some C-141s to a passenger configuration in late December and January to meet the closure requirements. As indicated in Table 3.3, the number of passengers carried on C-141s increased substantially from November to December and January.

As the United States deployed more and more forces, sustaining those forces through channel operations became increasingly important. As shown in Table 3.4, the number of airlift missions grew rapidly, from 8 in August to 885 in November (or approximately 30 per day). The steady increase in sustainment cargo can be seen plainly in Figure 3.1. Overall, airlift moved 30 percent of all the dry sustainment cargo, substantially more than the 10 percent anticipated before the crisis.

Table 3.4

Channel[*] and Unit Deployment Missions

Type	Aug 90	Sep 90	Oct 90	Nov 90	Dec 90	Jan 91	Feb 91	Total
Unit moves	1,545	1,640	871	506	1,544	2,020	1,429	9,555
Channel operations	8	265	552	885	1,098	1,122	1,361	5,291
Total	1,553	1,905	1,423	1,391	2,642	3,142	2,790	14,846
Channel as percent of total	1%	14%	39%	64%	42%	36%	49%	36%

[*]Scheduled supply and sustainment.
SOURCE: Lund and Berg (1993), p. 16.
NOTE: Totals are for 30-day periods. "Unit moves" are those missions scheduled against Unit Line Numbers in the TPFDL.

RAND#118-3.1-1293

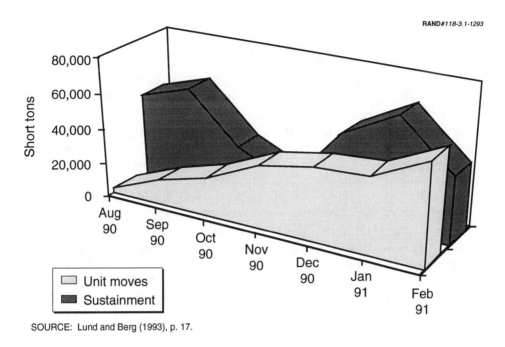

SOURCE: Lund and Berg (1993), p. 17.

Figure 3.1—Sustainment and Unit Cargo Tonnage

Phase III: The War, 17 January–28 February

In many ways, the start of the war did little to change MAC's operations; MAC had been effectively at war since 7 August. Nevertheless, the outbreak of hostilities did bring one new circumstance that seriously affected MAC operations: Scud attacks. The attacks by Iraqi Scud missiles on Saudi Arabian airfields and on Israeli cities led to two responses: one, many CRAF participants refused to fly into targeted areas at night (when the attacks occurred); and two, the President ordered the deployment of Patriots to Israel.

The missile attacks on Dhahran and Riyadh had long been anticipated. The greatest concern was that the warheads would carry chemical weapons. The airlines were most troubled by this prospect. Without chemical gear for their crews and reliable intelligence on the threat, many airlines refused to fly into these bases at night. This refusal complicated mission planning for MAC, but under the circumstances it agreed to accommodate the airlines.[14]

---

[14]This discussion is based on Mary E. Chenoweth, *The Civil Reserve Air Fleet and Operation Desert Shield/Desert Storm*, Santa Monica, California: RAND, MR-298-AF, 1993.

In response to the Scud attacks on Israel, President Bush ordered the deployment of Patriot batteries to that country. MAC and the Army responded swiftly, and within 24 hours the first fire units were deployed.[15] MAC diverted most of its C-5s (the only aircraft that can handle the many pieces of outsize equipment in a Patriot battery) and many of its C-141s (to carry missiles and other equipment) from other missions to support this move. Within days the deployment was complete. This experience highlighted the inherent flexibility of airlift and the significant contribution it can make in a rapidly changing operational environment.

Strategic airlift moved other vital cargo to the Gulf during the war. For instance, in January the Army found that its armored units did not have enough heavy equipment transporters (HETs), assets that would be critical to moving these units in preparation for the ground war. Since at that point shipping the HETs by sea would take too long, CENTCOM decided to move them by air. Only the C-5 could move this outsize equipment. Coming at the same time as the Patriot move, this placed a heavy demand on the limited C-5 fleet. Later, the Air Force needed to move the new GBU-28 "bunker buster" guided bomb to the Gulf quickly and secretly; organic strategic airlift was the answer. Throughout the war, unexpected requirements for high-priority items meant that airlift was constantly in demand.

Phase IV: Redeployment and Postwar Activities, March–August 1991

For MAC, the war did not end with the cease-fire. First, sustainment missions had to continue to support the half-million troops in the theater and to replenish spent stocks if fighting resumed. Second, most of the troops that deployed to the Gulf would need to be flown back home. The redeployment of troops would occur much faster than the deployment, eventually averaging over 5,000 passengers per day. Third, the United States began offering humanitarian aid to various groups in Iraq under Operation Provide Comfort. These various demands kept MAC's operational tempo high for many months. Not until the end of July 1991 did MAC complete the ODS missions. Forty-two days of combat required a year of airlift.

Performance Shortfalls in Strategic Airlift

Despite the many outstanding achievements of the ODS airlift, some have criticized the airlift *system* for failing to deliver its full capability or at least what they

---

[15]This speedy reaction was aided by the fact that a Patriot unit was already preparing for deployment to the Gulf.

believed this capacity to be.[16] These unmet expectations could be seen in many ways. Initial requirements for airlift passed down by CENTCOM were as much as three times larger than the capability MAC was able to provide. There were persistent complaints from personnel in transported units: that airlift was unreliable, coming too late or not at all; that units had little warning about when aircraft would arrive or what type of aircraft would be provided; and that payloads for the C-141 were substantially lower than planning factors.

Attention has been drawn to the various areas where airlift performed below planning factors. Utilization rates[17] fell well below expectations. The C-5 averaged only 5.7 hours per day, versus the commonly cited values of 11 hours for surged operations and 9 hours for sustained operations; the C-141 averaged 7 hours, versus 12.5 hours and 10 hours.[18] The average monthly rates can be seen in Figure 3.2. On average, only 67 percent of the C-5s were available, and at times only 50 percent were available; the C-141 performed better, with an average availability rate of 84 percent.

Payloads were below published wartime planning factors.[19] As shown in Figure 3.3, payloads for the C-141 averaged only 74 percent of its wartime planning factor, and for narrow-body civil aircraft (DC-8s and B-707s) only 57 percent. In passenger missions, only the wide-bodied civil aircraft (B-747s, DC-10s, and L-1011s) came close to planning factors, as seen in Figure 3.4.

These figures, verified by MAC, imply either serious inefficiencies in airlift operations, serious overestimation of capability in peacetime, a failure by people outside the deployment community to understand the planning factors, a lack of realistic training and exercises, or some combination of these factors. We believe the explanation lies in the combination.

---

[16]The shortcomings of the airlift system include those in the lift-requirements-setting process (CINC and supported components) and the priority-setting process (CINC) as well as those within the airlift commands themselves.

[17]Utilization (UTE) rate is the amount of flying time produced in a specific period expressed in hours per aircraft. This measures the productivity of the entire fleet, including aircraft not flown. One calculates UTE rate by aggregating the hours flown by all aircraft and dividing by all aircraft, whether or not they flew during that period. Thus, one counts non-mission-capable aircraft and mission-capable aircraft not flown. One senior USAF officer pointed out to us that UTE rates are skewed by the fact that some aircraft that count against the rate are "fenced" for use in higher-priority missions (e.g., presidential support, NASA, CIA, etc.).

[18]Aircraft that did fly in ODS missions attained UTE rates close to the expected rate of 10.1 hours for the C-141 and 9.7 hours for the C-5. However, these figures are not comparable. The UTE rate is supposed to already capture the effect of nonused aircraft (non-mission-capable aircraft and mission-capable aircraft not flown). Unless the existing plans assumed a 100 percent mission-capable rate, one would need to achieve a UTE rate *higher* than this to attain the desired UTE rate. For more information on how UTE rates are determined, see Captain Rick Gearing and Major Jim Hill, "UTE Rates Revisited," *Airlift,* Spring 1988, pp. 18–21.

[19]Planning factors as published in Department of the Air Force, *Military Airlift: Airlift Planning Factors,* Air Force Pamphlet 76–2, 29 May 1987.

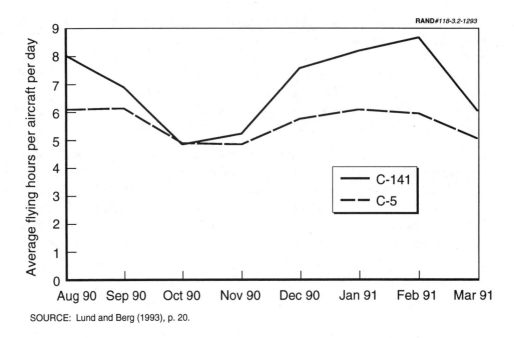

SOURCE: Lund and Berg (1993), p. 20.

Figure 3.2—Utilization Rates for the C-5 and C-141 Fleets

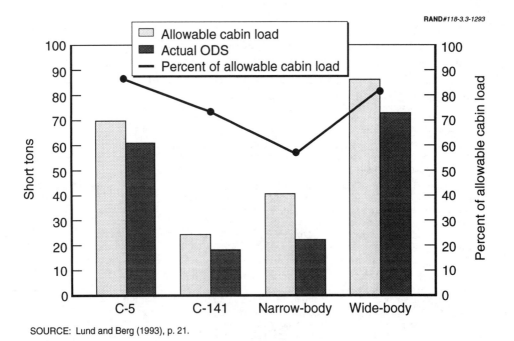

SOURCE: Lund and Berg (1993), p. 21.

Figure 3.3—Payloads: Actual Versus Planning Factors

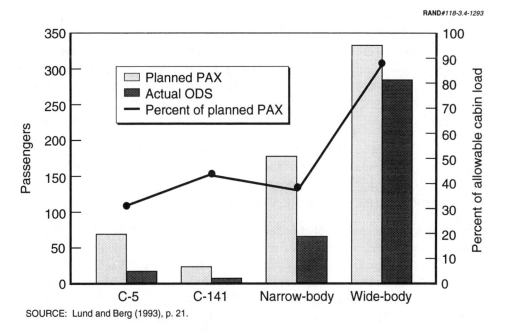

RAND#118-3.4-1293

SOURCE: Lund and Berg (1993), p. 21.

Figure 3.4—Passengers Carried: Actual Versus Planning Factors

FACTORS THAT SUBSTANTIALLY LIMITED STRATEGIC AIRLIFT OPERATIONS[20]

People often think of strategic airlift simply as a resource to be allocated. Yet airlift is also a system, consisting of many components that must work well together for the whole to function properly. To make efficient use of this limited resource, continual and careful planning is required to have aircraft where they are needed, when they are needed, and with as little idle time as possible. Prior to the aircraft's arrival at an onload base, a considerable amount of time and effort is needed to prepare the passengers and cargo for air shipment. Passengers must be briefed and manifested prior to boarding the aircraft. Cargo must be marshaled and evaluated prior to loading. Hazardous materials must be identified and sorted so as not to conflict with one another. Material must be placed on pallets, then secured to the pallets by netting or straps. Rolling stock (vehicles) must be prepared for air shipment, meaning that flammable fluids must be drained and purged. All cargo must then be weighed (both pallets and rolling stock), and with this information a load plan must be developed. The load plan is the sequence in which the aircraft is loaded, accounting for

---

[20]This analysis is taken almost verbatim from Lund and Berg (1993).

center-of-gravity and floor-load constraints. Prior to loading, this load plan must be approved by the aircraft's loadmaster. When the aircraft arrives, it must be unloaded, loaded, or both by trained personnel with specialized equipment. Aircraft must be serviced and maintained, requiring adequate supplies and the right ground crews. Aircrews must be available in sufficient numbers to support the flow, and they must be rested and prepared for their missions.

In ODS, RAND analysts found that problems existed in almost every component of the system, seriously constraining airlift operations. We have divided these problems into four broad categories: planning, aircrews, bases, and aircraft performance. We address each area in turn.

Planning. Operation Desert Shield began without a JCS-approved operation plan or feasible transportation plan. Requirements were defined as the deployment developed, and they changed frequently as the operational situation evolved. This lack of a stable, reliable requirement in the first weeks of the operation made it impossible to use the airlift fleet at peak efficiency. Exacerbating the problem, automated database processors and procedures often could not reliably keep up with CENTCOM's frequent changes to the requirements. Some of the apparent shortfalls in capability arose from people outside MAC who did not understand the assumptions underlying planning factors.

Aircrews. Roughly half of all MAC's strategic aircrews are in the reserves. Commonly cited utilization rates assume all these aircrews are available. However, the President did not authorize the call-up of reserves until 16 days into the deployment, and then only partially. The Secretary of Defense eventually authorized activation of all the reserve crews for the C-5s and three-quarters of those for the C-141. The late and incomplete call-up of reserve crews made it impossible to achieve full utilization of the fleet. Exacerbating the crew shortage was the lack of a crew rotation base in the Southwest Asian theater.[21] This meant that MAC had to use augmented crews—specifically, three rather than two pilots—for the Europe-theater-Europe leg of the mission, where crew duty days routinely reached 24 hours. The lack of a stage base at a time when aircrews were scarce could by itself explain a 20 to 25 percent shortfall in system performance.

Bases. MAC experienced various problems at onload, offload, and en route bases. Most deploying units were unable to prepare cargo within the time assumed in planning factors, especially when airlifters arrived at a rate of more than one per hour. This difficulty with cargo preparation meant that many

---

[21]The lack of a stage base in theater was the result of Saudi sensitivities and was not a planning failure.

missions were delayed or postponed, reducing the utilization rate of the fleet. The relatively few en route bases capable of handling the airflow made the entire system highly sensitive to any disruptions at those bases, such as weather, air traffic control delays, or ramp congestion. At Saudi insistence, offloads were largely limited to one location: Dhahran International Airport. This limitation constrained the throughput that could be attained and increased the sensitivity of the entire operation to problems there, such as limitations in the fuel system, ramp space constraints, and breakdowns in matériel-handling equipment. Although other bases were eventually used, Dhahran remained the dominant offload location.[22] At both onload and offload bases, old matériel-handling equipment proved to be unreliable, and this frequently caused delays or limited throughput.

Aircraft performance. On average, every ODS mission was delayed 10.5 hours, with aircraft reliability problems predominating. The C-5 in particular suffered from maintenance problems, with 33 percent of the aircraft deemed unavailable, on average (18 percent of those aircraft were unavailable because of maintenance problems). Of those planes available, the average delay per mission was 9.0 hours. This poorer-than-expected reliability of the C-5 significantly reduced its utilization level. It also meant that at certain times during the operation, the C-5 fleet could not meet the demand for outsize cargo capability. The C-141 had a better maintenance record, but its average payload was 26 percent below planning factors. Concerns about fatigue displayed in the inner-outer wing joint of the aircraft resulted in load weight restrictions. In some other areas, apparently poor performance actually reflects sensible operational decisions obscured in broad measures of efficiency. These decisions include the use of Desert Express, medevac withholds, and the use of narrow-body CRAF aircraft for smaller movements.

COMMERCIAL AND CRAF OPERATIONS[23]

CRAF (Civil Reserve Air Fleet) is a voluntary contract arrangement between the U.S. government and U.S. commercial airlines. It provides for government utilization of civil aircraft to supplement military airlift. The participating airlines receive certain benefits and guaranteed compensation in exchange for their commitment and their purchase of airlifters that have military utility. CRAF can be implemented in three stages, with Phase III encompassing the largest call-up of civil aircraft.

---

[22]A summary of Desert Shield/Storm airlift missions shows 57 percent terminated in Dhahran, 12 percent in Riyadh, 9 percent in Jubayl, and 22 percent at other airports of debarkation. (Data provided by John W. Leland of the USAF Air Mobility Command, 23 April 1993.)

[23]Chenoweth (1993).

During the first week of Operation Desert Shield, MAC tried to meet the growing gap in airlift capability by asking CRAF to volunteer aircraft and crews for military missions to the Gulf in the hopes of avoiding an activation of CRAF. CRAF carriers received an alerting message on 11 August warning them to prepare for the possible activation of either Stage I or II. A number of carriers did offer the use of aircraft in response to MAC's request. They provided a total of 6 to 10 passenger aircraft and 10 to 15 cargo lifters, but it soon became apparent that the airlift gap could not be closed by volunteerism alone. During the same period, carriers saw their commercial insurance for flights to the Persian Gulf region quadruple. The Commander in Chief of the U.S. Transportation Command, General Hansford T. Johnson, gave the order to activate CRAF Stage I on 16 August, with the call-up of 38 aircraft taking effect early on the 18th.

During the first days after call-up, short lead times provided to the CRAF "flow cell" in the MAC Crisis Action Team (CAT) resulted in short-notice requirements levied on the carriers. Many of these schedules were made only 24 hours in advance, and the airlines had to put aircraft and crews in the appropriate locations within this time window. After a few weeks of CRAF operation, this practice was replaced with a turnaround time of two to three days. In late October, MAC tried to give carriers up to five days' advance notice. Continuing scheduling improvement led to monthly scheduling by December.

Once the CAT screened an airlift requirement and found it CRAF-compatible, the order was passed to the CRAF cell. Here the requirement was translated into B-747 (cargo aircraft) equivalents and assigned mobilization value (MV) points. MAC assigned CRAF missions in much the same way it awards peacetime contracts, that is, through MV points. In this way, a company committing more aircraft of the type MAC most valued could expect to fly more of the missions. The next step was to receive budget authority for the mission and then place a "buy" with a CRAF carrier. MAC devised a system of mission slots and worked with the airlines to see that all were eventually assigned.

MAC worked out an agreement with the airline for each individual CRAF mission. The CRAF contract stipulated the airlift rates and the airline's commitment to fly missions. However, the actual procedures that evolved were a mix of volunteerism, with the tacit understanding that if the company did not "volunteer," it might be tasked to do so at a potentially less convenient time. MAC offered the airlines various mission slots and effectively asked the carriers to sign up for missions. If there was a mission for which no airline had volunteered, MAC then tasked it to the next carrier in line. In some cases, informal arrangements were made in which carriers agreed to fly more missions during certain periods of time in exchange for short blackout periods during which MAC agreed not to call on them.

For Desert Shield missions, MAC paid the airlines the same airlift rates used for peacetime contracts. On 1 November, the normal annual airlift rate increase took effect. If the mission was one-way, the airline received 1.85 times the one-way fare to compensate for the possibility of an empty return flight. The carriers were free to arrange a commercial flight on any unbooked return flight. Recognizing the mercurial nature of fuel costs, MAC's policy was to pay for any increase in cost beyond one cent of a standard rate and required reimbursement from the airlines if the cost dipped below the standard rate by a similar amount. Carriers thus were shielded from some inflation-related costs of operation.

In working with the airlines to set up a mission plan, MAC provided the carriers only with onload times, dates, and the final destination. It was left to the carrier to determine the route flown, staging areas, and estimated time of arrival at the airport of debarkation (APOD) (subject to MAC approval). Load requirements were confirmed before the mission was "bought" and checked again once the mission was assigned. There were a number of cases of aircraft arriving at the onload site only to find that the cargo had been shipped out on an earlier flight. Despite the double checks, the problem continued into late October, though less frequently.

As soon as the CRAF aircraft was airborne, the 21st Air Force at McGuire AFB assumed mission control. The carrier's operation center was responsible for monitoring its own flights and reporting back any known delays or problems. While most of the missions performed by CRAF aircraft were in direct support of Desert Shield, many were indirect in the sense that they filled in for MAC transports that were pulled from worldwide support missions. For instance, some of the Pacific routes previously flown by MAC transports were assumed by CRAF cargo carriers.

An Assessment of the Contribution of Commercial Airlift

One of the more important lessons learned from the first-time activation of the CRAF is that the concept works. Since 1952, the program has provided MAC extra airlift capability from commercial assets, but until Desert Shield, no one was sure how effective a start-up operation would be. By the end of November 1990, commercial jets had successfully completed 963 missions in support of the force deployment; 45 percent of these were passenger flights, the remainder cargo, as indicated in Table 3.5.

Table 3.5

Civil Airline Participation in Desert Shield and Storm

Airline	# of Aircraft[a]		Passengers			Cargo			Total Missions
	Passenger	Cargo	ODS	Channel[b]	Total	ODS	Channel	Total	
Northwest Airlines	3	2	75		75	24	12	36	111
Federal Express		8	4		4	9	86	95	99
American International		1				57	31	88	88
Evergreen		2				21	50	71	71
American Trans Air	1		70		70				70
Pan American Airlines	3		56		56				56
World Airways		1	30		30	18	4	22	52
Southern Air Transport		1				35	16	51	51
Rosenbalm Aviation[c]		4				34	16	50	50
Hawaiian Airlines			30	17	47				47
Air Trans International		1		1	1	24	20	44	45
Tower Air	1		37		37	1		1	38
United Parcel Services		2				15	20	35	35
American Airlines	2		30		30				30
United Airlines	4		27		27				27
Trans World Airlines	2		23		23				23
Korean Airlines						2	14	16	16
China Airlines	2		10		10				10
Servico Acorina de Transportes Aereos						2	8	10	10
Florida West							8	8	8
Eastern Airlines			7		7				7
Sun Country			6		6				6
Delta Airlines			5		5				5
Buffalo Airways						4		4	4
Trans Continental			3		3				3
Kuwaiti Airlines						1		1	1
Total	18	22			431			532	963

SOURCE: *PAF Assessment.*

[a]From July 1990 CRAF Capability Summary, Form 312.

[b]MAC commitments other than ODS.

[c]No longer in service.

MAC officers have told RAND analysts that the airlines, for the most part, lived up to their commitments. Most of the carriers gave high marks to MAC's handling of the operation, particularly its flexibility in working with the needs of individual carriers. By most accounts, activation proved beneficial to the airlines because it authorized the government to underwrite war risk insurance and, according to a number of carriers, helped management with labor relations in getting cooperation from the unions. The airlines also believe that activation helped spread the load: it was better to force all CRAF carriers to fly so that the burden was more evenly distributed. This latter point was important because of airline fears of loss of commercial market share while engaged in supporting the Gulf deployment. In spite of the generally excellent performance of CRAF and its interface with MAC, some airlines (those that remain after the current restructuring of the industry) are reconsidering their future participation in CRAF. Their fears are market oriented.

AERIAL REFUELING OPERATIONS DURING THE FORCE DEPLOYMENT[24]

Aerial refueling of the deployment and in-theater forces was a major contribution of the Strategic Air Command (SAC) to Operation Desert Shield.[25] Organizationally, Headquarters SAC, through its battle staff, monitored and controlled most SAC activities. Relatively early in the deployment, SAC supplied a general officer at the USCENTCOM forward headquarters in Riyadh, Saudi Arabia, to serve as adviser to the Air Force component command (CENTAF) on strategic forces and to control the tanker and bomber forces actually in the theater. The Eighth Air Force at Barksdale AFB, Louisiana, was the numbered air force involved with detailed planning of most operations and with most force "sourcing," i.e., determining which units would supply aircraft to meet requirements. The Eighth Air Force was responsible for the CONUS and Atlantic tanker "bridges," as well as for the initial B-52 deployment to Diego Garcia. The Fifteenth Air Force at March AFB, California, supported the Eighth Air Force with its tanker forces and ran the Pacific tanker bridges.

The magnitude of the tactical fighter deployment, coupled with other major refueling requirements for deploying bombers, electronic warfare, and special operations forces as well as strategic airlift, posed probably the most demanding set of aerial refueling challenges ever faced by SAC. Some 350 USAF fighters deployed from the United States, and another 68 deployed from USAF forces in Europe during the first phase of the deployment. As part of the deployment flow, the Marines deployed 110 fighters from the United States as well, for a total of 528 fighters requiring refueling support across the Atlantic tanker bridge.[26]

All of these fighter deployments occurred nonstop from either the east coast of the United States or Europe—except for the A-10s and Marine fighters, which

---

[24]This section draws heavily from *PAF Assessment*.

[25]Strategic Air Command was dissolved in the USAF reorganization of June 1993, with most of its tanker and lift aircraft transferred to Air Mobility Command (AMC). SAC bombers joined Air Combat Command (ACC).

[26]Headquarters TAC/DOXD working papers, 25 October 1990.

stopped at Rota or Moron, Spain, en route.[27] The general routing taken by deploying fighter squadrons took them from one of several east coast bases to a track near Lajes in the Azores, then around Gibraltar and through the center of the Mediterranean (skirting air traffic control areas), then southerly across Egypt, then east across the Red Sea into Saudi Arabia. Figure 3.5 shows the intensity of the refueling effort during the initial month of the deployment. In terms of numbers of receivers, Air Force and Marine fighters presented most of the refueling demand, with Marine assets moving in one compressed bulge. Continuous demand for airlift refueling occurred through the period, averaging about six C-5s or C-141s per day, most of which was supplied off the east coast of Saudi Arabia.[28]

The aerial refueling offload provided by SAC KC-10s and KC-135s totaled almost 71 million pounds. The number of refuelings required to take each fighter from the United States to the Gulf was extremely demanding, ranging from 7 (F-15) to 15 (F-4) to 21 (AV-8). The required total fuel offloads for all flight legs per deploying fighter varied from a low of about 51,000 pounds (USMC A-6s) to a high of almost 152,000 pounds (F-4G). These offload requirements were so large, in part, because most fighters carried full loads of munitions and external fuel tanks into the theater.

SAC UNIT DEPLOYMENTS

SAC provided virtually all its own airlift organically during the airlift-intensive portion of the deployment, using KC-135s and KC-10s. It was timely and effective. This self-deployment capability was very useful in Desert Shield because of the virtually complete commitment of MAC airlift assets to the movement of Army units and USAF and Marine tactical air force units. The lack of available MAC airlift and SAC's accelerated deployment to Diego Garcia resulted in the use of tankers in a purely cargo-carrying role. SAC tankers saw continued use in the cargo-only mode in supporting SAC forces at Diego Garcia. Using this method, it was able to maintain a 30-hour part resupply time from Castle AFB in California to Diego Garcia, in contrast to the MAC-supported nominal 72-hour part resupply time.

The effort that went into performing self-support airlift with organic SAC assets exceeded that experienced by MAC. The KC-135 is not equipped to handle standard five-ton cargo pallets. Consequently, the smaller and more labor-intensive cargo "skids" were used.

---

[27]Some Marine air units based in Japan flew to the Gulf via bases in the continental United States and then proceeded east over the Atlantic and the Mediterranean.

[28]Working papers, 8th AF/DOOK, Barksdale AFB.

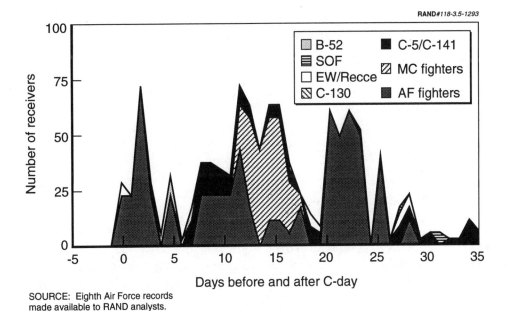

SOURCE: Eighth Air Force records
made available to RAND analysts.

Figure 3.5—Number of Aircraft Refueled During Initial Desert Shield Deployment

In addition to supporting the major deployments of a wide range of aircraft for Desert Shield, SAC also committed tankers to the direct support of ongoing US-CENTCOM operations. During the late summer and fall of 1990, these operations were mostly training and oriented to the defense of Gulf allies. In Chapter Six we discuss tanker support of the combat operations in Desert Storm. For now, we will describe the deployment of SAC tanker assets to support Desert Shield operations in theater.

As a backdrop for this discussion, one should remember that there was a history of SAC tanker operations out of Gulf bases to support a variety of U.S. exercises with Gulf security partners, tanker escort operations (Operation Earnest Will), and the episodic combat operations against Iranian forces in 1989. On C-day, there were already seven tankers in theater. By C+5, there were 70 in the Gulf region. To support its tanker operations during Desert Shield, SAC set up provisional tanker wings in the theater. At each base, a "lead tanker unit" provided most of the support personnel and equipment. This concept had been exercised before, but never to the scope that it was to encompass during the late summer of 1990.

A summary of KC-135 deployments on C+30 is presented in Table 3.6. The first three bases had only tankers on station. This required SAC to provide the "base support" normally provided by a host base. At each base, two tankers were on alert. Each base could generate three additional KC-135s within one hour.

Table 3.6

Summary of KC-135 Deployments on C+60

Location	KC-135Q	KC-135E	KC-135R	Total
King Khalid Int'l			20	20
Jiddah		18	10	28
Seeb			10	10
Al-Dhafra			3	3
Riyadh	10			10
Diego Garcia			6	6
Cairo West			3	3
Total	10	18	52	80

SOURCE: *PAF Assessment.*

As we have seen, SAC bombers arrived in the theater early in the Desert Shield Phase I deployment. Twenty-eight B-52s were scheduled for deployment to Diego Garcia, but competing requirements and shortages of ramp space limited the deployment to 20 aircraft. The primary factor enabling SAC to deploy so rapidly was SAC's prior practice and preparation. In 1986, SAC began to practice deployments to project its conventionally armed B-52s in the support of overseas theater commanders. The primary benefit gained by these overseas deployments was to train with the theater forces and mesh tactics. Valuable lessons were learned on interoperability, communications, and integration of effort. Deployed operations were made as realistic as possible with air tasking orders (ATOs, to be described further in the next chapter) to the overseas ranges with live weapons releases. A secondary benefit was the "desensitization of B-52 aircraft movements outside the United States."[29]

In spite of the seemingly smooth deployment of B-52s to overseas bases, evidence has emerged since the war that readiness and deployability standards were not always met. General Lee Butler, former commander of the Strategic Air Command, stated before the Senate Appropriations Committee that SAC was

> not as prepared for rapid deployment and conventional missions . . . in Desert Storm as we could have been.
>
> . . . going into the Gulf war, SAC's readiness spares kits were rated overall Not Mission Capable.[30]

---

[29] *PAF Assessment.* The movements included RAF Fairford in the UK, Moron in Spain, and Cedi Salmid in Morocco. In the Pacific, exercise deployments to Hawaii, Alaska, Guam, Australia, Japan, Thailand, and Diego Garcia were held.

[30] "B-52s Were Only Marginally Successful in Gulf War, Gen. Butler Says," *Aerospace Daily,* 28 January 1993, p. 155.

FIGHTER AND OTHER COMBAT UNIT DEPLOYMENTS

The magnitude and rapidity of the Desert Shield fighter deployment was unprecedented. USCENTCOM ordered its component commanders to "reprioritize and reduce airlift requirements. Priority remains on building combat power, *with minimum sustainment,* as quickly as possible."[31] Clearly, the emphasis was to get as much of the nation's tactical air forces to the theater as soon as possible.

Before discussing these deployments, we need to draw an important distinction between the rapid deployment of forces and the ability to conduct sustained combat operations on arrival. A fighter unit is more than its airframes and aircrews; it also consists of maintenance and support personnel and equipment, spare parts, fuel, weapons, and numerous combat support items. It takes time for this essential support to catch up to deploying aircraft—or if the support is prepositioned in theater, time for it to be broken out, moved to the support site, and mated to the deployed tactical fighter force. A useful metaphor is the fire engine that arrives rapidly at the fire scene only to find that hydrants are not available or that they lack sufficient pressure or suitable fittings. Thus, an aircraft arriving at an air base in the Gulf did not necessarily have any appreciable immediate combat capability, even if it deployed with its bomb and missile racks full.[32]

While carrier forces carry their initial support with them, they too are dependent on an early link-up with a logistics umbilical. A carrier battle group conducting contingency operations will look to refueling after a week of such employment. If it engages in high-tempo bombing operations, it will need to replenish munitions at about the same time.[33]

As we have noted, it was the great good fortune of the United States to have had access to a modern and extensive air base and supporting logistics infrastruc-

---

[31]USCENTCOM situation report, 14 August 1990 (emphasis added).

[32]For example, the aerial munitions for the assault echelon of Marine air units were loaded in maritime prepositioning ships. The aircraft could have been flown in early (assuming en route tanking was available), but they and their crews would have had to wait for the munitions and other support material to arrive, be unloaded, moved to the airfields, and made ready. As matters transpired, the delay in deploying Marine aircraft to the Gulf (because of higher priorities for the use of tankers) meshed with the arrival of their munitions in the maritime prepositioning ships. Air Force munitions were even more widely distributed between afloat prepositioning ships and depots in Oman and Bahrain (*CPGW*, pp. E-14/15). Early-arriving Air Force units had only the weapons they carried on their wing racks and whatever the Saudis and other hosts would let them use. (From interviews with RAND analysts, and staff officers who participated in the deployment.)

[33]Senior naval officers we interviewed emphasized that naval forces were ready for sustained combat operations on arrival and that the deployments to the Gulf were an extension of peacetime deployment practices. The logistics "train" supporting the early-arriving carriers during the Gulf War carried sufficient fuel and munitions to support 30 days of combat operations.

ture in the Gulf. Moreover, large amounts of prepositioned equipment and supplies were already in the region. Unlike an earlier contingency in the Middle East, en route staging bases and relatively unimpeded air access were available.[34] As indicated earlier, the urgency of the situation in early August 1990 persuaded General Schwarzkopf to deploy combat power to the Gulf rapidly and take a calculated risk that sustainability and other support could catch up before any additional Iraqi offensive action. He was convinced of the deterrent value of forces in place.

On 7 August, when the deployment execution message was received, the only air combat power in the Gulf region was the *Independence* battle group steaming in the Arabian Sea and the *Eisenhower* battle group steaming in the eastern Mediterranean. As important as their early presence was, they were nevertheless both distant from the threatened area of northeast Saudi Arabia and not directly visible to our Gulf allies. Land-based air forces were needed to defend Saudi airspace and defend our Gulf allies against Iraqi incursions.

Most of our discussion will focus on these land-based air forces, since the deployment and sustainment of Navy carrier battle groups was a straightforward expansion and extension of peacetime deployments. Two carriers were on station in waters adjacent to the Arabian peninsula on C-day and a third by C+30. By 6 January, six carriers were deployed in the Persian Gulf and the Red Sea.[35] The choice of routes for land-based air deploying to the Gulf was determined primarily by concerns about operational security and potential political constraints. The Air Force's Tactical Air Command (TAC) directed the deployment and wanted to avoid overflying any non-U.S. territory unless absolutely necessary. Egypt was the only country overflown, although bases in Spain were used en route by USAF A-10s and some Marine fighters. Standard procedures were used when setting up aerial refueling tracks to ensure that flights always had enough fuel on board to make it to an alternate field if necessary. Using tankers to "drag" the fighters is the TAC-preferred option, but in this case it was able to utilize this technique only about half the time.[36] In the other cases, deploying fighters were handed off from one group of tankers to another as they moved from west to east. This option allowed the tankers to

---

[34]During the 1973 Yom Kippur War, the U.S. aerial resupply of Israel was severely constrained by the refusal of some allies to make their bases available for airlift support.

[35]As a rule of thumb, the average aircraft load per carrier was 80, of which approximately 60 were fighter or attack aircraft.

[36]"Dragging" means that the refueler accompanies the fighters and provides multiple refuelings from the same group of tankers. After exhausting its transferable fuel, the tanker either returns to its originating base or to an en route base. The other method is to arrange rendezvous between tankers staging from en route bases and the transiting fighters.

operate from an intermediate staging base and not have dead time returning to the United States for the next fighter drag.

During the Desert Shield deployment, fighters were deployed from home bases throughout the United States, Europe, and Asia. All U.S.-based fighters staged through (and spent a night at) one of four bases in the eastern United States. Typical formations were six aircraft cells accompanying each group of tankers. Some aircraft (e.g., F-4Gs, AV-8Bs) went in two aircraft cells because of the frequency with which they had to be refueled.

Table 3.7 summarizes the Air Force fighter deployments during the first phase of Desert Shield. Of the 21 deploying units, 11 were able to complete the deployment (full closure) of all their assigned aircraft (24 to each unit) on the day that their first aircraft arrived in the theater. Most of the other units arrived less one or two aircraft (in most cases because of equipment malfunctions).

Figure 3.6 portrays the deployment of fighter aircraft of all services to the theater for the first month after C-day. Figure 3.7 shows the distribution by aircraft type of the 528 USAF and Marine fighters that deployed during the first phase, of which 460 came from the United States (350 USAF, 110 USMC) and 68 from USAF units in Europe. During this early period, two carrier battle groups were in theater. Even more impressive than these numbers are the distances the fighters had to fly and the times required to accomplish the deployment, shown in Figure 3.8. Flight times were a demanding 15–16 hours nonstop from the United States (except for Air Force A-10s and Marine AV-8s stopping overnight).

UK strike aircraft were almost as fast as the USAF and Navy aircraft in arriving. A squadron of Tornado fighters was committed on 9 August and was operational at Dhahran 48 hours later. These initial arrivals were followed two days later by a squadron of Jaguars with tanker support. Air force detachments from France, Canada, and Italy soon followed.

The Marine fighter deployment posed some special problems for supporting Air Force commanders. First, Marine commanders wanted to deploy their air as soon as possible after C-day. However, the CINC-determined priorities system, including the heavy commitment of tankers to other deployments, and the fact that Marine prepositioned support would not be in place until mid-August, put them further back in the tanker queue than the Marines preferred.[37] As a result, their deployment got under way around 20 August. In reconstructing these events, it appears that Marine planners first contacted SAC and indicated they were ready for aerial refueling support for their deployment after only minimal

---

[37]One source maintains that the Marine fighters and their support arrived in the theater at about the same time (*CPGW*, p. E-21).

Table 3.7

Summary of Early USAF Fighter Deployments

Deployed Base	Aircraft	Unit	Home Station	C+Days to Partial Closure	C+Days to Full Closure
Dhahran	F-15C	71 TFS	Langley	1	7
Dhahran	F-15C	27 TFS	Langley	2	11
Thumrait, Oman[a]	F-15E	336 TFS	Seymour-Johnson	3	11
Al-Dhafra, UAE	F-16C	17 TFS	Shaw	3	3
Incirlik, Turkey	F-111E			4	4
Al-Dhafra, Oman	F-16C	33 TFS	Shaw	4	26
Shaikh Isa, Bahrain	F-4G	561 TFS	George	10	19
King Fahd International	A-10	353 TFS	Myrtle Beach	11	11
King Fahd International	A-10	356 TFS	Myrtle Beach	13	19
Khamis Mushait	F-117A	415 TFS	Tonopah	14	14
Taif	EF-111A	390 ECS	Mountain Home	17	39
Taif	F-111F	492 TFS	Lakenheath	18	18
Al-Dhafra, Oman	RF-4C	106 TRS	Birmingham (ANG)	18	18
Tabuk	F-15C	58 TFS	Eglin	22	26
Doha, Qatar	F-16C	614 TFS	Torrejon	22	22
Al-Minhad	F-16C	4 TFS	Hill	23	23
King Fahd International	A-10	74 TFS	England	24	24
King Fahd International	A-10	76 TFS	England	25	25
Al-Minhad	F-16C	421 TFS	Hill	25	28
Taif	F-111F	493 TFS	Lakenheath	26	39
Shaikh Isa, Bahrain	F-4G	52 TFW	Spangdahlem	29	29

SOURCE: *PAF Assessment.*
[a]Originally deployed to Dhahran, then immediately redeployed.

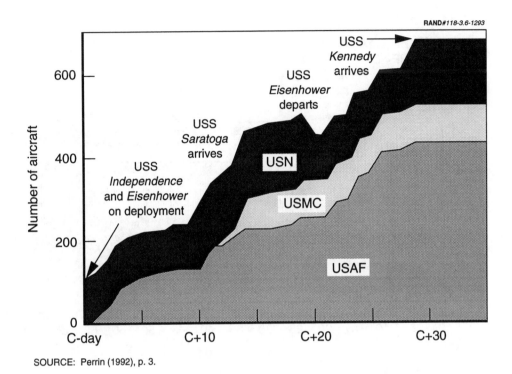

SOURCE: Perrin (1992), p. 3.

Figure 3.6—Arrival of Fixed-Wing Fighter and Attack Aircraft in Theater

internal planning. SAC quickly put them in contact with TAC deployment planners and coordinators. TAC had the collateral responsibility to move Marine aircraft, although staff personnel on board at the time had not performed this function for the Marines before, nor had they planned for this contingency. For example, TAC did not possess the flight parameters of Marine aircraft (e.g., maximum cross wind, maximum flight time, fuel flows). This information was obtained by direct liaison with Marine air units.[38]

Some Air Force units had their bed-down plans changed while en route.[39] A squadron of F-15Es from Seymour-Johnson AFB discovered, as it arrived in Saudi airspace, that Oman had denied it access to the planned bed-down base. The aircraft were diverted to Dhahran, but after two hours they were asked to leave (because of Saudi sensitivity at the time about basing offensive systems on their territory), and they deployed to Thumrait. The result was an exceptionally

---

[38]Marine air commanders respond that TAC and SAC had been moving Marine aircraft to Japan and Europe for many years and that movement planners should have been familiar with the flight parameters of USMC aircraft.

[39]Eliot Cohen, Director of the Air Force's Gulf War Air Power Survey, has stated that only 2 percent of deploying USAF aircraft deployed to the bases they had been assigned in prewar planning.

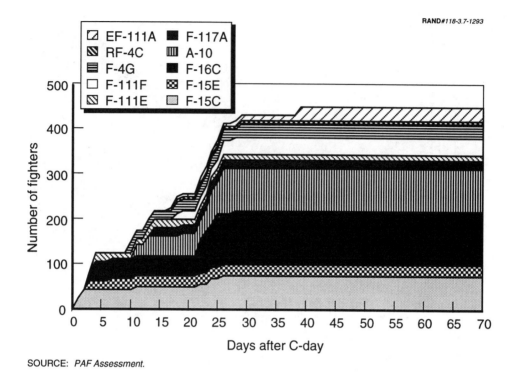

SOURCE: *PAF Assessment.*

Figure 3.7—First Phase Land-Based U.S. Fighter Deployments

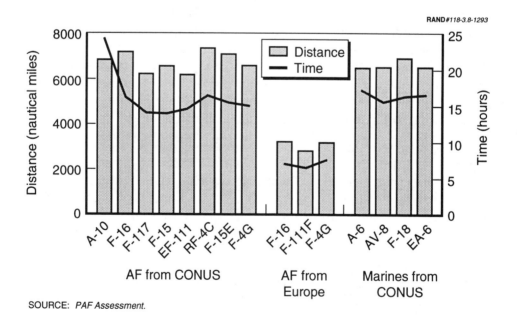

SOURCE: *PAF Assessment.*

Figure 3.8—Fighter Deployment Distances and Times

long deployment day. Difficulties were compounded by the failure of Saudi Arabia and Oman to agree on an overflight route, owing to an old border dispute. The solution was an extended flight via the United Arab Emirates.

WHAT IF SADDAM HAD INVADED SAUDI ARABIA IN AUGUST 1990?

RAND has conducted some analysis of the fighting capabilities that lie behind the numbers of U.S. tactical fighter aircraft deployed to the theater.[40] Could the U.S. forces in place during the early months of the deployment have defended Saudi Arabia against an Iraqi attack from staging areas in Kuwait? Analyses that respond to this sort of question are typically hedged with warnings and assumptions, and such is the case here. Nonetheless, it appears that effective combat power was established within about a week after the first deployed forces arrived. However, sufficient potential to stop the Iraqi air and armor threats was not in place until early September for the former and late September for the latter.[41] Deficiencies in preferred threat-capable munitions were the principal shortfall, rather than the numbers of deployed aircraft and flight crews.

However, deficiencies in numbers of aircraft and threat-capable munitions were not the only shortfalls during the early part of Operation Desert Shield. Robert Duncan has described the hand-to-mouth command and control situation in August and December 1990:

> In the early days of Desert Shield, U.S. and Coalition forces found themselves in a tenuous situation. The command was faced with the possibility of an imminent enemy armored offensive down the east coast of Saudi Arabia. . . . Opposing this force was a thin line of mostly Arab coalition forces, forward deployed with extremely limited munitions, while U.S. forces formed up in blocking positions north of the Saudi Arabian oil fields. Further aggravating the situation was the inchoate command structure of the Arab and other Islamic forces in early August 1990. Although U.S. air power in the region was increasing, the ability to use it to support these land forces was limited by their unfamiliarity with the concepts of close air support (CAS), fire support coordination lines (FSCLs), and air request nets, nor were there any air liaison officers (or their equivalents) to provide terminal control for CAS.

> The plan developed to deal with all of this, had war broken out at the time, was simple. Because of limited depth for defense and the ground force's lack of CAS command-and-control personnel and equipment, the command's primary ob-

---

[40] *PAF Assessment.* The analysis focused on USAF potential against representative Iraqi threat arrays. See Figures A.4, A.5, and A.7 in the appendix.

[41] The 7th Marine Expeditionary Brigade (MEB) had arrived on 24 August, and the first tanks of the 24th Infantry Division (Mechanized) arrived on 3 September. (*Triumph Without Victory*, p. 143.) *GWAPS*, p. 34, citing CENTCOM staff analyses, states that a successful defense could have been mounted by the end of August.

jective would have been to interdict the southbound army forces threatening Coalition ground forces and bases at Dhahran and King Faud air fields. It would have been a fight to survive.[42]

However, by the middle of September, Coalition air power in the theater totaled some 600 fighter and attack aircraft and was sufficient at that time to conduct an aerial offensive against Iraq and its forces in Kuwait while the ground buildup continued.[43] Phase II deployments resulted in a near doubling of allied air power in theater. These later deployments were more measured and conformed to an expanded bed-down plan using some two dozen air bases in and around the Gulf.[44] The thinking underlying the bed-down was to put the shorter-range and fighter interceptor aircraft forward in Saudi Arabia and the longer-range and support aircraft further back in Saudi Arabia and among the smaller GCC states.[45]

A RETROSPECTIVE ON THE DEPLOYMENT

In spite of the many problems (some of which we have examined; there were others), the deployment was a stunning achievement. All services deserve credit for their peacetime readiness and exercising and for their deployment planning. Innovation and workarounds were the order of the day. The over-lapping capabilities and redundancy built into the system from the beginning ensured success in the hands of good officers. While there may have been some excess capacity at some times and places, that capacity is what gave the planners and operators the ability to accommodate the unforeseen, the unplanned, and the occasional mistake, and to press on to get the force to the theater. Mass and speed were needed and available, and they served the country and the Coalition well.

---

[42]Robert E. Duncan, "Responsive Air Support," *Air Force Magazine*, February 1993, p. 75.

[43]The Chairman of the JCS was briefed by Brigadier General Buster Glosson (Horner's Director of Campaign Planning) on 12 September that the air campaign plan could be executed starting on 13 September. Horner and Schwarzkopf agreed. (Communication from Glosson.)

[44]For details of the bed-down, see *CPGW*, pp. 141–148.

[45]But this was not always possible, owing to airfield capacity limitations. For example, basing F-16s at al-Dhafra and al-Minhad in the UAE was dictated by space available, not optimal positioning.

Chapter Four

PLANNING THE AIR CAMPAIGN

> [T]o inquire if and where we made mistakes is not to apologize. War is replete with mistakes because it is full of improvisations. In war, we are always doing something for the first time. It would be a miracle if what we improvised under the stress of war should be perfect.
>
> —*Vice Admiral Hyman Rickover*

The Iraqi invasion of Kuwait gave the Air Force an unprecedented opportunity to translate its doctrine of air warfare into plans and ultimately into operations in a major regional contingency with little interference or guidance from senior command echelons or from its sister services. Indeed, as we will suggest in this chapter, the Air Force came to the Gulf conflict as the only DoD institution with an integrated theory of strategic air warfare and the doctrine and requisite systems for applying it. There were shortcomings in each of these constituent elements of air power, but there was a remarkable degree of consistency and compatibility among them. The gaps were few and could be managed during operations. Perhaps more importantly, there was a place in Air Force doctrine for the air units of the other services to add their contributions in a joint effort. The other services had different, more narrowly focused, and less ambitious concepts of air power's role and employment. USCINCCENT's prewar plans were more focused on a ground campaign and clearly envisioned the use of air power as an adjunct to ground operations for the defense of the region.

This chapter relies heavily on research working papers authored by Ted Parker and Don Emerson of RAND; Winnefeld and Johnson (1993); material in *CPGW* (chap. 6); James P. Coyne, "Plan of Attack," *Air Force Magazine*, April 1992, pp. 40–46; Horner (1991), pp. 16–27; Lieutenant Colonel David A. Deptula, USAF, "The Air Campaign: Planning and Execution (rev. 2)," a 1991 briefing for the Air Staff; Norman Friedman, *Desert Victory: The War for Kuwait*, Annapolis: U.S. Naval Institute Press, 1991, particularly pp. 169–192; and Palmer (1992a), particularly pp. 193–206. Interviews with principal planners, conducted as part of the research for the Winnefeld-Johnson book, provided a rich source of material for the description provided here.

In this chapter, we will discuss the state of preinvasion planning, the prewar planning for the Desert Storm air operations, and the planning done during the conflict itself. The focus is on not only the plans themselves, but the processes by which they were developed. We are primarily interested in force employment plans. Deployment plans were discussed in the last chapter, and logistics and intelligence planning will be discussed in later chapters. Along the way, we will address the different service and joint doctrines and practices on air campaign planning, since they did much to shape the plans and sometimes the controversy that attends them. In the last chapter we saw U.S. forces deploying to the Gulf, and in the following chapters we will examine command and control arrangements and the conduct of operations. Here we examine how air power means were linked to ends. It is a fascinating story that demonstrates both the strengths and weaknesses of the way the United States plans for wartime operations.

On 8 August 1990, General Schwarzkopf put a call through to General Michael J. Dugan, the Air Force Chief of Staff. Dugan was at MAC Headquarters, and the Vice Chief, General John ("Mike") Loh, took the call. Schwarzkopf had been tasked to develop an early offensive option for the President. He asked the Air Staff to develop an air plan that would give the President an option to take the initiative as an interim measure until theater ground forces could be built up to provide a balanced capability.[1] Loh said the Air Staff could do it, and thus began a chain of events that we shall describe shortly. First, however, we examine the state of U.S. regional planning before the Iraqi invasion.

U.S. REGIONAL STRATEGY AND PLANS

Throughout the late 1970s and the 1980s, the objectives of U.S. strategy in the Gulf were to maintain access to the area's petroleum resources, keep the Soviets out, and improve political stability in the region. During the early part of this period, the principal perceived threat was the Soviet Union.[2] The fear was that the Soviets would exploit regional instability and possibly U.S. engagement elsewhere to grab the oil resources of the Middle East. With the fall of the Shah of Iran in early 1979, the threat became more complex. Islamic fundamentalism, under the Iranian clerical leadership, gradually became the preeminent

---

[1] *GWAPS* notes that Schwarzkopf was not "predisposed to ask for assistance from a service staff. But at this time he had few forces available in the theater, and needed a way to retaliate against some new, hostile act by Iraq" (p. 86).

[2] For a typical Cold War formulation of these objectives, see the January 1987 *National Security Strategy of the United States*: "Our principal interests in the Middle East include maintaining regional stability, containing and reducing Soviet influence, preserving the security of Israel and our other friends in the area, retaining access to oil on reasonable terms for ourselves and our allies, and curbing state-sponsored terrorism" (p. 17).

threat of the early 1980s. However, the urgency of this threat was gradually attenuated as a result of the Iran-Iraq War. After initial Iranian successes in repulsing Iraqi invading forces, the war descended into a prolonged stalemate that was to exhaust Iran. At the end of the war in 1988, Iraq could claim victory. It emerged financially weakened but with forces that were large and powerful by regional standards. As the Soviet threat receded as a result of increasingly evident internal weakness and Gorbachev's more responsible foreign policy, Iraqi military might combined with a gangsterlike national leadership became the principal near-term threat to regional stability and U.S. interests. The Iranian threat remained, but it was much attenuated by that state's political transition and the losses suffered during the war with Iraq. By the fall of 1989, these developments had proceeded to the point where DoD planning shifted its principal emphasis to the defense of the Arabian peninsula.[3] Responding to direction from the Secretary of Defense and the Chairman of the Joint Chiefs of Staff, USCINCCENT in the spring of 1990 developed a draft operations plan for regional defense and then tested it in a command post exercise, "Internal Look 90," in July 1990. This draft operations plan became "USCINCCENT OPLAN 1002–90, Defense of the Arabian Peninsula." As we noted in Chapter Three, this plan was still in draft form, and the associated time-phased force deployment lists (TPFDLs) did not exist. Thus, a top-level plan reflecting requirements, force movements, and initial employment was available, but the critical details were missing.[4] The absence of these details probably complicated the timely and efficient movement of forces, particularly ground components, to the theater.[5]

But another aspect of this plan deserves mention. The plan was fundamentally a *ground defense* plan for the peninsula. Air forces were deployed and employed to defend peninsula airspace and to support engaged ground forces. An offensive option (Phase III of the plan) including air strike operations into Iraq was sketched out, but the planning was not completed before the August 1990 invasion of Kuwait.[6]

---

[3]*CPGW*, p. 42.

[4]Paul Davis of RAND reminds us that as important as TPFDLs are, they are unavoidably out of date when an occasion arises for their use. In his view, the ability to rapidly develop needed TPFDLs is more important than having the details of a baseline TPFDL worked out with great precision. We agree up to a point. The ability to develop TPFDLs rapidly and with high confidence did not exist in August 1990. We believe that if a roughly right TPFDL for OPLAN 1002-90 had existed in August 1990, many of the subsequent deployment problems would have been more tractable.

[5]Some officers we interviewed stated that the absence of detail in these plans provided for greater flexibility when a specific contingency arose.

[6]The staff work that went into sketching out the air operations for Phase III of OPLAN 1002–90 predated the Instant Thunder plan that would be developed by the Air Staff. In any event, that staff work was not as advanced as the Instant Thunder plan was by mid-August 1990.

On the plus side, exercise Internal Look 90, occurring weeks before the Iraqi invasion, provided an early and in-depth understanding of many of the problems that would be encountered. In a sense, OPLAN 1002–90 and Internal Look provided "just-in-time delivery" for the biggest U.S. force deployment since the Vietnam War.

THE EVOLUTION OF AIR DOCTRINE

In Chapter Two we discussed the larger context of the development of U.S. *military* doctrine in the post-Vietnam era. But to comprehend the development of the succession of air employment plans associated with Operations Desert Shield and Desert Storm, it is necessary to understand the evolution of service *air* doctrines since the Vietnam War. The focus of Army doctrine in the post-Vietnam years was "AirLand Battle." This doctrine contemplated the integrated application of air and ground power across the length and depth of the enemy front. The doctrine was and is based on mobility and deep-strike firepower delivered by both ground and air forces.[7] It carries the "blitzkrieg" concepts of the 1940s a step farther with emphasis on deep strikes. The Air Force, the putative Army partner in AirLand Battle, provided lukewarm support to the concept.[8] The Air Force saw support for some of its force structure in the concept, and its published doctrine supported it. At most levels, that service's officers saw it as a great improvement over "active defense" (AirLand Battle's predecessor) and as a thoughtful scheme for optimizing the efforts of U.S. Army forces in combat operations. The Marines saw AirLand Battle as a label for what they considered they had long been doing with their MAGTF (Marine Air-Ground Task Force) concept. The Navy, to the degree it paid any attention to the subject at all, considered AirLand Battle an esoteric doctrine of interest only to the Army and the Air Force.

The Army, though rarely addressing the subject head on, clearly believed that an air-only option or air campaign not in support of ground operations was a product of Air Force enthusiasm and doctrinal preferences, and that it did not reflect the realities of combat that required the Army to defeat the enemy on the ground. The Army—and Marine—view was largely carried over into the development of OPLAN 1002–90.

The Marine doctrine was built around the expeditionary qualities of the MAGTF. That organizational concept provided a balanced, initially self-sup-

---

[7]For a review of the Army's AirLand Battle doctrine, see Summers (1992), pp. 139–149.

[8]Summers (1992), pp. 146–149. Indeed, in the aftermath of the Gulf War, some USAF officials have gone to great lengths to disassociate the Coalition victory from AirLand Battle doctrine. See Hallion (1992), p. 252.

porting, nested set of capabilities that varied in size from a Marine Expeditionary Unit (MEU, a battalion supported by a composite air squadron), to a Marine Expeditionary Brigade (MEB, a regiment supported by a composite air group), to a Marine Expeditionary Force (MEF, a division supported by an air wing). In doctrinal terms, Marines came as an air-ground package with air clearly in a supporting role, and there was little, if any, consideration of using Marine air to conduct an air-only (or principally air) campaign.[9] Routine peacetime deployment plans were another matter, and Marine air, when embarked in carriers or based overseas, was given operational missions and objectives outside the MAGTF envelope.

The Navy, in the post-Vietnam era, used both classical sea power theory and its practical experience in contingency operations to develop its maritime strategy.[10] At its core, the maritime strategy was a rationale for the programs necessary to fight or deter a big war against the Soviet Union. The capabilities needed were adequate to perform a number of lesser included high-visibility missions generally grouped under the labels "peacetime presence" or "conops" (contingency operations). While the maritime strategy encompassed the need to perform deep-strike operations that might be a large part of an air-only option, it emphasized using the sea to project power ashore with expeditionary forces and to control the sea and its littoral to support larger operations by the forces of the other services. The Navy thought in combined maritime arms terms, not in terms of a strategic air campaign or extended support of a ground campaign. The result was a Navy that was prepared doctrinally for the big war with the Soviet Union at one extreme and short-duration contingency operations on the Libya and Grenada models at the other.[11] Thus, the Navy might contemplate strikes against the Kola complex and Petropavlovsk, but those strikes were for the purpose of denying the enemy the use of his sea power.

---

[9]The authors, in their review of Marine force employment literature prior to 2 August 1990, have been unable to find any mention of Marine Corps planning for, or contributions to, a predominantly air campaign. For typical discussion of the MAGTF concept, with emphasis on its combined-arms nature, see two articles from the *Marine Corps Gazette* of May 1990: Lieutenant General Bernard E. Trainor, USMC (ret.), "A Force Employment Capability," p. 31; and Major Thomas C. Linn, "MAGTF Capabilities in an Uncertain World," pp. 33–37. Also see Linn's "TACAIR: Marines Shouldn't Leave Home Without It," *Armed Forces Journal International*, August 1992, p. 37. The Marine Commander during the Gulf War, Lieutenant General Walter E. Boomer, USMC, did acknowledge the role of Marine air in a theater air campaign. (See the interview in *Armed Forces Journal International*, August 1992, p. 41.)

[10]The origins of this amalgam are admirably described in Richard Hegmann's "Reconsidering the Evolution of the U.S. Maritime Strategy, 1955–1965," *The Journal of Strategic Studies*, September 14, 1991, pp. 299–336.

[11]This gap in naval force employment concepts is implicit in Navy policy statements before 2 August 1990. See Admiral Carlysle H. H. Trost, USN, "Maritime Strategy for the 1990s," U.S. Naval Institute *Proceedings*, May 1990. Admiral Trost refers to relatively small-scale contingencies, such as escorting reflagged tankers in the Gulf in 1987–1988, and global war, but not to major regional contingencies on the Korea, Vietnam, and (future) Desert Storm models.

They were not considered "war winners" in their own right and did not include the use of large forces from the other services.[12]

The Marine Corps was part of the expeditionary component of the maritime strategy and satisfied with it. The Army and the Air Force saw this naval role as narrow, albeit necessary to bringing their own forces to bear. The principal "knocks" against the maritime strategy were that it was peripheral and did not go against the enemy centers of gravity, that the nonnuclear striking power of the forces was modest compared to larger Army and Air Force components, and that Navy and Marine Corps forces were vulnerable and lacked staying power for high-tempo operations of extended duration.

Air Force doctrine and planning preferences, as they were before Vietnam, remained grounded in a belief that air bombardment operating in support of a theater (joint) commander against an enemy's *center of gravity* (a term to be defined below) had the potential of contributing to victory as a primary force element and not solely as a supporting arm.[13] This doctrine gave priority to seizing control of the air and then using air power to pound the enemy into submission by destroying or holding at risk that which he held most dear. Missions such as supporting ground forces received less emphasis, and indeed were considered by some as a distraction to, and a drain on, planning and resources needed to pursue other, more important missions.[14]

Some Air Force officers, in most cases with a tactical fighter background, have taken exception to our portrayal of service doctrine and preferences. They believe that the "air-can-do-it-all" school was small and not influential ("zealots"), particularly after the Vietnam experience. We take their point, but believe there remained a pervasive service emphasis on the efficacy of bombing of targets at some remove from the land battlefield—some of which are "strategic" targets.[15]

---

[12]The Navy welcomed the availability of USAF tankers, AWACS, and B-52s for mining operations, but USAF support was not central to the tasks of the maritime strategy, and in a pinch might not be available because of conflicting USAF commitments.

[13]Whether the Air Force did or did not adjust its doctrine as a result of the Vietnam experience is a question on which there is continuing and lively debate. Clodfelter (1991, pp. 17–27) sees some change.

[14]For example, in USAF doctrine, the difficulties attending and inefficiencies of close air support to ground forces are emphasized. See *Basic Aerospace Doctrine of the United States Air Force,* Vol. II, pp. 165–168.

[15]General George Lee Butler, the last commander of the Strategic Air Command, gives some insight into the thinking of some of the Air Force officers we interviewed when he states that "Strategic Air Command was a nuclear outfit, had always been, and would always be . . . Strategic Air Command, which since its inception had been the heart and soul of the United States Air Force." SAC was disestablished *after* the Gulf War. See also Carl H. Builder, *The Icarus Syndrome: The Role of Air Power Theory in the Evolution and Fate of the U.S. Air Force,* New Brunswick, N.J.: Transaction, 1994, for a discussion of the roots and development of Air Force views on the role of strategic

As we will see, the Air Staff–developed strategic campaign plan (which was to be strongly criticized by Air Force field commanders) was approved at the highest echelons of that service before being sent to Tampa and Riyadh.

The Air Force benefited greatly during the post-Vietnam years by nurturing perceptive theoreticians of air power who saw the importance of the operational art of the air campaign in support of the theater commander, and the command and control needed to provide that support. Complementing the theorists were a large number of operators who laid the essential foundation of a workable doctrine. Although theory had not been translated completely to practice on the eve of the Iraqi invasion of Kuwait, impressive progress had been made in doctrine development (a draft of a new doctrine manual, Air Force Manual 1–1, and a growing number of joint publications on air operations), exercises (e.g., Red and Blue Flag), and in thinking through Air Force application in a wide variety of scenarios (e.g., the Checkmate institution).[16]

Thus, it is not surprising that when General Schwarzkopf wanted an air-only option, he went to the place he was most likely to find the necessary outlook, skills, plans, and doctrine: the Air Staff.[17] But this choice raises two related questions:

- Why was there not an offensive air campaign plan available off the shelf on 2 August 1990?

- Why did General Schwarzkopf have to go to the Air Staff to develop an outline plan to use as a basis for option selection and further planning (rather than to his own Air Force component commander)?

Before answering the first question—why no plan?—it is important to understand the difference between planning and plans. Planning for a counteroffensive (including an air campaign) had been undertaken by Schwarzkopf's staff as part of an overall campaign plan. Unfortunately, according to one report on the war, "it remained undeveloped because of the CENTCOM staff's uncertainty as to how the contingency might develop and their inability to de-

---

bombing. See also Clodfelter (1991), particularly pp. 27–28. Ziemke (1992) and Clodfelter have criticized the Air Force for learning the wrong lessons from Vietnam.

[16]For a more critical view of USAF preparedness to plan an offensive conventional independent air campaign against Iraq, see a statement attributed to Major General Robert M. Alexander (the Air Staff's director of plans) by Clodfelter (1991), p. 28. Hallion (1992), p. 144, alludes to the views of some Air Force officers who favored a gradualist approach to the application of air power.

[17]One senior Air Force officer informed the authors that in a separate action, the Chairman of the Joint Chiefs of Staff, General Colin Powell, requested that CINCSAC develop some early air attack options. It is not clear whether Schwarzkopf was aware of Powell's actions on this point.

fine the threat more fully."[18]   Moreover, it is arguable whether Schwarzkopf's staff had the expertise and system support needed to plan an air campaign. More to the point, such planning was more properly the domain of the prospective Joint Forces Air Component Commander (JFACC), of whom we will hear more in the next chapter.

Commander Ninth Air Force, in his COMCENTAF hat, had been the JFACC in the various CENTCOM exercises and might be expected to have had an air offensive plan on the shelf. Apparently he did not, except for the preliminary work done on Phase III of OPLAN 1002–90.   Indeed, one report says that CENTAF began planning an air campaign on 3 August.[19] There are several reasons for this gap in planning coverage. First, a component commander, such as CENTAF, develops campaign plans to support his CINC's plans; he does not normally have plans to go off and fight the war by himself.[20] Unfortunately, an air offensive option, if dropped into the peacetime planning environment before Desert Shield, would have raised all sorts of issues among the services and perhaps with the CENTCOM and Joint staffs. A second reason is that the CENTAF staff is built around the Ninth Air Force in peacetime, and it was neither manned nor supplied with the necessary system support to develop an air campaign plan along the lines pursued first by the analysts of the Air Staff's Checkmate organization and later by the "GAT cell" or the "Black Hole" in Riyadh.[21]   Finally, the focus of CENTCOM planning was on deployment of forces to the theater, since that represented more certainty than what they would do after they got there. Similarly, with the CENTAF staff deployed in theater and with Horner acting as USCINCCENT (Forward), the focus in theater

---

[18]See United States Congress, House Armed Services Committee, *Defense for a New Era: Lessons of the Persian Gulf War*, Washington, D.C.: U.S. Government Printing Office, 30 March 1992, p. 84. (Hereafter cited as HASC (1992).)

[19]*CPGW*, pp. 120–121. Another source states that Lieutenant General Horner, Commander USCENTAF, had already sketched an outline air campaign plan during his visit to Tampa on 2 August. (*Triumph Without Victory*, p. 55.) In reviewing the various accounts of air campaign planning, one is struck by the assertions of what commander and his staff did what and when, and ultimately how good the product was. The "Hail Mary" or "left hook" ground campaign plan also had many "fathers."

[20]CENTAF did have a "finely tuned and well rehearsed" plan (CENTAF OPLAN 1307) for the *deployment* of "show the flag" air forces to the Gulf. See Alan D. Campen, "Information Systems and Air Warfare," in Campen (ed.), *The First Information War*, Fairfax, Virginia: AFCEA International Press, October 1992, p. 25.

[21]This GAT (guidance, apportionment, and targeting) planning organization will be discussed in some detail later in this chapter. Some Air Force officers interviewed by the authors question whether the Ninth (or any numbered) Air Force staff had the needed planning capabilities. Those organizations were viewed primarily as logistics, training, and support organizations—not operational war planners and operators. They also observe that duty on numbered air forces was not considered a career-enhancing assignment and that the best officers were seldom assigned to them. Ongoing changes (starting in 1991) in the Air Force organization are intended, in part, to remove these impediments to sound war planning.

was on the immediate details of force reception and bed-down and the continuing changes in defense planning resulting from new force arrivals.[22]

With the CENTCOM and CENTAF staffs engaged in more pressing matters and not in a position to develop an air campaign plan, Schwarzkopf's options were to ask the Joint Staff for help or go to the service best equipped to fill the need. Apparently, the Joint Staff was not seriously considered as an option, and the initial planning job fell to the Air Staff. Before we continue with describing the Air Force, and later the joint, responses, we need to look at U.S. objectives in the Gulf War—because those objectives shaped the air campaign plan. We should note that these objectives were formulated after the Iraqi invasion of Kuwait and were not available to CENTCOM planners during the prewar period.

U.S. objectives in the Gulf can be viewed as a hierarchy. At the top level, U.S. national policy objectives were the following:

- Immediate, complete, and unconditional withdrawal of Iraqi forces from Kuwait.

- Restoration of Kuwait's legitimate government.

- Security and stability of Saudi Arabia and the Persian Gulf.

- Safety and protection of the lives of American citizens abroad.[23]

On 5 August, after a meeting by President Bush with his principal security advisers at Camp David, the military objectives of Operation Desert Shield were established as follows:

- Develop a defensive capability in the Gulf region to deter Saddam Hussein from further attacks.

- Defend Saudi Arabia effectively if deterrence fails.

- Build a militarily effective coalition and integrate coalition forces into operational plans.

- Enforce the economic sanctions prescribed by UN Security Council Resolutions 661 and 665.[24]

---

[22]Horner (1991), pp. 18–19; Coyne (1992b), p. 42. The *CPGW* report (p. 121) states that Schwarzkopf "determined it would not be advisable to divert the deployed CENTAF staff from organizing the arrival and bed-down of forces, while [also] preparing a plan to defend Saudi Arabia from further Iraqi aggression."

[23]*CPGW*, p. 38.

[24]*CPGW*, p. 40.

Lieutenant General Horner, who had briefed the President at the Camp David meeting, brought these more specific objectives back to his staff:[25]

• Force Iraq out of Kuwait.

• Destroy nuclear, biological, and chemical capability (5–10 year setback).

• Minimize loss of life (but do not draw out the war).

• Minimize civilian casualties.

These three sets of objectives together set the stage for the CINC's development of operational plans for both Desert Shield and Desert Storm. During Operation Desert Shield, the emphasis was on the defense of the Gulf states, to include making the necessary preparations to go over to the offensive, while the emphasis of what was later called Operation Desert Storm was the liberation of Kuwait and the destruction of Iraqi capabilities that endangered regional stability. The sequence of objective development is portrayed in Figure 4.1.

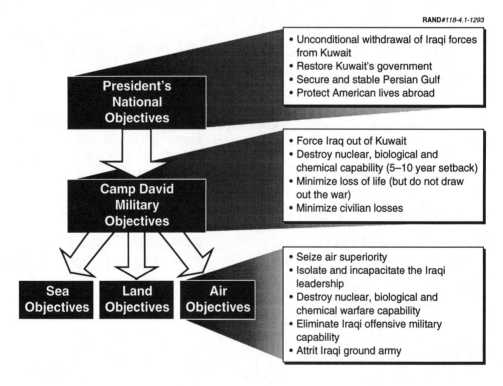

Figure 4.1—Origins of a Campaign

---

[25]These objectives have been provided to us by Lieutenant Colonel Richard B. H. Lewis, USAF.

It is now time to return to our story of the development of the air plans for the campaign, picking up with USCINCCENT's request that the Air Staff develop an air-only option.

THE EARLY ROLE OF CHECKMATE IN GULF WAR PLANNING

After the conclusion of the Vietnam War, a small office with the title "Checkmate" emerged within the planning directorate of the Air Staff. Checkmate, as it existed on 2 August 1990, was

> an organization set up in the late 1970s to provide Air Force budgeteers with long-range forecasts of service manpower and hardware requirements and how air power might be applied in future scenarios. These analysts also performed so-called bread and butter "Blue/Red" assessments that compared and contrasted Air Force weapons to their Warsaw Pact counterparts.[26]

Checkmate's interests were in evaluating vulnerabilities and high-payoff operational concepts. It was that rarity in Washington, a staff at a service headquarters that was competent to analyze options to guide and inform (if not do) campaign planning. Its limitations were more in the quantity than the quality of the staff available. In 1990 and 1991, Checkmate was led by its forceful, articulate, and often controversial chief, Colonel John A. Warden III. A recognized theoretician of air power employment, his special interest was in "operational art," the planning and execution of an air campaign.[27] Warden was (and is) a strong believer in the war-winning potential of a well conceived and executed strategic air campaign. Under his direction, Checkmate had been analyzing ways to conduct an air campaign against Iraq for some months before the Iraqi invasion of Kuwait. What was lacking was a specific planning context.

As bad luck would have it, Warden was vacationing on a cruise ship in the Caribbean when Iraq invaded Kuwait on 2 August. Debarking at his first opportunity, he arrived back in Washington on 5 August and immediately started the Checkmate staff to work on sketching out a plan for an air campaign against Iraq. When General Loh received the phone call from General Schwarzkopf on 8 August asking for help, Checkmate was already in a position to rough out a strategic air plan.[28]

---

[26]"Air Force Hopes to 'Checkmate' Future Enemies," *Defense Week*, 2 December 1991, p. 3.

[27]Warden's 1988 book, *The Air Campaign,* op. cit., was well known to air planners and analysts.

[28]There is some disagreement between Coyne (1992b) and the *CPGW* report on the dates of this and the immediately following events. We use the dates Warden gave one of the authors in an interview in the fall of 1991.

After briefing the Air Force Chief of Staff, a small team led by Major General Robert M. Alexander, the Air Staff's director of plans, and with Warden as the briefer, presented the concept plan, now called "Instant Thunder," to General Schwarzkopf at MacDill AFB in Tampa, Florida. As Coyne writes,

> The plan was based on concepts set forth by Colonel Warden in his 1988 book *The Air Campaign.* In the book, Colonel Warden postulated five concentric "rings," or centers of gravity," for strategic planning. The center ring, the most important, was the enemy's leadership. Outside that was key production—oil and electricity, for example. The third ring was infrastructure: roads, railroads, and lines of communication. The fourth ring was population. The outside ring was fielded military forces.[29]

Figure 4.2 portrays this conceptual basis for "inside out warfare."[30] Warden's plan at this stage of its development has been misunderstood by some of its critics. First of all, it was an outline plan—with objectives, an initial list of target sites, phases of force application, and a first approximation of force requirements. Secondly, it was intended to fill an immediate need for a basis for national policy decisions; it was not intended to provide guidance for the immediate formulation of an air tasking order. Third, it omitted classes of targets important to the CINC and did not include important details necessary to keep air losses within acceptable limits. It was a strawman and a skeleton of a plan.[31] It reflected its Air Staff origin and did not include attacks on Iraqi ground forces. It is easy from this distance to criticize its omissions and errors. What is important is not the major changes made to the plan as staffs in Riyadh improved it, but the degree to which the underlying concept carried over to provide the basis for the *first phase* of the air campaign in the late winter of 1991.

Because victory has many parents and defeat is an orphan, there are many both inside and outside the Air Force who are quick to criticize the Checkmate-developed plan. Lost in this scramble for credit as to who authored the "real" plan is the fact that the Checkmate plan was a pretty good effort made with little notice and under the press of time. There is no question that the final plan was better—but it took months, not days, to develop. A more fundamental (and in

---

[29]Coyne (1992b), p. 42.

[30]This figure is drawn from a briefing by Lieutenant Colonel David Deptula, USAF, who headed up the Iraq planning cell in the "Black Hole" in Riyadh during the Gulf War. It was borrowed from Warden (1988). Lieutenant General Glosson, who served as Director of Campaign Planning during the war, has emphasized to us that this diagram does not portray his approach to the targeting philosophy actually used during the war. He believes there are in fact only three rings: leadership/C^3 (at the center), infrastructure/production, and military forces/structure. He maintains that that campaign was designed to start either from inside out or outside in—or both simultaneously.

[31]*GWAPS*, pp. 36–37.

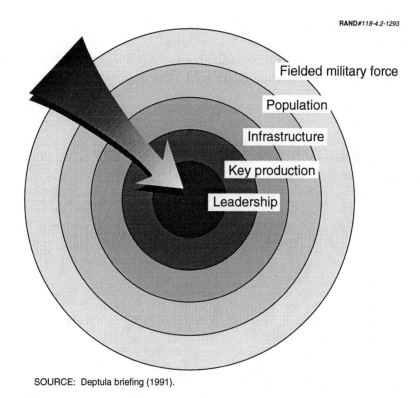

SOURCE: Deptula briefing (1991).

Figure 4.2—Conceptual Basis for "Instant Thunder" Campaign Plan

our view justified) criticism of the Checkmate plan is that its focus on the Iraqi leadership was unexecutable in the event the Coalition air forces were unable to find and hit that leadership. Moreover, there is now evidence that the real center of gravity may have been the Republican Guards—and they were not targeted in the Checkmate-developed plan.

In any event, Schwarzkopf accepted the Air Force plan developed by Checkmate as a basis for further planning and obtaining concurrence from higher authority. The Chairman of the Joint Chiefs of Staff, General Colin Powell, was briefed the next day. He ordered that the planning become joint at that point—under the nominal supervision of the Director of Operations (J-3) of the Joint Staff. As a practical matter, planning continued in Checkmate spaces in the Pentagon, and the other services detailed groups of planners to help. Over one hundred officers and specialists from all services, the Joint Staff, and the intelligence community were involved. The product was a plan that bore a heavy Air Force stamp, but also reflected the expertise, interest, and concerns of the planners of all services and the Joint Staff.

Warden briefed an expanded plan to General Schwarzkopf on 17 August. He was directed to take the plan to Riyadh, brief General Horner (who was then also acting as USCINCCENT (Forward)), and "hand it off to him." This was done by a small team from the Air Staff led by Warden on 19 August.

Although polite in hearing Warden out, Horner took strong exception to the content of the Instant Thunder plan, believing it to be a doctrinaire strategic bombing plan that was out of touch with regional realities (e.g., failure to target Iraqi ground forces).[32] After thanking the briefers he asked that the briefing team (except Warden) stay in Riyadh to help in further planning. Soon thereafter he called Brigadier General Glosson (who was on the Commander Joint Task Force Middle East flagship) and conveyed his displeasure with the Instant Thunder plan and asked him to come to Riyadh to help him plan the air campaign. Glosson was briefed by Lieutenant Colonel David Deptula (a member of Warden's team who stayed in Riyadh) the next day. Glosson, referring to notes made at the time, has provided his reaction to the plan.

> Think piece. Excellent to outstanding intell. Too fast—doesn't relate to real war. World War II bomber mentality alive and well. Eighty-four targets unrealistically few. Plan not a bad place to start.[33]

THE INSTANT THUNDER PLAN

Instant Thunder was a concept plan designed to form the basis for CENTCOM's more comprehensive Operation Desert Storm air campaign. As briefed by Warden in Riyadh in mid-August, it was an amalgam of service (principally Air Force) and joint planning and the distilled experience of a number of exercises and war games. Its name was intended to distinguish it from its Vietnam War cousin, "Rolling Thunder," the latter described by the *CPGW* report as "a prolonged, gradualistic approach to bombing North Vietnam."

The intent of Instant Thunder was not signaling, but massive, rapid, and precisely delivered attacks against Iraq's centers of gravity. These attacks, to be scheduled over six days, were focused on 84 targets centered on Iraq's leadership (e.g., C^3I), key production facilities (e.g., electricity and oil refining), infrastructure (e.g., bridges, railroads, and ports), and selected fielded forces (e.g., air defenses). Attacks on Iraqi ground forces were not included in the plan.

The reasoning behind and flaws in the Instant Thunder plan can only be understood against a backdrop of the Gulf scenario as it unfolded in August and

---

[32]*GWAPS* states that "General Horner thought the plan seriously flawed in its operational aspects and disapproved of its relative neglect of Iraqi forces in Kuwait" (p. 37).

[33]Communication from Glosson.

September, of Air Force doctrine as interpreted by John Warden, and of a task laid on by Schwarzkopf—to provide an offensive option to the President prior to the buildup of sufficient ground combat power in theater. The initial concern was in countering an Iraqi thrust into Saudi Arabia. The resources then available were not the full-blown force that launched an onslaught on Iraq and Iraqi forces in Kuwait on 17 January 1991, but the much smaller forces associated with the initial Phase I deployments described in Chapter Two. The Instant Thunder plan's shortcomings—its initial absence of focus on opposing ground forces, its failure to adequately reflect the political importance of the Scud threat, and its aura of "air can do it all"—are all rooted in Schwarzkopf's tasking, in its early single-service origin, short time-lines, and the size of forces available in August and September. The air planners did what they had been taught to do: they planned a campaign in keeping with air power doctrine, and they did it under the direction of an officer who had a strong belief in the importance of an air campaign.

Ground forces, including Republican Guard elements, were not included in the original Instant Thunder plan. Several reasons have been advanced for this omission. Air Force critics believe that the service was convinced it could win the war with air efforts alone, and that forces that could have been used to attack Iraqi ground forces were used for more doctrinally comfortable tasks.[34] Other observers believe the original plan focused limited air assets on a manageable target set, and that after the initial air campaign's objectives were realized, attacks would be made against Iraqi ground forces.[35] Whatever the merit of these views, General Schwarzkopf added Republican Guard units in Kuwait and southern Iraq to the target list because of the threat they posed to Iraq's neighbors.[36]

Before leaving our discussion of Instant Thunder, one might ask: What were the alternatives during August and September 1990? Two come to mind. The air planners could have focused on a "roll back the defenses" plan. Such a plan would have used the limited air assets available to peel away Iraqi air defenses to enable subsequent strikes against Iraqi military targets. Some Air Force and

---

[34]From conversations with Navy and Army officers familiar with Gulf War air campaign planning.

[35]RAND's Natalie Crawford observes (based on interviews with Warden) that Warden contemplated a three-phase campaign: Phase I was the strategic air campaign, and Phase II was a transition phase to Phase III that involved supporting ground forces. Phase I of Instant Thunder was done in some detail and continually revised. Phases II and III were far less complete and essentially placeholders in the event Phase I was insufficient to defeat Iraq.

[36]Based on our interviews with officers in a position to know, we believe the *CPGW* (p. 122) incorrectly attributes this decision to the Secretary of Defense. Deptula, in conversations with one of the authors, said that adding the Republican Guards to the Instant Thunder target plan was not inconsistent with the initial concept, since the Guards were an essential support element for the Iraqi leadership. See also Palmer (1992a), p. 25.

Navy planners held this view. That type of plan was consistent with much Cold War planning for strikes against Warsaw Pact targets, where NATO was precluded from planning for other than defensive operations. A second possible plan would have targeted Iraqi forces and staging areas in Kuwait that threatened Saudi Arabia. This type of plan appealed to many ground officers. The distinctive feature of the Instant Thunder plan was that it bypassed these potentially important considerations and went right to the heart of the Iraqi ability to conduct war. In a sense, it was a gamble that one could defeat the enemy by a successful attack on his head and nervous system (assuming one knew where they were) and leave the arms and legs until later.

AIR CAMPAIGN PLANNING

As will be described in more detail in Chapter Five, in-theater air planning was under the direction of the Joint Forces Air Component Commander, Lieutenant General Charles Horner, USAF. Given the necessary authority by General Schwarzkopf over the operations of the other air components and consistent with emerging joint doctrine, General Horner directed three planning evolutions concurrently.[37] First, as General Schwarzkopf's representative in theater until late August, he had to provide for the defense of Saudi Arabia—both air defense and support of defending ground forces. Second, he had to plan and support the deployment of all air forces to the theater because he had an important voice in requirements and priorities and because he had to coordinate the bed-down and support of arriving forces. We have discussed elements of this story in the last chapter. And finally, he had to plan for offensive operations necessary to achieve the larger U.S. security objectives. These three planning efforts were interrelated and in some cases competitive for the same pool of assets (tankers, for example).

However, at this point in our narrative we are most interested in the development of the initial daily master attack plans (MAPs) and associated air tasking orders (ATOs) for the first few days of offensive air operations. These plans were developed by a special planning group (SPG) in Horner's headquarters in Riyadh. Called the "Black Hole" because of the security involved, this group was led by Brigadier General Buster Glosson, USAF.[38] The core of this staff was

---

[37]In Chapter Five we will discuss the nature and extent of this authority, since it became a matter of dispute after the war.

[38]Glosson was a Deputy Commander to Commander Joint Task Force Middle East before the war and continued in that billet until early December 1990. On 16 August, Horner (with Schwarzkopf's concurrence) told Glosson he was going to have him transferred to Riyadh to build an air campaign plan. On 19 August, Horner told him to come up and get started. (Communication from Glosson.) See also Palmer (1992c), p. 26. The impetus for diverting Glosson to work on an air campaign plan was the specter of having a Washington-developed plan imposed on CENTAF.

made up of officers detailed from various echelons throughout the Air Force. It was supplemented by Navy and Marine Corps officers attached to service component staff elements in Riyadh, as well as by a few RAF officers.

The staff of the Black Hole was relatively junior when measured against the importance of the task at hand: most of its members were majors and lieutenant colonels and their Navy equivalents. The total was rarely more than 30 officers. It was not a joint staff; it was an Air Force staff with officers seconded from the other services. Although all views were heard by the staff's Air Force leadership, the decisions made not surprisingly reflected in the main the views of that leadership. Nevertheless, over long hours and days of planning, tension, and dispute, the staff developed a certain esprit de corps and style of its own.

Glosson's chief of plans during the later stages of the force buildup was Colonel Tony Tolin. Under Tolin was Lieutenant Colonel David Deptula, who directed the Iraqi targeting cell. Deptula had been a member of Warden's Checkmate planning group, which had briefed General Horner on Instant Thunder on 19 August and Glosson on 20 August. Their task was to take the Instant Thunder plan, merge it with ongoing CENTAF planning, and make it responsive to the CINC's dual needs for an initial counterattack option and the leading edge of a Coalition strategic counteroffensive.

The planning activity that followed the tasking given to Glosson has attributes of both the conventional and unconventional. The initial work consisted of modifying the Instant Thunder concept. Important modifications were made early in the planning process and included more emphasis on night operations, attacking many targets simultaneously for shock effect, attacking the Republican Guard formations on D-day, making it "smarter" to reduce anticipated U.S. casualties, and making it supportable (e.g., tankers). Coyne describes this first order of business:

> General Glosson's Black Hole group conceptualized five basic objectives. They were to isolate and incapacitate Saddam's regime, gain and maintain air superiority, destroy his weapons of mass destruction (nuclear, biological, and chemical weapons and production facilities), eliminate Iraq's offensive military capability, and render the army in the Kuwaiti theater of operations ineffective.[39]

A fundamental principle in plan development was to pit Coalition strength against Iraqi weakness. Key nodes were to be hit, nodes that if hit successfully, had the potential of taking down an entire system. Initially, there were not enough air assets to "brute force" the enemy by an attack across the breadth

---

[39]Coyne (1992b), p. 45.

and depth of most systems. This activity involved a great deal of conventional target planning—"weaponeering," timing, and providing tanker support, among many other functions. Figure 4.3 suggests the planning paradigm.

But in our view, the most important product of this initial planning in the Black Hole was the decision to attack almost all the key targets as near simultaneously as possible. Even if there is an agreed target set (as there was in this case), the timing, priority, and level of effort against particular targets are the key decisions in the exercise of operational and grand tactical arts. The earlier thinking by the CENTAF planning staff had been traditional. That is, the planning concentrated on opening holes in the radar net, rolling back defenses, and blasting a path to the targets. The traditional method required the attainment of high damage expectancies against each key target. This approach would quickly soak up attack resources and leave some important targets unhit in the first attacks. What the planners settled on instead was to spread attacks all across Iraq—"that is to stun the entire system and then exploit the delayed reactions of

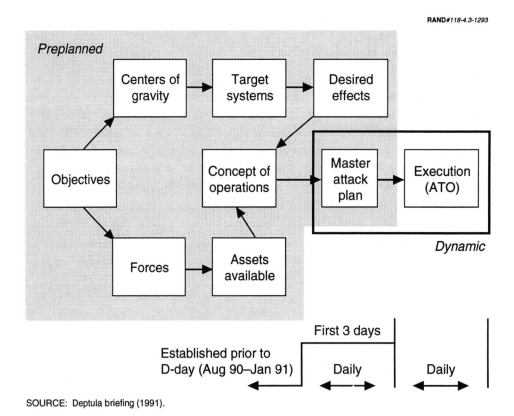

RAND#118-4.3-1293

SOURCE: Deptula briefing (1991).

Figure 4.3—Planning Phases: Concept to Execution

the stunned opponent to win control of the air."[40] The risk in this approach of sacrificing higher damage expectancies to broaden the base of the attack was that some time-urgent targets might not be knocked out in the early attacks. This was a key risk that was accepted. The essential hardware in making the risk acceptable was the F-117 (and, to a lesser extent, cruise missiles). Their surprise value and the ability to apply small packages of resources in precision strikes against key targets made the difference between success and failure.[41]

During this period of planning initial operations, the short pole in the tent was the availability of sufficient numbers of aircraft with laser self-designation capability:

> At first, planners could rely on fewer than 75 long-range aircraft with a laser . . . capability: 18 F-117As and 55 A-6Es. The mid-August decision to deploy 32 F-111Fs was the first major expansion in the laser-guided bombing capability. After the November decision to deploy additional forces [Phase II], the number of aircraft so equipped increased to more than 200 F-117As, F-15Es, F-111Fs, and A-6Es.[42]

Nevertheless, a shortage of laser designator equipped aircraft continued to be a major factor both in shaping the plan and in Desert Storm air operations that followed.

By early September, the Black Hole had delivered what Horner considered an executable plan,[43] that is, one that reflected the agreed objectives and with sufficient resources available to carry it out. From then on, the plan was updated and modified to reflect targets added to the list (the list grew from Instant Thunder's 84 to more than 300 by January before the campaign began) and the additional air power streaming into the theater.[44] The planning quickly became more complex, and the dangers of mutual interference and fratricide were very much on the planners' minds. Coordinating the operations of several thousand

---

[40]We are indebted to RAND's Chris Bowie for this quote and for his pointing us to the critical attack timing decisions in the development of the initial master attack plan.

[41]Some have observed that a "truly joint" JFACC staff would have been unable to develop and sell such a risky plan; that is, it took a staff of airmen (from one service) to think of and put such a plan together. In their view, a joint staff would have required that each service have a piece of the action. We are not convinced on this point. It depends on the quality of the personnel assigned to the staff. Joint and combined staffs in the past have been able to put together daring and unconventional plans quickly and execute them well. See Winnefeld and Johnson (1993), pp. 31–36.

[42]*CPGW*, p. 125.

[43]Horner (1991), p. 22.

[44]Not just in theater, but outside it as well. Committed SAC bomber numbers increased, and the possibility of using USCINCEUR air assets from Turkish bases came more clearly into view. Palmer (1992c) quotes Glosson as stating, "We never changed the plan after the 13th day of September, . . . the only thing we did . . . was to do more of the plan simultaneously." We note that some targets had multiple aimpoints.

aircraft in Saudi, Kuwaiti, and Iraqi airspace became a major management problem. The vehicle for operationalizing the plan and for minimizing the potential for mutual interference was the air tasking order (ATO) and the software used to help build and deconflict it. We will address those topics in Chapter Five.

The evolution of the air campaign plan is best summed up by Figure 4.4, a briefing chart drafted by Lieutenant Colonel Deptula as he reflected on the Operation Desert Storm experience. The figure illustrates the continuing growth in the number of targets from the August Instant Thunder plan to that executed on 17 January. Some of the growth was the result of adding the Republican Guards and the Iraqi army in Kuwait. Through December, phased execution was planned because there were insufficient forces, but during December, the plan evolved to one of simultaneous execution of the first three phases.[45] The air campaign planning that occurred during the period from August to mid-January was heavily weighted to developing the attack plans for the first 72 hours, but included a strategy and possible options for follow-on attacks. This emphasis on the front end of the plan was premised on the expectation that following the initial attack a dynamic situation would exist, reattacks would be needed, and enemy responses would have to be countered.

THE DESERT STORM AIR CAMPAIGN PLAN

To this point, we have considered the process for developing the initial strike plan; now we turn to the plan itself. As indicated earlier in this chapter, the President identified four U.S. objectives in the Gulf. We have seen how planners translated these into five air campaign objectives. These five campaign objectives were then linked to twelve target sets and a concept of operations comprising four phases.

The Air Campaign Objectives and Target Sets

The *CPGW* report provides a crosswalk from objectives to target sets.[46]

1. Isolate and incapacitate the Iraqi regime:

---

[45]Just because the first three phases started at the same time does not mean that each received equal effort. The controversy over timing and targeting that was to arise in late January was not about whether the three phases were proceeding together, but the *weight of effort apportioned to each*. The air campaign plan (assuming good flying weather) envisaged a three-week air campaign with six days needed for strategic air operations (Phase I), one day for establishing air superiority over the KTO (Phase II), and 20–24 days to prepare the battlefield (Phase III). (Communication from Glosson.) See also *CPGW*, pp. 133–134.

[46]*CPGW*, pp. 125–126. For associated numbers of targets, see Table A.10 in the appendix.

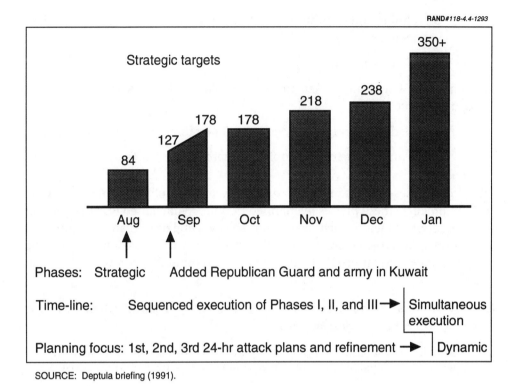

RAND#118-4.4-1293

Figure 4.4—Evolution of the Air Campaign

- Leadership command facilities

- Crucial aspects of electricity production facilities that power military and military-related industrial systems

- Telecommunications and C^3 systems

2. Gain and maintain air supremacy to permit unhindered air operations:

- Strategic IADS, including radar sites, SAMs, and IADS control centers

- Air forces and airfields

3. Destroy NBC warfare capability

- Known NBC research, production, and storage facilities

4. Eliminate Iraq's offensive military capability by destroying major parts of key military production, infrastructure, and power projection capabilities:

- Military production and storage sites

- Scud missiles and launchers, production and storage facilities

   - Oil refining and distribution facilities, as opposed to long-term produc-
     tion facilities

   - Naval ports and facilities

5. Render the Iraqi army and its mechanized equipment in Kuwait ineffective,
   causing its collapse:

   - Railroads and bridges connecting military forces to means of support

   - Army units to include Republican Guards in the KTO

The four phases of the campaign are portrayed in simplistic fashion in Figure
4.5. In practice, these phases overlapped in time. What varied was the amount
of effort apportioned to each over time. The evolving draft plan was subjected
to rigorous, iterative analysis to see that it was executable, could achieve the
posited objectives, and could be carried out with minimal aircrews and civilian
casualties.[47]

Some observers have referred to a single documented air campaign plan. But as
the *Gulf War Air Power Survey* notes,

> No single "air campaign plan" recognizable as such existed. Rather the air cam-
> paign plan executed by Coalition forces at the outset of the Gulf War consisted
> of three elements:
>
> (1) a broad statement of purpose, including the idea of a four-phased war;
>
> (2) extremely detailed air-tasking orders for the first two days of the war,
> plus additional staff work on the third day of operations; and
>
> (3) a more diffuse set of expectations about how the air war would unfold
> and what it would accomplish against any given target set.
>
> . . . Nonetheless, the result was a unified conception for applying air power
> against Iraq.[48]

Constraints

A major constraint on planning involved casualty avoidance, both to Iraqi
civilians and to Coalition aircrews. Some targets were placed off limits because

---

[47]At the request of General Mike Loh, Acting Chief of Staff of the Air Force, a team of RAND analysts
conducted a three-day game of the plan to independently analyze its strengths and weaknesses.
RAND concluded that the plan was basically sound but that the attack on Republican Guards and
the army in the Kuwaiti theater of operations would be the most effective part of the campaign,
since the Iraqi ground forces were Saddam's primary center of gravity. Colonel John Warden
disagreed with this assessment when it was presented to General Loh and Secretary Rice in October
1990. General Loh supported the RAND assessment. The RAND analysis also pointed out the
importance of the Scud missile threat to Coalition cohesion.

[48]*GWAPS*, p. 28.

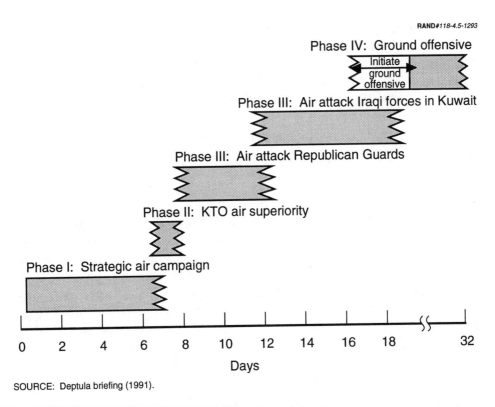

RAND#118-4.5-1293

SOURCE: Deptula briefing (1991).

Figure 4.5—Planned Phases of the Air Campaign

of their proximity to politically sensitive buildings such as schools, hospitals, mosques, or cultural treasures.[49] Every candidate target had to meet those carefully drawn criteria before being placed on the list. Targets in the heavily defended central Baghdad area were hit almost exclusively by F-117 "stealth fighters" with laser-guided weapons or Tomahawk missiles. Against heavily defended targets outside Baghdad, the planned strikes contained heavy air-defense suppression packages. The demand for these "SEAD" (suppression of enemy air defenses) assets exceeded the supply, and thus constrained the numbers of highly defended targets that could be hit simultaneously.

A similar resource constraint that posed the most difficult challenges in the planning process was the availability of tanker support. The fact of the matter was that there were more aircraft in theater (some at remote airfields or aircraft carriers) that needed tanking than there was tanking support for them. But this point is easily overdrawn, since one can reasonably anticipate higher losses of

---

[49]John A. Humphries, "Operations Law and the Rules of Engagement in Operations Desert Shield and Desert Storm," *Airpower Journal*, Fall 1992, pp. 30–32.

fighter-bombers than of tankers.[50] Moreover, there are more major performance and mission differences among classes of fighters and bombers than is the case with tankers.[51] The needed mix of fighter aircraft can change over time, so a larger number is needed than would be apparent from a snapshot of requirements at a given point in time.

TRANSLATING THE PLAN FOR THE FIRST 48 HOURS TO AIR TASKING ORDERS

The master attack plan whose development was the object of so much attention throughout the fall of 1990 and into the winter of 1991 covered the first 72 hours of the air war. Subsequent planning, obviously subject to many variables and unknowns, was to be done on the fly as the early part of the campaign unfolded. Horner has stated publicly that the reason the air campaign's early ATOs covered only several days is that he wanted the staff to recognize and react to the dynamics of combat and not be stuck with a plan that would constrain their planning flexibility.[52] By all reports, the shift from the prewar planning to the dynamics of in-war planning was very difficult, and was made more difficult by the onset of bad weather.[53] By D+10, however, most of the difficulties (except battle damage assessment and targeting, to be discussed below) had been solved or made tractable.

The master attack plan for initial operations was closely guarded and was not released to those who normally developed the air tasking orders. That translation job was done by a special team from the Black Hole during slack periods of everyday Desert Shield air tasking order writing (the latter covered, inter alia, defensive combat air patrols and surveillance missions). The product of the planning evolution was ATO coverage of the first two days of combat air operations. Changes were made in these ATOs right up until the last days before 17 January as targets and aircraft available for the operation changed. How the initial attack was carried out is dealt with in Chapter Six. Suffice it to say here that it was a textbook example of good planning and airmanship and a demonstration of the advantage of having the initiative in military operations.

---

[50]There is some evidence that the House Armed Services Committee, in considering the ODS experience, may have overstated the tanker shortage relative to weapons delivery aircraft. See HASC (1992), p. 35.

[51]For some missions, an F-15C is preferred over an F-16 or an A-6 over an F-18—and vice versa.

[52]Remarks at Naval Institute symposium.

[53]Some Air Force officers attribute the problems encountered to the unequal distribution of the most talented officers between the GAT and ATO cells of the staff.

IN-WAR PLANNING

While the master attack plan for the first 72 hours was the object of months of attention and intelligence gathering and processing, the subsequent master attack plans were developed during the heat of battle. Typically, three were in view at one time: the first addressed the day after tomorrow and reflected CINC apportionment decisions and targeting preferences, while the second addressed tomorrow and was the subject of review and revision based on today's operations as it was transformed into an ATO. A third master attack plan was reflected in today's ATO; changes were made to the ATO in execution rather than to the undergirding master attack plan.[54]

Any discussion of in-war strike planning is necessarily intertwined with the discussion of command and control and information in Chapters Five and Six. The command and control interface centers on *who* does the planning, *how* the weight of the air effort is apportioned against classes of targets, *which* targets are hit and *when*, *what* air assets are employed, and *how* they are supported. The information/intelligence interface centers on *what* information is available *when*, *how* needed information is obtained and interpreted, and *who* is responsible for providing intelligence support. Both the command and control and intelligence interfaces with planning were the sources of a lively debate before, during, and after Operation Desert Storm.

The Command and Control Interface

According to joint doctrine, the Joint Force Air Component Commander (the JFACC, Lieutenant General Charles Horner) had the responsibility for "planning, coordination, allocation, and tasking based on the joint force commander's [General Schwarzkopf's] apportionment decision."[55] The implementing mechanisms for these planning responsibilities were the CENTAF staff as augmented by officers seconded from the other services and Coalition partners, and the CINC's Joint Target Coordination Board (JTCB).

The CENTAF planning mechanism was centered in the guidance, apportionment and tasking (GAT) cell and the air tasking order (ATO) cell of the staff. This organization and the attendant responsibilities are set out in Figure 4.6. The GAT cell generated and received target nominations and developed appor-

---

[54]The best description of the process of plan development is in a publication by Lieutenant Colonel Richard B. H. Lewis, USAF (who served on Glosson's staff), *Desert Storm—JFACC Problems Associated with Battlefield Preparation,* Carlisle Barracks, Pennsylvania: U.S. Army War College, 1993.

[55]JCS Pub. 3–01.2, *Joint Doctrine for Theater Counterair Operations,* p. III-4.

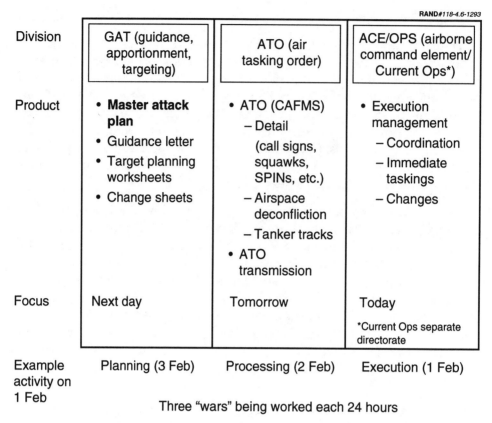

RAND#118-4.6-1293

Division	GAT (guidance, apportionment, targeting)	ATO (air tasking order)	ACE/OPS (airborne command element/ Current Ops*)
Product	• **Master attack plan** • Guidance letter • Target planning worksheets • Change sheets	• ATO (CAFMS) – Detail (call signs, squawks, SPINs, etc.) – Airspace deconfliction – Tanker tracks • ATO transmission	• Execution management – Coordination – Immediate taskings – Changes
Focus	Next day	Tomorrow	Today *Current Ops separate directorate
Example activity on 1 Feb	Planning (3 Feb)	Processing (2 Feb)	Execution (1 Feb)

Three "wars" being worked each 24 hours

SOURCE: Deptula briefing (1991).

Figure 4.6—Organization: Directorate for Campaign Plans

tionment recommendations for the JFACC to discuss with the CINC. Since the service components were represented by liaison officers in the GAT (as well as other) cells, it was joint in an ad hoc fashion. The components were heard as targets were nominated and decided on, strike tasks were allocated to component forces, scarce support assets (e.g., tankers, SEAD) were spread across requirements, and guidance was prepared for the ATO writers. But these JFACC decisions were decisions that usually reflected the CINC's priorities and Air Force preferences and practices.[56] We will continue our discussion of the ATO and how it was written in Chapters Five and Six.

---

[56]See the discussion in Winnefeld and Johnson (1993), pp. 163–183.

The Intelligence Interface

The in-war planning process was intended to proceed along the lines shown in Figure 4.7. The key steps in the process were developing battle damage assessments (BDA) and revisions to the master target list. Suffice it to say that bomb damage assessment remained a problem throughout the air campaign, forcing the planners to work on suspect assumptions and data and to set up arrangements to pull useful data out of the system rather than having it "pushed" to them. As we will see in Chapter Eight, this was a sensor problem, an architecture and systems problem, and an organizational problem. The upshot was that planning was made much more complicated and problematic in the absence of timely and accurate intelligence. This difficulty is portrayed in Figure 4.8.

But going beyond organization diagrams and information flows, there were some fundamental cultural and perceptual problems that created and exacerbated the gap between planners and intelligence officers. One study attributes the ensuing difficulties to the Checkmate origins of the original attack plan, the "closed shop" nature of the Black Hole, and a fundamental failure to communicate between organizations within (or associated with) the CENTAF staff.[57]

Issues in Apportionment and Targeting

Apportionment is defined in the JCS dictionary as

> The determination and assignment of the total expected effort by percentage and/or priority that should be devoted to the various air operations and/or geographic areas for a given period of time.[58]

According to joint doctrine, apportionment is a CINC prerogative. In practice, the JFACC has the key voice in recommending apportionment to the CINC. The service component commanders are sometimes consulted, but field commanders rarely are. The mechanism whereby apportionment options are staffed and presented to the CINC and the way in which targets are designated became contentious issues during Desert Storm. After the early days of the strategic air

---

[57]There is criticism of this situation in *GWAPS*, pp. 128–132. For a parallel critical Navy view, see Commander Daniel J. Muir, "A View from the Black Hole," U.S. Naval Institute *Proceedings*, October 1991, pp. 85–86. However, Black Hole veterans point out that the problem was one of performance, not turf. They needed good intelligence quickly, and in their view it was not forthcoming through regular intelligence channels.

[58]The Joint Chiefs of Staff, *Dictionary of Military and Associated Terms* (JCS Pub. 1), 1 June 1979.

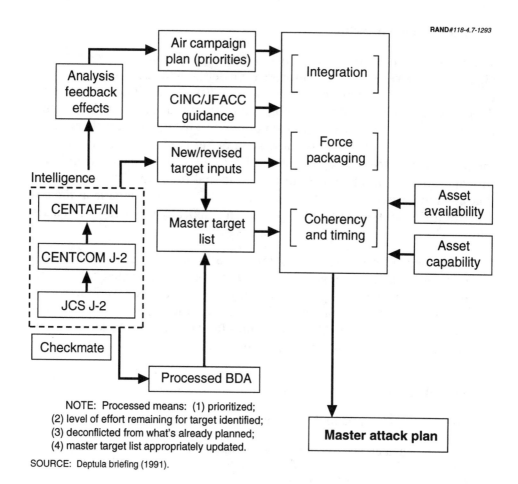

NOTE: Processed means: (1) prioritized;
(2) level of effort remaining for target identified;
(3) deconflicted from what's already planned;
(4) master target list appropriately updated.

SOURCE: Deptula briefing (1991).

Figure 4.7—Anticipated Dynamic Planning Process

campaign, the Army and Marine component commanders became concerned
that the prospective battlefield in Kuwait and southern Iraq was not receiving
the weight of effort they wanted. The allegation was along the lines that the Air
Force was running its own autonomous show and not paying sufficient attention to the needs of other services dependent on Air Force support. Air Force
commanders and planners vehemently deny this allegation. They contend that
the Marines and Army either did not know how to use the system for requesting
target servicing or chose not to use it because of a preference for delivery by
own-service systems. The DoD report on the conduct of the war put the issue
more diplomatically:

> The theater Commander-in-Chief has the key role in theater-level targeting, but
> this role is not clearly defined in joint doctrine. This lack of definition caused
> confusion and duplication. Ground force commanders expressed discontent

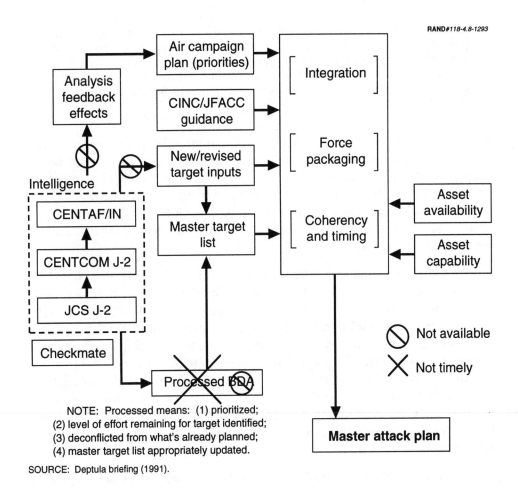

RAND#118-4.8-1293

NOTE: Processed means: (1) prioritized;
(2) level of effort remaining for target identified;
(3) deconflicted from what's already planned;
(4) master target list appropriately updated.

SOURCE: Deptula briefing (1991).

Figure 4.8—Reality: Planning Process

with the JFACC targeting process for not being responsive to pre-G-Day targeting nominations. On the other hand, the JFACC targeting process reacted to
CINC direction regarding priorities and maintenance of the overall deception
plan. Difficulties were experienced in nominating and validating targets.[59]

But sharper language in the report expresses the depth of this discontent:

CINCCENT established priorities for air preparation of the battlefield. Although
the ground commanders made recommendations regarding targets and timing
of the operations, CINCCENT aligned it with the overall theater plan. Ground
tactical commanders found this discomforting, since they were most concerned
about the forces immediately to their front and had only limited information on

---

[59]*CPGW*, p. 246.

how CINCCENT was using air power to shape the entire theater. Additionally, by CINCCENT direction, air operations did not initially emphasize destruction of front line Iraqi forces in the KTO until just before the ground offensive. This was done in part to enhance the deception plan. This also concerned the ground commanders, who naturally wanted air power to degrade the Iraqi units immediately in their line of advance.[60]

The issue did not center on whether JFACC-apportioned aircraft were hitting battlefield targets; they were, having hit them as early as the first day of the air campaign. The issue was the weight of effort assigned to battlefield preparation and to which targets were hit. Thus, the argument centered on the CINC's judgment and on the JFACC's responsiveness. For Air Force officers, this criticism challenged the heart of their service's doctrine and threatened to constrain the JFACC's authority to wield the air weapon.

The ad hoc solution to these differences was to move the location of the JTCB meetings and have the deputy CINC, Lieutenant General Calvin Waller, USA, act as its single spokesman for ground force commanders. Waller was responsible for integration and priority ranking of the target nominations by ground force commanders. All service components had membership on the board. Waller created the "DCINC" target list, a list separate from the master target list maintained by Horner for Schwarzkopf. The DCINC list contained targets of special interest to ARCENT and MARCENT.[61] Thus, an organization external to the JFACC was inserted into in-war air campaign planning. This solution met the minimum needs of those most concerned, but it remained a source of dissatisfaction and friction.[62]

Once one got beyond the headquarters in Riyadh and the deployed ground forces corps headquarters, another problem emerged. Subordinate air commanders, while appreciating that there was a coherent targeting strategy, were not always aware when and how the emphasis in that strategy changed. The field (and afloat) staffs could have been more effective if they had been kept up to date on the priorities each day.[63]

---

[60]*CPGW*, p. 345. If the explanation is valid, it suggests a breakdown in communication between Schwarzkopf and his ground commanders, or some muleheadedness by the latter in arguing for local support at the expense of larger theater considerations. See Lewis (1993), p. 79, note 54, in support of the former view.

[61]Lewis (1993), pp. 6–7. ARCENT and MARCENT are the Army and Marine Corps component commands, respectively, of CENTCOM.

[62]Based on numerous interviews with officers who served on the service component and JFACC staffs. Whether the JTCB should answer to the CINC or the JFACC remains a lively topic of discussion among joint and service staff officers.

[63]Rear Admiral Dan March, the Arabian Gulf Battle Force Commander, has suggested that in the future the ATO contain a "short simple status report on the overall campaign plan each day together with each unit's part in the plan." As officials in Riyadh saw matters, one of the functions

As we shall observe in Chapter Six, the weight of effort from Phases I and II of the air campaign began to shift to Phase III (battlefield preparation) by D+5, but it was not until the five-week point in the campaign (roughly 14–20 February) that the weight of these attacks shifted to the Iraqi tactical echelon units.[64]

A Critique of the Strategic Air Campaign Plans

The daily master attack plans developed for Operation Desert Storm have received a great deal of praise for their objectives orientation, their logical formulation, their mating of system and force capabilities to objectives—and, not least, for their generally perceived success. This praise has not just come from the Air Force, which understandably saw the plans as proof of the efficacy of its doctrine on the employment of air power, but also from many analysts and public officials who see this type of force application as a new and cheaper way of providing needed defense capabilities.[65]

Some observers, from both left and right, have been more critical of the plans. William M. Arkin, an analyst with Greenpeace International, contends that "the strategic air war was largely unnecessary because the Iraqi army was demoralized and defeated in the Kuwaiti theater of operations by massive tactical bombing."[66] Arkin has no substantial quarrel with the efficiency of the strategic air campaign, only with its relevance to the outcome. However, Arkin (in his reported comments) does not address the degree to which elements of the strategic air campaign made tactical bombing more effective (or even decisive).

Other critics of the plans are concerned that their apparent success will be misinterpreted. Carolyn Ziemke of the Institute for Defense Analyses and military affairs author Jeffrey Record believe that the air campaign, as waged against Iraq, was a continuation of the application of Air Force strategic-bombardment theory and paid too little attention to what they believe really won the war: the

---

of service liaison officers to the JFACC was to apprise their sponsoring commands of these matters. However, it is unlikely that these relatively junior officers would have access to much of this information, and even if they did, they were so involved in the details of attack coordination that they had little time to develop and communicate the big picture to their remotely located service component seniors.

[64]*CPGW*, pp. 119, 190. Lewis (1993) argues that pressures by ground commanders forced a premature scaling back of Phase I operations.

[65]For example, see HASC (1992); Representative Les Aspin, "An Approach to Sizing American Conventional Forces for the Post-Soviet Era," House Armed Services Committee document, 25 February 1992 (Aspin proposed a Desert Storm air package equivalent as the principal U.S. reinforcement of Korea); Blackwell, Mazarr, and Snider (1991), pp. 12–13; and "Changing Our Ways," Carnegie Endowment National Commission, Washington, D.C., 1992, p. 63.

[66]"Defeat of Iraq Sparks Debate on Which Air Role Was Crucial," *Aviation Week & Space Technology*, 27 January 1992, p. 60. Jeffrey Record makes a similar point. See his *Hollow Victory: A Contrary View of the Gulf War*, Washington, D.C.: Brassey's (U.S.), 1993, pp. 106–107.

neutralization of the Iraqi army, first by air power and then by ground forces.[67] Norman Friedman, writing for the U.S. Naval Institute, makes a similar argument:

> Because these implicit goals (reducing but not destroying Iraq's military power and eliminating Saddam) underlay the explicit objective (liberating Kuwait), the strategic air war was particularly important. But one fact made clearer since the original publication of *Desert Victory* is that the strategic air war very largely failed to achieve any of its goals.[68]

Thus, Friedman sees a disconnect between the plans and the campaign's objectives. The plans were feasible (it could be done) and acceptable (the losses were not inordinate), but they were not suitable (did not realize the objective). But this is a stiff test of plans that were not intended by the CINC to be sufficient to liberate Kuwait and overthrow Saddam.[69]

In our view, the plans for the first 72 hours of the air campaign were soundly conceived, explicitly tied to military and larger political objectives, clearly reflected the operative constraints (e.g., minimize Coalition aircrew losses), and optimally employed the available forces. The plans weren't perfect, but they represented an excellence in military judgment that will be difficult to equal in future campaigns.

After the first 72 hours, the problems encountered lay not so much in the planning mechanism as in the timely availability of the needed targeting and battle damage assessment information. We will return to this subject in Chapters Six and Eight.

PLANNING IN PERSPECTIVE

While major planning difficulties were encountered—both prewar and in-war—the outside observer is struck by the inherent resilience of the airmen and systems that were plugged together almost in Tinkertoy fashion to develop a total system and organization that was up to the challenge. True, there was time to prepare, and yes, a more resourceful enemy might have stressed the system to the breaking point, but the product of the planning mechanism met the test. RAND's Paul Davis has observed that the resilience of the system is

---

[67]Ziemke (1992); Jeffrey Record, "Why the Air War Worked," *Armed Forces Journal International*, April 1991; see also Summers (1992), pp. 196–199.

[68]From the second edition of Friedman's *Desert Victory*, published 1992 (p. 441).

[69]Friedman takes issue more with Air Force strategic bombardment advocates, who are alleged to have seen the strategic air campaign as a war winner largely by itself, than with the air campaign planners.

best demonstrated by the ability of the Riyadh planners to take a useful but flawed concept (the Instant Thunder plan) and over time turn it into an effective tool for neutralizing an army in the field.

It is somewhat easy at this remove to say this or that could have been done better, but some of this is postoperative sour grapes associated with Washington-level budget and force planning issues and with zealous guardians of service doctrine.[70] This is not to say that we cannot do better next time, only that the air planners and their plans were the key ingredient in designing the U.S. victory in the desert war.

---

[70]Gelman (1992); Molly Moore, "War Exposed Rivalries, Weaknesses in Military," *Washington Post*, June 10, 1991, p. A1.

Chapter Five

COMMAND, CONTROL, AND ORGANIZATION

> The Pentagon's command, control and communications (C^3) equipment and procedures withstood the strain of hard use despite being cobbled together "virtually from scratch."
>
> —Defense Week, *20 April 1992 (p. 8)*

We agree with the above assessment. Hard use and cobbling together there were—together with the attendant friction. But the Gulf War was the first conflict since World War II in which U.S. theater air forces enjoyed a large measure of unity of control exercised by a single air commander. The command failures experienced in Korea, Vietnam, and lesser combat operations were not duplicated in the desert war, and the essential elements of unity of effort in combat air operations were put in place and used effectively. This chapter describes this major achievement and puts it in the context of experience in earlier conflicts. While air command, control, and communications comprised a success story (though not without difficulties), the unique environment in Operations Desert Shield and Storm is not likely to be repeated. The unique factors, combined with the difficulties in controlling Coalition air forces—particularly the U.S. component of those forces—suggest a degree of skepticism regarding assertions that effective joint command and control has been achieved. What makes the performance of the command and control system in Desert Storm look particularly good is the comparison with the command and control difficulties experienced during earlier joint operations.

This chapter relies heavily on Winnefeld and Johnson (1993); unpublished RAND working papers by Leland Joe and Daniel Gonzales, and by Major Robert Butler, an Air Force Fellow at RAND before and during the war; interviews with participants in Operations Desert Shield and Storm; and the following documentary sources: *CPGW*, chaps. 3 and 6 and app. K; Coyne (1992a); Friedman (1991); Center for Naval Analyses, *Desert Storm Reconstruction Report, Volume II: Strike Warfare* (U), 1991, and *Volume VIII: C^3/Space and Electronic Warfare* (U), 1992; Major Michael R. Macedonia, U.S. Army, "Information Technology in Desert Storm," *Military Review*, October 1992, pp. 34–41; Humphries (1992), pp. 25–41; and other works as cited.

PROLOGUE

Since their inception during World War II, joint air operations have been troubled by defective command and control arrangements. The issues have centered on the fact that the different services have had different doctrines and priorities for the employment (and hence the control and subordination) of air power. In short, each of the four services was loath to subordinate its air units to the control of an officer of another service or to commit its forces to missions that were the preeminent domain of another service. The result was, with few exceptions, a hodgepodge of command arrangements that represented uneasy compromises between opposing views.[1] While it is convenient to state that the differences among the services were based on narrow service interests, the fact of the matter is that each service's doctrinal paradigm was correct for a specific set of circumstances. The arguments centered on whether that set of circumstances pertained in a given operation.

Nevertheless, a growing body of experience in operating together led to the conclusion that a single air "commander" or controller or coordinator was needed at the minimum to prevent mutual interference and at the maximum to make unity of effort possible. This convergence and the growing realization that there would be few occasions when a single service could fight alone resulted in a series of agreements from 1965 to the late 1980s that closed much of the gap among the services. There was general agreement that a single air authority was needed for air defense in the theater, that an airspace coordinator or controller was needed where air operations among the services overlapped, and that theater-level targeting needed central direction. But each service mapped out special preserves for itself. For example, the Marines were successful in retaining control of their air forces to serve ground Marines—with "excess" sorties being made available by the joint forces air component commander.[2] A bow to the CINC's ultimate authority provided a means whereby Marine air could be diverted to serve other purposes if the CINC believed it necessary. These arcane arrangements, and others, became the treaties among the services that served as the joint organizational edifice for Operation Desert Storm.

In the run-up to that conflict and in the commentary since, much has been made of the importance of the Department of Defense Reorganization Act of

---

[1]Some notable exceptions were the Solomons, Philippines, and Okinawa campaigns of 1942–1945. In these operations a lead service was identified and the 1940s equivalent of a joint forces air component commander *served by a joint staff* was established. For an analysis of the Solomons experience, see Winnefeld and Johnson (1993).

[2]This so-called omnibus agreement was enshrined in the 1986 joint publication, JCS Pub. 3–01.3, p. III-4.

1986 (hereafter cited as "Goldwater-Nichols"). This landmark legislation, among other things, formalized the growing power of the regional unified commanders (CINCs) in the military command structure and provided the Chairman of the Joint Chiefs of Staff with new authority at the expense of the services' chiefs. Insofar as command and control of air operations is concerned (not specifically mentioned in Goldwater-Nichols), the main effect was to provide the CINC with indisputable authority to organize his command as he sees fit.[3] Moreover, the new legislation strengthened the Chairman of the Joint Chiefs of Staff's authority for "developing doctrine for the joint employment of the armed forces."[4] As we shall see in the discussion to follow, these powers of the CINC and the Chairman created a new framework for joint air operations in the desert war.

At this point, we must digress from this line of discussion to define some terms that had come into use before Operation Desert Storm to define command and control authorities relevant to joint forces, including air forces.

A commander, including a joint commander, may, depending on the authority he is given, exercise one of three types of command or control over forces. The first of these is

> **Combatant Command (COCOM).** Nontransferable command authority established by title 10, United States Code, section 164, exercised only by commanders of unified and specified combatant commands. Combatant Command (command authority) is the authority of a Combatant Commander to perform those functions of command over assigned forces involving organizing and employing commands and forces, assigning tasks, designating objectives, and giving authoritative direction over all aspects of military operations, joint training, and logistics necessary to accomplish the missions assigned to the command. Combatant Command (command authority) should be exercised through the commanders of subordinate organizations; normally this authority is exercised through the service component commander. Combatant Command (command authority) provides full authority to organize and employ commands and forces as the CINC considers necessary to accomplish assigned missions.[5]

Note that this type of command may be exercised only by the CINC. It is what gives him the unique power to organize his forces and set up subordinate joint commanders, including a joint forces air component commander, and to em-

---

[3]10USC 163–164. General William Westmoreland, Commander of Military Assistance Command, Vietnam, did not have this authority and was hamstrung by contrary JCS and service interests until early 1968 in his efforts to get unity of control of air forces of the various services operating in his area of responsibility. See Winnefeld and Johnson (1993), pp. 72–73, 172–183.

[4]10USC 153(a)5.

[5]JCS Pub. 1–02, *Dictionary of Military and Associated Terms*, 1987.

power them with the authority necessary for them to accomplish their missions. This is the "shotgun in the closet" that the CINC has for dealing with less-than-forthcoming service component commanders.

The next level of command and control authority is operational control, or OPCON, defined as follows:

> **Operational Control (OPCON).** Transferable command authority that may be exercised by commanders at any echelon at or below the level of combatant command. Operational control is inherent in combatant command and is the authority to perform those functions of command over subordinate forces involving organizing and employing commands and forces, assigning tasks, designating objectives, and giving authoritative direction necessary to accomplish the mission.... Operational control normally provides full authority to organize commands and forces and to employ those forces as the commander in operational control considers necessary to accomplish assigned missions.[6]

This type of control is the key lever below the CINC level. Historically, operational control of the forces of one service by another service has occurred infrequently, since it involves major elements of command authority. To have OPCON of forces is to have effective command, but it also entails responsibility for logistics and administrative support that have best been provided along service rather than joint lines.[7]

The third level of command and control is tactical control, or TACON:

> **Tactical Control (TACON).** The detailed and usually local direction and control of movements or maneuvers necessary to accomplish missions or tasks assigned.[8]

This lesser level of control still provides major authority for command in combat. It should be noted that OPCON or TACON can be limited to certain functions, areas, or force types. These intricate definitions aside, it is perhaps more useful to think of COCOM as *owning* forces, OPCON as *leasing* forces, and TACON as *renting* forces on a short-term basis.[9]

With these definitions in hand, let us now turn to a command function of great importance during Operations Desert Shield and Storm: the authority exer-

---

[6]JCS Pub. 1–02, *Dictionary of Military and Associated Terms*, 1987.

[7]There are exceptions. During the Gulf War, a theater logistics command, with the Army as the lead service, was established to provide for common items and to establish priorities among different users. See William G. Pagonis, with Jeffrey L. Cruikshank, *Moving Mountains: Lessons in Leadership and Logistics from the Gulf War*, Boston: Harvard Business School Press, 1992, p. 97.

[8]JCS Pub. 1–02, *Dictionary of Military and Associated Terms*, 1987.

[9]*CPGW*, p. K-8.

cised by the joint forces air component commander or JFACC. The JFACC is not a new concept. It was used, but without that name, as early as September 1942 during the early battles for Guadalcanal.[10] In those early days, the Air Force (then the Army Air Forces) had fought the concept of a single air commander (unless he was an Air Force officer). However, as it became apparent in later years that its assets would comprise the largest component of any joint air force, the Air Force returned to its doctrinal heritage and supported the concept of a joint forces air component commander. This commander was a "functional" component commander as opposed to a "service" air defense commander.[11]

The concept of a functional air component commander made its first joint doctrinal appearance in 1964 with the publication of the *Joint Doctrine for Air Defense* (JCS Pub. 3–01.3). This manual provided for an "area air defense commander." His mission was to "coordinate and integrate" the joint air-defense effort. Note that this commander did not exercise what we now call OPCON or TACON. This antecedent of a joint air commander grew into the JFACC in a somewhat misleadingly titled 1986 publication, *Joint Doctrine for Counterair Operations*.[12] Since counterair goes beyond air defense to include attacks on enemy airfields and air support facilities, an entering wedge was put in place for providing for a joint air commander with authority beyond the counterair mission.

The JFACC's duties, to be defined by the CINC, would normally include the "planning, coordination, allocation, and tasking" of service component air sorties based on the CINC's apportionment decision. The words "allocation" and "apportionment" are terms of art very specific and full of meaning because they are the source of power and authority.

As noted earlier, apportionment is

> The determination and *assignment* of the total expected effort by percentage and/or priority that should be devoted to the various air operations and/or geographic areas for a given period of time.[13]

---

[10]With the quaint name of "COMAIRCACTUS," Cactus being the code name of Guadalcanal. The "Cactus Air Force" (later COMAIRSOLS) was a joint force composed of air units of all services. See Winnefeld and Johnson (1993), pp. 26–29.

[11]The most prominent theorist of the air functional component commander concept is Colonel Thomas Cardwell, USAF; see Cardwell (1984). But Cardwell had been anticipated by others, perhaps most importantly General William M. Momyer, USAF; see Momyer (1978), particularly pp. 65–110.

[12]JCS Pub. 3–01.2.

[13]JCS Pub. 1–02, *Dictionary of Military and Associated Terms.* Emphasis added.

Apportionment authority lies with the joint force commander, normally a theater CINC.[14] It is a major authority, and its exercise and the advice leading to the CINC's apportionment decision was to become a point of discussion during Operation Desert Storm, since the principal source of advice on apportionment comes from the JFACC (who was an Air Force officer in that case).

Allocation is only slightly less controversial. Allocation is the translation of the apportionment decision into total number of sorties by aircraft type available for each operation/task.[15] It is a JFACC task. In Desert Storm, the master attack plan (MAP) reflected apportionment decisions, and the air tasking order (ATO) translated them into allocation. Service component commanders had an intense interest in what and how many sorties were tasked for missions in support of the apportionment decision. Disagreements among the components and with the JFACC were not uncommon—nor unexpected. However, for the most part, satisfactory working agreements were reached because senior officers involved were of one mind about winning the war.

Note that while called a "commander" in his title, the JFACC is more an executive agent of the CINC who "controls" or "coordinates" air operations rather than "commands" air forces.[16] His power to control flows from the CINC's apportionment decision (on which the JFACC can exert a powerful influence) and from his own allocation decision that determines the important details of implementation.[17] As we will see, the JFACC did not exercise OPCON (except for selected forces in his parent service) and only partial TACON in Desert Storm.

Having beaten a path through this definitional jungle, we might ask what it all means for the exercise of command and control of air operations in Operation Desert Storm. We finish our examination of the Desert Storm prologue with a description of how USCENTCOM had implemented these and other joint concepts before August 1990.

USCENTCOM was a direct successor of the Rapid Deployment Joint Task Force (RDJTF) set up during the Carter administration to provide a basis for possible intervention in the Gulf in the aftermath of the Soviet invasion of Afghanistan

---

[14]JCS Pub. 3–01.2, p. III-6.

[15]Ibid., p. B-3.

[16]Marine airmen strongly believe that the word "control" does not accurately describe the JFACC's authority. They believe coordination or synchronization is the proper term, and cite Annex J ("Command Relationships") of the 16 December 1990 CINCCENT Operations Order for Operation Desert Storm as confirmation of their view.

[17]The precise meaning of the JFACC's duties and authority were the subject of some rancor within the staff and among the services who helped develop DoD's *CPGW* report. (From discussions with officers on the *CPGW* report staff and cognizant officers on the Joint and service staffs.)

and the overthrow of the Shah of Iran. Essentially it was made up of a planning staff, and between crises it had few if any forces of any real consequence.[18] The principal tools of USCINCCENT were exercises (mostly limited to U.S. forces) and an extensive set of military-to-military contacts with the Gulf Cooperation Council (GCC) states. Both were to prove invaluable in getting forces rapidly to the Gulf and siting them on the regional support structure.

However, USCINCCENT assumed major operational responsibilities and the attendant control of forces for the first time during the 1987–1988 tanker reflagging and escort operation (Operation Earnest Will) and the 1988 operations against Iranian forces (Operation Praying Mantis).[19] These operations and the exercises that were conducted in the summer of 1990 just before the Gulf War were to provide useful experience for conducting major combat operations effectively.

Two exercises that occurred just on the eve of the conflict warrant mention. The first was a USCINCCENT-sponsored command post exercise called Internal Look (described in Chapter Four). It was conducted over a two-week period in mid-July 1990. Intended to set the stage for a major deployment planning effort, Internal Look also further exercised the JFACC concept. Earlier exercises conducted under the previous CINC, General George B. Crist, USMC, had smoothed off many of the rough edges of interservice cooperation. Internal Look was to serve as a dress rehearsal for the command arrangements employed during the U.S. force deployment that started a few weeks later.

The second exercise was a field exercise called Ivory Justice, a combined exercise with the United Arab Emirates designed to practice refueling operations with USAF tankers supported by AWACS. Brigadier General Buster Glosson, Deputy Commander of the Joint Task Force Middle East (under Rear Admiral Fogarty), was put in charge of the exercise.

This description of events leading up to Operation Desert Shield suggests that the USCENTCOM staffs and assigned forces had extensive experience in the region, had a toolbox of tested command and control arrangements tailored to the deployment and employment of forces, all led by officers—Schwarzkopf, Horner, and Glosson—who had operated in the region and with staffs who were to become major actors in the Gulf War drama about to unfold.

---

[18]There was the Navy's Middle East Force, and during and after the tanker war of 1988, the "Commander Joint Task Force Middle East." That task force was composed of a few Navy escort units operating in or near the Gulf and some transient Air Force tankers and AWACS ostensibly on training missions with Gulf state forces. See Michael Palmer, *On Course to Desert Storm: The United States Navy and the Persian Gulf,* Washington, D.C.: Department of the Navy, Naval Historical Center, 1992, chaps. 11 and 12 and app. A.

[19]Ibid., pp. 133–149.

THE COALITION COMMAND STRUCTURE

The Coalition command structure and its relationship to command and control of Coalition air forces is shown in Figure 5.1. Political sensitivities played a large part in dictating the parallel U.S.-Saudi command structure for the overall effort. Arab forces were kept under Arab "command" in the person of Lieutenant General Khalid bin Sultan bin Abdul-Aziz, Commander, Joint Force/Theater of Operations (CJFTO, later called the Joint Forces Command or JFC). Other forces, predominantly from NATO states, were placed under CINCCENT's operational control. These non-Arab forces were initially under TACON of the Saudi commander but later under the TACON of either ARCENT or the JFACC for Desert Storm. *Note that while there was no overall supreme commander for the operation, the JFACC was the single authority (coordination or control, depending on one's point of view) for air operations.*

Coordination between the two command structures occurred through the mechanism of the Coalition Coordination, Communications, and Integration Center, or C³IC.[20] The jointly (that is, U.S.-Saudi) manned C³IC served as the coordination point for training and firing ranges, logistics, frequency management, and planning activities, as well as the mechanism for the sharing of intelligence and strategic and tactical reconnaissance.[21]

The U.S. chain of command went from the President and Secretary of Defense to USCINCCENT, General H. Norman Schwarzkopf, USA.[22] Schwarzkopf, reflecting his command's exercise experience, organized USCENTCOM to include four service component commands (which exercised OPCON over their assigned forces), a subordinate joint command—SOCCENT—and the Joint Forces Air Component Commander. The JFACC, in the person of Lieutenant General Charles Horner, was also Commander, Ninth Air Force and COMUSCENTAF.[23]

---

[20]*CPGW*, pp. K-20/25.

[21]*CPGW*, p. K-25.

[22]The Chairman of the Joint Chiefs of Staff (General Colin Powell during the Gulf War) is not in the chain of command. That officer advises the President and Secretary of Defense and passes their orders and guidance to the CINC. In spite of the careful wording used in the Goldwater-Nichols Act to describe his role, the Chairman exercises a powerful influence in planning and directing military operations.

[23]Military jargon on organizational matters is nearly opaque to the outside eye. Commander, Ninth Air Force, headquartered at Shaw AFB near Columbia, South Carolina, is a distinct USAF command responsible for the readiness and training of assigned USAF forces. COMUSCENTAF is the USAF component command of USCENTCOM. In his Ninth Air Force "hat," General Horner was responsible ultimately to the Chief of Staff of the Air Force; in his CENTAF hat, he was responsible to USCINCCENT, General Schwarzkopf, for assigned USAF forces. In his third hat, JFACC, he was also responsible to General Schwarzkopf for the planning, coordination, and tasking of *all* USCENTCOM fixed-wing apportioned sorties regardless of service. Loading up one officer with all these hats can lead to conflicts of interest. As we will see, that charge has rarely been leveled at General Horner except in the way he organized and manned the JFACC staff. It is worth noting that

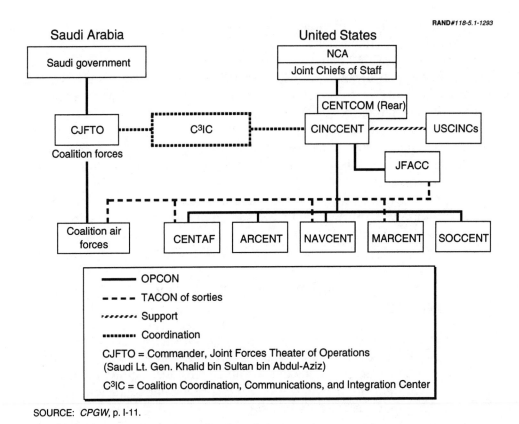

Figure 5.1—Coalition Forces Chain of Command for the Air Campaign

The other component commanders for Desert Shield, and with one exception for Desert Storm also, were:

- Lieutenant General John Yeosock, Commander Third Army and COMUS-ARCENT.

- Vice Admiral Henry Mauz, Commander Seventh Fleet and COMUSNAV-CENT.[24]

- Lieutenant General Walter Boomer, Commander I Marine Expeditionary Force and COMUSMARCENT.

---

the JFACC could have been a senior officer inside or outside the service component organizations, and indeed it could have been a Navy or Marine officer. The choice was General Schwarzkopf's to make. He chose Horner because he had JFACC experience, because he was in Riyadh, and because the Air Force provided most of the air units in theater.

[24]Succeeded by Vice Admiral Stanley Arthur on December 1, 1990.

Each of these officers had intense interest in the planned air operations, and each attempted to shape them to suit the interests of his service component in furtherance of the CINC's mission. Horner had a major advantage in this interaction: He was in Riyadh with Schwarzkopf; he had been designated by the CINC to plan and direct air operations; and the state of doctrine at the time was such as to give him fairly specific authority to do so. Boomer was at al-Jubayl, and Mauz (followed by Arthur) was in his flagship at sea. Mauz and Boomer were represented in Riyadh by one-star and two-star officers, respectively, with small staffs. This imbalance in representation (vis-à-vis the Air Force), when combined with doctrinal issues and preferences, was to be the source of problems. The fact that solutions or workarounds were devised and that a large measure of unity of effort was achieved should not obscure the importance of the command and control issues raised.

COMMAND AND CONTROL IN CENTCOM's SERVICE COMPONENT COMMANDS

Under General Schwarzkopf's COCOM were the air forces of three services.[25] Each had a service-distinct role, doctrine, organization, and set of hardware. There were some overlaps among them in all dimensions. For example, a Navy F/A-18A could perform most of the same tasks of a comparably equipped Air Force F-16C. What was different were the concepts of employment that guided their training, munitions, tactics, and employment priorities. In the discussion that follows, we look at the organizational and command and control components that shaped each service's air force.

The Air Force Component Command Structure

As if his three hats were not enough, General Horner was also designated as Commander, USCENTCOM (Forward), in Riyadh from 6 to 26 August 1990.

---

[25]We refer to the fixed-wing forces of the Air Force, Navy, and Marine Corps. There were also the large rotary-wing (helicopter) forces of the Army and Marine Corps, and the somewhat smaller Navy and Air Force helicopter units. As indicated earlier, we have drawn the somewhat artificial distinction between these two types of forces to simplify our story and to focus on the forces that were the source of most of the interest across services. There were some on the USCENTAF staff who believed that the JFACC's control should have extended to rotary-wing forces as well, and even to some artillery and missile forces on the theory that they too utilized airspace. In general, these attempts to gain control of vehicles and weapons beyond the fixed-wing category failed for practical reasons rooted in the realities of detailed coordination with surface forces. (From discussions with officers on the JFACC staff.) For Air Force views on this issue, see Deputy Chief of Staff, Plans and Operations, *JFACC Primer*, Headquarters, U.S. Air Force, August 1992, pp. 24–25 (hereafter cited as *JFACC Primer*).

Horner, as the first senior CENTCOM representative in Riyadh, had major responsibilities for the overall force reception and in setting up a hasty defense for the Kingdom of Saudi Arabia. In addition, he had to provide for the bed-down of arriving U.S. land-based aircraft, which included aircraft of all services. Schwarzkopf remained at his headquarters in Tampa during these early weeks, directing the planning and implementation (almost simultaneously) of force deployments from CONUS.

As we saw in Chapter Four, the planning for the offensive air campaign (which was to become such an important part of Operation Desert Storm) was con-ducted in Washington during this early period. And as we discussed in Chapter Three, much of the early deployment effort was oriented to the defense of Saudi Arabia from a possible Iraqi invasion. Given the C^3I infrastructure limitations in theater, headquarters staffs back in the United States had to carry a heavy load in the planning for the deployment and support for deployed forces. In CENTAF's case, the staff left at Shaw AFB was not prepared in personnel, sys-tems, or time to deal with such a massive deployment. Accordingly, on 12 August 1990, the staff of the Air Force's Tactical Air Command (TAC) at Langley AFB was designated "CENTAF (Rear)." This large staff was well equipped to deal with day-to-day tactical aircraft operations and their support. They had a battle staff structure and support system that was well connected to a wide va-riety of supporting commands, including the intelligence community. In effect, they provided the needed support that COMUSCENTAF was unable to provide from his own staff resources.[26]

Originally, the CENTAF organizational structure was centered on provisional wings. But because of the size of the deployment and intended operations in the Gulf, a different structure, oriented around provisional air divisions (more than one wing) for different specialties, began to be used in December 1990.[27] This organization, portrayed in Figure 5.2, served USCENTAF well. Brigadier General Glosson, who had moved over from the Joint Task Force Middle East staff to the USCENTAF staff in mid-August, served in a dual capacity: he was the commander of the 14th Air Division and CENTAF's Director of Campaign Planning.[28]

---

[26]This practice of having a deployed tactical operations staff forward (often called advanced echelon or "ADVON" in USAF parlance) and a housekeeping staff to the rear has a long history in aerial warfare. The Marines used it in the Solomons campaign of 1942–1944, and MacArthur's Air Forces under General Kenney used it in the southwest Pacific during the same period.

[27]*CPGW*, p. K-12.

[28]Brigadier General Profitt, the commander of 15th Air Division, was double-hatted as Glosson's deputy in the CENTAF Campaign Planning organization.

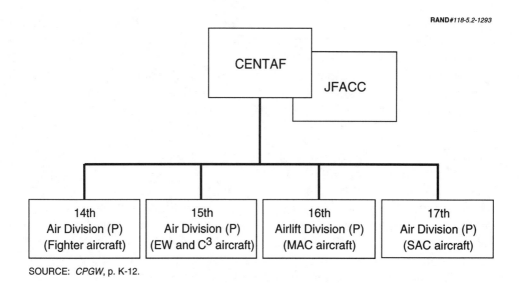

RAND#118-5.2-1293

SOURCE: *CPGW*, p. K-12.

Figure 5.2—CENTAF Command Relationships

So far this sounds fairly straightforward—once one is removed from the intersection of Lieutenant General Horner's disparate collection of responsibilities. However, the command relationship of deploying USAF forces to Horner and his provisional air division commanders was not at all clear. Some USAF forces were under Horner's command, some were under his TACON, and some were in neither category. After the war, Air Force Chief of Staff General Merrill Mc-Peak cited this mixture of command arrangements within the deployed Air Force component as unacceptable.[29] While not tidy, those arrangements apparently worked because of cooperation on all sides.

A somewhat different case was provided by Proven Force. This force was a joint task force that was deployed to Turkey on the eve of Desert Storm. Aircraft in this force were in action on D-day. However, they were under the OPCON of USCINCEUR. Nevertheless, their sorties were conducted under the TACON of COMUSCENTAF. If we were to show the Proven Force wing in Figure 5.2, it would be with a dotted TACON line from the COMUSCENTAF (in his JFACC hat) to that wing.[30] That is, the Proven Force wing was given targets or regions

---

[29]Tony Capaccio, "USAF Chief Pans War's Chain of Command," *Defense Week*, December 2, 1991, p. 1. He stated that General Horner "had only actual command of some of his fighters and electronic warfare assets but did not have actual command of his other fighters.... In the case of bombers he did have operational control. But SAC has never given up operational control of its tankers."

[30]We will discuss the command arrangements of Proven Force in more detail in Chapter Six.

of responsibility to conform to the JFACC's tasking. While the size of the Proven Force effort was small compared to the bulk of the effort directed by Horner and his staff in the Gulf, the composite air wing in Proven Force provided a needed capability to cover a region remote from bases in or near the Arabian peninsula.

The Air Force then and now has carefully avoided associating the Proven Force operation with the route package concept that was discredited, in its view, on the basis of its experience in Korea and Vietnam.[31] The entire concept was anathema to General Horner and his CENTAF staff. Yet Proven Force was a form of route package, albeit under somewhat different rules than obtained in the earlier conflicts. Although under separate *command*, the Proven Force wing was more integrated in the C^3 and planning structures than were its counter-parts in the Korean and Vietnam conflicts. The experience with Proven Force suggests that flexible organizational arrangements can be workable—even if they involve some degree of geographic separation.

The Navy Component Command Structure

The Navy and Marine command structures were markedly different from the Air Force structure. Both services kept their component commanders in the field or at sea, leaving relatively small staffs to represent their interests in Riyadh. While this conferred operational advantages on their commanders, it incurred serious representational disadvantages and resulted in overburdened operational staffs with theater-level support and coordination problems.

At the time of the Iraqi invasion of Kuwait, COMNAVCENT was the second hat of the Navy's Commander Middle East Force. No senior flag officer, say a three-star fleet commander, had been designated as COMNAVCENT in the event of a major force deployment or conflict. True, Commander Joint Task Force Middle East was a naval officer, but after 2 August 1990 the rules changed and that officer's role was subsumed in the overall CINCCENT role. Thus, the Navy had two problems in organizing its command structure for Operation Desert Shield: It had to bring in a new commander and one who had not before been subordinated to USCINCCENT, and it had to juggle the problem of operational control of its forces while representing the command's interest to the CINC in Riyadh. These challenges and their resolution were to cause the Navy significant problems in interfacing with the JFACC structure and in staffing up to meet the new requirements.[32]

---

[31]"Route packages" involved carving up an area of operations and giving subordinate or parallel organizations responsibility for operations therein. USAF doctrine, with its emphasis on unity of *air* command, is directly opposed to such a concept. See *JFACC Primer*, pp. 4–5, 24–25.

[32]*CPGW*, pp. K-13/15.

The Navy command structure is shown in Figure 5.3. This structure is relatively straightforward except for the somewhat anomalous position of NAVCENT, Riyadh. This officer, who was a junior battle group commander, removed to Riyadh where with a small staff he served the Navy component's interest in advising the CINC and the JFACC. The first incumbent, Rear Admiral Tim Wright, was a naval aviator who was well acquainted with the air command and control and planning issues that dominated the naval interface with Riyadh. On 1 November 1990, he was relieved by Rear Admiral Conrad L. Lautenbacher, Jr., a surface warfare officer. His job was, inter alia, to ensure that Navy air operations and support requirements meshed with the emerging master attack plan being developed in the Black Hole and that the air tasking order promulgated by the JFACC reflected Navy requirements and capabilities.[33] This was a large order, and it stretched the small Navy staff and its support system close to the breaking point once combat operations started on 17 January 1991.

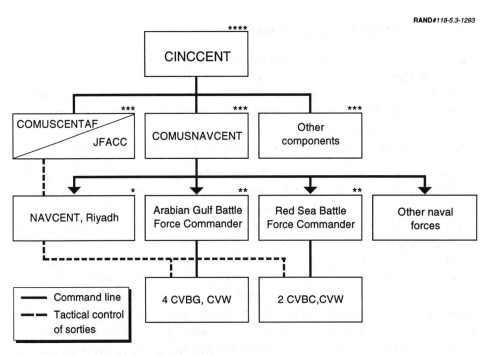

RAND#118-5.3-1293

SOURCE: Winnefeld and Johnson (1993), p. 113.

Figure 5.3—Navy Command Arrangements for Desert Storm

---

[33]He also had major responsibilities for advising USCINCCENT on the ongoing maritime intercept operations.

In practice, most communications on air operations flowed from the NAVCENT Riyadh staff (really, the Navy liaison officers serving with the CENTAF staff) to strike cells of the Arabian Gulf and the Red Sea carrier battle force staffs. Thus, Rear Admirals March and Mixson respectively ran the carrier side of the air war using the staff of Rear Admiral Lautenbacher in Riyadh as an information and coordination conduit with the JFACC.[34] The reality, however, was more complex than this simple description, since both COMNAVCENT and individual carrier battle group commanders were all netted by communications links and participated in the give-and-take of recommending and tasking sortie assignments.

The Marine Corps Component Command Structure

Like Lieutenant General Horner, but unlike Vice Admiral Mauz on 2 August, Lieutenant General Walter Boomer, the commanding general of the 1st Marine Expeditionary Force (I MEF), was a service component commander in the pre–Desert Shield period. But like Vice Admiral Mauz, he was not an aviator. The Marine organization is portrayed in Figure 5.4.

Command arrangements for Marines in Saudi Arabia were made more complex by the existence of a separate large contingent embarked in amphibious shipping under the command of the amphibious force commander and ultimately COMNAVCENT. However, General Boomer established a general officer afloat ("MARCENT (Forward)") on the COMNAVCENT flagship *Blue Ridge* and coordination was relatively smooth. The Marines enjoyed an advantage over the Navy in Riyadh: their interests were represented at the two-star level ("MARCENT (Rear)") by Marine aviators. Moreover, as we shall see, the Marines were better connected in communications and system support than their Navy colleagues. In spite of these advantages, the Marine interface with the Air Force–run JFACC staff was less harmonious.[35]

In their relationship with the JFACC, Marine lines of coordination in theory flowed up from the 3rd Marine Air Wing to I MEF, thence to the JFACC at Riyadh through MARCENT (Rear). In practice, record communications usually

---

[34]Interviews with Rear Admirals March, Mixson, and Lautenbacher.

[35]This point is substantiated by our interviews with many Air Force and Marine officers who were close to the interface. The sources of disharmony centered on control of air space adjacent to Marine ground forces and the weight of effort (and its timing) given to battlefield preparation. However, the presence of a USAF liaison officer on the 3rd Marine Air Wing staff and very able Marine representation in Riyadh worked to resolve differences once they were raised.

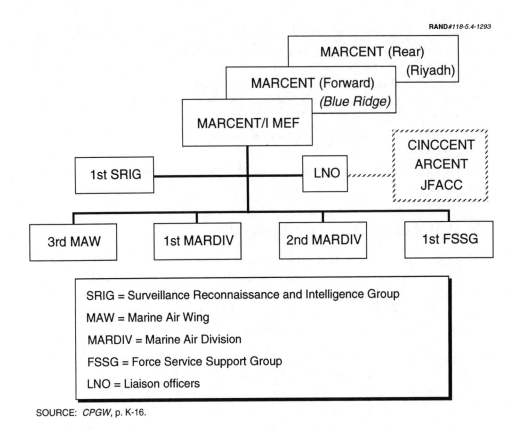

SOURCE: *CPGW*, p. K-16.

Figure 5.4—MARCENT Command Structure

went directly from 3rd Marine Air Wing to the JFACC, with "info copies" to I MEF and MARCENT (Rear). Voice communications were usually between Marine operations staff in 3rd Marine Air Wing and MARCENT (Rear) representatives attached to the JFACC staff.

To this point in our narrative we have moved the pieces into place for a discussion of the JFACC himself, his staff, and the way his functions in planning and operations were discharged during the Gulf War. We have already discussed some of these matters when we examined plans and planning in Chapter Four. Here we will focus more on organizational and staffing matters: how and by whom control and coordination of air operations were exercised.

THE JFACC ORGANIZATION

First off, there was no JFACC "staff" as such. The only person on the US-CENTAF staff with a JFACC hat was General Horner himself. His CENTAF staff performed JFACC duties in addition to their normal CENTAF duties. Thus, the

"JFACC staff" was from top to bottom an Air Force staff: organized on USAF lines, using USAF staffing practices, supported for the most part by single-service Air Force systems, and buttressed by a supreme confidence in the effectiveness of air power.   This Air Force staff, assisted by a collection of "component liaison officers" from the other services and allies, planned and directed Desert Shield and Storm air operations.

Horner's staff was made up of many directorates and staff offices, but in this discussion we focus on only two: campaign (or combat) plans and combat operations.   Figure 5.5 portrays these important command and control elements.   Under Horner was his deputy chief of staff for operations (DO), Major General John A. Corder.   Under Corder were the Director of Campaign Planning (Brigadier General Buster Glosson) and the Director of Campaign Operations (Colonel Jim Crigger), as well as several other offices not discussed here.   Glosson's deputy was Brigadier General Profitt.

We have already noted that Glosson and Profitt were also commanders of key air division force elements. The somewhat convoluted arrangement of double-hatting Glosson and Profitt with staff as well as command positions suited Horner.   It gave his two senior planners direct access to him (and vice versa) and provided Horner with tight personal control over key operations and processes both within his staff and over key subordinate commands.

In this organization, Glosson occupied the key role under Horner, particularly during the planning that was conducted starting in early August 1990. But this focus on plans and planning should not take away from the critical importance of the conduct of day-to-day operations under the direction of Major General Corder and Colonel Crigger. Planning gets the ball rolling in the right direction and speed, but operations keeps it on its path to provide strikes. The fact that the plans were executed so successfully is a testimonial both to the plans themselves and to the operations staffs who directed their execution.

The role of the liaison officers from the other services (and the Coalition partners) is an interesting story in itself. These liaison officers were attached to their parent service component commands (e.g., MARCENT (Rear)) in Riyadh and seconded to CENTAF (actually Glosson's plans shop) to help that staff perform JFACC functions. These officers had no official status in the CENTAF/JFACC staff other than as liaison officers. There was no joint staff as such, though the existence of component liaison officers gave the appearance of one. These liaison officers took on jobs as either "action officers" or planners in specified CENTAF staff offices or "cells"—or they performed in a consultant or advisory capacity.

The component liaison officers were there to represent their service interests, to inform the JFACC staff on their service's operational characteristics, and to

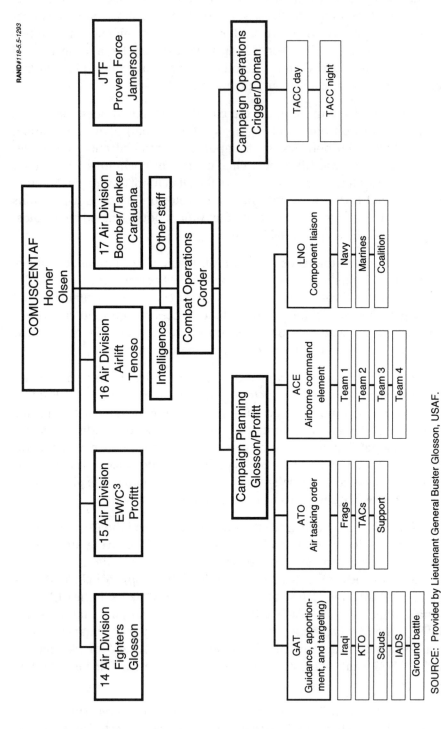

RAND#118-5.5-1293

SOURCE: Provided by Lieutenant General Buster Glosson, USAF.

Figure 5.5—CENTAF/JFACC Headquarters Staff Organization

perform an external "sanity check" on planning that included aircraft of their service. When they thought their service or their views were being short-changed, they would complain, and in some cases these complaints reached General Horner. Thus, in most cases, they performed in an advisory, coordinating, and requesting role rather than as full-fledged members of the staff. In interviews by the authors with the officers of the other services who were involved in this system of single-service dominance, the respondents to a man found the system flawed. Air Force respondents fell into two groups. The first believed that a single-service organization is the most expedient one and ensures that the commander will receive frank views from attached liaison officers from the other services. The second believed that a joint staff is better, provided there is time to form and staff one.

But arguments in favor of a joint JFACC staff can, of course, be taken too far. Some have observed that to insist on a joint JFACC staff is to play by "Little League rules": everyone gets to play. In a more serious vein, some critics of joint staffs have correctly argued that the objective is not "jointness" for its own sake, but rather to use tools and service forces that are best suited to the job. But these views are not inconsistent with (1) recognition of the major (though we would suggest narrowing) differences among the services on the subject of air doctrine, (2) the fact that joint staffs build confidence and encourage teamwork among members of the service components that do not furnish the joint commander, and (3) historical evidence that joint air staffs have been very effective in combat under circumstances much more difficult than those of Desert Storm. In sum, arguments for or against a joint staff should not be suggested or rejected on the basis of single-service precedent or convenience.

It is easy to be critical of the Air Force's dominance of the JFACC "staff," but in the early days there was no practical alternative. Even though the JFACC concept had been used and exercised, no provision had been made for a joint staff (or a deputy JFACC provided by another service) in prewar planning. The reason for this is not clear, but the answer probably lies in two sources. The Air Force was comfortable with a single-service organization supplemented by liaison officers from the other service components, and the other services were leery of providing officers to man "joint" billets in an Air Force–dominated staff. What is less easy to explain is that in the months following the Iraqi invasion, apparently no attempt was made either by General Horner or the other component commanders to insist on a joint JFACC staff.[36]

---

[36]General Horner has said that he felt the single-service nature of the JFACC staff was necessary under the circumstances. But he also believes there are strengths to the liaison officer concept: Such officers are more likely to frankly state their parent service views if they are in a liaison capacity than if they are assigned as joint staff officers. (Interview with General Horner.)

HOW THE COMMAND AND CONTROL SYSTEM WORKED

The Black Hole was served by a variety of conventional and ad hoc intelligence sources. Among the latter, the most publicized was the linkage back to the Air Staff's Washington Checkmate organization headed by Colonel John Warden (see Chapter Four). That organization served as a fusion center for intelligence available in the Washington-based intelligence community and a conduit to the Black Hole in Riyadh. Although ad hoc in nature, this system worked well and filled an important operational need. Less publicized (and arguably more important) was Glosson's direct liaison path to Rear Admiral Mike McConnell, the head of the Defense Intelligence Agency (DIA) and the J-2 on the Joint Staff in Washington.

The principal product of the Black Hole was the master attack plan. During the Desert Shield phase, while the attack plan for the first three days of combat operations was being developed, the staff of the Black Hole also used the ATO cell's automated systems to translate the plan to air tasking order format. Liaison officers worked in both the ATO cell and the airborne command element (ACE) cells. In this function they represented their components' interests in writing the ATO and (through the Combat Operations directorate) in providing guidance to the airborne command element. Although various control elements—AWACS and ABCCC aircraft, ASOCs, and the Marine DASC (all described in Chapter Six)—could make the on-the-spot decisions needed to execute the ATO, the normal process was for Combat Operations to control and provide guidance during the execution of the ATO to all commands and headquarters elements.

There were two types of liaison and coordination chains flowing from the CENTAF/JFACC staff in developing the master attack plan and ultimately the ATO, which was the instrument of JFACC control:

- The various service component liaison officers communicated with their parent commands, sometimes in very innovative ways because of a mixed bag of communications links. Secure voice was perhaps the most common method (e.g., STU-III, INMARSAT).

- USAF officers on the CENTAF staff communicated with the various provisional air divisions and directly with the wings at the large number of bases in the theater. These voice circuits were more firmly established and more reliable than those used by the liaison officers.

The common element shared by these two types of links was the interactive nature of establishing what missions the CENTAF/JFACC felt obliged to fly to support the CINC's apportionment decision and the master attack plan and what the units in the field or with the fleet were capable of providing (or in some cases wanted to provide). Robert Duncan sums up the process as follows:

> The term "Air Tasking Order," however, is somewhat misleading. U.S. and Coalition forces performed their missions after a process of dialog and give-and-take, not the simple issuing of orders. Integration was achieved by asking each Coalition force, through liaison cells in the Tactical Air Control Center (TACC), what they could contribute, given the taskings and targets to be struck, and what targets they could best attack. This dialog ensured that no Coalition forces were sent against targets they did not feel well suited to handle.[37]

Hence, most of the communications represented a brokering session among requirements, capabilities, and service desires that were often rooted in doctrine and operating practices. But in a positive sense, these communications permitted the wings to participate in the planning process and propose changes on short notice. Nevertheless, this type of activity provided a fertile field for misunderstandings and doubts about the motives of other services. Below we list some examples of the resulting misunderstandings and disagreements:[38]

- The Navy generally wanted a stronger combat air control (CAP) package with its strikes than the JFACC's staff was willing to provide tanker support for—given the latter's perspective of total theater needs and capabilities.

- Air Force officers in the CENTAF/JFACC staff wanted more Navy and Marine EA-6B jammer assets supplied for JFACC tasking than either service had available or wished to divert from its own strike packages (outside the MAP, but inside the ATO).

- Some naval aviators perceived Air Force bias in favor of giving Air Force units the more desirable missions (e.g., CAP stations with a better chance of getting air-to-air kills of Iraqi aircraft) or preferential assignment of tankers.

- Air Force officers believed that the Marines were holding back sorties for missions they preferred to fly in support of ground Marines.

- The fact that Brigadier General Glosson was both the JFACC Director of Campaign Planning and the commander of the CENTAF air division of fighter aircraft planted further suspicions among Navy and Marine planners and commanders (e.g., preferential assignment of sorties to USAF units).

---

[37]Duncan (1993), pp. 74–75. Duncan served during the Gulf War in the TACC's directorate of plans. He wrote CENTAF's Desert Shield and Desert Storm concept of operations for command and control of tactical air forces in support of ground forces.

[38]It is to the credit of all the service component commanders that these disagreements and misunderstandings did not become major issues. In our view, the genius of Horner lay in his ability to see that grievances were addressed and that he took no more control of air operations than was necessary to do his job. (Winnefeld and Johnson (1993), pp. 146, 196.)

- Air Force officers criticized Army staffs for not fully exploiting the available systems for requesting air support, and for using unrealistic BDA accounting rules.

A more serious source of concern was the fact that ground commanders focused on, and nominated for attack, targets of immediate tactical importance to them, while JFACC and CINCCENT understandably kept a theaterwide perspective. This meant that targets directly affecting each individual ground commander's area of responsibility did not always receive the priority established by each ground commander. Ground commanders, as a result, complained of insufficient air support in their sectors, and in the Marine case, tended to withhold Marine aircraft from assignment in the master attack plan in order to accomplish missions that they deemed most important.[39] For example, Marine AV-8Bs flew sorties in MARCENT area of responsibility (AOR) and stood close air support alert for Marine and pan-Arab ground force commanders. By agreement between Generals Boomer and Horner, they were not included in the master attack plan and were scheduled in the ATO by Marine liaison officers to ensure sorties were available to service targets of Marine interest.[40] Generally, Navy sorties over water (principally for maritime defense), and Marine sorties in direct support of Coalition troops were not included in the master attack plan. The fact that misunderstandings, disagreements, doubts, and differences in service practice were confined to the one-star and two-star level and below is testimony to the statesmanship of General Horner and his service component counterparts.[41]

In addition to the voice linkages between the CENTAF/JFACC staff and the component air commanders, there was a data link serviced by the Air Force's Computer-Aided Force Management System (CAFMS). This system, composed of hardware and software and supported by compatible communications systems, had been developed to help air operations staffs build an air tasking order. It provided set formats for the necessary operations data and provided a framework for associated software to deconflict the large number of flights involved.[42] It was an interactive planning tool that under near-ideal circum-

---

[39]For an Air Force view of this point, see Hallion (1992), p. 208, and Lewis (1993).

[40]In addition to serving as a tasking order, the ATO served as a deconfliction and support coordination device. Hence, AV-8B sorties were not "JFACC-tasked," but were included in the ATO to avoid mutual interference with other forces. Some have said the Marines "gamed" the ATO, as we will discuss in Chapter Six.

[41]Apparently, these issues were rarely taken up to the component commander level. This result is at marked variance with the experience of the Korean and Vietnam conflicts. (From authors' interviews with the various air planners and commanders involved. See also *GWAPS*, pp. 145, 153.)

[42]The CADS (Combat Airspace Deconfliction System) "automatically compiles the Airspace Control Order and inserts it into the . . . CAFMS . . . where it becomes one element of the daily ATO" (Campen (1992), p. 34).

stances would permit air tasking order writers to communicate in set formats with unit operations personnel. Its weaknesses were its outdated and somewhat awkward software, its high demand on communications capacity when netted, and its limited acceptance and use outside the Air Force (and even within the Air Force). Navy and Marine air task order writers did not have CAFMS before Operation Desert Shield and were not familiar with using it. Indeed, some Air Force units did not have the equipment or the experience to use it.

During Desert Shield, the Air Force provided a CAFMS unit to the 3rd Marine Air Wing along with staff proficient in its use. Given the relatively good communications enjoyed by the Marines in their link with Riyadh, CAFMS served MARCENT and CENTAF/JFACC well. With the Navy it was another story. CAFMS terminals were ultimately supplied to all six Navy carriers on station in the region. Aside from some unfamiliarity with using the system, the major drawback was that the carrier flagships did not have sufficient communications capacity to provide a serviceable data link with CAFMS in Riyadh. As a result, the Navy-CENTAF/JFACC planning link was a fluid, often ad hoc, and largely voice circuit coordination affair. The ATO that resulted from these processes had to be delivered in hard copy and disk form by air to the carriers daily.[43] Given the 43-hour lead times in ATO preparation and the delay in delivery, it is understandable that the Navy would complain about the ATO's lack of flexibility.[44] The ATO's flexibility, or lack of it, is a subject of lively debate. In execution, the ATO was structured to fit changed circumstances. For example, untasked (e.g., strip alert) sorties could be (and were) loaded into the ATO to meet emerging requirements. We suspect there are hidden agendas on both sides of the argument. The pro-ATO group sees criticism of the ATO as an attack on the need for an empowered JFACC and an attempt to carve out dedicated airspace for service component commanders. It also argues that the ATO must be evaluated in the context of its associated battle management system, a system designed in part to modify the ATO on the fly as circumstances dictate. The anti-ATO group does not question the need for an ATO-like coordination document, but does question the rigidity and long lead times in its preparation, and sees it as a wedge to facilitate JFACC control over matters best left to local commanders. Both groups agree that improvements are needed in the ATO development process and system support. But even under the best of conditions, the ATO required modification in execution, as we shall see in Chapter Six.

---

[43]The Navy lack of communications capacity for receiving the daily ATO and the need to fly it to the carriers each day has been widely publicized. Less known is that the ATO also had to be flown to some Air Force commands. See the interview with Major General Larry Henry, USAF, in "Getting USAF C^3 on the Ground," *Jane's Defense Weekly*, 22 May 1993, p. 25.

[44]This lead time figure was supplied by Leland Joe and Dan Gonzales of RAND. Others use slightly longer or shorter figures. As the war progressed, lead times were reduced.

AIR DEFENSE COMMAND AND CONTROL

CENTAF was given four joint functions under the CENTCOM command structure: he was to serve as JFACC, airspace control authority, interdiction coordinating authority, and air defense commander.[45] We will discuss airspace control later in this chapter. Because the Iraqi air threat was of such short duration, it is easy to forget that it was a major concern to Coalition commanders at the onset of Desert Storm. This concern was sharpened because of anxiety over potential Iraqi use of air-delivered chemical and biological weapons.

The air-defense system used by the Coalition included U.S., European, and Soviet-built systems. The challenge to the command and control system was to provide effective air defense while preventing fratricide—all in the context of truly massive flight operations that exacerbated the usual problems of distinguishing friend from foe.

The command and control structure for air defense consisted of "national system," airborne, and ground-based elements. These were involved in surveillance, generating and disseminating a coherent air situation display, and controlling air defenses. Because with few exceptions Iraqi air operations were limited to Iraqi airspace, detections were made mostly by USAF AWACS and Navy E-2 aircraft. In some cases electronic warfare assets made the initial detection.

There were at least four AWACS airborne at any one time—with three covering the Iraqi border with Kuwait and Saudi Arabia. Navy E-2 aircraft mainly operated over the Gulf and Red Sea areas. Coalition SAMs, both on the ground and at sea, were kept under close control. An effective system of coordination with air controllers aloft and on the ground prevented any Coalition SAM firings against friendly aircraft.

A noteworthy feature of the Navy-Marine part of the integrated air-defense system is that Navy E-2s flying from carriers in the Gulf were integrated through the Marine TACCs, which in turn coordinated with the Control and Reporting Center at Dhahran. However, this became a tenuous link on occasion, and Navy commanders' access to the complete air picture suffered accordingly.

USAF AND MARINE APPROACHES TO AIRSPACE CONTROL

Perhaps nowhere were differences in the Air Force and Marine approaches to command and control as apparent as in the JFACC's exercise of his responsibility for airspace management. General Horner and his staff believed that cen-

---

[45]*CPGW*, p. 56.; Duncan (1993), p. 74.

tralized control of airspace was necessary because there were so many users from different commands. Failure to control airspace could result in friendly fire both between aircraft and between air and ground units. Moreover, it would result in an inefficient application of the air effort. But there was a special factor at work during Operation Desert Storm: multiple simultaneous uses of airspace over a given land area. The achievement of air supremacy gave the airspace manager the opportunity to set ceilings and floors within a given airspace section for a given piece of territory. Thus, strikes flying from Saudi bases could proceed into Iraq at 25,000 feet, while strikes on targets in Kuwait were being conducted at 12,000 feet in the same geographic location.

The Marines wanted what was in effect a lease on airspace adjacent to their ground forces, so as to optimize Marine operations and reduce the amount of prior coordination required with Riyadh and to respond quickly to the needs of engaged ground forces if required. They called these areas high-density air control zones, or HIDACZs. These zones would be controlled by the Marine Tactical Air Control Center. The Air Force staff at Riyadh argued that they should control that airspace and that the Marines should ask to use it when they needed it. Their position was founded more on that service's preferences (and prerogatives associated with the JFACC mission) than on operational necessity in the circumstances of the Gulf War. By the start of the ground campaign, an agreement had been reached that gave the Marines the control they sought up to designated high altitudes that the Air Force retained under its control for the routing of transiting aircraft.[46]

MARINE CLOSE AIR SUPPORT

One of the reasons the Marines give for wanting their own HIDACZs was to be in a position to effectively render rapid close air support (CAS). As matters turned out, relatively few close air support sorties were required because much of the enemy strength was neutralized before the start of the ground campaign, rapid movements characterized the ground campaign, and ground units appeared to have sufficient firepower of their own. Nevertheless, an elaborate close air support command and control system was put in place—and only partially used. RAND's Ted Parker and Don Emerson have calculated that slightly under 4,400 CAS sorties were flown during Desert Storm, out of 112,000 total sorties. Even this CAS figure is probably inflated, since many sorties were likely miscategorized.[47] The close air support function and associated re-

---

[46]*CPGW*, p. 195. The size and shape of HIDACZs were a matter of continuing negotiations, particularly in the period just before and after the commencement of the ground campaign.

[47]As they were during the Vietnam War. Our judgment on this matter rests on interviews with deployed operations staff members and RAND analysts familiar with the sortie data.

sources, so often a bone of contention among the Air Force, Army, and Marine Corps, were not really put to a stiff test during Operation Desert Storm.[48]

THE SPECIAL OPERATIONS FORCES (SOF) INTERFACE

The 1989 operation in Panama (Operation Just Cause) aside, Desert Storm was the first opportunity to test SOF command and control in extended combat against a major opponent. It is safe to say that the services and most joint commands have never been happy with congressionally mandated command arrangements that place Special Operations Forces outside service component command chains. Critics maintain that a resource allocation problem has been solved at the expense of unity of command and in further muddying the waters of a difficult force management problem. The DoD after-action report, while laudatory of the SOF contribution, suggests that this intermeshing of political differences between the Congress and the DoD showed up on the battlefield.[49]

But our interest in Special Operations Forces is limited to their participation in the air campaign—either as strike forces or as supporting forces. Two SOF missions are of particular interest: direct action (DA) missions and combat search and rescue (CSAR).

Direct Action Missions

These missions either overlapped the air campaign or provided direct support to the campaign. For example, two key Iraqi radar sites near the Saudi border were destroyed just before H-hour to breach the Iraqi air-defense barrier and open the gate for the large-scale aerial attacks that were to flow over and around it. Although those attacks were carried out by SOF helicopters, others were launched from fixed-wing attack aircraft such as AC-130 Spectre gunships. Fixed-wing air missions were contained in the ATO, and most deep helicopter missions were coordinated with the ATO, controlled or monitored by the AWACS, and supported by fixed-wing SEAD aircraft.[50]

---

[48]For a ground-level perspective of the effectiveness of Air Force CAS arrangements for support of the Army during ODS, see John M. Fawcett, Jr., "Which Way to the FEBA?" *Airpower Journal*, Fall 1992, pp. 15–24. Fawcett (an Air Force officer serving with the Army) points out two principal problems in controlling CAS in the Gulf War: coordination of CAS beyond the fire support coordination line (FSCL) during fast-moving ground operations, and the delays experienced in the receipt of ground commanders' fire support element (FSE) priorities.

[49]*CPGW*, p. J-2.

[50]*CPGW*, p. J-16.

Combat Search and Rescue

CENTAF was designated by USCINCCENT as the combat search and rescue co-ordinator.

> Because SOF aircraft were best suited to conduct long-range personnel recovery missions, the SOCCENT commander was designated as commander of combat rescue forces. SOF provided 24-hour, on-call CSAR for Coalition aircrews.[51]

Thus, SOCCENT was in effect another component commander for the JFACC to deal with. Note that CENTAF's role was as a CSAR *coordinator*. JFACC staff officers were openly critical of the JFACC interface with SOCCENT and looked on the separateness of the latter command as an artificiality that got in the way of effective direction.[52] In many respects, this difficulty was in microcosm similar to the Air Force–Marine relationship. That is, a task-oriented, combined-arms task force had requirements and capabilities that overlapped what the Air Force saw as the legitimate responsibilities and authorities of a single air commander.

COMMAND, CONTROL, AND ORGANIZATION IN PERSPECTIVE

Command and control as exercised by CENTCOM during the Gulf War was an amalgam of emerging procedures and doctrine and ad hoc arrangements built on the fly. The major changes from previous conflicts were the establishment of a single air control or coordinating authority (the JFACC), a single master attack plan disseminated in a single ATO, and the crafting of a tight network of integrated procedures and nets that tied system components together. There were important unresolved issues in command and control, and the system was not subjected to the test posed by an able and competent enemy.[53] Nevertheless, the Gulf War was the first to demonstrate that effective theaterwide command and control is attainable and not necessarily a hostage to special interests.

---

[51]*CPGW*, p. J-16.

[52]Discussions with Air Force officers who served with the CENTAF staff. For a more evenhanded assessment, see General Loh's comments at the Air Force Association's Symposium on Air Warfare, Orlando, Florida, 30–31 January 1992 (reported in *Inside the Pentagon*, 6 February 1992, p. 6).

[53]See *JFACC Primer*, pp. 21–26.

Chapter Six

OPERATIONS

OVERVIEW: EXECUTING THE AIR CAMPAIGN

The Desert Storm air campaign was the most intense air war conducted since World War II. Some 88,500 tons of bombs were dropped over a six-week period on targets in Kuwait and Iraq in support of the Coalition's political and military objectives. It was fought initially against a backdrop of minimal supporting surface combat operations. The success of the air campaign's execution ultimately would be critical to the outcome of the ground offensive, especially in terms of its duration and the casualties suffered. Minimizing both was very important to sustaining Coalition unity and public support.

The enemy that the Coalition faced across the Saudi-Iraqi border looked formidable. The Iraqi army was usually considered the fourth largest in the world, and many also considered it to consist of battle-hardened troops and experienced commanders after its eight-year war with Iran, an impression that would seem less credible in retrospect. But it did possess a formidable array of tanks, armored personnel carriers, and artillery, as well as modified Scud ballistic missiles, already used against Iran during the Iran-Iraq War, and chemical weapons, also used against Iraqi Kurdish villagers in rebellion against Baghdad. Some therefore feared that Iraq was prepared to use chemical weapons if necessary to defend Kuwait. Saddam Hussein was also known to be pursuing biological weapons research, as well as a nuclear research program, both of which posed, if not immediate threats, long-term threats to Iraq's neighbors and to regional stability. Reducing this long-term threat was one of the war's objectives.

This chapter draws heavily on an unpublished RAND working paper by Fred Frostic, "Air Campaign Against the Iraqi Army in the Kuwaiti Theater of Operations"; unpublished RAND working papers by T. M. Parker and Donald Emerson, Stephen T. Hosmer, Leland Joe and Daniel Gonzales, Richard Mesic, and Raymond Pyles, and by Major Robert Butler and Major Thomas Marshall, Air Force Fellows at RAND during and after the Gulf War. It also draws on *CPGW;* Coyne (1992a); Friedman (1991); Hallion (1992); unclassified portions of Volumes I and II of the Center for Naval Analyses's *Desert Storm Reconstruction Report; GWAPS;* and other works as cited.

Of more immediate concern to the air war planners was Iraq's extensive and sophisticated air-defense network. Built on a Soviet model with a combination of Soviet and Western technology, Iraq's integrated air-defense system (IADS) consisted of some 7,000 radar-guided surface-to-air missiles (SAMs), lethal against high-altitude aircraft, 9,000 infrared (IR) low-to-medium altitude SAMs, and 7,000 antiaircraft artillery (AAA) pieces. Iraq also possessed 800 combat aircraft, including advanced Soviet and Western models, such as Soviet-made MiG-29 Fulcrum air-defense interceptors and French Mirage F-1s. Although the Iraqi air force was not considered to be on a par with the best U.S. and European forces, it was not insignificant, and the Coalition expected to lose aircraft and pilots to Iraqi air defenses.

The Desert Storm air war may be divided broadly into four chronological stages:[1] the body blow delivered on the first night of the war, 17 January, and continuing through the first 24 hours; the next two weeks of the campaign, when the effort focused on gaining air superiority and continuing the strategic air campaign; the next three weeks or so, when emphasis shifted to the task of cutting off the Iraqi forces in the Kuwaiti theater of operations (KTO) and reducing their effective fighting strength through continuous bombardment of their positions, in preparation for the ground campaign; and, finally, air operations in support of the short ground campaign. These phases had considerable overlap: for example, attacks against Iraqi ground force positions in the KTO began on the first night, and the strategic campaign continued, albeit at a lower level of effort, throughout the final weeks of the war. Nonetheless, this description of the stages is a useful general characterization of how the air war unfolded.

This chapter focuses on the conduct of air operations throughout the campaign. Operations includes numerous topics that cut across all phases of the air campaign, including training; in-war planning, tasking, and control of forces; the effect on operations of problems with bomb damage assessment and weather; refueling support; and the operations of the Turkey-based Joint Task Force Proven Force. In short, this chapter picks up from Chapter Four to describe how the daily master attack plans were executed, and from Chapter Five to describe how command and control was exercised from the point of view of air units and operators. We conclude with a review of the results of the air campaign, comparing its execution to the objectives and plan that guided it.

---

[1]Our use here of four chronological stages should not be confused with CENTAF's four-phase campaign plan described in Chapter Four. CENTAF's four phases were originally intended for sequential execution; in fact they were executed more or less simultaneously, and had complementary and sometimes overlapping target sets. Our characterization of the air campaign is intended to be both narrative and analytic, and provides the framework for the remainder of this chapter's discussion of air operations.

TRAINING FOR WAR

As we pointed out in Chapter Two, the combination of the professionalization of the U.S. military in the 1980s and the extensive and realistic training programs employed by U.S. forces in the same period resulted in well-trained units, tactically and technologically proficient, that were able to adapt to unexpected changes in plans and circumstances and to exploit the high-technology systems entering the force during this time. This training ranged from large-scale operational deployments, to interoperability demonstrations, to command post exercises to evaluate plans and procedures, and to competitive system proficiency exercises.

After the Iraqi invasion in August and the Coalition deployment to the Gulf, units conducted training under wartime conditions both at their home bases and in the theater. Squadrons designated for Gulf duty underwent a training program focusing on aspects of operations that were considered politically unacceptable in densely populated Britain, for example, unsafe, too costly, or environmentally hazardous for regular peacetime training. These included nighttime air-to-air refueling, very-low-altitude flight, and heavy load flying.

Once in theater, pilots continued to train with even more realism, including a heavier dose of night operations and flying in strike and air-defense packages made up of aircraft from the various members of the Coalition, all conducted over mostly featureless desert terrain that placed heavier demands on navigational accuracy. Complex procedures for managing the airspace and safety practices were worked out and learned by allied flight and ground control crews.

As plans developed and the Iraqi air-defense threat was further assessed, aircrews began practicing for specific missions and adapting training to the threat environment, including medium-altitude bombing. Fighter-bomber aircraft of all services conducted "mirror-image" flights that duplicated the actual flight ranges, profiles, and weapons delivery that would be required once combat operations commenced.

Predeployment training for most of the air forces had emphasized high-speed, low-altitude attacks on targets, due to the presumed threat from Iraqi high-altitude SAMs. The high-altitude SAM threat was suppressed very quickly, but the Coalition lost aircraft to low-altitude SAMs and to antiaircraft artillery throughout the war. This led the air commander to limit operations below 10,000 feet. Since aircrews had not trained and were not equipped for effective precision strikes at this altitude (with the exception of laser-guided bombs), there was some loss in accuracy, as we will see.

THE FIRST TWENTY-FOUR HOURS

Desert Storm began officially at 0300 local time on the night of 17 January. Actual commitment to hostilities had begun earlier. On the morning of 16 January, at 0630 local time, seven B-52G bombers armed with conventionally armed air-launched cruise missiles (ALCM-Cs) took off from Barksdale AFB, Louisiana, for the Persian Gulf. At 0130 on the 17th, Navy ships in the Gulf launched Tomahawk cruise missiles toward their targets in Iraq. Shortly before H-hour, Air Force Special Operations Pave Low helicopters led Army Apache helicopters in attacks against two Iraqi early-warning radars. F-117A Stealth fighters had already swept undetected past the border into Iraq. The F-117s attacked Iraqi air-defense sites, and together these two attacks punched a hole in the Iraqi air-defense network that allowed the attacking armada to sweep into Iraq. F-15C and F-14 air superiority fighters led follow-on waves and established combat air patrols (CAP) to intercept any opposing airborne Iraqi aircraft—of which there were only twenty. Some F-15s had pushed into Iraq early in response to a scramble by the Iraqi air force. Although the Iraqis sent up their best air-defense aircraft the first night—MiG-25s, -29s, and Mirage F-1Es—they had limited nighttime capability and inferior weapons, and they were trounced.[2]

Nearly 700 combat aircraft from the United States, Britain, France, and Saudi Arabia, including almost 400 strike aircraft, sortied against the first night's objectives in Iraq and Kuwait. They were supported by 160 tankers, flying in preassigned tanker tracks the length and width of Saudi Arabia, three USAF AWACS aircraft and two Navy E-2C Hawkeyes as flying command posts, and an RC-135 Rivet Joint electronic eavesdropping plane.[3] Strike packages were as large as 50 aircraft, made up of a dozen or more strike aircraft such as F-16s accompanied by F-4Gs for defense suppression, Navy/Marine EA-6Bs or Air Force EF-111s for jamming, and F-15s, F-14s, or F/A-18s as fighter escorts. The 37th Tactical Fighter Wing's F-117A Stealth fighters, however, sortied alone with no support except for tankers (although there is some dispute over the extent to which they benefited from jamming that was intended to support other aircraft). Figures 6.1 and 6.2 show the Iraqi situation just before H-hour, and the first night's attacks.

The first night's objectives were to deliver a quick disabling blow to three critical functions: to the Iraqi integrated air-defense system (IADS), to Saddam

---

[2]Analysis by RAND's Fred Frostic. As he has pointed out, this had to be discouraging to the remaining Iraqi pilots, and perhaps helps explain the limited response of the Iraqi air force and even the flights to Iran later on.

[3]Coyne (1992a), pp. 3–11; *CPGW*, pp. 149–159.

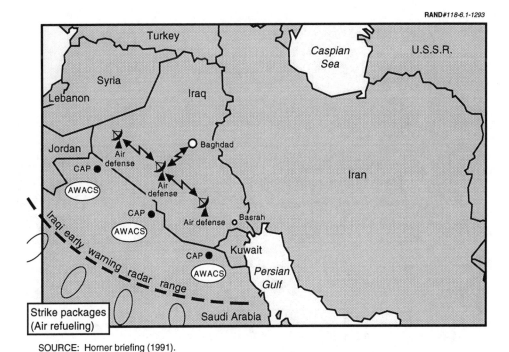

SOURCE: Horner briefing (1991).

Figure 6.1—Iraqi Situation Before H-Hour

Hussein's command, control, and communications network, and to the electric power generation and transmission facilities that support modern communications, computers, and other military functions. The initial attacks included "more than a dozen key leadership targets, a similar number of air-defense and electric distribution facilities, 10 C³ nodes," and a dozen targets in other categories, including airfields and fixed Scud missile sites in western Iraq.[4] As described in Chapter Four, the plan relied on simultaneous, closely coordinated strikes all across Iraq to stun multiple critical systems at once. The execution relied on simultaneity, surprise, and flawless execution. Using stealth technology, Tomahawks, and other systems, all coordinated in the ATO, the plan was successfully executed.

To suppress Iraq's air defenses—the crucial first step for the success of the night's attacks—more than 200 High-speed Anti-Radiation Missiles (HARM) were fired against Iraqi radar sites, almost half by USMC F/A-18s, the rest by USAF F-4Gs.[5] Other aircraft jammed enemy radars and military communica-

---

[4] *CPGW*, p. 156.

[5] *CPGW*, p. 158; United States Navy (1991), p. 37.

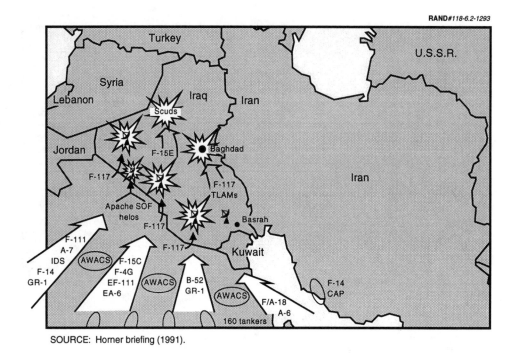

SOURCE: Horner briefing (1991).

Figure 6.2—The First Night's Attacks

tions. The B-52s launched 35 ALCM-Cs against eight targets, including power
generation and transmission facilities and military communications sites. One
hundred sixteen ship-launched Tomahawk missiles (TLAMs) attacked sixteen
heavily defended electric power and C^2 targets in Baghdad. F-117s attacked key
leadership targets in Baghdad, air-defense sites, and other strategic targets such
as Iraq's NBC weapons research, production, and storage sites.[6]

In the first three hours of combat, between 0230 and dawn, the Coalition's 400
attack aircraft sortied against more than 100 targets in Iraq and Kuwait. As day
broke, attacks continued with other aircraft suited to daytime operations,
including A-10s and F-16s.

By the end of the first day the Coalition had inflicted serious damage to the C^3
network, key leadership facilities, and parts of the known NBC capability. Electricity was also knocked out, with 85 percent of Baghdad's electrical power cut
by the end of the third day. Most significantly, air superiority was achieved
early. The Iraqi air-defense network's sector control centers were damaged, cut
off from centralized control, and forced to attempt to operate autonomously—

_____

[6]*CPGW*, p. 154; United States Air Force (1991), p. 21.

which they could not do. The Iraqis were unable to coordinate defensive operations, flying only 50 air patrols during the first day and even fewer in the days following.[7] This success was to prove crucial to continuing the air campaign's relentless pounding of Iraqi targets.

The one notable dark cloud overhanging the first day's successes consisted of the Iraqi Scuds. Planners had been unable to determine the success of F-15E attacks against fixed launch sites, and in any event it appeared that they had not set back the Iraqis' ability to launch from mobile launchers.

THE FIRST TWO WEEKS: ACHIEVING AIR SUPREMACY AND THE STRATEGIC AIR CAMPAIGN

"Perhaps the most important factor in the entire campaign was the early establishment of air superiority."[8] The achievement of air supremacy in the KTO was one of the Coalition's first objectives, paving the way for increasingly intense attacks against Iraqi forces in the theater. The SEAD (suppression of enemy air defenses) campaign consumed a major part of the first three days of the air campaign, with the most important attacks coming in the first 24 hours as Coalition forces sought to knock out the Iraqi air-defense network in one overwhelming blow.   Ultimately, the result was the achievement of air supremacy by D+10 (27 January). This achievement was the precondition for the successful prosecution of the next phase of the campaign, the destruction of enemy ground forces. Without air supremacy, the neutralization of the Iraqi army in Kuwait would have been much more difficult, time-consuming, and costly, and Coalition casualties during the ground war would have been much higher than they were.

Similarly, attacks against strategic targets—leadership and command and control targets, energy production, weapons of mass destruction, and Iraqi military capabilities—were heaviest in the earliest days of the war, and fell off after the first two weeks as the weight of effort shifted to attacks against enemy ground forces in preparation for the ground offensive (although attacks against enemy ground forces began on the very first day of the war, using AV-8s, A-10s, and B-52s). The goal of the strategic campaign was to deliver a swift disabling blow to Iraq: to paralyze Saddam Hussein and the Iraqi leadership, crush their ability to control the army and population, and eliminate their most important current and potential military capabilities.

---

[7]*CPGW*, p. 162.

[8]Unpublished RAND research by Fred Frostic, op. cit.

Weather

Bad weather settled in on the third day of the war, and remained a problem for the next several days, causing diversion and outright cancellation of many sorties and complicating the transition from the first three "scripted" days to day-to-day planning starting on Day 4. The weather was much worse than had been predicted. In fact, over the 43-day course of the war, cloud cover exceeded 25 percent almost three-quarters of the time, 50 percent half of the time, and approached 75 percent on nine days.[9]

This posed a problem because the Coalition's rules of engagement demanded positive visual identification of targets before weapons release to avoid collateral damage and casualties. Targeting was thus made more difficult, and so sorties were less effective than planned. For example, the hit percentage for the F-117s averaged 70 percent during the war's first three weeks, and rose to 86 percent after the weather improved. Laser designators did not work as well in low cloud cover and in rainy or foggy conditions. Overall, half of scheduled sorties were diverted or canceled due to weather.[10] The strike system that performed its mission regardless of weather conditions was the Navy's Tomahawk sea-launched cruise missile.

The weather not only slowed the pace of the war, it also degraded assessment of the air war's progress. Damage assessment from overhead imagery was impaired by the cloud cover. Mission results often could not be assessed for several days. Weather would again be a factor during the ground campaign. Low cloud cover forced Coalition aircraft to operate at low altitudes, where they were more vulnerable to Iraqi air defenses. Thick, oily smoke from oil pipeline and wellhead fires set by the retreating Iraqi forces compounded the difficulties during ground operations.

Achieving Air Supremacy

Iraq's air-defense network was built on the Soviet model, with multiple, internetted layers that included antiaircraft artillery (AAA), surface-to-air missiles (SAMs), and fighter-interceptors, centrally controlled by a network of hardened underground command and control facilities. Significant modifications had been made by Western, especially French, firms. The overall architecture and

---

[9]Hallion (1992), pp. 176–177. USAF planners had assumed 13 percent cloud cover on average, based on the record of previous years. According to *GWAPS* (p. 9), this prediction may have been biased by poor data: "It is not clear that the Coalition actually encountered unusually poor weather. Planners may have simply had excessively optimistic expectations because of the poor quality of the climatological data for the region."

[10]Hallion (1992), p. 177; *GWAPS,* pp. 6–8.

specific details of much of the system became available to Coalition planners through foreign governments and firms involved in its design and construction; these data were analyzed by both the CENTAF staff and the Navy and were extremely important to the effectiveness of early attacks in knocking out the system.[11]

The first blow came 22 minutes before H-hour, when three Air Force Pave Low helicopters from the First Special Operations Wing, equipped with night-guidance equipment, guided nine Army Apache helicopters over the border to two Iraqi early warning radar sites. The Apaches launched their Hellfire missiles against the sites, punching a hole in the Iraqi defense network for F-15Es to pass through on their way to their D-day targets in western Iraq. F-117s destroyed other Iraqi defense sites, including an air-defense operations center in southern Iraq.

Numerous systems participated in the campaign to suppress the enemy's air defenses, and SEAD was truly a joint operation. USAF F-4G Wild Weasels and Navy/Marine Corps F/A-18s firing HARM (AGM-88) missiles destroyed radar emitters; EF-111s and EA-6Bs jammed radars; Air Force EC-130 Compass Call aircraft disrupted the air-defense command and control network;[12] and critical C^2 nodes were destroyed, principally by precision-guided munitions launched by F-117s and F-15s and with Navy Tomahawks.

Early on, SAM sites with known locations were subject to preemptive laydown attacks by general-purpose ground attack systems and occasionally by Navy Tomahawks. For the rest, a "bait-and-kill" tactic was employed: standoff jamming aircraft jammed Iraqi electronic warfare and ground control intercept (EW and GCI) radars, then shut off just as drones were launched toward Baghdad. As Iraqi SAM operators tried to shoot down the decoys, HARM antiradiation missiles launched from USAF F-4G Wild Weasels and Navy and Marine Corps F/A-18s homed in on the radars and destroyed them. Together, these attacks were highly effective, minimizing EW and SAM radar emissions within a week after the start of the air campaign, as shown in Figure 6.3.

---

[11]United States Air Force (1991), p. 5. In our view, the contribution of the Navy's SPEAR (Strike Projection Evaluation and Antiair Research Agency), whose mission included detailed analysis of air-defense systems of potential opponents, has not been sufficiently recognized in the popular literature on the Gulf air war. SPEAR had the most complete and accurate analysis of the Iraqi air-defense system of any organization in DoD. See Eric Rosenberg, "Pilots Identify Capability Shortfalls," *Defense Week*, 16 September 1991, p. 5; also *GWAPS*, p. 125. Some USAF officers interviewed stated that SPEAR's contribution was not unique and that similar information was available from other sources.

[12]USAF Compass Call communications-jamming aircraft crews are among the many unsung heroes of the air war. The Air Force is the most advanced service in performing this important mission. See *Inside Defense Electronics*, 1 February 1991, p. 3.

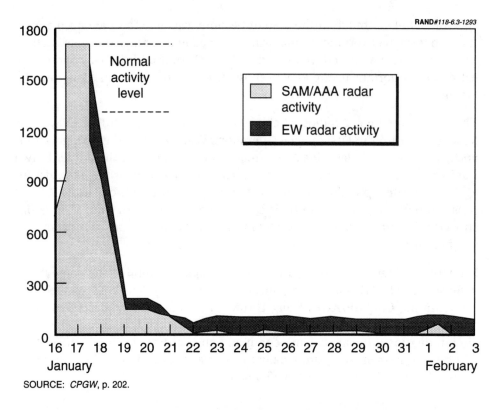

SOURCE: *CPGW*, p. 202.

Figure 6.3—Iraqi Air-Defense Radar Activity

In the first two weeks of the war, when the SEAD campaign was most intensive, the Air Force, with 62 F-4Gs and 22 EF-111s, flew some 1,151 SEAD missions. The Navy and Marine Corps together flew another 1,012 missions. Over time the Air Force flew proportionally more SEAD sorties—approximately 70 percent altogether.[13]   The HARM missiles were the most important element in "hard" suppression of enemy air-defense radar sites. The Air Force fired 1,067 HARMs during the course of the war, and the Navy and Marine Corps another 894. Air Force F-4Gs had the ability to launch HARMs in the more effective "range-known" mode, while the Navy and Marines employed preemptive launch of missiles toward the potential target array, with the missile homing in on emitters as and if they started transmitting.

The Navy's EA-6B area-jamming aircraft, along with the Air Force EF-111, saturated remaining radars with electronic "noise," hiding the flight path of the strike aircraft they accompanied behind what is sometimes referred to as a

---

[13]Analysis by RAND's Christopher J. Bowie, and T. M. Parker and Donald Emerson. See Tables A.6 and A.7 in the appendix.

"wall of electrons" and allowing them to penetrate to their targets safely. Jamming of enemy radars by EF-111 aircraft was successful against Saddam's older-vintage air defenses, including the Spoon Rest and Flat Face radars and SA-2 and SA-3 missiles.[14]

The SEAD operation continued throughout the war, although it quickly became apparent that the first night's attacks had had a devastating effect. Over time, the resources devoted to fighter support of strike packages and defense suppression were reduced, and more aircraft were devoted to strike missions. According to one RAND analyst,

> Following the initial intensive SEAD campaign in the KTO, at least two F-4Gs, EF-111s, EA-6Bs, and a Compass Call EC-130 were kept on station in the KTO continuously to provide threat warning and engage those emitters which came up periodically. In addition to the organized SEAD effort, attack flights devised a series of tactics to discourage and suppress reactions by AAA sites.[15]

The Coalition was highly effective in suppressing the use of radar-guided SAMs; Iraqi operators feared turning on their radars, knowing they would be attacked by the HARMs. Thus, contrary to prewar expectations, the medium- and high-altitude air environments provided a virtual sanctuary for allied aircraft. The low-altitude air-defense environment (IR-guided SAMs and AAA), however, remained highly lethal. According to Major General John Corder, director of combat operations for CENTAF, "Aircraft self-protection systems worked perfectly against radar-guided missiles. The people who were shot down were hit by guns or infrared missiles."[16] The persistence of the low-altitude threat caused General Horner to order that Coalition aircraft operate at altitudes greater than 15,000 feet, later lowered to 10,000 and then 8,000 feet. This was one of the most significant changes in allied strike planning, since peacetime training for most of the contributors of air power (including the most important, the United States and the United Kingdom) had emphasized low-level delivery of weapons. Medium- and high-level bombing altitudes reduced the effectiveness of some attacks, notably against runways, but against other targets as well. For F-16s, for example, CEPs[17] for unguided bombs went from 30 feet (in peacetime low-altitude training) to 200 feet. Significant bombing errors for B-52s were also recorded.[18] These accuracy degradations came as a surprise to

---

[14]Rear Admiral R. D. Mixson, "Navy's Version of Carrier Contribution to Desert Shield/Desert Storm," *Armed Forces Journal International*, February 1992, p. 44.

[15]Frostic, op. cit.

[16]Coyne (1992a), p. 98.

[17]CEP is "circular error probable," a measure of bombing accuracy.

[18]Hallion (1992), p. 212, and Mixson (1992). The degradation in B-52 bombing accuracy was attributable to three factors: (1) the unaccustomed use of high-altitude bombing tactics, (2) a shortage of low-drag conical bomb fins necessary for high-altitude bombing, and (3) the failure of

planners, and were the result of both aircraft system and training deficiencies. For example, there had been little peacetime training in medium-altitude delivery. In effect, a significant loss of accuracy was the price paid to limit aircrew losses.

In parallel with SAM suppression and jamming, the Coalition also carried out intensive attacks against Iraqi airfields to ground the Iraqi air force. Although during the first few days' operations the Iraqis launched only 30 fighter sorties a day on average, CENTAF and CINCCENT were concerned that the Iraqis were husbanding their resources to mount an offensive later, perhaps against Coalition positions in Saudi Arabia, and possibly with chemical weapons. Navy commanders in the Persian Gulf were concerned by the remaining Iraqi F-1s armed with small, fast, and hard-to-detect Exocet missiles that had proved so deadly in the past.[19] By the end of the first week, General Horner concluded that runway attacks were unnecessary because of the reduced numbers and effectiveness of the Iraqi air force and the potential high cost of low-level attacks. As a result, he ordered allied aircraft to operate at higher altitude, and switched tactics. The Iraqis had built 594 hardened shelters in which to hide their aircraft, and it was to "shelter-busting," using F-111Fs and F-117s carrying laser-guided 2,000-pound bombs, that the effort now turned. As would often prove to be the case, conclusive evidence of the success of these attacks remained elusive during the conduct of the war, although the circumstantial evidence was significant: the Iraqis began dispersing aircraft to residential neighborhoods and other areas where they were less vulnerable (because of Coalition collateral damage restrictions), but where operations support was minimal or nonexistent. Starting three days after the shelter campaign began, some 80 Iraqi combat aircraft fled to Iran. What the motivation was remains unknown, but the result—since the Iranians seized the planes and thus removed them from the war—was, from the Coalition's point of view, largely salutary.[20] Moreover, the Coalition established barrier air patrols to shoot down fleeing aircraft, downing several. By the end of January, after another round of flights to Iran was countered by allied air patrols, the Iraqi air force was seemingly completely out of the war. Three hundred seventy-five of the 594 shelters were destroyed or damaged. Postwar inspection of damage to shelters indicated that

---

avionics software to correct for wind conditions at higher altitudes. See "B-52s Were Only Marginally Successful in Gulf War, Gen. Butler Says," *Aerospace Daily*, January 28, 1993, pp. 155–156.

[19]An Exocet fired by an Iraqi jet severely damaged the USS *Stark* and killed 37 of its crewmen in 1987, during the Kuwaiti tanker reflagging escort operations.

[20]Navy commanders in the Persian Gulf remained concerned about Iraqi aircraft in Iran, however, because of restricted sea maneuvering room and because little warning of an attack passing through Iranian airspace would be available.

the attacks had been quite successful in destroying aircraft when they were inside.[21]

On 27 January, CINCCENT declared allied air supremacy over Kuwait and Iraq. A few operations centers and SAM sites remained operational, and as late as the fifth week of the war the Coalition lost five aircraft, including two A-10s engaged in low-level attacks against Republican Guard forces operating mobile SAMs. Nonetheless, compared to earlier wars and given the dense threat environment that existed before the war, the allied air forces operated with virtual impunity over enemy airspace for most of the conflict.

The Strategic Campaign

Iraq's leadership, its command, control, and communications systems, its war-supporting infrastructure, and its capability for producing and employing weapons of mass destruction were among the principal targets in the early phase of the war. These, along with the Republican Guard, were the Iraqi "centers of gravity" targeted in General Horner's plan, as described in Chapter Four. Destroying these target sets would, it was thought, seriously cripple Saddam Hussein's ability to wage war and to control his own country.

The original plan for this phase of the air campaign had envisioned a two-week intensive strategic phase, dropping off from 700 sorties per day to less than 100 after the first week for restrike of targets hit earlier. In fact, the buildup of air power in the second phase of Desert Shield permitted Horner to schedule nearly 1,200 sorties per day in the first week against strategic targets, falling thereafter to around 200 sorties per day until the start of the ground campaign. The increased sorties were also attributable to a growing target list, as discussed in Chapter Four: the Air Staff plan Instant Thunder's 84 targets had grown to over 300 strategic targets by the beginning of the war. Figure 6.4 shows the weight of effort assigned to each strategic target category.

The results were gratifying from the allies' perspective. Iraq's oil refining and production capability was essentially shut down by the end of the first week, forcing Saddam Hussein to rely on his prewar inventory. Crude production was not attacked, in order to spare the civilian population undue hardship after the war. The naval blockade prevented the import and export of refined petroleum products.

The nation's electric power grid was also knocked out. Again, Coalition planners for the most part concentrated their attacks on transmission nodes, rather

---

[21]*CPGW*, p. 206.

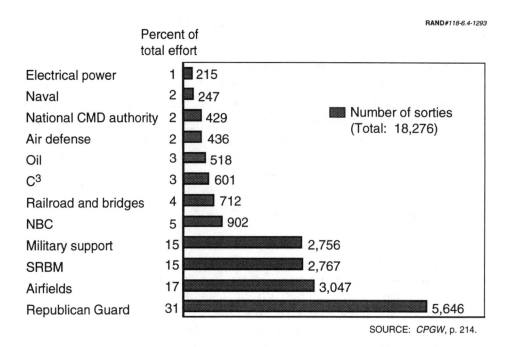

Figure 6.4—Strategic Air Campaign Level of Effort

than on power generation halls themselves, so that the basic capability could be restored quickly after the war. Some generator halls were incidentally struck, however, because units did not receive specific aimpoints in the ATO, and standard targeting manuals specified generator halls among the nominal targets to strike. The Baghdad water supply and sewage facilities were also disrupted as a result of the attacks on the electric power supply. Overall, this strategy required follow-up attacks throughout the remainder of the war, but power was indeed restored to Baghdad relatively quickly after the cease-fire.

The collapse of the national electrical grid combined with the attacks on critical communications facilities to severely disrupt the Iraqi leadership's ability to communicate with its own population and with its forces in the field. Several key nodes, including the so-called AT&T building, were attacked in downtown Baghdad by F-117s and TLAMs in the war's first 48 hours. The civilian telephone system was knocked out, overloading the regime's military system. Attacks on bridges, as part of the effort against resupply of the Iraqi army in the field, also downed fiber-optics communications cables carrying message traffic from Baghdad to Basra and the army in the KTO. Nevertheless, the Iraqi communications network was heavily redundant and dispersed, and it required repeated follow-up attacks. Although communications were never totally blacked out, they were severely disrupted, and the leadership was obliged to use less secure means of communication, principally radio, subject to interception and jamming. By the time of the ground campaign, Saddam and his military leadership in Baghdad had a serious shortage of timely information from their front-line commanders, which probably significantly affected the course of the war because decisions were made in Baghdad with virtually no initiative left to front-line commanders.[22]

One objective of the campaign against Iraqi ground forces was to deprive them of sustainment. This aspect of the campaign consisted of a heavy effort against road and railroad bridges early in the campaign, as well as attacks against railroad marshaling yards, fuel depots, and supply depots. Air attacks against the very large rear supply areas (one supply complex extended over more than 10 square miles) proved only moderately effective, but as described in more detail below, Iraqi resupply of the front-line troops in the KTO was degraded because distribution of supplies in forward areas was impeded. The truck and tanker fleet to move them to forward positions was under constant attack, and drivers were often afraid of being attacked by Coalition aircraft and so refused to move in daylight.

Supply lines of communication were also attacked, especially vulnerable choke points such as bridges, beginning in the second week of the war. Navy F/A-18s and A-6s flew over 70 percent of bridge interdiction sorties in the first two weeks, along with RAF Tornados and Buccaneers, but the absence of a laser capability limited the F-18s' role, and they were replaced with LGB-capable aircraft (A-6Es, F-117s, F-111Fs, and F-15Es with LANTIRN pods).[23] Precision-guided munitions were key to the success of the bridge campaign, which damaged or destroyed 50 of the 54 fixed bridges across the Tigris and Euphrates rivers (the other 4 were deliberately left standing), and 32 pontoon bridges.[24] As early as D+18 (February 4) it was estimated that the supplies reaching Iraqi forces in the KTO were below the level needed to sustain offensive combat operations.

The Iraqi nuclear, biological, and chemical weapons programs (including the airplanes and missiles to deliver the weapons), as potentially the most dangerous elements of Iraq's arsenal and the regional threat it represented, were among the air campaign planners' top priorities. Attacks against such targets were scheduled and prioritized to maximize their impact on the war effort. Thus, storage areas were attacked first to preclude the use of ready weapons,

---

[22]Based on information provided by Stephen Hosmer of RAND.

[23]Frostic, op. cit.

[24]Frostic, op. cit., and the McPeak briefing (1991). *GWAPS* states that about half of the known 126 highway bridges and 9 railroad bridges south of Baghdad were targeted. Of these, 37 highway and all the railroad bridges were destroyed by the end of the war. (*GWAPS*, pp. 92–93.)

then production facilities so that the destroyed weapons and missiles could not be replaced, and finally research and development facilities to cripple the Iraqis' future potential for building and deploying such weapons.[25]

Damage to both the Iraqi nuclear weapons program and to Scud storage and production facilities eventually proved to have been much less than was widely believed during the war. Numerous facilities had simply not been detected, and in other cases much of the equipment or production was moved before the start of the war without detection. NBC warheads are small and thus easy to conceal and disperse, so confidence in their destruction could never have been high. The disappointing result of the NBC effort bears strong similarities to the results of the counter-Scud campaign.

The Scud Hunt

Beginning on the first day of the air campaign, Iraq launched the first of some 88 Scud missiles against Israel and the Coalition forces in Saudi Arabia. Initial planning had envisioned attacks against Scud fixed launch sites and against production, storage, and support facilities. These attacks were initially thought to have been successful. The problem centered on the mobile launchers that Iraq had developed and deployed, which were more numerous and in some respects operationally superior to what U.S. intelligence had expected. The "Scud hunt" took on great significance, not just because of the sensational media coverage it received, but also because it diverted resources away from other targets.

The intelligence community's failure was at both a strategic level and a more narrowly technical level. The number of missiles and mobile launchers and, importantly, of presurveyed sites for mobile launches was simply underestimated and not taken into account in planning. U.S. intelligence had estimated that Iraq possessed some three or four dozen Scud launchers. In fact, later analysis concluded the total was probably closer to 225.[26] In addition, the intelligence community also overestimated the time it would take for the Iraqis' mobile launch vehicles to leave their launch sites after firing. Rather than the half-hour analysts thought would be necessary, actual dispersal came in five to six minutes. Moreover, the Iraqis devised some clever operational techniques for deception, effectively using decoys to divert attacks from actual launch vehicles.

---

[25]Richard Mackenzie, "A Conversation with Chuck Horner," *Air Force Magazine*, June 1991, p. 64.

[26]Hallion (1992), p. 179. *GWAPS*, p. 87, concludes that the total was more likely close to the original estimate.

At another level, however, the military intelligence community (as well as planners in Washington and Riyadh) discounted the importance of Scud missiles because they were felt to be *militarily* insignificant: that is, because they were inaccurate and prone to break up on reentry, they posed little *military* threat to Coalition forces. (In the event, however, Scuds demonstrated their potential for destruction when one struck a barracks in Dhahran on 25 February, killing 28 U.S. soldiers: the single most lethal Iraqi military action of the entire war.) It is questionable whether the military judgment was correct, given the potential impact of chemical weapons on airfields or ports, but it also ignored or missed the larger strategic implications that proved so important and led to the use of some 2,500 sorties to suppress further launches.

The use of these weapons was significant for several reasons. First, while they were inaccurate and usually caused only minor damage, they were psychologically and politically threatening. Even without chemical or biological warheads, they created an atmosphere of anxiety and fear among the population and troops against whom they were targeted. Armed with nonconventional charges, they had the potential to sow panic and widespread destruction.

At a political-strategic level, their use against Israel was intended to bring that country into the war against Iraq, which would have placed severe strains on the bonds holding together the diverse members of the Coalition. In this, Saddam was very nearly successful.[27] It might have been difficult or impossible for Arab members of the Coalition to continue to fight against a fellow Arab country that was at war with Israel.

Finally, because they had such political and psychological importance and received so much attention from the media, considerable effort was spent trying to find and destroy the mobile Scud launchers. This presented a technical and technological challenge to the U.S. and allied military, and it diverted resources from pursuit of the rest of the planned air campaign.

In the end, despite considerable diversion of sophisticated resources, few if any mobile Scud launch vehicles (known as transporter-erector-launchers or TELs) were destroyed.[28] For one thing, it proved very difficult to actually locate and distinguish Scud TELs. Prior to the war, it appears the Iraqis dispersed many or most of the launchers, missiles, and support equipment. TELs were often deployed in urban areas in warehouses or garages, making it impossible to locate

---

[27]General Schwarzkopf states that the Israelis at one point had 100 aircraft in the air for an attack against Scud launch areas, but were dissuaded at the last minute by the U.S. administration from actually sending the aircraft into Iraq. (H. Norman Schwarzkopf with Peter Petre, *It Doesn't Take a Hero,* New York: Bantam, 1992, pp. 416–417.)

[28]Unpublished RAND working paper by Richard Mesic, James C. Rogers, and Gerald Stiles. See also *GWAPS,* p. 83.

and identify them. Operationally, the Iraqis exposed TELs only very briefly for launches, dashing them fully fueled and armed from cover and then returning them to cover quickly after launch. Thus, the time available to locate a TEL after a launch was very limited before it was once again moving or hidden.

In terms of resources used, the level of effort was quite high. Since over 80 percent of Scud launches occurred at night, two to four F-15Es were kept on combat air patrol each night. From D+6 (January 22) until the first day prior to the ground war, 30–40 A-10 sorties were tasked daily to search for and destroy Scud launchers. This amounted to approximately 20 percent of the available A-10 sorties, reducing the level of effort against the Iraqi army in Kuwait.[29] Altogether, 2,493 sorties were launched as part of the Scud hunt, including fixed sites, representing by some estimates perhaps a week's worth of effort. By CINCCENT's own estimate, fully a third of the daily sorties were diverted to Scud hunting at the height of the campaign.[30] Had it not been for the abundance of strike aircraft available to him, this might have forced some more difficult force apportionment decisions.

Like the NBC effort, the disappointing results of the counter-Scud effort is one of the strategic air campaign's notable failures. The U.S. intelligence agencies focused a great deal of effort and resources against Iraq's nonconventional weapons programs—they were a major targeting priority of the strategic campaign—and yet they could probably have been reconstituted and continued with at most a couple of years' setback. The failure of the Scud campaign bears many similarities to the shortcomings of the NBC campaign. In the end, despite the level of effort, there were no confirmed kills, although the Air Force has claimed that it did manage to keep enough pressure on to suppress more launches.[31] Both efforts demonstrate that air power can destroy known targets, but it is critically dependent on accurate intelligence. In this instance, it was also defeated by relatively simple but clever efforts at concealment by the Iraqis.

TANKER SUPPORT[32]

A RAND analyst has summarized well the extent of the refueling support operation provided by Strategic Air Command tankers:

---

[29]Frostic, op. cit.

[30]Schwarzkopf (1992); also confirmed in RAND analysis by Rich Mesic and Fred Frostic. See also Friedman (1991), p. 171.

[31]A conclusion that the Gulf War Air Power Survey concurred in. See Eliot A. Cohen, "The Air War in the Persian Gulf," *Armed Forces Journal International*, June 1993, p. 13.

[32]This section draws on a RAND working paper by Major Tom Marshall. See the appendix for further statistics relating to refueling operations in Desert Shield and Desert Storm.

Tankers are needed to support almost any air operation and Desert Storm was no exception. In fact, the distances between bases and targets were so great that aerial refueling was needed for almost all combat and many support missions. Strategic Air Command tankers refueled aircraft from all services and nations.

To meet this demand the Air Force committed nearly half of its tanker fleet to Desert Storm—some 300 aircraft. These tankers flew nearly 15,000 sorties, refueling 46,000 aircraft, and delivering 700 million pounds of fuel.

Tankers deployed from 21 CONUS bases to 21 overseas bases to support Desert Storm. SAC effectively doubled its number of tanker bases and operated them with no increase in personnel. Many of the overseas bases required considerable development to bring them up to operating standards.

Airspace congestion imposed the largest single limitation on tanker operations. This in turn limited the numbers of attack and support aircraft in raid packages. This problem worsened as the focus of air operations shifted from Iraq to the KTO where more aircraft occupied less space. It is remarkable that there were no mid-air collisions, although there was a relatively large number of near collisions.[33]

We might add that the task of marrying strike and support aircraft to tankers was done each day *by hand* in the JFACC ATO cell. Changes from the plan (which were inevitable) placed great stress on airborne command and control. As one RAND analyst put it, getting strike packages through the tankers was one of the most emotional events of the day.

While the extent of the operation is impressive, there were some shortcomings. Air Force tankers are equipped with a single refueling boom, optimized for high transfer rates (1,000 gallons of fuel per minute). For tactical strike packages, however, the single boom meant that some aircraft would have to wait for others to finish refueling. The RAF had tankers with three drogues that were better suited to refueling formations of three tactical aircraft. To get around this problem while taking advantage of the number and capacity of Air Force tankers, smaller Navy tankers often refueled from the big Air Force tankers and then in turn fueled Navy tactical aircraft, in effect multiplying the number of available hoses. Navy combat aircraft were not compatible with the standard Air Force boom refueling system. The Air Force was obliged to attach a refueling hose to the boom prior to takeoff to accommodate Navy aircraft directly.[34]

Apportionment of tankers occasionally appeared to reflect some interservice tensions. Navy F-14s operating from carriers in the Red Sea required enormous tanking support merely to fly to the KTO. But tankers were assigned on the basis of bomb damage capabilities, not distance, which meant that the Navy got

---

[33]Marshall working paper, pp. 33–34.

[34]Friedman (1991), pp. 195–196.

fewer tankers than it sought.[35] Navy aircraft sometimes went on missions with less than desired ordnance loads because they had to carry additional fuel.[36] As carriers in the Gulf were able to move further north, their need for land-based tankers decreased, and Navy tankers met most of the requirement.

Communications were also a problem during Desert Shield: the Air Force's KC-135s did not have radios compatible with allied aircraft and ground controllers. A crash program located and installed compatible radios beginning in November, with all in-theater tankers equipped by mid-January.[37]

THE KEY TO EFFECTIVE OPERATIONS: THE AIR TASKING ORDER

As the master attack plan defined the scope and content of the air war, the air tasking order was its execution order.[38] It was the principal instrument for allocating the use of air power in the theater, translating the MAP into specific wing taskings and instructions. The ATO covered almost all fixed-wing aircraft sorties in the theater.[39] In addition to assigning aircraft against targets in the MAP, the ATO also gave instructions as to procedures, airspace coordination, communications frequencies and call signs, search and rescue procedures, and targets precluded from attack, and it tasked noncombat and support missions such as airlift, escort, and refueling.

The ATO preparation cycle was long: from first planning meeting to first sorties usually took over 40 hours. The process began at JFACC's daily 7 a.m. staff meeting, where the previous day's results and CINCCENT's objectives were reviewed. The new guidance served as the basis for developing the plan for the day after, taking into account BDA, weather reports, intelligence, and other factors. Strategic targets were assigned first, and the most difficult of these went to F-117As, which, because of their stealth and accuracy, were the only manned aircraft to hit targets in downtown Baghdad. Tomahawks were used to complement and fill the gaps in F-117 coverage in the first few days of the air campaign. Other strategic targets went to F-111s. Scuds were assigned to F-15Es

---

[35]Coyne (1992a), p. 98.

[36]"Desert Storm Naval Air War," *NAVY International*, April 1991, p. 115.

[37]Coyne (1992a), p. 136.

[38]This section draws heavily on RAND work by Leland Joe and Dan Gonzales, and by Fred Frostic. See Chapters Four and Five on wartime planning and the master attack plan. See also Winnefeld and Johnson (1993), pp. 104–110.

[39]Helicopters flying below 500 feet and naval aircraft operating over water were exempt from direct JFACC control. Sorties from Turkey as part of JTF Proven Force were also exempt, but they were coordinated with the ATO. *GWAPS*, p. 5.

and F-16s with LANTIRN pods for night attacks.[40] Navy and Marine aircraft were assigned to targets in all categories except downtown Baghdad.

The plan was approved by the Director of Campaign Planning, Brigadier General Glosson, at 8 p.m. each evening. From there, the detailed targeting work was accomplished, designating aimpoints (known as DMPIs, for designated mean point of impact) for each target. By 4:30 a.m. the target details were handed over to the team that processed the ATO, and they worked out all the myriad details of deconfliction, IFF (identification friend or foe) codes, tanker rendezvous points, and the like to finalize the operations order. Finally, in the late afternoon, the ATO was delivered to the wings for execution the following day. At any given moment, therefore, three ATOs were in the works: one was being executed, another was being transmitted ("fragged") to units for the next day, and a third was being prepared for execution two days hence.

Transmission of the voluminous ATO (often 300, sometimes as many as 900 pages) to the wings was slow. CAFMS—the Computer-Aided Force Management System—was the primary USAF system for production and dissemination of the ATO. It consisted of mainframe computers at TACC and remote-receive terminals at the wings with limited processing capability. The system was out of date and not user-friendly, and TACC and the wings developed workarounds to compress the ATO to speed transmission and to edit the order at the wings using personal computers. Transmission of the ATO was also slowed because of inadequate interoperability, particularly with the Navy, which did not have the requisite super high frequency (SHF) terminals on board its carriers, and with B-52 wings (which did not have CAFMS). As a result, the ATO in hardcopy was delivered to carrier air wings by courier; Navy liaison officers regularly phoned carrier air wings with preliminary information to give them a head start.[41]

At the wing level, mission planning was accomplished by a mission planning cell, with responsibility for providing mission leaders and flight members with flight plans, maps, and mission data cards. Extracting information from the ATO was something of an art, and each wing devised its own methods. A wing received the entire ATO and had to extract from it the pertinent information and instructions, using personal computers to edit it. Often, wings complemented the data with their own intelligence files, which were frequently quite extensive. Wing commanders frequently requested changes to the ATO based on their own intelligence and situation assessment.

---

[40]Coyne (1992a), p. 88.

[41]A practice replicated by wing liaison officers from all services.

In addition to its problems with timeliness, the ATO received criticism from non–Air Force participants, especially the Marines but also the Navy, for inflexibility. As noted in Chapter Five, the ATO reflected USAF doctrine and experience preparing for a large-scale war. The MAP and ATO process reflected a centralized, theater-level view of the air campaign. Navy mission planning, in contrast, is optimized for small-scale contingency operations, usually involving a single carrier task force. Navy strike planning is self-contained at the unit level, rather than integrated and centralized. Similarly, the Marines' integrated air-ground concept (MAGTF) emphasizes organic air assets tailored for support of their own troops.

Marine commanders stated that the ATO was well-adapted to a "set-piece" air campaign with a nonresponsive enemy, but was ill-adapted to a fluid battle involving ground forces. Since their planning revolved around integral air support of Marine ground troops, Marine aviators sought to "game" the ATO to ensure that they had sufficient sorties from their own air assets to provide air cover to their troops. To do this, they "stuffed" the ATO with large numbers of sorties—bypassing the planning/apportionment phase of the ATO development cycle and going directly to the ATO writers—which they could then cancel if they were not needed, or divert to other purposes.[42] Navy commanders did the same thing to meet their own requirements, for instance overhead CAP flights.

The efficient and safe management of the strategic air campaign, as well as the apportionment of air assets according to the CINC's campaign plan, required the centralized coordination that the ATO provided. Planning on this scale necessarily took place in advance of execution. On the other hand, "the dynamic nature of battlefield targets placed a premium on timely execution."[43] The interface between the ATO and the dynamic nature of operations was the job of the Combat Operations directorate.

---

[42]Lieutenant General Royal N. Moore, Jr., "Marine Air: There When Needed," U.S. Naval Institute *Proceedings*, November 1991. As General Moore, commander of the I MEF's airborne command element, says in this interview, "What I did to make it work for us—and I think the Navy did the same thing—was write an ATO that would give me enough flexibility to do the job. So I might write an enormous amount of sorties . . . and I might cancel an awful lot of those. This way I didn't have to play around with the process while I was waiting to hit a target. I kind of gamed the ATO process."

[43]Frostic, op. cit.

CONTROLLING AIR OPERATIONS[44]

Managing airspace and controlling air operations was no easy task. One writer has described its magnitude well:

> There were as many as 980 daily sorties to be deconflicted during Desert Shield and over 2800 . . . during . . . Desert Storm. These sorties involved 122 different air refueling tracks, 660 restricted operating zones, 312 missile engagement zones, 78 strike corridors, 92 combat air patrol points, and 36 training areas alone, spread over 93,600 square miles.
>
> All of this had to be superimposed upon and thoroughly coordinated with the continually shifting civil airways of six independent nations. This civil coordination step involved placing 357 USAF controllers, 55 of which were liaison personnel, at the air traffic control and ground control intercept facilities of the host nations in the Gulf region.[45]

The Combat Operations directorate, under Major General John A. Corder, controlled and provided guidance for the execution of the ATO to all players. The air command and control system in Desert Storm consisted of both ground and airborne elements. On the ground, the Tactical Air Control Center (TACC) at the air component level (under JFACC) had the overall responsibility for real-time force allocation. Two Control and Reporting Centers (CRCs) helped manage the air situation picture, and wing operations centers provided control. Air Support Operations Centers (ASOCs) were Air Force planning elements located at Corps Tactical Operations Centers, and they participated in the daily Corps planning process. The ASOCs, with their immediate picture of the battlefield, worked through the TACC to dynamically adjust mission allocation among Corps sectors inside the fire support coordination line (FSCL), which defines the area in which air units must coordinate with friendly ground units. The ASOCs developed an informal procedure for working among themselves when time did not permit working through the TACC, instead directing sorties through airborne control elements or through direct communications with incoming attack flights to allocate forces, informing the TACC for approval after decisions were executed. Wings placed great value on the up-to-date information and intelligence obtained from the ASOCs. The Marines' Direct Air Sup-

---

[44]This section draws heavily on Frostic, op. cit. See also Duncan (1993) for an excellent description of the air command and control system.

[45]Campen (1992), p. 34. Navy commanders point out that their antiair warfare commander system (AAWC, the officer designated by the OTC—officer in tactical command—to direct the antiair efforts of the command) made a major contribution to this success under difficult conditions. During the Gulf War, that officer was the skipper of the Aegis cruiser that was farthest north in the Gulf. His responsibilities included tracking and identifying all aircraft in his zone of responsibility, vectoring intercepts if warranted, releasing missiles if warranted, etc. An aviator flew over the Gulf at his peril unless he had checked in with the AAWC. Rear Admiral Dan March told us that the AAWC in the Persian Gulf deconflicted over 65,000 sorties with no incidents.

port Centers (DASCs) performed a similar role in the MARCENT area of responsibility.

Airborne elements included the Airborne Warning and Control System (AWACS), the EC-130 Airborne Command and Control Center (ABCCC), and the Joint Surveillance Target Attack Radar System (JSTARS), as well as forward air control (FAC) aircraft. The different airborne control elements had different functional and geographical responsibilities, which changed over time. Changes were reported in the ATO's Special Instructions (SPINS) section. AWACS, ABCCC, the ASOCs, and the Marine DASCs could make on-the-spot decisions to execute the ATO (although Combat Operations normally was in charge).

AWACS controlled operations north of the KTO, in the so-called flight lead control interdiction area (see Figure 6.5). Separate AWACS aircraft operating in Saudi airspace exercised control in each of three zones—east, central, and west. Their primary mission at the start of the war had been air defense, identifying the location and heading of Iraqi aircraft, directing Coalition interceptors against them, and alerting allied aircraft to threats. After the Iraqis stopped flying, AWACS acted as a traffic controller, clearing strike aircraft in and out of zones, linking them up with tankers, and managing other support aircraft. Once airborne, strike and air-defense aircraft would check in with the appropriate AWACS and get clearance to their CAP station or into Kuwaiti or Iraqi airspace to attack their targets. As the campaign evolved, AWACS' "view of the air situation and the lack of an air threat enabled the TACC to use AWACS controllers to help manage the combat airspace in the KTO."[46]

Each AWACS carried on board an airborne command element (ACE), a small staff headed by an Air Force colonel directly representing JFACC, and including a Navy liaison officer. The ACE program was the responsibility of Campaign Planning (under General Glosson), but Combat Operations executed the day-to-day war, coordinating, tasking, and recommending last-minute changes to the ATO to respond to the changing combat situation, aircraft availability, and fast-breaking intelligence.[47] One of the ACE's most important jobs was tanker management as tankers aborted their missions, strike aircraft refueled from the wrong tanker, or emergencies or diversions arose.

While the ASOC and DASC were responsible for air power employment inside the FSCL, the ABCCC was primarily responsible for the control of ground-strike missions, including interdiction and close air support, initially just beyond the

---

[46]Communication from RAND's Joe and Gonzales.

[47]ACE authority did not extend to changing targets (authority exercised by Glosson), but did include target-on-top (TOT) times, tanker and CAP support, and similar matters.

RAND#118-6.5-1293

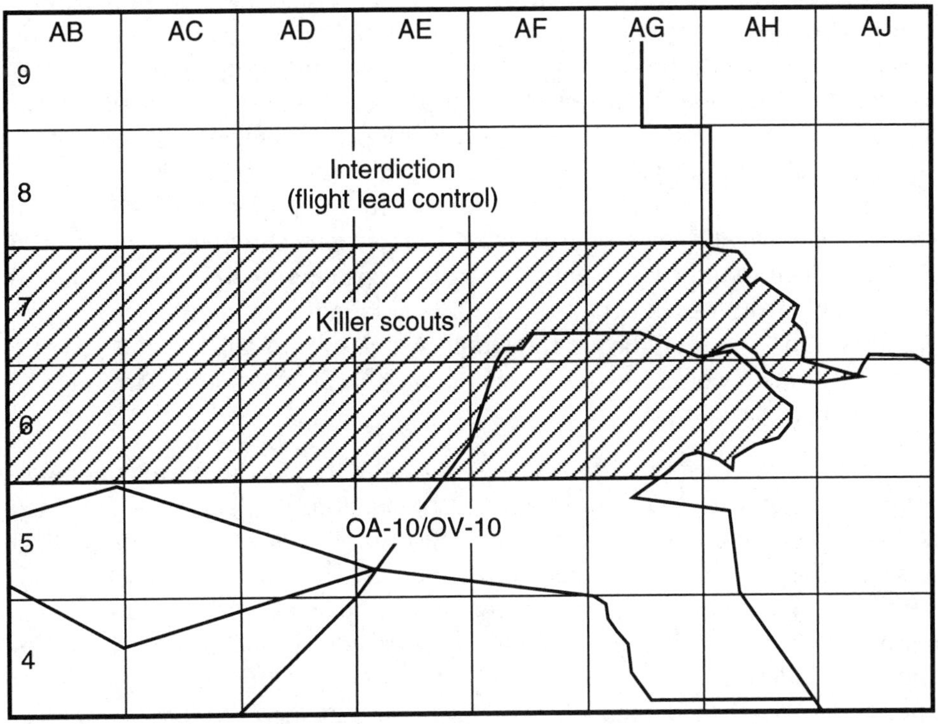

SOURCE: Unpublished RAND working paper by Fred Frostic.

Figure 6.5—Organization of Airspace Control in the Kuwaiti Theater of Operations

FSCL in the KTO, south of the AWACS's area of responsibility. The area of
responsibility for ABCCC was reduced during the course of the war as limitations on its capabilities for force allocation were identified. Communications
were a constraining factor,[48] as was the ability to correlate the ATO (loaded onto
optical disks aboard the ABCCC) with the real-time picture developed through
in-flight reports and surveillance/reconnaissance assets. The ABCCC was thus
less effective and timely than had been demonstrated in less dense
environments. The F-16 "killer scouts" took over much of their role later on
(see below).

Deployment of the E-8A JSTARS came after a lengthy debate on the feasibility
and desirability of deploying an untested, in-development system into an actual

---

[48]At least in part because the rules of engagement had always foreseen attack aircraft operating at
altitudes below the ABCCC. When the attack aircraft were operating at the same or higher altitudes,
the ABCCC's antenna was shielded and communications were poor—another artifact of operating
at higher altitudes. We thank Natalie Crawford for pointing this out.

combat theater.[49] The aircraft, a modified Boeing 707, is equipped with a multi-mode, side-looking radar with a range of over 155 miles. Its original mission was limited to nighttime surveillance of enemy ground equipment movement, using its mobile target indicator (MTI) to pass likely targets to the ABCCC for allocation to attack sorties. However, as the war progressed, F-15Es and later F-16s were tasked in the ATO to work directly with JSTARS to identify and attack targets, including possible Scud launchers. After taking off, the F-15s would check in with AWACS to be cleared into the target zone and then turned over to JSTARS, which would provide them with the target coordinates. The F-15s and F-16s and JSTARS would communicate by secure radio to identify the target's exact location, and then the aircraft would switch over to talk to either AWACS or ABCCC, which would clear them in and out of "kill boxes" and warn them of other traffic.[50]

The kill box system was one means devised to add flexibility to the air campaign against the Iraqi army. The boxes were 30 × 30 nautical mile grids established across the center of the KTO (see Figure 6.6). Aircraft were assigned in the ATO to search for and destroy targets within a kill box (or quadrant of a kill box). Because strike aircraft could be assigned to operate in a kill box only for a short period, continuity had to be provided by a system of forward air controllers known as killer scouts. This consisted of two USAF F-16s or USMC F-18Ds operating in daylight in each kill box. These aircraft surveyed planned targets and looked for lucrative alternative targets, and eventually were tasked to assign attack flights to targets, acting in effect as airborne forward air controllers (AFACs). The ABCCC was not allowed to divert aircraft into kill boxes covered by the killer scouts without their permission.

The Damage Assessment Problem

The killer scouts and other AFAC-type units were also eventually tasked with assisting with battle damage assessment (BDA), which proved to be one of CENTCOM's biggest headaches during the war.[51]

> During Desert Shield, CENTCOM, CENTAF, and the intelligence community ... built an imagery dissemination architecture to meet the CENTAF mission planners' perceived needs, which at that time were based on a 72-hour cycle that included a 36-hour ATO cycle, as specified in USCENTAF Regulation 55-45, and another 36 hours for BDA results to be incorporated into the ATO planning that was in process at the time the BDA results were reported ...

---

[49]A technical but accessible description of JSTARS is set out in John Haystead, "JSTARS—Real-Time Warning and Control for Surface Warfare," *Defense Electronics*, July 1990, pp. 31–34.

[50]Coyne (1992a), p. 90–91.

[51]BDA is discussed in more depth in Chapter Eight.

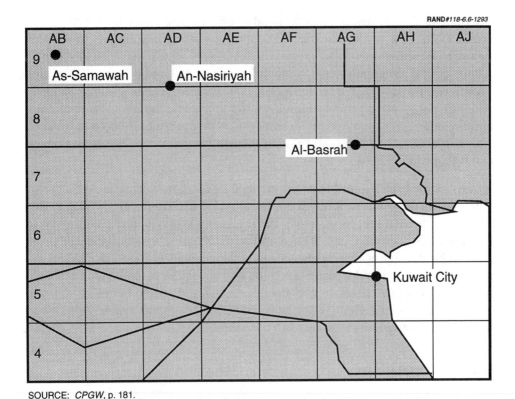

SOURCE: *CPGW*, p. 181.

Figure 6.6—Kill Box Structure in the Kuwaiti Theater of Operations

However, things began to change after just one day of hostilities. These changes were driven by the GAT's desire for BDA on the same day as the attack in order to develop the plan for the next day's attacks. Limits on the number of overhead collection assets, the geographical separation of collection and exploitation facilities in the theater and in CONUS, the communications capacity for transmitting information in theater, and poor weather all affected the intelligence community's ability to meet the GAT's desire for quick turn-around of BDA information . . . [and] "same-day" BDA to support restrikes. When the GAT realized that the existing intelligence resources in theater could not meet its desires, it turned to other sources for confirmatory BDA information. These included video imagery from the wings for assessing physical damage from GBU [guided bomb units, e.g., laser-guided bombs] strikes, and all-source, functional damage assessments from DIA.[52]

As Chapter Eight will make clear, one of the war's most serious problems was the lack of a BDA architecture with attendant system support. The word

_____

[52]RAND working paper by Major Robert Butler, USAF. Glosson points out that video imagery was arranged prior to D-day.

"architecture" is a misnomer. National overhead assets, set up for the U.S.-Soviet Cold War confrontation, were not sufficiently responsive to theater tasking. Washington's infatuation with overhead assets had virtually eliminated tactical reconnaissance capabilities such as the Air Force RF-4s and TARPS-equipped Navy F-14s. Both were available in extremely limited supply, and had many calls on them. Moreover, the secondary imagery dissemination and transmission capabilities were inadequate, creating a bottleneck in Riyadh, where intelligence of potential value to the wings piled up in "boxes and boxes of hardcopy in the halls."[53]

All this created timing problems for damage assessment within the ATO cycle. Since the ATO for the next day was disseminated the afternoon of the day the BDA input was supposed to arrive, there was not enough time to integrate it into the ATO. The GAT had to take up the slack by incorporating intelligence and working with Combat Operations to make changes to the ATO. GAT planners came to rely on pilot mission reports and especially aircraft video imagery to determine if any critical targets needed restrikes, or could be removed from the list. Last-minute changes to the ATO were often made by telephone with the wings. Photographs were faxed to the wings.

Coalition Operations

Forces from many nations deployed ground, naval, and air forces to the Gulf to fight the Iraqi invasion. The RAF provided five tactical fighter squadrons as well as helicopters, reconnaissance aircraft, tankers and transports. The Royal Canadian Air Forces deployed air superiority and ground attack fighters available for defensive counterair missions and support of ground forces. The French air force provided three tactical strike squadrons, air superiority fighters, tankers, transports, reconnaissance aircraft, maritime patrol aircraft, and helicopters. The Italian air force deployed a squadron of attack fighters, transports, tankers, and reconnaissance aircraft, available to conduct and support air intercept and interdiction missions.

The Gulf Cooperation Council states provided logistics and operational support, as well as air superiority and ground attack fighter aircraft available to fly offensive counterair, defensive counterair, and interdiction sorties. Air forces also were available to conduct refueling, airborne command and control, reconnaissance, utility, and airlift missions.[54] Table 6.1 shows the contribution of allied forces to the total allied air order of battle at D-day.

---

[53]Rear Admiral Dan March, communication with the authors.

[54]*CPGW*, p. 148.

Table 6.1

Coalition Aircraft at D-Day

Country	Fighter/ Attack	Tanker	Airlift	Other	Total
United States	1,323	285	175	207	1,990
Saudi Arabia	276	15	38	10	339
Kuwait	40	—	3	—	43
Other GCC[a]	64	—	—	—	64
United Kingdom	57	9	3	4	73
France	44	3	12	7	66
Italy	8	—	—	—	8
Canada	26	—	—	2	28
New Zealand	—	—	3	—	3
Total	1,838	312	234	230	2,614

[a]Other Gulf Cooperation Council states are Bahrain, Qatar, Oman, and United Arab Emirates.
SOURCE: Hallion (1992), p. 158.

Different allied forces operated under different constraints and rules of engagement, brought about both by equipment, training, and political considerations. Canadian aircraft, for instance, could not fly air-to-ground missions, and could not overfly the battle area, but did fly CAP in the Persian Gulf, taking pressure off organic Navy assets. Initially, French air forces were restricted to Saudi airspace, although this restriction was lifted later on and French aircraft flew missions in Iraq in mixed packages with other Coalition aircraft.[55] Not all allied equipment was night or all-weather capable.

But allied forces also brought considerable capabilities to bear, and willingness to cooperate and participate.[56] British Tornadoes and French Jaguars, for example, while not equipped for night operations, used their laser-guided bombs against Iraqi bridges and airfields to great effect during the daylight hours. Altogether, the allies flew nearly 16 percent of all sorties. According to RAND analysis, allied aircraft flew approximately 12 percent of air-to-ground missions, concentrating most heavily on airfields, military support targets in both Iraq and the KTO, and petroleum storage sites, in each of which they contributed disproportionately. They were also frequently assigned to bomb Iraqi forces in front of allied positions, especially in the MARCENT sector. In addition, non-U.S. forces flew nearly 20 percent of all reconnaissance and offensive

---

[55]At the time of the invasion, the French Defense Minister was Jean-Pierre Chevènement, a founding member of the French-Iraqi Friendship Society, and an opponent of the war. He was replaced on 29 January by Pierre Joxe, who supported the allied intervention.

[56]The Coalition's command and control arrangements are discussed in Chapter Five.

counterair missions, and over 40 percent of all defensive counterair sorties.[57] Thus, while their overall numbers were not large compared to the U.S. forces, in certain areas their contributions were significant.

THE SECOND AIR FRONT: JOINT TASK FORCE PROVEN FORCE

On the initiative of a group of planners at U.S. European Command (EUCOM) headquarters in Germany, an air task force was organized for basing at Incirlik AB, Turkey, with the overall mission of opening a second air front in northern Iraq. The concept was to keep pressure on Saddam Hussein in an area where he may have thought he had a sanctuary from allied attacks, and to prevent him from concentrating all his forces in southern Iraq against the Coalition forces. Moreover, the distance from air bases in Saudi Arabia to strategic targets in northern Iraq was considerable compared to the distance from Incirlik, and would have required a large diversion of tankers and other support aircraft.[58]

Air Force operations in Proven Force were organized as a single composite wing, the 7440th Combat Wing (Provisional), with all combat elements collocated under a single wing commander. The forces were assigned from U.S. Air Forces Europe, and were under the operational control of EUCOM, but all sorties were under the tactical control of CENTAF. Normally, Air Force wings are organized by "mission design series" (MDS), that is, with aircraft of a single type. The organization of a "composite" wing with different types of aircraft put to the test an idea advanced by some Air Force planners and the Chief of Staff. The Task Force consisted of over 130 aircraft, including 28 F-15Cs for air superiority, 46 F-16C, F-111E, and F-4 strike aircraft, 32 F-4G, F-16C, and EF-111A for SEAD and electronic warfare, and over 30 other support aircraft, including AWACS, RF-4 reconnaissance, KC-135 tankers, and intelligence aircraft.[59] Notably absent from the Proven Force wing were F-117A stealth fighter-bombers and aircraft capable of dropping laser-guided bombs.

Although included in the MAP, Proven Force had its own ATO that was coordinated with JFACC's ATO through the master attack plan. In practice,

> mission type orders were used only during the first few days of the air campaign. However, the Joint Task Force staff developed its own mission type orders with which to develop and prioritize targets for the wing during the two to three weeks after the initial air campaign. More often, the wing was given

---

[57]Data supplied by RAND's Parker and Emerson. See the appendix for further details.

[58]Much of this section is based on an unpublished RAND working paper by Raymond Pyles, "Composite Wings in Wartime: The Experience of Joint Task Force Proven Force (U)." See also Coyne (1992a), pp. 57–61; *CPGW*, pp. 147–148.

[59]United States Air Force (1991), p. 23; *CPGW*, p. 147.

target type orders, both by the Joint Task Force Staff, and later, by the CENTAF staff. Those orders specified nothing more than which targets were to be attacked next, without specifying the size and composition of the mission packages. This allowed the wing to allocate its own resources to mission packages and plan integrated mission tactics based on its current understanding of effective tactics for each [type of aircraft] and on its estimates of the enemy's capabilities.[60]

In contrast to CENTAF's 40-hour ATO cycle, Proven Force, with only a single wing to coordinate, was able to build an ATO within 28 hours.[61]

Those target type orders became especially important when CENTAF began to concentrate more of its effort on attacking ground targets in the Kuwait Theater of Operations, drawing effort away from critical nuclear and missile design and production facilities in the north of Iraq. As the war neared its end it became clear that the Coalition wanted to achieve some specific military, political and economic objectives that required more centralized direction than could be achieved with broad mission type orders. At that time, CENTAF's taskings became more specific, first eliminating whole classes of targets, then identifying more and more specific targets to be attacked.[62]

Proven Force continued to concentrate on strategic targets as the forces based in Saudi Arabia shifted the weight of their effort to tactical targets and battlefield preparation.

A RAND analyst who studied Proven Force operations in depth concludes:

Proven Force demonstrated the responsiveness of the composite wing to support either mission type orders or target type orders. The composite wing's ability to respond quickly to target changes was more robust than an equivalent single-MDS wing organization because it was able to divert a complete previously formed package rather than assemble a mission from several existing missions while maintaining the original package's mission integration. Thus, Proven Force was able to assemble a complete package at the last moment with greater confidence than CENTAF.

Perhaps more important, Proven Force also demonstrated the improved mission integration that can be achieved by a composite wing, both in learning and quickly correcting for new situations, and in new tactics that enhance strike communications security and reduce the pre-strike tanker hunt confusion.

Proven Force also demonstrated composite wings' ability to coordinate with a wide variety of collateral and supporting forces. Early in Desert Storm, B-52s and F-117s attacked targets in the same areas as Proven Force aircraft with

---

[60]Pyles, op. cit. One might add that the strengths and weaknesses of the composite wing concept paralleled long Navy and Marine Corps experience with a similar organizational arrangement.

[61]Brigadier General Lee A. Downer, "The Composite Wing in Combat," *Airpower Journal*, Winter 1991, p. 9.

[62]Pyles, op. cit.

minimal coordination and deconfliction between units. Later, Proven Force conducted operations further south, using target type orders. In those operations, Proven Force mission packages were not integrated directly with CENTAF's, but they contributed to a coordinated effect on the enemy in accordance with CENTAF's objectives.[63]

WEEKS 3–5: ATTACKING ENEMY GROUND FORCES

By the second week of the air campaign, Phase III was under way in earnest. The objective in this phase was to render the Iraqi forces in the Kuwaiti theater ineffective prior to the ground campaign. General Schwarzkopf set as a goal reducing the Iraqi army's "combat effectiveness" by 50 percent (and higher in certain key breaching areas), principally by the destruction of armored vehicles, tanks, and artillery, but also by degradation of communications and resupply, and by sapping the troops' will to fight. The success of this phase of the air campaign was central to the rapid and virtually casualty-free victory achieved by Coalition ground forces.

The battle against the Iraqi forces in the KTO had begun at the very outset of Desert Storm. As the campaign proceeded, it became more focused, and the number of sorties continued to grow over time as objectives from the other phases of the campaign were met. The number of attack sorties in the KTO grew from approximately 400 per day, divided between strategic air offensive targets and the Iraqi field army, to over 1,000 sorties per day focused directly on the Iraqi forces. The emphasis of the sorties changed to exploit successful tactics and weapon systems. Figure 6.7 shows the weight of effort between strategic targets and enemy ground force targets. Ultimately, some 35,000 attack sorties were directed against Iraqi forces in the KTO—60 percent of all Desert Storm attack sorties—including 5,600 against the Republican Guard. The target planning for all sorties against Iraqi ground forces was conducted by the KTO cell of the Campaign Planning directorate.

Assessing Attrition

CINCCENT determined during the planning for the ground offensive that the combat effectiveness of the Iraqi army in Kuwait should be reduced by 50 percent before ground operations would commence. Nominally, this meant a 50 percent attrition of armor—tanks and armored personnel carriers (APCs)—and artillery. Attrition goals were higher for key breaching areas, where the goal for artillery was set at 90 percent. Other information in addition to the attrition of enemy armor, including resupply rates, troop conditions and morale, and

---

[63]Ibid.

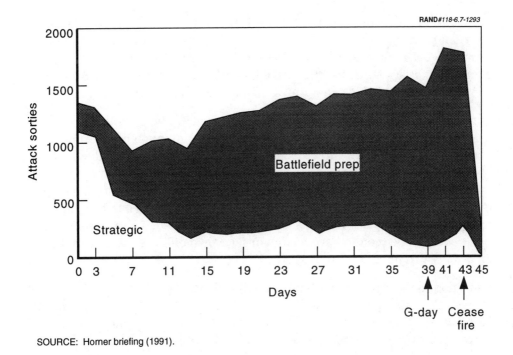

RAND#118-6.7-1293

SOURCE: Horner briefing (1991).

Figure 6.7—Strategic and Battlefield Preparation Sorties

enemy prisoner of war and deserter debriefings, informed CINCCENT's judgment about the fighting condition of the Iraqi forces. In the end, these other
criteria—the degradation of command and control, the disruption of Iraqi
ground force logistics, and especially the collapse of morale—would contribute
at least as much to CINCCENT's decision as the equipment attrition results.

Considerable uncertainty and dispute arose during the war, and continue to
this day, on estimates of damage to Iraqi armor and artillery. The uncertainty
begins with disagreements on the baseline against which damage was computed—i.e., the starting Iraqi order of battle. ARCENT G-2 was assigned overall
responsibility for evaluating attrition to enemy armor and artillery. Its original
estimates of equipment, based on fully manned and equipped divisions, were
on the order of 4,900 tanks, 3,100 APCs, and 3,200 artillery tubes.[64] CENTCOM
estimates in January 1991 put the levels at 4,200 tanks, 2,800 APCs, and 3,100
artillery tubes.

Adding to the confusion were problems with the methodology and effectiveness
of attrition estimates. ARCENT used pilot reports or onboard imagery from

---

[64]Based on Frostic, op. cit.

only four aircraft types: A-10s, F-111s, F-15Es, and AV-8s. Video imagery of laser-guided bomb deliveries was used to back up pilot reports, as were reports from the F-16 killer scouts and Marine "Fast-FACs." Other aircraft types conducting attack sorties against Iraqi ground forces—F-16s, A-6s, B-52s, and F/A-18s, as well as foreign aircraft—were not even counted.[65]

Further adding to the uncertainty, ARCENT revised the factors used for evaluating a functional "kill" during the ground campaign, although no revisions were made to the cumulative earlier estimates. ARCENT reduced credited kills to one-half for F-111s and one-third for the A-10s. National intelligence sources based in the United States also used conservative criteria for confirming a "kill," in part because of limitations on the resolution from national overhead imagery to determine the type of vehicle and the damage inflicted. A tank, for example, that could not be seen to have had its turret blown off or to have been flipped on its back was not a confirmed kill.

Reflecting the disagreement about the original Iraqi order of battle, Table 6.2 shows the attrition percentages for the ARCENT and CENTCOM estimates, based on ARCENT's estimate that, prior to the start of the ground campaign, air power destroyed 1,772 tanks, 948 APCs, and 1,477 artillery tubes.[66]

Against this background of uncertainty about the effectiveness of the battlefield preparation phase, compounded by uncertainty and disagreements over how many pieces of equipment the Iraqis had even started out with, ground commanders, concerned about their areas of responsibility during the ground campaign, sought increased levels of effort against enemy forces facing them. The timing of the transition from the strategic phase to the battlefield preparation phase of the air campaign was a source of friction between the Army and Marine components on the one hand and CENTAF on the other. Ground commanders naturally were concerned about the enemy they would have directly in front of them during the ground offensive. The JFACC apportioned effort according to General Schwarzkopf's theater campaign objectives, at least one of which was to maintain deception as to the timing and location of the ground offensive. Despite withholding forces from the ATO to devote to battlefield preparation, the Marines met difficulties in achieving the attrition goals in the MARCENT sector, due to aircraft shortages and equipment shortfalls: insufficient night-attack capabilities (not enough A-6s and no LANTIRN night-targeting pods) and tank-killing capability (Mavericks).[67] Approximately 10 days before the start of the ground campaign, Glosson requested General

---

[65]Hosmer, op. cit.

[66]Tables A.11 and A.12 in the appendix provide more detail on attrition.

[67]Although the Marines repeatedly stressed that tanks worried them less than artillery.

Schwarzkopf's permission (with MARCENT concurrence) to use Air Force and Navy assets to help meet the attrition objectives in the MARCENT area of operations.[68]

Table 6.3 shows attrition results for tanks, armored personnel carriers, and artillery in each sector and by echelon, based on ARCENT's final estimates and using ARCENT's original order of battle. Two points emerge from the table. First, although overall results did not meet the 50 percent objective (at least according to this estimate), it was generally met or exceeded against front-line Iraqi units directly facing Coalition forces (the tactical echelon). Second, the Marines were clearly less successful in attriting equipment in their sector. Their emphasis on killing artillery, rather than tanks, is also evident.

Table 6.2

Percentage Attrition of Iraqi Armor and Artillery in the Kuwaiti Theater of Operations Based on Various Estimates of Baseline Forces

	Tanks	APCs	Artillery
Order of battle estimate			
ARCENT	4,922	3,125	3,256
CENTCOM January 91	4,200	2,800	3,100
ARCENT kills	1,772	948	1,477
Resulting attrition percentages			
ARCENT	36%	30%	45%
CENTCOM January 91	42%	34%	48%

SOURCES: Frostic; *GWAPS*, p. 8.

Table 6.3

Attrition Percentages on G-Day

Area of Operations and Echelon	Tanks	APCs	Artillery
ARCENT	50	39	52
Theater	43	24	27
Operational	46	39	58
Tactical	70	87	62
MARCENT	14	20	32
Theater	2	5	6
Operational	8	4	11
Tactical	23	53	54
Total KTO	36	30	46

SOURCE: Frostic, based on ARCENT BDA reports.

---

[68]Communication from Lieutenant General Glosson; also, Lewis (1993) p. 11.

Iraqi armor and artillery, however, were not the only targets of bombing in the KTO. The air campaign also focused on Iraqi defensive fortifications. Coalition aircraft attacked Iraqi defensive fortifications in key breaching areas, including the use of napalm against Iraqi fire trenches. F-117s attacked the pumps that supplied oil to the trenches. Even B-52s were used in a "tactical" role to clear out minefields by dropping large-area munitions over them and to bomb other Iraqi defensive works.

The Coalition had two other important target sets in the KTO: logistics and distribution of supplies, and battlefield communications. Perhaps most important of all, however, was the bombing campaign's effect on the morale and behavior of the Iraqi defenders.

The allies conducted an extensive campaign against the lines of communication linking the front to Baghdad (the bridge campaign described above) and against rear-area supply depots. Thirty percent of military production facilities in Iraq were damaged, and the inventory of stored matériel in Iraq and Kuwait was "moderately" reduced.[69] Attacks against the logistics and communications of forward-deployed Iraqi units, however, were more important to the final outcome. The really severe damage was caused by the disruption of redistribution of supplies to troops on the front lines, resulting from the destruction from the air of supply trucks and fuel and water tankers. Trucks and other thin-skinned vehicles were more vulnerable to attack than tanks and other armor, and as a result, "the air campaign effectively interdicted LOCs within the KTO and destroyed thin-skinned tankers and other vehicles that supplied food and water."[70]

Communications between Iraqi rear-area headquarters and the front-line troops, and even among units along the front lines, were severely disrupted by the air attacks. The national command authorities probably were unaware of the degree of destruction wrought against their forces, and the forces were out of touch with the overall theater situation. Battlefield communications along the front lines were also disrupted.

In addition to the destruction of equipment, supply interdiction, and the disruption of communications, the most important effect of the campaign against the Iraqi army was on the morale and behavior of Iraqi soldiers. The air campaign in the KTO further battered the already low Iraqi troop morale, confirming their concerns about their military inferiority, intensifying their hardships,

---

[69]"Supply depots were so numerous and large that they could not be eliminated; however, they were methodically attacked throughout the war, resulting in moderate reduction in stored materials" (*CPGW*, p. 213). See also Hosmer, op. cit., p. ix.

[70]*CPGW*, p. 211; Hosmer, op. cit., p. 131.

and sowing concern for their own and their families' safety. Coalition psychological operations (PSYOPS) reinforced these fears. One result was that the Iraqi troops distanced themselves from their equipment when they realized that it was a Coalition target. The Iraqi troops were so pinned down that it was virtually impossible to move, either by day or night, or to practice using or maintaining their equipment, especially tanks, APCs, and artillery, which were constant targets of allied attack.[71] It was safer to leave the equipment dug in (where precision munitions were generally less effective) and avoid being caught in it if it were hit. To be dug in was to suffer slow attrition; to move, however, was to invite swift destruction. This air-supported maneuver dominance was an important contributor to the Coalition success during the ground war.

As G-day approached, it became apparent that the Iraqi troops were disorganized, demoralized, and seriously weakened in their fighting strength. The various pieces of evidence contributed to CINCCENT's judgment that the Coalition was ready to begin the final phase of Operation Desert Storm: the ground campaign.

THE FINAL WEEK: SUPPORTING THE GROUND CAMPAIGN

The air operations for Phase IV of the campaign were planned to provide support for ground offensive operations. In the event, very little close air support in the traditional sense was conducted or needed, since "the classic situation for close air support—troops in contact with the enemy—rarely developed."[72] This phase of the operation was characterized by engagement and destruction of Iraqi units well forward of allied ground forces as the former maneuvered to counterattack and defend, and the attack of elements of the Iraqi army attempting to retreat from Kuwait. Most fighting between ground units consisted of armor and artillery engagements, with little close combat. A more accurate characterization of this phase, therefore, would be the simultaneous engagement by allied ground and air forces in a joint campaign against different elements of the Iraqi army.[73] Part of the explanation lies in the increasing range and lethality of Army direct fire ground force weapons and attack helicopters, which have to some degree replaced the earlier reliance on CAS provided by the Air Force, and by the Army's doctrinal emphasis on mobility and the avoidance of static lines.

For the most part, then, allied air was used more for air interdiction, either engaging enemy forces in the line of the allied advance or attacking retreating

---

[71]Hosmer, op. cit., pp. 140–149.

[72]Coyne (1992a), p. 168. See Figure A.13 and Tables A.6–A.8 in the appendix for sortie statistics.

[73]Frostic, op. cit.

forces, than for traditional close air support. Movement of Iraqi forces was detected by U-2 or TR-1 aircraft, RC-135s, or JSTARS, which then resulted in the call-in of interdiction air strikes. JSTARS, for example, on the second day of the ground campaign, detected an Iraqi blocking force headed toward the 3rd Egyptian Mechanized Division and called in air attacks to disrupt the counter-attack. The Iraqi III Corps, retreating toward Basra and entangled with elements of the occupying force, presented a lucrative target for air attacks also detected by JSTARS.

With the fast pace and confusion of events, fratricide was always a concern, and partially helps explain why air units operated well forward of ground forces. Because of the speed of the Coalition advance, airborne control elements and FACs improvised to apprise pilots of the fast-moving FSCLs (fire support coordination lines), which tended to quickly outrun their planned positions disseminated in the daily ATO. Liaison officers and FACs from three services moved with the ground troops to guide in air attacks when they were needed. Because most of the air support provided during the ground campaign was interdiction rather than CAS, for the most part aircraft operated in kill boxes controlled by airborne FACs in F/A-18Ds or USAF OA-10s. (The Marines operated OV-10s as forward air controllers and for reconnaissance within the FSCL, but the F/A-18s were faster and less vulnerable, and the Marines eventually abandoned the use of the OV-10s after two were shot down.) Close in to the line of engagement, air attacks required the permission of the ground commander. The F-16 killer scouts acted as buffers between CAS and air interdiction operations, and they controlled the airspace about 30 nautical miles out from the FSCL.

As described in the previous chapter, the commander of the I MEF (Marine Expeditionary Force) negotiated with JFACC a special high-density air control zone (HIDACZ) for his AOR, which gave him control of the airspace in front of his position and allowed him to coordinate and control the use of all aircraft, rockets, and artillery within it. The Marines employed a system called "Push CAS" in support of their ground forces. Two fully loaded attack aircraft arrived on station every 7.5 minutes and were assigned to targets by the "Fast-FACs"—Marine F/A-18Ds. If there were no CAS targets, the strike aircraft would be cleared into kill boxes in the interdiction area.

The Air Force used a mirror-image concept. Duncan describes it this way:

> Fighters would launch at maximum sustainable sortie rates and receive targeting from the ... ABCCC.... Should coalition forces need CAS, they were to forward the requests directly to the ABCCC, which would *divert* interdiction assets from the flow on a priority basis.... Though we concentrated on inter-

diction, the directive was that no units on the ground would go without CAS—if it could get the request to an ABCCC.[74]

Friendly-Fire Casualties

One of the war's tragic ironies was that, with overall Coalition casualties well below almost anyone's expectations or even hopes, many of them were inflicted by so-called friendly fire. Of the 146 U.S. personnel killed in action, 35 were killed in friendly-fire incidents; 72 of the 467 wounded were the victims of friendly fire. Altogether there were 28 incidents involving U.S. forces, of which nine were the result of air-to-ground engagements, resulting in 11 deaths and 15 wounded. Seven of the dead were the result of the strike by an A-10-fired Maverick missile against a Marine Corps light armored vehicle during the battle of Khafji. U.S. A-10s also accidentally struck British armored personnel carriers, killing several British soldiers during the ground campaign.

Remarkably, there were no cases of air-to-air fratricide. Control of the airspace was the responsibility of JFACC, through the Airspace Coordination Center, part of the Combat Operations directorate. Primary responsibility for airspace de-confliction lay with the airborne control elements, notably AWACS. Procedures and rules of engagement were specified each day in the ATO, including IFF codes for those aircraft equipped with IFF transponders. Rules of engagement required dual-source confirmation of targets before firing. Other mechanisms, such as the FSCL, the Marines' HIDACZ, and kill boxes, were all designed to ensure that collisions and fratricide did not occur. That no allied aircraft shot down (or collided with) any other is testimony to the effectiveness of the process.

Many factors contributed to the air-to-ground incidents during the ground campaign, including extremely poor visibility due to the low cloud cover and heavy black smoke from oil well fires, the very rapid and nonlinear ground advance, nighttime operations, and the featureless desert terrain.[75] Perhaps the

---

[74]Duncan (1993), p. 76 (emphasis added). The author was on the Campaign Planning directorate staff and wrote CENTAF's concept of operations for command and control of tactical air forces in support of land forces. Nothing so vividly illustrates the difference between the Air Force and Marine close support doctrines than the differences in priorities between USAF and USMC concepts. Although in a perfect world the results might be the same under either system, as a practical matter there were bound to be differences in the respective weapons load-outs under different priorities. Moreover, air (and ground) Marines did not want to rely on the ABCCC to get CAS. Some Air Force pilots also reportedly preferred other control centers (ASOC, DASC) to ABCCC. While in our view there are advantages to both concepts, we believe the Air Force concept was more suitable to the particular circumstances of this war.

[75]CPGW, p. 197.

single biggest problem was "mislocated" ground forces.[76] While aircraft could use IFF transponders to identify other aircraft, no such interactive system existed for identifying ground forces, since the enemy could use it for the same purpose. When they lacked a highly accurate system such as GPS (the Global Positioning System, which allows vehicles or individual soldiers to identify their geographical position within a few meters anywhere on the globe), ground forces occasionally simply lost their way in the desert terrain. More often, the speed of the ground offensive found Coalition forces behind Iraqi positions on the battlefield. Pilots and even ground-based forward air controllers mistakenly took them for enemy forces as a result.

Various methods were sought to prevent friendly-fire casualties, including marking Coalition vehicles with an inverted "V" on the tops and sides. This was most effective for encounters with other ground forces, but less successful for aircraft operating at high speeds, medium altitudes, and in haze and smoke. U.S. personnel—FACs, Special Operations teams, or ANGLICOs—were assigned to Coalition units to coordinate with U.S. forces.[77]

Beginning in early February, DARPA began a crash effort to develop a system to prevent air-to-ground kills, resulting in the development and deployment of the so-called DARPA light, or AFID (antifratricide identification device), a battery-powered infrared beacon visible from the air. The DARPA light was deployed in limited numbers beginning 26 February. Much more numerous were the simpler infrared beacons known as "bud lights," delivered at the same time.

RESULTS OF THE AIR CAMPAIGN

The air campaign had several goals, and was organized into separate (but overlapping) phases. It is thus possible to assess the results from several perspectives. To begin, in Table 6.4 we present data on targets and planned and flown sorties grouped by the air campaign's objectives.

The more meaningful but elusive measures of effectiveness are the functional damage wrought on the enemy, in terms of the campaign objectives—that is, not simply the number of targets destroyed in a given category, but the effect of the destruction on the enemy's ability to wage war. To begin to evaluate the role and performance of air power in more functional terms, numerous analysts and commentators have used the broad distinction between strategic and battlefield preparation phases of the air campaign; that is, between on the one

---

[76]"Horner Calls GPS Key to Reducing Fratricide in Future," *Aerospace Daily,* 2 March 1992, p. 339. Air-to-ground communications or IFF are considered the answer by some.

[77]Coyne (1992a), p. 103.

Table 6.4

Targets, Sorties Planned, and Sorties Flown by Target Category

Campaign Objective	Associated Target Categories	RAND Expanded MTL Targets	Sorties Planned	Sorties Flown
1. Isolate and incapacitate the Iraqi regime	Command, control, communications	202	1,049	601
	Leadership	48	340	429
	Electric power	39	241	215
2. Gain and maintain air supremacy	Strategic air defenses	115	847	436
	SAMs	128	310	n/a
	Airfields	64	3,690	3,047
3. Destroy NBC capabilities	NBC weapons and facilities	43	1,039	902
4. Eliminate Iraq's offensive military capability	Scuds and SRBM support	78	3,594	2,767
	Naval bases and forces	36	362	247
	Oil refining and production	49	574	518
	Other military support and production	150	3,538	2,756
5. Render the Iraqi army in the KTO ineffective	Republican Guards	105	6,987	5,646
	Other ground forces in KTO	n/a	28,401	29,354
	Railroads and bridges	131	1,168	712
	Breach: fire trenches and minefields	34	178	n/a
Total		1,222	52,140	47,630

NOTE: Scud targets include only fixed targets; sorties include sorties against mobile Scud launchers.

SOURCE: RAND working paper, "The Desert Storm Air Campaign: An Overview," by T. M. Parker and Donald Emerson, pp. 8, 34. Based on CENTAF's daily MAP and JTF Proven Force strike mission records. The RAND Expanded Master Target List includes targets from the daily MAP as well as daily ATOs, unit missions reports, and change sheets.

hand the campaign against the major sources of Saddam Hussein's power (or his "centers of gravity," in the phrase of the Checkmate planners) and on the other the effort devoted to weakening and destroying his army in Kuwait preparatory to the final ground offensive.[78] We have described major aspects and results of the air campaign in these terms in this chapter. In Chapters Eleven and Twelve we offer some global assessments of the performance and the role of air power in all its aspects during Operations Desert Shield and Desert Storm. Let us here merely summarize some of air power's accomplishments and deficiencies during Desert Storm.

---

[78]Friedman (1991), pp. 446–447, divides the air campaign into three components: strategic, tactical, and interdiction.

Assessing the Strategic Campaign

The strategic campaign's most important results were achieved in the first 24 to 72 hours of the war for most target sets, notably the complete collapse of the Iraqi air-defense system and attacks on the leadership's command and control facilities and communications network. While the latter was never completely destroyed or incapacitated, it was put under severe pressure in the opening, scripted days of the air campaign, and the follow-up attacks in the ensuing weeks kept the communications network under pressure and prevented its reconstitution. Similarly, the primary electric power grid, especially for Baghdad, was seriously damaged in the opening days of the war, and this had widespread and cascading consequences for Iraqi battle management and operations and for the quality of life in Baghdad (not only was electricity cut off, but water and sewage facilities, which depended on electric supply, were incidentally disrupted).

For some other strategic targets, the results were disappointing. The most important instances, already discussed above in some detail, were the mobile Scud campaign and the Iraqi NBC program. Not only did air power fail to destroy any mobile Scud launchers, but the Iraqis had also dispersed a considerable amount of their production equipment and components, and the actual damage to the Scud production program and fixed-launch facilities was less than had been thought. Similarly, although attacks against known Iraqi NBC production facilities were generally successful, postwar inspections by the United Nations revealed that a large number of nuclear and chemical weapons facilities had not been targeted and attacked. Some targets had not been known to Coalition intelligence, and some elements of the program had been dispersed prior to the war. Some facilities were also emptied out during the war, implying that the concentration of attack against this target set was not as great as it could have been. The setback to the Iraqi program was thus not nearly as significant as had been hoped. In sum, the Iraqis were able to thwart the Coalition's intelligence capabilities and thus protect at least some of their valuable national assets from destruction.

In short, the strategic portion of the air campaign registered the greatest success in its spillover effects on Iraqi battlefield operations—the degradation of communications and resupply, and the neutralization of the Iraqi air force. Success in reducing Iraq's long-term military/strategic assets—Scuds, NBC programs, and even Republican Guard forces—was less impressive.

The Air Campaign in the KTO

In contrast to the strategic campaign, the success of which relied on precision intelligence and precision attacks, the success of the theater campaign can in large measure be attributed to its sheer mass and relentlessness (although precision strikes against Iraqi armor were a notable feature). Table 6.2 (above) gives some measure of the scale of the pounding the Iraqi army took, compared to the strategic campaign's relative economy (in most instances): well over half of strike sorties were directed against ground forces in the KTO, and additional sorties struck related or directly supporting targets such as supply and transportation targets and battlefield communications.

From the perspective of the Iraqi troops in the KTO, the "air campaign's psychological damage exceeded [its] physical damage":

- It was ubiquitous—there were always aircraft overhead;

- It was intense—bombing went on around the clock, day in and day out;

- It was accurate; and

- It was impossible to defend against.[79]

The Iraqi army was probably considerably understrength at the start of the war, and the fear engendered by the relentless air campaign probably led to a considerable desertion rate. Rather than the 540,000 troops that might have been deployed had all units been fully manned, the Coalition more likely faced a force of perhaps 336,000, and perhaps as few as 240,000 by G-day.[80]

Enemy deserters and, more importantly, prisoners of war gave little evidence of belief in their cause. Analysis of enemy prisoner of war interviews led RAND's Stephen Hosmer to conclude that "many, if not most, of these remaining forces were prepared to offer minimal or no resistance to the Coalition forces that were about to attack them."[81] Iraqi troops began deserting even before the ground campaign began, and very often surrendered very quickly once it did begin. Over 85,000 enemy prisoners of war were either captured or surrendered during the ground campaign.

As noted above, the air campaign in the KTO attrited Iraqi armor and artillery inventories, disrupted distribution of supplies to front-line forces, and most importantly, reduced the size and morale of the forces facing the Coalition. Iraqi commanders were also blinded by the grounding of their air force and its reconnaissance and surveillance aircraft. As a result, Iraqi commanders didn't know the disposition of Coalition forces or what their movements were. Gen-

---

[79]Hosmer, op. cit.

[80]The higher figure is from *GWAPS*, p. 8; the lower figure, which is a lower bound, is from Hosmer, op. cit. The two are not necessarily inconsistent, since the former number is for the beginning of the air war, and the latter for the eve of the ground campaign, implying that perhaps 25–30 percent of Iraqi troops deserted during the air campaign.

[81]Hosmer, op. cit.

eral Schwarzkopf could hardly believe that the Iraqis had not detected the massive movement of troops for the "left hook," but indeed they apparently remained completely ignorant of it.

Air power effectively interdicted maneuver during the ground campaign. Once again, without any countervailing air-to-air capability, the Iraqi ground forces were at the mercy of the seemingly all-seeing, omnipresent Coalition air forces.

The result was light opposition from front-line units, limited opposition from rear-area units, the nonengagement or surrender without a fight of other units, including elements of the Republican Guard, abandonment of huge amounts of Iraqi equipment, and low casualties *on both sides*.[82] These phases of the air war were an unqualified success and key to the swift allied victory on the ground.

---

[82]Ibid.

Chapter Seven

TACTICS

> I have always regarded the forward edge of the battlefield as the most
> exclusive club in the world.
>
> —*Sir Brian Horrocks*

The Gulf War served more to validate the existing tactics of the air services than
to foster major tactical innovation. The Iraqi threat, as formidable as it was
prior to the onset of Desert Storm, was more of an early 1980s threat than a
state of the art 1990s threat. In effect, it was a derivative of the Soviet threat as it
had existed about ten years earlier.[1] Given the usual intelligence lag times and
training lead times, the U.S. forces in the Gulf met the threat they had been
trained to defeat.[2]

The biggest change in tactics since the Vietnam War resulted from the prolifer-
ation of precision-guided munitions. These munitions and their antiradiation
missile cousins were just coming of age when the Vietnam War ended in the
early 1970s. In the Gulf War, they played the preeminent role—whether in the
form of Tomahawk missiles fired from warships or GBU-27 laser-guided bombs
dropped from a F-117A stealth fighter. Antiradiation missiles played a particularly important role during the first 48 hours of the air campaign as the Iraqi
integrated air-defense system was neutralized and largely destroyed. As the
campaign progressed, carriage of these missiles became more oriented to
"policing" Iraqi and Kuwaiti airspace than to providing direct strike support.

In this chapter we examine, within the limits of classification, the tactics that
were used by Coalition aircrews as they systematically took out the Iraqi ability
to make war and destroyed their forces in the field. In some ways, this chapter

---

[1]Air Vice Marshall R. A. Mason, RAF, "The Air War in the Gulf," *Survival*, Vol. 33, No. 3, May/June
1991, p. 213.

[2]Hallion (1992), pp. 121–124.

is a pilot's-eye view of the air war and provides some of the details underlying our discussion of air operations in the previous chapter.

THE FIRST TWO DAYS: THE INTERFACE BETWEEN THE PLAN AND TACTICS

The strike plan for the first night, indeed for the first 48 hours, was a study in "grand tactics." Lieutenant General Horner wielded the air weapon under near-ideal conditions, with a well-trained professional force. He and his staff orchestrated the initial attack to exploit Iraqi weaknesses and Coalition strengths simultaneously. Although strategic and operational surprise were largely lost as a result of the deliberate and escalating pace of the diplomatic situation, Horner managed to achieve tactical surprise: the timing and locations for the initial attack.[3]

To achieve tactical surprise required getting hundreds of allied aircraft into the air undetected, refueling them, marshaling them outside of Iraqi radar range, and then dispatching them en masse into Iraqi and Kuwaiti airspace in waves and under conditions that involved blinding the Iraqi integrated air-defense system and systematically suppressing its radar emitters and SAM launchers. The attack was launched at precisely the time that the E-3 AWACS aircraft on station aloft was being relieved by the oncoming E-3. To an observer at an Iraqi air-defense radar scope, the scene would have been no different from that of many previous nights at about the same time. No different, that is, until Coalition missiles and F-117-dropped bombs started to rain down on air-defense system nodes. What followed was an aerial onslaught with no pause.

The initial "laydown" of weapons was phased to have stealthy and long-range standoff weapons delivered first.[4] The initial punch had three prongs: F-117s delivering laser-guided bombs in time-urgent attacks against sensitive command and control and air-defense nodes, complemented by 52 Tomahawk missiles launched from U.S. Navy ships, and 35 conventional cruise missiles (ALCMs) launched from seven B-52 bombers.

Other strikes followed closely and were configured in conventional strike packages consisting of primary weapons delivery aircraft supported by defense suppression aircraft, such as Air Force F-4G "Wild Weasels" or Navy/Marine EA-6B

---

[3]*Triumph Without Victory* (p. 243) attributes this judgment to General Colin Powell. Lieutenant General Glosson told us that H-hour (not D-day) was selected in September 1990 and never changed.

[4]The exception was "Task Force Normandy," a team of Army and Air Force helicopters tasked with knocking out Iraqi air-defense radar sites blocking the path to the main air attack. These sites were knocked out 22 minutes before H-hour (see p. 125).

Prowlers. Covering these strikes were fighter sweeps and combat air patrols furnished by fighter aircraft of all services.

Air Force informational literature distributed after Operation Desert Storm compares a "standard" mission's composition with a similar stealth mission, as shown in Figure 7.1. Note that the standard mission as portrayed does not show AWACS, Compass Call, combat search and rescue, and poststrike reconnaissance aircraft. Strike and support aircraft were refueled both before going into and after coming out of Iraq. In the case of aircraft whose home airfields were in remote parts of the Arabian peninsula, multiple refuelings were used. Overseeing and guiding the entire operation were Air Force E-3 AWACS, whose job it was to ensure strike aircraft were cleared into and off the tracks to their targets with minimum mutual interference, and to warn the strikes of air threats while guiding friendly fighters to intercepts.

To a large degree, the tactics for the first 72 hours were dictated by the ATO described in Chapter Six. The diverse capabilities of the air weapon were blended in such a way as to provide the best opportunity of a safe weapons delivery and preventing mutual interference—the latter no small charge when over 650 aircraft were crammed into a small slice of theater airspace as they were on

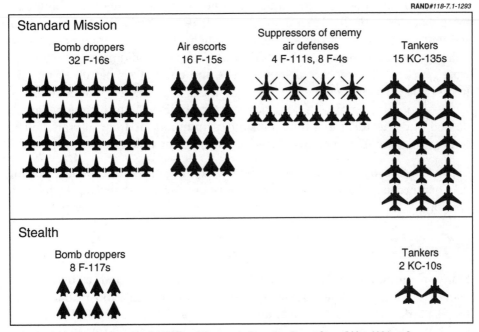

RAND#118-7.1-1293

Standard Mission

| Bomb droppers
32 F-16s | Air escorts
16 F-15s | Suppressors of enemy
air defenses
4 F-111s, 8 F-4s | Tankers
15 KC-135s |

Stealth

| Bomb droppers
8 F-117s | | | Tankers
2 KC-10s |

SOURCE: *Air Force News,* Special Edition: "Airpower in Operation Desert Storm," May 1991, p. 8.

Figure 7.1—Comparison of Stealth and Standard Mission Packages

"opening night." Nevertheless, individual flight leaders had to make rapid decisions to deal with unfolding situations that the scripted ATO did not and could not anticipate. Such instances included the "target that was not there" (having already been destroyed), the "bogey" whose identity could not be sufficiently determined to warrant a blind shot with an air-to-air missile, the missed rendezvous with a tanker, and a host of other similar instances that required a high degree of judgment and airmanship.

The guiding principle in the weapons delivery tactics was to place the aircraft in the best possible position for good visibility (e.g., smoke blowing away from the shooter) with minimum detectability (e.g., "pop up" delivery at high speed when using low-altitude attack profiles) and unpredictability (e.g., shooters approaching the target from different directions). Time over or near the target was compressed to the absolute minimum. In the case of laser-guided munitions, this minimum was affected significantly by the need to keep the target illuminated until weapon impact.

KILLING THE IRAQI AIR FORCE

The Iraqi air force was first blinded, then pinned down, then chased in part to Iran, and finally destroyed where it chose to hunker down in its shelters. The early attacks on the Iraqi integrated air-defense system effectively blinded a force that was critically dependent on centralized control and execution. Subsequent attacks against the airfields did much to deny the Iraqi air force its ability to get large numbers of aircraft aloft. Those that did manage to take off were quickly killed by U.S. fighter sweeps and combat air patrol. When the Iraqis chose to avoid destruction by remaining in their shelters, the Coalition air forces went after them with deep penetrating bombs. With this refuge largely denied and the toll mounting, substantial numbers of Iraqi aircraft fled to Iran—with a number of them being shot down during this retreat.

Because we have already discussed the attack on the IADS and shelter-busting in Chapter Six, this discussion will focus on runway denial and air-to-air combat.

Runway Denial Tactics

Many of the initial attacks on Iraqi airfields were conducted at low altitude using cratering and other runway denial munitions. While most Coalition air forces participated at one time or another in airfield attacks, the RAF had some of the best weapons for this purpose and was given a central role in the denial mission.

On 15 August 1990, President George Bush meets with his top Department of Defense and national security advisers in the Pentagon Gold Room to receive a briefing on the status of U.S. military deployments to Saudi Arabia in response to the Iraqi invasion of Kuwait. Shown, left to right, are: General H. Norman Schwarzkopf, U.S. Army, Commander in Chief, U.S. Central Command; Secretary of Defense Dick Cheney; President Bush; and Chairman of the Joint Chiefs of Staff, General Colin E. Powell.

The senior leadership of the Desert Shield/Desert Storm campaigns. Front row, left to right: Paul Wolfowitz, Under Secretary of Defense for Policy (OUSDP); General Colin L. Powell, Chairman of the Joint Chiefs of Staff; Secretary of Defense Dick Cheney; General H. Norman Schwarzkopf; and Lieutenant General Calvin Waller, Deputy CINCCENT. Back row: Lieutenant General Walter Boomer, USMC; Lieutenant General Charles A. Horner, USAF; Lieutenant General John J. Yeosock, USA; and Vice Admiral Stanley R. Arthur, USN. The colonel is unidentified.

Nevada-based F-117 stealth fighters line up at Langley AFB, Virginia, for an overnight stay before deploying to Saudi Arabia during Desert Shield.

An F-15E Strike Eagle fighter aircraft deployed from the 4th Tactical Fighter Wing (TFW), Seymour Johnson AFB, North Carolina, during Desert Shield.

U.S. Air Force photo by TSgt Hans Deffner.

Marine AV-8B Harrier aircraft from the 513th VMA, Yuma Marine Corps AB, Arizona, fly in formation during Desert Shield.

Newly arrived soldiers from the VII Corps in Stuttgart, Germany, wait in the sand by the holding area tents for transportation to their Desert Shield deployed location. Behind them is a C-130 aircraft.

Official USAF photo by SSgt Lee Corkran.

Two aviation ordnancemen move a skid loaded with multiple ejector racks past a Carrier Airborne Early Warning Squadron 115 (VAW-115) E-2C Hawkeye aircraft on the flight deck of the aircraft carrier USS Midway (CV-41) during Desert Shield.

General Schwarzkopf and other senior military commanders are briefed on 15 January 1991 by Lieutenant Colonel David A. Deptula, one of the architects of the air campaign. Left to right: General Olson (CENTAF/CV), General Horner (partially hidden), General Glosson, General Schwarzkopf, and Lieutenant Colonel Deptula.

Official USAF photo, courtesy of Lt. Col. Deptula.

Official USAF photo by TSgt Marvin Lynchard.

F-16C fighter aircraft sit on the parking ramp on 16 January 1991, the day of the UN deadline for Iraq to exit Kuwait. The F-16Cs are from the 388th TFW, Hill AFB, Utah.

At a private aviation terminal somewhere in Saudi Arabia, nearly 230 C-130s flew around the clock for three days to move the 82nd Airborne.

Official USAF photo by SSgt Dean Wagner.

An F-16 aircraft from the 614th TFS, "Lucky Devils," flies over the Saudi-Kuwaiti border during Desert Storm.

A Marine F/A-18 returns after a bombing mission on enemy targets well into the third week of the air campaign.

Official USAF photo by MSgt Bill Thompson.

An A-10 close ground support aircraft from the 23rd TFW, England AFB, Louisiana, loaded with 30mm cannon ammunition, Mk-87 cluster bombs, AGM-65 Maverick missiles, and AIM-9 Sidewinder missiles.

Official USAF photo by MSgt Kit Thompson.

B-52s from the 1708th BMW prepare for a mission on a flightline in Saudi Arabia.

Official USAF photo by TSgt Rose Reynolds.

EF-111 aircraft from the 366th TFW, Mt. Home AFB, Idaho, move in for refueling over Saudi Arabia during the air campaign.

An E-3 Airborne Warning and Control System (AWACS) aircraft operates over northern Saudi Arabia during the air campaign.

A SAC RC-135 reconnaissance aircraft from the 55th SRW, Offutt AFB, Nebraska, flies near the Iraqi border.

The prototype JSTARS, used to locate and track moving ground targets and relay that information to air and ground commanders.

A Navy intelligence specialist evaluates aerial photographic images returned from a combat mission flown from the deck of the USS *John F. Kennedy* (CV-67).

The USS *Saratoga* steams continuously while on patrol in the Red Sea, launching strikes at Iraqi positions.

The USS *Saratoga* operates in the Red Sea during the air campaign and launches its aircraft for attacks, day and night.

Elements from the *Kennedy's* Carrier Air Wing Three's strike support group, two EA-6Bs from Electronic Warfare Squadron 130 and an F-14 from Fighter Squadron 32, refuel from a USAF KC-135 tanker while en route to new targets over Iraq and Kuwait. Strike support provided the radar jamming and fighter intercept necessary for the safe delivery of ordnance by the light attack bombers embarked with CVW3.

Official USN photo by CDR John Leenhouts.

While en route from the USS *Kennedy* to targets in Iraq and Kuwait during Desert Storm, five A-7E Corsair aircraft from Attack Squadron 72 (VA-72) and an A-6E Intruder aircraft from Attack Squadron 75 (VA-75) rendezvous with a KC-135E Stratotanker aircraft for in-flight refueling. The A-7E aircraft third from the top is carrying AGM-88 HARMs (high-speed antiradiation missiles); the others carry Mk-83 1000-pound bombs and AIM-9 Sidewinder missiles.

The battleship USS *Wisconsin* (BB-64) fires a Tomahawk missile during operations in the Persian Gulf in support of Desert Storm.

An F-111 fighter aircraft from the 48th TFW, RAF Lakenheath, England, returns from sorties over Iraq and Kuwait.

Official USAF photo by SRA Chris Putman.

F-4G Wild Weasel aircraft from the 35th TFW, George AFB, California, fly in formation over Saudi Arabia.

Official USAF photo by MSgt Bill Thompson.

An intercept officer aboard an F-15E aircraft from the 4th TFW, Seymour Johnson AFB, North Carolina, relaxes during refueling above the Saudi Arabian desert.

Lieutenant General Horner was both the air component commander (COMUSCENTAF) and the Joint Forces Air Component Commander (JFACC) during Desert Storm.

Lieutenant General Royal N. Moore, Jr., USMC, was the Commander, 3rd Marine Air Wing, during Desert Storm.

Rear Admiral Riley D. Mixson, Red Sea Battle Force Commander, aboard the USS *Kennedy* during Desert Shield.

Rear Admiral Daniel P. March, USN, was the Arabian Gulf Battle Force Commander during Desert Storm.

Operations in the "Black Hole": Brigadier General Buster Glosson, USAF, and his team discuss targeting and mission planning during the air campaign.

Technicians sort through Iraqi Scud missile debris in a private company's parking lot after it was shot down by a Patriot missile.

Extensive internal damage is evident in an Iraqi shelter that was bombed by the U.S. Air Force.

General Norman Schwarzkopf and Lieutenant General Prince Khalid, head of the Saudi forces, discuss cease-fire matters with Iraqi officers, Lieutenant General Mohammed Abdez Rahman Al-Dagitistani and Lieutenant General Sabin Abdul-Aziz Al Douri, on 3 March 1991.

NOTE: Unless otherwise noted, all photographs are courtesy of the Office of Public Affairs, Department of Defense.

Several RAF flight leaders have described the tactics used. Tornado GR Mark 1 aircraft would approach the target at almost 600 knots at 200 feet along the terrain using terrain-following radar. The terrain-following radar, linked to a Doppler radar, autopilot, and attack computer, guided the aircraft to the preset weapons drop point. At that point, two JP233 canisters under the fuselage launched 490 parachute-retarded bomblets. The bomblets were in two categories:

> The larger—the SG357 runway-cratering bomb . . . weighed fifty seven pounds. Each time one struck a runway or taxiway, a shaped charge punched a small circular hole in the concrete surface. A fraction of a second later, a second warhead was blown through the hole and into the foundation, where it detonated. The force of the secondary explosion, confined between the foundation and the concrete surface, blasted a cavity topped with a circular area of "heave"— cracked and broken concrete pushed up from below. . . . To make repairs difficult and dangerous, the dispensers also release 430 HP876 area-denial mines . . . to provide interruption times for anyone trying to clear the area and effect repairs.[5]

Six Tornados were lost, all during the first four nights of the conflict. But only one was lost on a low-altitude runway denial sortie. Each aircraft loss was unique and not necessarily related to the altitude used in weapons delivery.[6] In any event, the rapid neutralization of the Iraqi air force made runway denial missions unnecessary for most of the remainder of the Gulf War.

Air-to-Air Combat Tactics

During the early days of the air war, the Iraqi air force averaged only some 30 fighter sorties per day. Nine Iraqi aircraft were shot down during the first day's operations and six more on the third day.[7] These small numbers reflect the low level of Iraqi air activity rather than any deficiencies in U.S. fighter commitments and tactics. Coalition losses in such combat were either zero or one.[8]

Fighter tactics included dedicated sweeps to attack any Iraqi aircraft detected by AWACS aircraft, fighter escort of strikes, and combat air patrols on designated stations to both defend Saudi airspace and shoot down any Iraqi aircraft

---

[5]Alfred Price, "Tornado in the Desert," *Air Force Magazine*, December 1992, p. 43.

[6]Ibid., pp. 45–46.

[7]Coyne (1992a), p. 51.

[8]A dispute flared up in September 1992 between the DoD and a professor at Johns Hopkins University about whether one Saratoga F/A-18 loss was the result of air-to-air combat or to an Iraqi SAM. The evidence, to say the least, is inconclusive. But lost in the dispute is that whatever the facts, Coalition losses to air-to-air combat were either zero or very small (*CPGW*, p. 167). See *GWAPS*, p. 58, footnote 10, for speculation on the loss of this aircraft.

that eluded the sweeps.[9] Most of these sweeps concentrated on areas close to Iraqi military airfields and enjoyed the most success in air-to-air operations. Fighter sweeps immediately followed the first wave of F-15E and F-117A strike aircraft in the attack on the first night. This tactic greatly assisted the fighter crews in separating the egressing strike aircraft from the scrambling Iraqi fighters.[10]

A major difficulty in the Coalition's prosecution of air-to-air combat were the stringent rules on beyond-visual-range (BVR) shots. The large number of Coalition aircraft in the air at any given moment raised justifiable fears of fratricide. Accordingly, a target aircraft had to be identified visually as enemy or had to have backup corroboration of its enemy status. More than 40 percent of the air-to-air kills during the war were BVR shots. Most of them were cleared by E-3A AWACS corroboration of the target's hostile status.[11]

THE SCUD HUNT

The "Great Scud Hunt" was the premier unscheduled event of the air war in the Gulf. The DoD report on the Gulf War states: "The amount of effort and the length of time required to deal with the Scud threat was underestimated." In Chapter Six we discussed Scud hunt operations. Here we focus on tactics. No tactics to counter mobile Scuds had been developed prior to combat operations in the Gulf.[12] Consequently, tactics had to be developed on the fly to deal with this threat, a threat that was always more political than military—and for that reason of critical importance in a coalition war.

Scud hunting was done either by armed reconnaissance missions (frequently AC-130 gunships) or by aircraft on CAP (mostly F-15Es, F-16s, and, during daylight, A-10s). Early-warning satellite detections of Scud launches were relayed by voice link to CENTCOM, and thence to JSTARS or to aircraft on CAP, which were then sent to search for the Scud launcher.[13] Toward the end of the war, Air Force flight crews claimed a kill against a group of Scud launch vehicles that were later identified as fuel trucks.[14]

---

[9]For a vivid description of one of these sweeps, including the tactics used, see *Triumph Without Victory*, pp. 250–254.

[10]Coyne (1992a), p. 52.

[11]*GWAPS*, pp. 59–60.

[12]*GWAPS*, p. 43.

[13]Hallion (1992), pp. 181–183.

[14]*GWAPS*, p. 86.

It is worth noting that some favorable factors were at work, specifically the lack of significant Iraqi air defenses or jamming. However, the risk from AAA fire was enough to keep planes operating at higher altitudes (10,000 to 15,000 feet) that further degraded the discrimination power of their sensors. Bad weather also frequently made locating TELs difficult.

The tactics used are summarized in the DoD report in addressing the last week of January:

> The next week saw an intense effort in western Iraq to eliminate the mobile SCUD launchers. B-52s bombed suspected SCUD hide sites and support facilities at H-2 and H-3 airfields in western Iraq during the day and at night. During the day, A-10s and F-16s patrolled the area; at night, LANTIRN-equipped F-16s, F-15Es, and FLIR equipped A-6Es took up the task. Pilots often received target coordinates or patrol areas, based on the most up-to-date information, as they headed out to the planes. Using Defense Support Program (DSP) early warning information and other indications, CENTCOM directed aircraft to attack the launchers. JSTARS helped . . .[15]

STRIKE TACTICS

As important as F-117A, Tomahawk, and anti-Scud operations were to the success of the air campaign, the heart of that campaign was the day-in and day-out strikes conducted by the many different bomb and missile shooters of the Coalition air forces.

B-52 Tactics

The first strike aircraft to take off the first day of Operation Desert Storm were seven B-52s from Barksdale AFB in Louisiana. These aircraft launched the first-ever ALCM attack in combat. Their tactics were straightforward and centered on their flight planning and missile programming. In the opinion of Air Force leaders, that attack is a harbinger of the new dimensions of bomber deployment in regional contingencies.[16]

The tactics consisted of a high-altitude launch of 35 AGM-86C ALCMs from outside Iraqi airspace to hit eight targets in Iraq, including power generation and transmission facilities and military communications sites.[17] Because these

---

[15]*CPGW*, p. 226.

[16]See "The Air Force and U.S. National Security: Global Reach—Global Power," Department of the Air Force White Paper, June 1990, pp. 8–10; and "Enhancing the Nation's Conventional Bomber Force: The Bomber Roadmap," Department of the Air Force, June 1992, pp. 4–5.

[17]*CPGW*, p. T-179.

same targets were hit by other systems, the effectiveness and contribution of the ALCM strikes cannot be determined.[18]

But these initial operations by the B-52s were merely a precursor for sustained bomber operations over the entire period of the Gulf War. As we saw in Chapter Three, B-52s deployed early to Diego Garcia and subsequently to the United Kingdom, Spain, and elsewhere. Most of the sorties were used against "interdiction" (i.e., deep) targets (as opposed, for example, to close air support or offensive counterair). Most of the interdiction sorties were flown against the Iraqi army in the KTO.

Most sorties were flown at high altitude (between 30,000 and 40,000 feet) and the weapons load consisted of a large number of medium to large gravity bombs. Some Air Force officers interviewed suggested that the main (and possibly unique) contribution of the B-52s was in demoralizing the dug-in Iraqi army in the KTO. There is some POW interview evidence to suggest that this outcome was at least as important as the systematic air attack on Iraqi armored and artillery forces. Thus, their role largely paralleled the heavy bomber role in the Korean and Vietnam Wars, with the difference that the targets were more visible and accessible and the targeted troops were more susceptible to psychological warfare used in conjunction with heavy bombing attacks.

Because of the necessarily long flights from bases both inside and outside the theater to the target area, changes were often made in the target assignments while the bombers were en route. Changes occurred in about 25 percent of the missions. The flight crews readily accommodated these changes, though not without some difficulty, and there is no evidence of mission failure because of changes received en route.[19]

A tactic unique to Desert Storm was the use of B-52s to assist in mine-clearing operations. Ten percent of the total B-52 sorties flown during the war were committed to that mission. The intent was to blast an attack path through opposing minefields by detonating them with a dense pattern of bomb blasts. The evidence (and opinion) on their effectiveness in this role is mixed.[20]

---

[18]This was a not uncommon phenomenon of the Gulf air war, in which critical targets were hammered by several different systems within minutes.

[19]Defenders of the ATO cite this and other examples of changing missions and targets on the fly as evidence of the ATO's flexibility. We believe the more relevant question is not whether the ATO can be changed—it can and was—but whether the system used for its development can accommodate a shorter (than 48-hour) cycle time and thus provide a better and more responsive blend of deliberate and quick reaction planning. For B-52s (as in this case) this would mean the ability to get the bombers armed and launched with shorter lead times and the ability to switch weapon loads at the last minute.

[20]CPGW, p. 196.

In spite of the overall success of B-52 operations, it is clear that the performance of the B-52 force was a disappointment from the standpoint of bombing accuracy. One news report based on Air Force congressional testimony summarizes the experience this way:

> Whereas SAC crews had trained for low-level nuclear attack missions into the Soviet Union, they had a hard time adjusting to the high altitude, "more survivable" tactics of the Gulf War, and this threw off their accuracy.... The offensive avionics software on the B-52s also didn't properly correct for windage when dropping from high altitude, causing "bombing inaccuracy from high altitude," Butler said. The problem wasn't corrected until the war was over.[21]

Battlefield Preparation

"Battlefield preparation" involved attacks on the Iraqi army in both Kuwait and Iraq with the objective of destroying its combat effectiveness. One shorthand index of achieving the objective was the 50 percent destruction criterion applied by USCINCCENT to tanks, armored personnel carriers, and artillery. Battlefield preparation was a mission engaged in by air and ground elements of all four services. It was also a controversial mission—it being charged that the needed weight of effort was not applied soon enough and that it was not sufficiently responsive to the needs of some individual ground commanders.[22] In our discussion of this subject, we focus principally on air operations before G-day (24 February) that kicked off the four-day ground offensive.

In fundamental terms, there were two target arrays: the Iraqi army that was heavily committed to defending the Saudi-Kuwaiti border region, and the Republican Guards who were serving as the theater operational reserve in northern Kuwait and southern Iraq. Some tactics (e.g., "tank plinking") were much the same in both areas, while others differed (e.g., barrier clearance operations were localized in southern Kuwait, and attacks on Iraqi army supply truck convoys were mostly in northern Kuwait and southern Iraq).

After the opening days of the air war, most air strikes were conducted from medium altitude (in the vicinity of 10,000 feet) to reduce losses. This limitation

---

[21]"B-52s Were Only Marginally Successful in Gulf War, Gen. Butler Says," *Aerospace Daily,* January 28, 1993, p. 155. For a more upbeat view, see Doug Fries, "The BUFF at War," *Air Force Magazine,* June 1992, pp. 44–49.

[22]We have discussed these charges and responses to them in Chapter Five. For a succinct official review of this topic, see *CPGW,* pp. 246, 345. Senior Air Force officers (serving in responsible positions during Operation Desert Storm), respond that there was plenty of air available; all ground force commanders had to do was ask for it, using the JFACC (Air Force) system of processing requests. But the problem goes beyond misunderstandings about procedures and includes doctrinal preferences and operational priorities, as pointed out in Chapters Five and Six.

required that incoming aircraft attempt to locate their targets at considerable distance and often in conditions of low visibility. Moreover, because of their short time in the target area and limited tactical reconnaissance assets, the strike crews had little opportunity to familiarize themselves with the topography and the appearance of target arrays. To facilitate control of incoming strike sorties and clear them on to targets, a kill box system was set up, as described in Chapter Six.

Air Force FACs flew these missions in F-16 (called killer scouts) and OA-10 aircraft, while Marines used two-seater OV-10s and F-18Ds. In each case, the incoming flight (from whatever service) was handed off from the ABCCC C-130, ASOC, or DASC to the appropriate airborne FAC.[23] The FAC either confirmed the prebriefed target and gave cueing information and updates, or put the incoming flight on a more recently developed target, often designating it with a smoke rocket or other ordnance. Many of the attacks against vehicles and artillery were conducted using the AGM-65 Maverick with electro-optical, infrared, or laser seekers.

Use of gravity weapons at medium altitude was a chancier exercise. Most crews had not had much training in medium-altitude drops, and the hit rate was not good.[24] However, Coalition aircraft losses were minimal.

Coalition airmen soon developed innovative tactics for destroying tanks and other armored vehicles with weapons that had been designed for other tasks:

> Aircrews learned that desert conditions created some unique opportunities for weapons that use thermal imaging or IR seekers. In early February, F-111 crews returning to base near sunset noted the presence of buried armor could be detected by FLIR [forward-looking infrared] equipment, because metallic surfaces cooled slower than the surrounding sand. On 8 February, F-111Fs tried a new tactic that informally became known as "tank plinking" in which an F-111 carrying four GBU-12 500 lb LGBs located and bombed individual Iraqi tanks.[25]

Other aircraft types soon adopted this practice and the toll on Iraqi tanks climbed steeply. Many battlefield preparation attacks were conducted using

---

[23]We should note that these FACs were only occasionally used as forward air controllers in the close air support sense. Rather, they were controlling strikes in enemy-held territory at some considerable distance from friendly ground forces (i.e., in an interdiction role).

[24]Hallion (1992), p. 212, states that F-16 bombing accuracy was about 30 feet CEP during low-altitude delivery and 200 feet during medium-altitude delivery. CEP, or circular error probable, is a circle around the aimpoint in which half of the bombs dropped will be within the circle and the other half outside it.

[25]*CPGW*, pp. 184–185. General Horner reminds us that aircrews in F-111Fs, F-15Es, and F-16Cs had detected armed vehicles in the desert at night in a series of exercises conducted before the start of the war in January 1991.

laser-guided weapons. Unfortunately, the numbers of aircraft equipped with laser designator equipment were limited, though many could carry and drop laser-guided weapons. All F-111Fs and A-6Es had laser designators, but there were fewer than two dozen LANTIRN pods with a laser designator capability available for the large number of F-15 and F-16 aircraft in theater.[26] Occasionally, these shortages were overcome by launching laser-guided weapons on signal from an LGB aircraft accompanying an aircraft with a designator. For example, A-6Es illuminated targets for LGBs dropped from accompanying A-7 and AV-8B aircraft, as did RAF Buccaneers for Tornado aircraft.

DEFENSE SUPPRESSION TACTICS

In one sense, the bulk of the first night's air activity was an exercise in defense suppression: taking down the Iraqi IADS. As we have seen in Chapter Six, it was successful. But in spite of that success, parts of the Iraqi air-defense system survived, in many cases under a form of local control, and took Coalition aircraft under fire. Suppressing these residual, but important, capabilities then fell to SEAD aircraft in the suppression of enemy air defenses role.

The enemy air-defense threat was an imposing one. Figure 7.2 portrays a system more dense than that fielded by the Warsaw Pact in Eastern Europe during the 1980s.

The principal weapons in SEAD were electronic jamming and HARM missiles. Air-defense jamming was conducted by EF-111s and EA-6Bs.[27] HARMs were fired by USAF F-4Gs (Wild Weasels), F/A-18s, and EA-6Bs. (EA-6Bs can both jam and launch HARMs.) Operational modes included

- **Autonomous operations.** Attacks against targets in designated geographic areas to reduce the enemy air-defense threat or roll back enemy air defenses.

- **Direct support operations.** SEAD support of a specific strike.

[26]A complete LANTIRN system consists of two pods: a navigation pod and a targeting pod. The latter carried a laser designator. F/A-18s did not have a laser designator capability in any form.

[27]A Navy adjunct to these systems was the tactical air-launched decoy (TALD) intended to stimulate Iraqi air defenses so that they could be targeted and destroyed. An Air Force adjunct was the EC-130 Compass Call aircraft that jammed Iraqi communications. Army systems were also used in the SEAD role—witness the Task Force Normandy operation that opened the air war and the Army's use of its ATACMs to suppress SAM defenses closer to the battle line. (*CPGW*, pp. 158–159, 218.) A-10s accompanied by F-4G Wild Weasels were also used in the SEAD role for suppression targets that were not deep in Iraq.

- **Area suppression operations.** SEAD support to a number of closely scheduled strikes occurring in one area.[28]

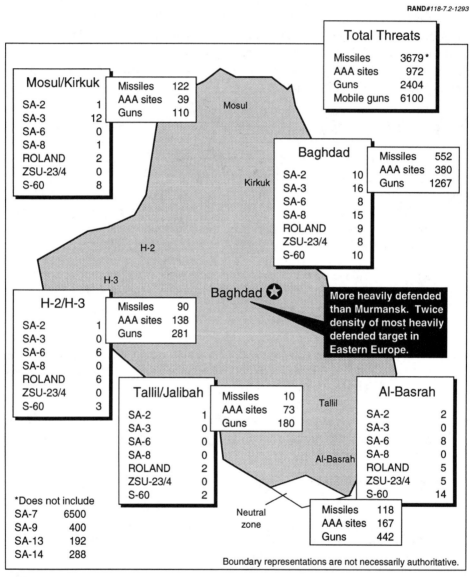

Figure 7.2—Iraqi SAM/AAA Threat, January 1991

---

[28]*CPGW*, p. T-49.

The mode of operation and tactics varied over time. All three modes were used on the first night of the war, but gradually autonomous and area suppression became the preferred options as Iraqi air defenses were systematically destroyed. Direct support was limited to the most heavily defended targets. There was an initial difference in HARM-shooting philosophy among the services, a difference that narrowed as the air-defense threat was reduced.

> For Navy and USMC HARM-shooters, initial tactics were based on the preemptive use of HARMs and electronic countermeasures. Typically, the use of HARMs in the preemptive mode was more common when supporting attacks on heavily defended strategic targets inside Iraq. The target of opportunity mode was more frequently used during operations against less well-defended targets and fielded forces in the KTO. More than half of all HARMs used were expended during the first week of the war, with another third expended from 6 to 13 February when the emphasis on attacking Iraqi forces in the KTO increased.... By the end of the conflict, reactive HARMs and ECM became common as a result of combat experience and the perceived need to husband HARMs.[29]

The Navy-Marine practice was founded on its experience in contingency operations in which lavish use of HARM was warranted over a short period in order to eliminate aircrew losses. The Air Force usage was based on the concept of a longer conflict where use of HARM had to be balanced against the threat over time. The Gulf War followed the USAF model, and hence its tactics were more relevant in this case *after the first days of the war*.[30]

The DoD report sums up the Desert Storm SEAD experience by stating that the Coalition SEAD effort defeated most Iraqi radar systems, thereby enabling Coalition aircraft to operate in the middle altitudes with relative safety. Nevertheless, they faced a threat from infrared and electro-optically guided SAMs while at low-to-medium altitudes. With sortie rates relatively constant,

> approximately half of its fixed-wing combat losses ... [occurred] during either the first week of Operation Desert Storm (17 aircraft), before enemy defenses had been suppressed, or during the last week (eight aircraft), when aircraft were operating at lower altitudes in the IR SAM region.[31]

---

[29]*CPGW*, p. 217.

[30]See Friedman (1991), pp. 164–168, for a discussion of different SEAD philosophies and tactics. See Coyne (1992a), p. 71, and *CPGW*, p. 158, for a description of SEAD employment and tactics during the first night of strike operations. Coyne states that at one time 200 HARMs were in the air at the same time.

[31]*CPGW*, p. 242.

CLOSE AIR SUPPORT

Close air support tactics during the Gulf War were, for the most part, a departure from post–World War II experience. The closest analog was the breakout from the Normandy beachhead in late summer 1944, when fast-moving U.S. armored forces moved to encircle retreating Nazi troops. Instead of fixed, slow-moving, or sometimes indeterminate battle lines that characterized most of the Korean and Vietnam Wars, the ground war in the desert was one of rapid movement. Except for the two Marine divisions entering southeastern Kuwait, there was little need for classical close air support in which air weapons were used in close proximity to U.S. ground formations. Moreover, Coalition ground units were lavishly supplied with their own close as well as deep support weapons, including attack helicopters and MLRS (and ATACMS). Ground commanders in effect had sufficient support capabilities integral to their units.

The effect of these circumstances was that air systems planned and tasked for close air support missions were frequently diverted to other missions. Even the A-10, which was designed for CAS, was used in a strike role, against Scuds, and even in suppression of enemy air defenses.

Close Air Support of Army and Coalition Forces

According to data compiled by RAND, 4,393 close air support sorties (out of a total of 112,235 for all missions) were tasked during Desert Storm. The vast majority of these were flown during the ground war period of 23–27 February.[32] Of these, 1,461 were flown by Air Force aircraft—mostly in support of U.S. Army and Coalition forces and typically to accomplish an alternative interdiction mission. Marines provided almost all of their own close air support. Navy aircraft were prepared to fly CAS missions, but were rarely called upon to do so—in part because an amphibious assault operation was not conducted and because Marine assets were adequate for I MEF ground operations. Coalition partners did not fly any CAS missions.

Because Army forces were executing the famous "left hook" or "Hail Mary," they moved rapidly. Iraqi resistance was seldom prolonged in any given location and was dealt with for the most part with ground forces firepower. Typically, CAS sorties, operating under the "push CAS" or "push flow" concepts, were either on-station airborne under the control of a Fast-FAC aircraft or were handed off to a forward air controller accompanying the ground forces. Other aircraft stood strip alert and "scrambled" to meet emerging requirements. The

---

[32]Some were flown in support of the Khafji and al-Wafra battle on 29 January 1991. (Data provided by Ted Parker and Don Emerson of RAND.)

tactics used were not new. It is likely that some sorties counted as close air support were, in fact, strikes at some distance in the Iraqi rear. Speaking of Army force movement, Coyne states:

> They moved forward so rapidly that the classic situation for close air support—troops in contact with the enemy—rarely developed.[33]

Allied forces did rely on close air support, because they had lighter forces—and, in the case of the French, had little artillery support. During the first three days of the ground war, 46 USAF CAS sorties were flown in support of the French.[34] Marines flew CAS sorties in support of the pan-Arab forces.

Close Air Support of Marine Forces

The Marine situation was different. CINCCENT's plan did not envision their fighting a war of rapid movement; they were tasked to proceed directly to Kuwait City in the face of entrenched Iraqi forces. Moreover, their air support was built into their ground movement plan, and not an adjunct to it. Accordingly, it is not surprising that Marines logged two-thirds of all Desert Storm CAS sorties:

> The basic CAS plan during the ground offensive involved multi-sortie surge operations, particularly by those aircraft designed for CAS operations and operating from forward operating locations (FOLs) near the battlefield. . . . USMC aircraft began increased operations into Kuwait two days before the ground offensive . . . based on a system in which fixed wing aircraft were launched according to schedule, instead of against specific targets, and flew to a series of stacks or holding points.[35]

After arriving at the stacks and if no CAS was needed, the strike was sent deeper into the KTO and obtained alternate targets from an F/A-18D Fast-FAC overseeing a kill box.[36]

Since the Marine air-ground coordination problem differed considerably from the situation faced by Army forces farther west, the Marines set up a high-density air control zone (HIDACZ) to control air strikes in close proximity to Marine ground operations.[37] As we have seen in Chapter Five, this was to be

---

[33]Coyne (1992a), p. 168.

[34]Ibid., p. 167–168.

[35]*CPGW*, p. 195.

[36]Although these flights were still logged as CAS.

[37]Air Force officers view this as a matter of service preference rather than as a different coordination problem.

the cause of some disagreement between the JFACC and I MEF staffs. Nevertheless, doctrine and tactics were successfully meshed.[38]

REFUELING

Refueling operations were every bit as massive as the weapons-delivery operations during Operation Desert Storm. It was the largest and most intensive aerial refueling operation ever conducted. Tactics involved trying to cram (safely) a large number of tankers and their customers into a very limited airspace, attempting to increase the number of offload points available to efficiently transfer fuel, and juggling assets to ensure that the right kind of fuel was available for users with different requirements.

Tanker "tracks" (flight paths) planning, although computer assisted, was meticulously done by hand and included in each daily ATO. Refueling coordinators were put aloft in AWACS aircraft to ensure that the refueling plan went smoothly and that unforeseen events (e.g., a missed rendezvous, a tanker abort, emergency tanking for combat-damaged strike aircraft) were accommodated by adjusting the ATO "on the fly."

Low-altitude air refueling (LAAR) was conducted on occasion when tankers had to operate close to the Iraqi radar horizon. But since the Iraqi air threat was quickly neutralized, this was not common practice. There were several reports that refueling was conducted in Iraqi airspace when the combat situation dictated. Fortunately, this hazarding of valuable and vulnerable tanker assets was not countered by the Iraqis.

Tanker requirements were greatly reduced by the tactic of having Coalition aircraft operating from bases remote from Iraq and Kuwait stage through friendly bases closer to their targets. The aircraft could refuel and rearm and squeeze more sorties per day out of a given pool of aircraft. This tactic was used as early as World War II, and was continued in the Korean and Vietnam conflicts.[39] As carriers moved deeper into the Gulf, tanking requirements for their air wings were also greatly reduced.

---

[38]Interviews with both Lieutenant General Horner (JFACC) and Lieutenant General Boomer (I MEF) confirm that this was a problem between the staffs, each of which was trying to suboptimize force application for their own missions. Other interviewees suggest that it was a case of the Marines "going off the reservation" (the USAF view) or "Riyadh trying to control that which it didn't have the capability to control" (the USMC view).

[39]During the Solomons campaign, 1942–1944, Navy aircraft conducted combat missions off carriers, staged through allied shore bases, rearmed and refueled, and struck targets repeatedly during a single day's operations. Navy shore-based aircraft did the same in occasionally providing CAP coverage for carriers whose air wings were striking Japanese targets, recovering on board for refueling, flying their mission, and returning to their shore bases. During the Korean War, Air Force and Marine aircraft based in Japan would occasionally cycle through UN-held Korean airfields.

AIR CONTROL

Some attributes of air control tactics have already been discussed. The sheer numbers of Coalition aircraft airborne at any given time and the confines of the target array required careful control to avoid mutual interference, but control was not so tight that flexibility was lost. The usual practice for strike and fighter aircraft was to check in with the appropriate AWACS immediately after takeoff to ensure that the strike was identified and "painted" on the AWACS scopes. The primary mission of the AWACS was air defense. Accordingly, it was important to separate friends from potential enemies as early as possible. CAP and aircraft on strikes into Iraq would remain under AWACS control. Aircraft scheduled to strike targets within the KTO were shifted to ABCCC (a specially configured USAF C-130) or TACC or USMC DASC control. The strike might then be shifted to a forward air controller. Battle management in the KTO beyond the fire support coordination line was conducted normally by the ABCCC. The AWACS retained overall airspace control, provided for fighter cover, and deconflicted incoming and outgoing strikes from other operations on or near their tracks. When the Iraqi air threat had all but disappeared, the AWACS became more of a traffic advisory agency, assisting in rendezvous and in the direction of combat SAR efforts.[40]

All of these procedures had been employed before. What was different during the Gulf War was the size of the operation and the procedural discipline required. The interfaces between three different air control systems—Air Force, Navy, and Marine—were not always smooth, but the large number of control assets and a largely neutralized air threat were sufficient to make it work.[41]

CONSTRAINTS

Altitude

The success of the Coalition air forces in taking down the Iraqi air-defense system and neutralizing the Iraqi air force led directly to a change in tactics.[42] The DoD report on the war states:

> Perhaps the most significant tactical issue to arise in planning the air campaign concerned Coalition aircraft flying above the AAA and hand-held SAMs threat.

---

[40]Coyne (1992a), pp. 98–99.

[41]General Michael J. Dugan, USAF (ret.) has remarked to us that the interfaces among the various tactical air control and air-defense systems are well developed and that they are usually smoothly operated. What is not "smooth," in his opinion, is determining who is in charge.

[42]The RAF's early loss of four GR-1 Tornados on low-level airfield attack missions was probably a big factor in Horner's decision. But U.S. losses and battle damage were not insignificant and probably played a role.

Despite the strong peacetime emphasis on training for low-level delivery tactics, which exploit the terrain to reduce aircraft detectability to radar and hence vulnerability to SAMs and to increase weapons delivery accuracy under the weather, the density of the Iraqi AAA and the dangers posed by unaimed barrage fire to low flying aircraft drove some aircraft to higher altitude delivery tactics.[43]

There were significant consequences to setting a medium-altitude floor under allied air operations over Kuwait and Iraq:

> By attacking from altitudes of approximately 10,000–15,000 feet (above the reach of anti-aircraft artillery) survivability increased, but at the expense of bombing accuracy. Given the conditions of this war and the need to minimize casualties, the move made sense. However, a consequence of this restriction was the need for higher weather ceilings in order to bomb visually (the most accurate method); thus, there was a higher-than-anticipated incidence of mission changes because of the weather. Air Force planners estimated that by 6 February, three weeks into the war, approximately half of the attack sorties into Iraq had been diverted to other targets or cancelled because of weather-related problems. Not only did the weather impede accuracy, it hampered accurate bomb damage assessment.[44]

There were, of course, exceptions in close air support and some other specialized missions. The result of this policy was to force aircrews to use weapon delivery methods in which they had had less peacetime training.

Targeting Limitations[45]

There were two major targeting constraints: the need to minimize Iraqi civilian casualties, and the requirement that special cultural and religious sites be spared. The first constraint category posed major problems for target planners because some support facilities served both civilian and military uses (e.g,. electrical power stations, bridges). This limitation required that Coalition aircraft take special measures in bomb delivery. For example, aircraft tracks were routed to minimize the effect of target misses on the adjacent civilian population, even though some of those tracks would put the aircrew in greater danger or reduce chances of weapon effectiveness. Only laser-guided munitions and Tomahawks were used against targets in downtown Baghdad. This, in effect,

---

[43]*CPGW*, p. 167. Coyne (1992a) cites an initial floor of 15,000 feet (p. 91), later reduced to 8,000 feet (pp. 78, 91). After G-day there were no altitude restrictions, and aircrews operated at altitudes consistent with optimal weapons delivery.

[44]*GWAPS*, p. 16.

[45]This discussion is largely drawn from *CPGW*, pp. 131–133.

meant that such targets were mostly attacked at night (and the Iraqis could thus use them in the daytime with little fear of attack except by Tomahawk missiles).

Some areas were exempt from any weapons because of their proximity to sites of cultural or religious value. Thus, targets near mosques, historic buildings, and archeological "digs" were not struck, and there is ample evidence that the Iraqis took advantage of this restraint to locate otherwise targetable functions or material adjacent to such sites. In a tactical sense, target planners and flight crews had to be aware of the proximity (less than six miles) of such sites while conducting attacks on other targets, lest a "miss" on the target become a "hit" on a restricted site.

Availability of Support Aircraft

The two "short poles" in the JFACC "tent" were the availability of SEAD aircraft and tankers.[46] Arabia had an overlay of "tanker tracks" that required tight management. Strike package composition was heavily affected by tanker availability. The Navy, the Red Sea Battle Force in particular, preferred to include at least a division of F-14s with each Red Sea Battle Force strike package. When those packages originated from the Red Sea carriers, the refueling requirements often exceeded the number of tankers available, and the package had to be retailored. As the air threat declined, the Navy reduced its fighter cover requirements and brought refueling requirements into closer alignment with tanker aircraft available. But every service had its own gas guzzlers: for the Navy, it was F-14s; for the Air Force, it was F-4G Wild Weasels. Other aircraft were also relatively short-legged (e.g., F-16, F/A-18), and their tanker requirements often required adjusting strike composition.

Similarly, the availability of SEAD aircraft would determine what targets could be hit, with what size package, and how often. No strike aircraft covered by SEAD aircraft was ever downed by Iraqi radar-guided SAMs.[47]

ASSESSMENT OF TACTICS

Most tactics employed were either already in use before the Gulf War or were adaptations of existing tactics to fit the special circumstances of the war. The quantity and quality of fielded air systems gave the Coalition considerable opportunity to experiment and do it effectively. Perhaps the greatest disappointment—and the result of system limitations rather than unimaginative tactical

---

[46]Lieutenant General Royal Moore has remarked to us that, with respect to SEAD, the real shortage was in jammer aircraft, not HARM shooters.

[47]*CPGW*, p. 172.

thinking—was the inability to come up with a tactical answer to the mobile Scud threat. The greatest tactical successes were in SEAD and tanking, where the problems of supporting massive operations against a nearly first-rate threat (at least initially) were successfully solved.

Chapter Eight

INFORMATION ACQUISITION AND MANAGEMENT

> First we're going to cut it off. Then we're going to kill it.
>
> —*General Colin Powell on the strategy for*
> *dealing with the Iraqi army, January 1991.*

THE FIRST INFORMATION WAR

Most people hearing General Powell's statement might conclude that it described a U.S. strategy to separate the Iraqi army logistics train and other links to Baghdad through concentrated bombing and strikes. However, carrying that interpretation a bit further, one might conclude that U.S. forces would seek to deny the Iraqis access to information about Coalition force strength, disposition, and other information necessary to conduct effective military operations. To accomplish this would require separating the Iraqi army from its "head," i.e., its centralized command and control system, and severing the "nerves" linking the head with the rest of the body. The accomplishment of such an objective would require not only bombing such obvious targets as the bridges over which Iraqi troops would cross, but also attacking electronic networks (e.g., by introducing a computer virus into the Iraqi computer system, as was reportedly done), destroying satellite data-receiving stations (to deny their ability to access weather or multispectral imaging data, for example), and denying them the

---

This chapter relies on the following sources: Winnefeld and Johnson (1993); unpublished RAND working papers by Major Robert Butler (former RAND Air Force Fellow), Leland Joe, and Daniel Gonzales; *CPGW,* chap. 6 and apps. C, K, and T; Coyne (1992a); unclassified portions of US-SPACECOM, *United States Space Command Operations Desert Shield and Desert Storm Assessment,* January 1992; USSPACECOM, "Space Operations for Desert Shield/Desert Storm," unpublished paper, n.d.; United States Congress, House Armed Services Committee, *Intelligence Successes and Failures in Operation Desert Shield/Desert Storm,* U.S. House of Representatives, 103rd Congress, 1st Session, August 1993 (hereafter cited as HASC (1993)); *GWAPS;* Bruce W. Watson et al., *Military Lessons of the Gulf War,* London: Greenhill Books, 1992; Lewis (1993); and other sources as cited.

ability to "read the battlefield" by maintaining dominance of the skies over Iraq. This is what was achieved.

From the perspective of U.S. and Coalition forces, a successful Desert Storm air campaign required the acquisition, management, and integration of information from a myriad of ground-based, airborne, and space-based sources. A combination of circumstances—high-technology information systems, imaginative and innovative approaches to circumventing existing organizational impediments and communications shortfalls, and an inept enemy—enabled the Coalition to achieve "information superiority" over the Iraqis. Desert Storm represented the first modern "information war," in that every aspect of military operations depended to some degree on information provided by many systems operating in various media and at all echelons. Not only was the information process critical to moving a sizable military force halfway around the world, it had to adapt from a peacetime footing to the needs of theater warfare, all the while integrating and exploiting strategic and national systems with their not always compatible tactical counterparts to support Gulf operations. Furthermore, as described above, the Coalition was able to dominate Iraqi information acquisition and exploitation by effectively negating its command and control system in the early stages of the air war. Here was an effective demonstration of synergism between information and weapons: the use of information systems to support the critical needs of the air campaign, and the exploitation of the air weapon to eliminate the Iraqi access to information and to protect the Coalition's own access.

To use a simple analogy, in the past the military commander relied on sensors—his eyes—that processed information from a relatively limited view and relayed it to his brain, a distance of perhaps two inches. His mouth and hands were "enablers" which allowed him to communicate that information to his troops in the field. The information was "enhanced" by the height he could raise himself to, perhaps sitting on his horse at the top of a hill, certainly not a limitless range. Furthermore, he was able to communicate orders to his troops in his immediate proximity. Battles were conducted on a relatively small geographical area, usually lasting no more than a day, depending on the stamina of the forces and their support. Today's commander faces a much different situation: he controls, manages, or coordinates simultaneous operations in play over thousands of square miles and involving perhaps thousands of forces, a feat made possible by the aid of his sensors—space-based and airborne systems providing intelligence and conditional (i.e., dynamic) data—and "enabled" instantaneously by speed-of-light technologies. His "view" of the battlefield extends, in essence, for whole theaters and even continents. The focus of this chapter is the interplay of the systems and processes providing the information necessary for him to make critical military decisions.

For the first time in modern warfare, intelligence and space systems were actively—if not perfectly—integrated into every phase of military operations. They performed the functions of tactical ballistic missile (TBM) warning, surveillance, navigation, weather support, communications, and remote sensing for mapping and other purposes. Also, the contributions made by personal computers (PCs), facsimile machines (faxes), and STU-IIIs (secure telephone communications)—products of the revolution in computing and communications—were key to processing and moving information. These systems were instrumental in bypassing the more traditional means of communication, which became saturated soon after the start of Desert Shield and never fully recovered.

However, three points must be made about how well this integration of intelligence/space systems and military operations worked in the larger scheme of information management. First of all, there was not then (nor is there now) an overarching architecture for the use of offboard (overhead and aircraft) sensor systems for intelligence, surveillance, battle damage assessment (BDA), or any other aspect of information collection and management. Moreover, the enabling subsystems such as communications were not in place. Second, there was no system or plan for secondary imagery dissemination. While there were means to gather information (and vast amounts of it), there were problems getting it to the right individual in the right place at the right time. Finally, no one was in charge of the overall architecture. Many organizations were involved in producing intelligence estimates and reports; however, many of these products were, from a combat commander's perspective, too broad, nonpredictive, caveated, and contradictory with each other to be of direct assistance to combat operations. Military space systems were controlled by one group of operating agencies, and their products were used by another group—all, for the purposes of Desert Shield and Storm, under the combatant command (COCOM) of the U.S. Space Command (USSPACECOM). These three points describe critical information-related deficiencies that unless resolved will continue to pose problems in any future military operations, whether or not they are the size and scope of Desert Shield and Storm. However, these deficiencies should not diminish the contributions made by the information sensors and processes in achieving information superiority over the Iraqis and supporting Coalition objectives for the war.

The chapter is organized as follows. Our discussion will begin with prewar threat assessments and deployment activities and the organization of the intelligence community to support the air campaign. Next, we describe the various sensors and "enabling" systems, i.e., those systems that facilitated the conduct of the air campaign. Communications—the means by which information was passed from the sensors and "enablers" to the commander and his forces—is then addressed. We then progress to targeting and mission planning, and battle damage assessment. Finally, we will examine information acquisition and management *in toto*, identifying its strengths and weaknesses and problems encountered during Operations Desert Shield and Storm.

PREWAR ACTIVITIES

Throughout the 1980s, U.S. military forces and support infrastructures had undergone extensive expansion and modernization. As we saw in Chapter Two, there were a number of new players in the information acquisition and management arena: AWACS, JSTARS (deployed as prototypes in Desert Storm), new weapon systems employing advanced technology guidance and terrain-mapping systems, and complex—but mostly user-friendly—computer, navigation, and communications systems. These "high-tech" capabilities provided U.S. military commanders with force multipliers that provided a critical edge in the Gulf War, and they changed the more traditional approaches to operational planning and military force management. They were also critical to denying the Iraqis the ability to hide force buildup. What surprise there was to the U.S. leadership and intelligence community was due more to human fallibility than to a failure in technology.

Given the number of agencies involved in the intelligence process in the United States, it should come as no surprise that the intelligence community was not of one mind on the threat that Iraq posed to its neighbors in the late 1980s and early 1990. Some of this was fostered by American policy toward Iraq, by conflicting evidence of the expansion of Iraqi military capabilities coupled with bluster from Saddam Hussein himself, and by a longstanding but slowly shifting focus on the threat from the Soviet Union to the region. These factors had an effect on the air campaign in terms of the intelligence and space communities' preparedness for supporting targeting, battle damage assessment, and other activities.[1]

The intelligence community continued to monitor the Iraqi buildup of forces and their emerging nuclear, biological, and chemical (NBC) weapons programs (including obtaining the critical elements purchased overseas for those programs). However, the regime's penchant for extreme secrecy and severity of punishment for transgressions made it difficult to determine Iraq's intentions toward its neighbors and the true extent of its military capabilities. It was believed that the outcome of the Iran-Iraq War had left Iraq with a battle-

---

[1]See Douglas G. Armstrong, "The Gulf War's Patched-Together Air Intelligence," U.S. Naval Institute *Proceedings*, November 1992, p. 109, for an assessment of the intelligence community's difficulties and shortcomings in reorienting from Soviet and Iranian threats to an Iraqi threat.

hardened force capable of taking on just about anyone in the region except perhaps the Israelis. Nevertheless, by late 1989–early 1990 the Bush administration and the intelligence community were distracted by unfolding events in Germany, Eastern Europe, and the Soviet Union, and intelligence-collection activities oriented to Saddam's regime were given relatively low priority.

The Navy's intelligence organization known as SPEAR (Strike Projection Evaluation and Antiair Research) was probably the most advanced organization in evaluating Third World air and ground defenses. Although not immediately available to the air war planners, its analysis of Iraq's integrated air-defense system (IADS) was completed just prior to the invasion of Kuwait.[2] This analysis later proved to be valuable in preparing the aircrews for the air campaign.[3]

The modest size of the American presence in the region also resulted in reliance on strategic systems for access to denied areas. While tracking the Iraqi order of battle was extensive and accurate, those systems could only provide a snapshot of activities over a period of days. Employed in functions such as strategic indications and warning (I&W) and treaty monitoring, they were not designed to be responsive to a theater commander in the tactical sense. This reliance on strategic systems contributed to an overestimation of the size and quality of Iraqi forces and to an underestimation of how the Iraqis might use those forces.[4]

During the prewar period, military planning and preparations had focused on the Soviet threat and a possible invasion of Iran. Consequently, in the summer of 1990, U.S. forces were not adequately prepared in an information sense to operate against the Iraqi threat. Maps illustrating current topographical information were not available. Intelligence, space support, and battle damage assessment activities were not incorporated into existing operational plans, nor had they been adequately exercised prior to the conflict. As one observer noted, while the United States had extensive foreknowledge of Iraqi equipment capabilities, one of the biggest problems during Desert Shield and Desert Storm was determining the location of the Republican Guard and Scud missiles, their state

---

[2]See the discussion of the Iraqi IADS, and USN, USAF, and Coalition tactics to counter it, in Friedman (1991), pp. 147–168.

[3]As noted earlier, some USAF officers interviewed believe SPEAR's contribution, while useful, paralleled efforts by other organizations.

[4]Gerald W. Hopple argues that the Iraqi invasion caught "virtually everyone in the Western intelligence community by surprise. That community documented the Iraqi buildup, but completely missed Baghdad's real intentions until August 1st." See Hopple's article "Indications and Warning (I&W) and Intelligence Lessons" in Watson et al. (1991), p. 146. Also, Friedman (1991), pp. 443–444, points to the Iraqi use of landing craft and civilian boats, rather than traditional minelayers, to mine Persian Gulf waters; this resulted in the *Princeton* and *Tripoli* incidents.

of readiness, and their willingness to deploy and engage Coalition forces.[5] Several prototype intelligence systems were deployed during Desert Shield to provide direct support to CENTCOM headquarters; these prototypes (generally ground systems) supported TR-1 and U-2R reconnaissance aircraft equipped with imagery intelligence (IMINT) sensors capable of near-real-time intelligence collection.[6]

Information technologies were crucial in the early days of the Desert Shield deployment. At MacDill AFB, where CENTCOM headquarters was located, staffs were equipped with computers and facsimile machines that were extensively used to keep track of force deployments, to keep the Pentagon abreast of developments, and to communicate with other members of the Coalition. Cable News Network (CNN) was monitored to keep the command aware of crisis developments in Southwest Asia. Partly because of the information capabilities resident in CONUS, CINCCENT did not deploy to the theater immediately. Rather, as one participant noted, it was an irony of the modern information age that CINCCENT "could gather more intelligence information and more effectively control his forces 7,000 miles away from the theater of operations than from the Saudi MOD [Ministry of Defense].... Not only did CENTCOM have to await the build-up of its forces but also the development of a communications infrastructure to fight the war."[7]

ORGANIZING TO SUPPORT THE AIR CAMPAIGN[8]

Not only is it important to have advanced sensor and information systems, it is important to be able to exploit them in the most effective manner possible. Effective exploitation is achieved partly through an efficient organization and management of resources. However, for a variety of reasons, the organization and focus of the U.S. intelligence community at the time of the Gulf War was characterized by a plethora of agencies and perspectives, not necessarily consistent with each other. Consequently, no umbrella organization existed to serve the CINC in coordinating the collection, analysis, and dissemination activities of the community, nor was any single agency in charge. The lack of a central responsible organization had the effect of encouraging informal relationships among people and organizations across more traditional chains of command for the purposes of obtaining and exploiting intelligence. In spite of

---

[5]Armstrong (1992), p. 109.

[6]Ibid., p. 110.

[7]Macedonia (1992), p. 35.

[8]This section relies heavily on *CPGW; GWAPS;* Daniel M. Hoffman, "A Beltway Warrior Looks at Gulf War Intelligence," U.S. Naval Institute *Proceedings,* January 1993; Armstrong (1992); Campen (1992); and other sources.

those shortcomings, American forces were provided with the best intelligence capabilities available and were better informed than any forces that had fought before the Gulf War. But there was still plenty of room for improvement in the organization and process.

As it became clearer that the United States would become militarily involved in response to the Iraqi invasion of Kuwait, the resources of most of the U.S. intelligence community were brought to bear in support. Given the scope of the air campaign, Horner and his planning staff required extensive intelligence information about Iraqi targets and order of battle. To accomplish their goals, they relied extensively on CONUS-based intelligence organizations rather than theater ones, in large part because the necessary expertise and broad range of resources were resident there and because theater intelligence staffs suffered from a lack of qualified personnel. The security arrangements imposed on Black Hole operations further separated the theater intelligence staffs from the air planners, as did their physical location.[9] Furthermore, the Black Hole planners believed that theater intelligence was not as responsive to their requests as they felt was necessary, especially in providing imagery in a timely manner. The Black Hole staff's compartmentalization and lack of familiarity with imagery tasking and prioritization exacerbated the problem as well.[10]

CONUS-Based Intelligence

Figure 8.1 illustrates the defense intelligence community organization at the national level in support of Desert Shield and Storm. It is obvious that the organization was not a model of simplicity or efficiency, and was probably the result of competition and "turf fights" among agencies for the control and dissemination of intelligence. In order to consolidate duplicative efforts within the defense intelligence community, the Defense Intelligence Agency (DIA), located at Bolling AFB near Washington, was designated the lead DoD agency for oversight of the production of threat estimates, imagery, and battle damage assessment.[11] Early on in the Desert Shield deployment, the DIA activated an Intelligence Task Force (ITC) in the National Military Intelligence Center (NMIC) in the Pentagon. The role of the ITC was to support the Joint Chiefs of Staff (JCS) and to act as a "clearinghouse" for requests for information (RFI) transmitted to the NMIC. DIA also augmented the Operational Intelligence Crisis Center

---

[9]The Black Hole was located in the basement of the Royal Saudi Air Force headquarters, while CENTAF's intelligence group was located in a large tent on a soccer field next to the RSAF building. *GWAPS*, p. 130.

[10]*GWAPS*, pp. 130–131.

[11]Hoffman (1993), p. 88.

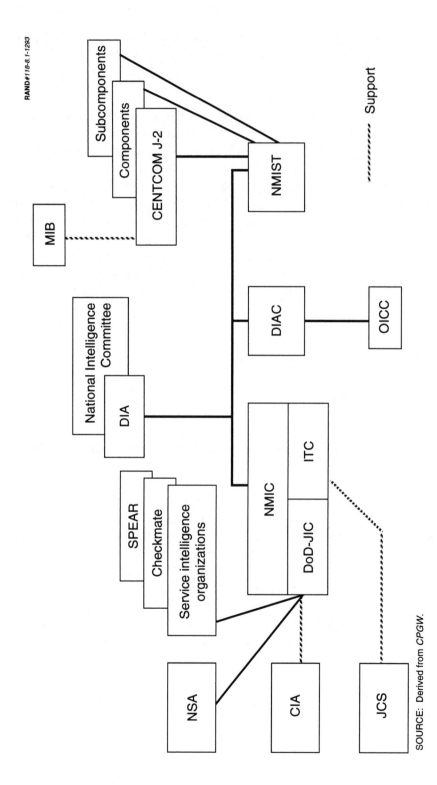

SOURCE: Derived from *CPGW*.

Figure 8.1—Organization of National-Level Defense Intelligence Support to CENTCOM

(OICC) at the Defense Intelligence Analysis Center (DIAC) at Bolling AFB. The OICC acted as the analytical house for responding to the requests for information received by the ITC and provided specialized targeting packages. DIA also deployed a National Military Intelligence Support Team (NMIST) to Riyadh in early August. The NMIST eventually grew to 11 teams and provided a network directly back to DIA for the dissemination of imagery and intelligence information to the theater. As the *CPGW* report notes, the NMIST network was critical to the intelligence staffs of CENTCOM because it became

> the sole dedicated intelligence communications capability between the CENTCOM J-2, the component and subunified command intelligence staffs, and the national intelligence community. These teams were vital sources of timely information, to include imagery, especially when the existing communications circuits between the United States and the theater became saturated with operational message traffic.[12]

Support and advisory organizations to CENTCOM included the Military Intelligence Board (MIB), which directed the deployment of intelligence personnel, systems, and equipment to fill in gaps at CENTCOM. The MIB is made up of the directors of DIA, NSA, and the service intelligence organizations, and, for Desert Shield and Storm, several nonvoting representatives of the JCS C^3 directorate and the Defense Support Program Office.[13] It also served to help set up CENTCOM's intelligence staff organization by deploying a joint service team to Saudi Arabia in early November.[14] Individual service intelligence organizations developed analyses to support the air, ground, and maritime campaigns. In particular, the Air Force Intelligence Agency supported Checkmate's planning and targeting development, while SPEAR performed similar activities for the JFACC staff and the Navy. Checkmate itself became a conduit and fusion center for intelligence and operational information from DIA/J-2 and other intelligence agencies and offices in the Washington area to the Black Hole staff. Since many air planners deployed from Air Staff assignments, they were familiar with individuals on the Checkmate staff, which increased Checkmate's importance to the planning process in Riyadh.[15] Other members of the intelligence community such as the National Security Agency and the Central Intelligence Agency provided extensive support, including detaching specialists to the theater.

---

[12]*CPGW*, p. C-4.

[13]Ibid., p. C-5.

[14]Ibid., p. C-6.

[15]*GWAPS*, p. 131.

A notable development was the establishment of the DoD Joint Intelligence Center on 2 September in the NMIC in the Pentagon. The DoD-JIC brought together analysts from the DoD, the NSA, and service intelligence staffs into one location with one reporting chain of command and with the purpose of providing a single Defense-wide intelligence view to the theater commander and the NCA.[16] Liaison personnel from the CIA also participated in the DoD-JIC.[17]

Theater-Based Intelligence

In the early phases of Desert Shield, CENTCOM lacked organic resources, personnel, and organizational structures to provide intelligence support adequate to the size of the deployment and the subsequent air campaign.[18] CENTCOM relied heavily on the CONUS-based intelligence community, particularly the MIB, to help establish an intelligence organization. This organization became the Joint Intelligence Center, shown in Figure 8.2. The purpose of the JIC was to provide the overall lead and collection manager for intelligence in the theater, maintaining linkages with component and subunified intelligence organizations. It also provided a focal point for daily meetings between the theater and component collection managers, and maintained contact with appropriate elements in the national intelligence community. Within the JIC were organized a Combat Assessment Center and a Joint Reconnaissance Center. The Combat Assessment Center was composed of two cells: the Combat Assessment Cell, which provided assessments of enemy intentions 24–96 hours in the future, and the Battle Damage Assessment Cell, which assessed the outcome of strikes and made targeting recommendations based on intelligence received from the intelligence staffs of CENTAF, NAVCENT, and ARCENT.[19] The Joint Reconnaissance Center was placed in the JIC to better coordinate reconnaissance and airborne intelligence assets with the rest of the intelligence community, rather than in the J-3/Operations Directorate, its usual place in unified and specified commands. Another means of deconfliction between intelligence collection and surveillance operations among the CENTCOM components and Coalition partners was the Daily Aerial Reconnaissance and Surveillance (DARS) conference conducted by CENTCOM.

---

[16]*CPGW*, p. C-5. General Glosson has told us that by far the most important source for him was his direct link with Rear Admiral Mike McConnell, J-2 and head of DIA.

[17]According to HASC (1993), pp. 9–10, the CIA refused to join the JIC because it ostensibly lacked the staff and also needed to maintain an independent perspective for providing intelligence assessments to senior decisionmakers. At the working level, however, CIA analysts were in daily contact with their counterparts in theater.

[18]For example, just days after the Iraqi invasion, the Marine Corps' RF-4B photographic reconnaissance squadron, VMFP-3, was deactivated on schedule. (Armstrong (1992), p. 111.)

[19]*CPGW*, pp. C-6, C-7; *GWAPS*, p. 132.

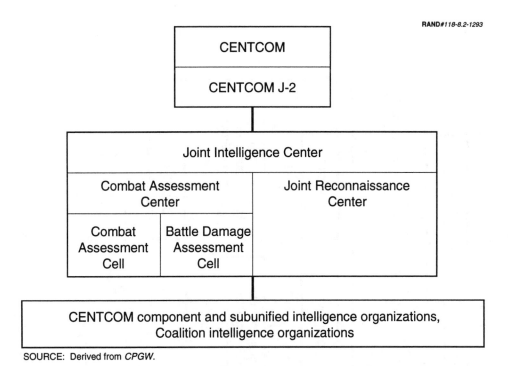

RAND#118-8.2-1293

SOURCE: Derived from *CPGW*.

Figure 8.2—CENTCOM Intelligence Organization and Relationships

CENTCOM's component intelligence support was organized along the lines shown in Figure 8.3. Of notable interest is the separate intelligence network provided by the European Command (EUCOM) to the Joint Task Force Proven Force in Turkey, and the Joint Air Intelligence Center (JAIC) that supported the JFACC. The latter organization was composed of intelligence officers from all services and based in Riyadh. Unfortunately it was set up in January 1991, too late to provide effective support to the planning process for the air campaign, but it did serve as a clearinghouse for intelligence in support of campaign air operations. During the campaign, the CONUS-based Air Force Checkmate and JCS J-2 intelligence organizations were instrumental in providing intelligence support and fusion (again, largely due to personal relationships established from the top down).

The development of intelligence relationships across institutional boundaries was also facilitated by the use of STU-IIIs, secure faxes, and other "tools" of information and communication technologies. These capabilities greatly increased the ability of the air planners to incorporate BDA and other information into the ATO planning cycle in a more timely, effective, and secure manner. They also made possible the bypassing of traditional organizational chains, which could and often did result in some confusion. The effect of these new

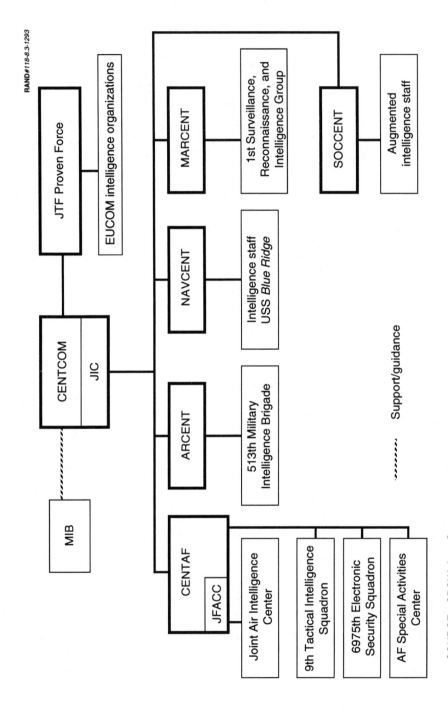

SOURCE: *CPGW*, App. C.

Figure 8.3—Component and Subunified Intelligence Support to CENTCOM

information technologies on the speed and scope of activities in the planning and execution process was not anticipated before the war.

THE SENSORS AND THE "ENABLERS"

Continuing with the analogy we described earlier, the military commander possesses several sets of "sensors," such as warning sensors and human intelligence (HUMINT), which provide data that are then transformed and fused into information necessary for the conduct of military operations. He also possesses "enabling" sensors providing conditional or dynamic information, such as navigation and positioning data and weather, that are likely to be transitory in nature.[20]   After processing this information, he relays it to his forces through essentially instantaneous means of communication. This section describes the sensors, enablers, and communications links.

Sensors: Tactical Ballistic Missile (TBM) Warning

Early warning of ballistic missile attack against the United States is provided by dual phenomenology sensor systems, i.e., both radar and infrared. Because the Iraqis possessed a tactical ballistic missile capability that they stated publicly they would use against Coalition forces in the Gulf and against Israel, U.S. surveillance capabilities were put to the task of monitoring the region. The primary infrared (IR) sensor performing this surveillance task was the Defense Support Program (DSP). DSP's primary mission is early warning of intercontinental ballistic missile (ICBM) and submarine-launched ballistic missile (SLBM) launches.

DSP provided early warning of Iraqi tactical ballistic missile launches, performing far better than expected for its age or level of technology but still not adequately for responsive targeting purposes. The information DSP provided coupled with the deployment of Patriot anti-TBM systems to Israel enabled Coalition leaders to persuade that nation to stay out of the war. Of course, the exploitation of DSP in the Gulf was not an overnight success, for it required a change in "mind-set" among DSP operators and alterations of certain operating procedures to facilitate tactical warning while still performing the system's primary mission.

As in other areas of planning and operations, U.S. and Coalition forces benefited from the five-month delay before the onset of the air campaign, for it facilitated the collection of critical warning data, the development of "Scud

---

[20]This is not meant to imply that HUMINT and warning are not transitory or conditional in nature, but to distinguish them from sensors monitoring a dynamic environment in real time.

alert" modifications to existing ICBM/SLBM warning and communications protocols, and the exercise of the TBM warning process before combat began. Warning reaction times were driven by the short flight of the Scud missile. USCENTCOM required sufficient warning time to react to an impending Scud attack (e.g., for personnel to protect themselves from possible gas warfare). US-SPACECOM, the supporting unified command, and its component commands relayed voice warning messages from the Space Command Center (SPACC)[21] to CENTCOM. Data messages were sent over the TERS alerts (Tactical Event Reporting System).

Sensors: Airborne Reconnaissance and Surveillance

Any and all airborne reconnaissance and surveillance assets, whether their roles were strategic reconnaissance or tactical, were used to gather information about the Iraqi forces. Airborne reconnaissance and surveillance activities were truly joint and combined and were conducted at all altitudes by USAF E-3B AWACS, U-2R, TR-1, RF-4C, and RC-135 Rivet Joint aircraft, Navy reconnaissance units such as the F-14 TARPS, the prototype JSTARS, Navy E-2C, P-3, EP-3, and S-3 aircraft, USN and USMC EA-6B aircraft, and surveillance unmanned aerial vehicles (UAVs) of all services.[22] In addition, VTRs on fighter aircraft provided important and timely poststrike BDA.

The Air Force provided the bulk of the airborne surveillance and reconnaissance missions. The E-3B AWACS maintained one to three 24-hour surveillance orbits during Desert Shield; during Desert Storm combat operations, this was increased to five U.S. orbits (four over Saudi Arabia and one over Turkey) and one to three Royal Saudi Air Force orbits. SAC's U-2R and TR-1 met those collection requirements that could not be met by other capabilities, flying at high altitudes and for extended-duration flights. They carried a variety of sensors,

---

[21]The SPACC was designated the center for issuing Scud alerts, whereas the Missile Warning Center, located in Cheyenne Mountain and which normally issues ballistic missile warning messages, was dedicated to the strategic warning mission. However, the Missile Warning Center served also as the backup center to the SPACC. (Information provided by USSPACECOM.)

[22]See Palmer (1992a), pp. 105–106, for the important contribution of UAVs to reconnaissance. While the UAVs made interesting and useful contributions, their employment points out some of the problems of joint operations. The Navy, Marines, and Army all brought UAVs of the same general type. The Navy used its UAVs for adjusting naval gunfire, and the UAVs reported back to the ship. The Marines used them for BDA and target acquisition for air strikes, and they reported back to the Marine TACC. The Army used its UAVs to surveill the area in front of its positions, and they reported back to the requesting units. Essentially, there were three separate systems providing important intelligence data to their parent units, data that in the main went no further up the intelligence chain. Before the conflict, the Air Force did not see any need for UAVs, and that service's commanders in the Gulf were crying for BDA information.

including infrared, radar, and long-range optical systems, and could be flown both day and night in all weather.[23]

In coordination with raiding F-15s, Tornados, and F/A-18s, SAC's RC-135 Rivet Joint electronic reconnaissance aircraft tested the Iraqi IADS during Desert Shield in preparation for the air campaign. The F-15s, Tornados, and F/A-18s would fly close to the Iraqi border to trigger the Iraqi radars, and Rivet Joint would monitor the Iraqi communications and radar response. These operations were also used as dress rehearsals for the air campaign.[24] For low-altitude reconnaissance, reliance was placed on tactical reconnaissance provided by the Air Force's RF-4C. Although few in number (a total of 24 USAF aircraft), the RF-4C provided reconnaissance information using the long-range oblique photograph (LOROP) camera and other systems.[25] The Coalition also relied on British Tornado aircraft, Saudi RF-5Cs, and a mixture of attack aircraft used in reconnaissance roles (F-16s, French and British Jaguars, F-14s, A-6s, and F/A-18s).[26]

Two prototype JSTARS were used to locate and track moving ground targets and relay that information to air and ground commanders. The *CPGW* report states that

> JSTARS tasking for the air campaign was to locate and target high-value armor, army forces, and resupply activity in the KTO (including the area encompassing the Republican Guard and secondary echelon forces). JSTARS also was tasked to find and target Scud locations, gather intelligence on the movement of forces within the KTO and eastern Iraq, and validate targets for other weapons systems. For the ground campaign, JSTARS was tasked to locate and target movement within the second echelon forces with emphasis on the Republican Guard, provide intelligence on the movement of forces within the KTO and eastern Iraq, and respond to immediate requests for support of engaged ground forces.[27]

The Navy provided some of the electronic reconnaissance assets used to develop the campaign against the Iraqi air-defense system. Real-time intelligence was gathered by Navy E-2C aircraft, which were among the first airborne early warning assets in the theater. During Desert Shield they operated from land bases in Bahrain, filling the coverage gaps of the AWACS, but Desert Storm saw them located on the carriers. They assisted in fusing tactical and strategic intelligence from the AWACS, ship-based Aegis, and other systems to provide a

---

[23]Coyne (1992a), pp. 119–120.

[24]Ibid., p. 119.

[25]Ibid., p. 120.

[26]*GWAPS*, p. 195.

[27]*CPGW*, pp. 235–236.

comprehensive intelligence picture of the KTO, as well as performing tailored tactical control and aircraft deconfliction for Navy and Coalition strike packages.   The roles of these aircraft emphasized battle group indications and warning (I&W), prestrike and poststrike reconnaissance, threat warning to strike packages entering Iraqi airspace, and HARM targeting, as well as providing information to the USAF AWACS, EC-130H Compass Call, and Rivet Joint aircraft. Furthermore, selected Navy F-14s were transformed into reconnaissance assets by equipping them with the Tactical Aerial Reconnaissance Pod System, or TARPS. TARPS sensors included high-resolution cameras and infrared systems.[28] Normally employed at low-to-medium altitudes for strike planning and real-time BDA, the threat of the Iraqi air defenses led to the employment of TARPS at higher altitudes.[29] TARPS imagery was collected and exploited by the carriers, such as the *Kennedy* in the Red Sea, but could not be passed to the JFACC because of communications network overloading and conflicting priorities. This proved to be a bottleneck in imagery dissemination.[30]

Red Sea carrier battle group reconnaissance support was provided by the EP-3s. Friedman notes that they were tied directly to E-2, EA-6B, and S-3B aircraft to identify and triangulate electronic targets for general reconnaissance and for HARM targeting. The Mediterranean EP-3Es provided signals intelligence in support of JTF Proven Force strikes and of long-term monitoring of the shipping lanes in the Mediterranean leading to the Suez Canal and the Gulf.[31]

Sensors: HUMINT

Overall, the human intelligence that we know about (HUMINT, i.e., spies, intelligence agents/sources) was inadequate, owing to several factors. One was that the U.S. intelligence community had been evolving toward a dependence on advanced technology sensors on space-based, ground-based, and airborne platforms for intelligence gathering and away from espionage networks. Another factor was that regional conditions made establishment of an effective

---

[28]*CPGW*, p. 236; for an account of a BDA mission against an Iraqi nuclear weapons component manufacturing site by an F-14 equipped with TARPS, see Mark Meyer, "Going Up to Big Al," U.S. Naval Institute *Proceedings*, July 1991, pp. 77–79. Armstrong (1992) points out: "The first three generations of aerial reconnaissance had one element in common: aircraft had to be launched and recovered before any information collected during a mission could be exploited. . . . In the early fall of 1990 . . . planners were able to assemble a few—very few—fourth generation [near-real-time information] prototype systems to provide direct support to U.S. CENTCOM Headquarters" (p. 110).

[29]Coyne (1992a), p. 119; Friedman (1991), p. 167.

[30]Communication to the authors by Major Robert Butler, USAF.

[31]Friedman (1991), pp. 167–168.

human intelligence network very difficult. While sensors can provide extremely sophisticated images of sites and events at particular points in time, they cannot discern intentions in ways that HUMINT may; however, both are necessary and complement each other if employed appropriately. Friedman asserts that despite available intelligence resources, the United States was unable to determine with any degree of certainty when the Iraqis had abandoned their air-defense efforts. This uncertainty resulted in the dedication of a substantial amount of air attack assets upon the air-defense target set that Friedman argues probably went on far longer than needed.[32] HUMINT about the numbers of Iraqi troops in Kuwait that Coalition troops were expected to face proved to be inflated.[33] Furthermore, to be on the operationally safe side, military commanders believed it more prudent to continue to bomb the Iraqi AAA and SAMs.[34]

The *CPGW* report notes that what information was gathered by HUMINT proved valuable in improving the targeting and destruction of significant military facilities in Baghdad, including the Ministry of Defense and various communications sites, as well as attacks against troops and logistics targets. For example, Colonel John Warden and the Checkmate staff were able to interview Western industrial officials to obtain blueprints of critical targets in Iraq, as well as American and Coalition officers who had been stationed there, to gain the first-hand knowledge that was necessary for the air campaign. That information was provided to Lieutenant Colonel David Deptula when he joined General Glosson's staff in the Black Hole.[35]

The Enablers: Environmental Monitoring (Weather)

As discussed in Chapter Two, the weather throughout the region turned out to be the worst experienced in that part of the world in more than a decade, causing about 15 percent of the total air sorties to be canceled during the first ten days of the air campaign.[36] Air sorties would be planned around the predicted weather over the target. The extent to which a strike mission was affected by weather was determined by the type and location of the target, the flight profile,

---

[32]Ibid., pp. 8–9.

[33]Ibid.; see also Hopple (in Watson et al. (1991), p. 154), who states that U.S. planners were told Iraq had moved 540,000 troops into the KTO, half of them in Kuwait, while (according to him) the actual numbers were 250,000 and 150,000, respectively.

[34]General Glosson has responded, "As long as they fire AAA and SAMs, they get hit. Period." (Communication to the authors.)

[35]Communication to the authors by a senior Air Force officer.

[36]*CPGW*, p. 227. See also Vice Admiral William A. Dougherty, "Storm from Space," U.S. Naval Institute *Proceedings*, August 1992, pp. 51–52. Weather conditions continued to be poor during the ground campaign as well.

and the particular weather phenomenon encountered, including interference from cloud or smoke with normal forward-looking infrared (FLIR) or visual targeting.[37] Consequently, daily weather reports were critical for mission planning and daily operations.

Weather support was provided by a number of satellites owned by the United States, Japan, the European Space Agency, and the Soviet Union (see Table 8.1). The Defense Meteorological Satellite Program was the DoD's primary meteorological satellite system for the war. Before and during the period of hostilities, three DMSP satellites in polar sun-synchronous orbits were available to provide twice-daily coverage of the Earth and data relating to atmospheric vertical temperature and moisture profiles, cloud images, and other environmental effects. Data were transmitted to six Mark IV DMSP receiving vans deployed throughout the theater.[38] In addition, selected Navy ships staffed with meteorological personnel and equipped with DMSP terminals received data directly, while others with personnel but without appropriate DMSP equipment relied on civil meteorological systems. Other means of getting DMSP data to the theater were also used:

> TFU managed Mark IV operations at Riyadh and produced a standard weather report transmitted by high frequency (HF) radio to Army and Air Force (USAF) users in theater. Weather images were faxed from the USAF Mark IV van to USAF units by land lines. Army units received weather images from non-military weather satellites through a commercial receiver which could only receive a civil weather broadcast. The Army chose to use these receivers because the Mark IV van required considerable airlift space (75 percent of a C-141 load) and, therefore, could not meet Army mobility requirements.[39]

DMSP "provided data for weather and sandstorm predictions that optimized force deployment, weapon loads, laser-guided munitions, the application of aircraft, and provided data critical to the timing of the ground offensive. DMSP also helped program cruise missiles for effective deployment and assisted in the determination of appropriate surveillance platform configurations."[40] Furthermore, the importance of DMSP to the air campaign cannot be over-

---

[37]Communication from CNA.

[38]*CPGW* notes that one Air Force van was deployed to Riyadh and provided data to the CENTCOM staff and a Tactical Forecast Unit (TFU), while the remaining five vans were deployed with Marine forces in support of Marine aviation and amphibious operations. The deployment of Air Force and Army terminals occurred later because of the need to deploy higher-priority items. See *CPGW*, p. T-219; also, communication to the authors by Commander Theresa Dorphinghaus, USSPACECOM.

[39]*CPGW*, p. T-219.

[40]Dana J. Johnson, Max Nelson, and Robert J. Lempert, *U.S. Space-Based Remote Sensing: Challenges and Prospects*, Santa Monica, California: RAND, N-3589-AF/A/OSD, 1993, p. 17.

Table 8.1

Weather Support Provided to Desert Shield and Storm

Satellite	Owner	Orbit	Coverage*
DMSP (DoD)	U.S.	Polar	Overhead 0610L and 1810L
DMSP (DoD)	U.S.	Polar	Overhead 0735L and 1935L
DMSP (DoD)	U.S.	Polar	Overhead 0930L and 2130L
NOAA/POES	U.S.	Polar	Overhead 0723L and 1923L
NOAA/POES	U.S.	Polar	Overhead 0206L and 1406L
GMS	Japan	Geostationary	Hemisphere 140° E
METEOSAT	ESA	Geostationary	Hemisphere 50° W
METEOSAT	ESA	Geostationary	Hemisphere 0° W
METEOR	USSR	Polar	12 sats available

*Coverage times are approximate, within ±1 hour.
NOTE: See pp. xix–xxvi for abbreviations.
SOURCE: Information provided by USSPACECOM.

estimated, for it helped the JFACC plan the most effective use of air assets whose systems were affected by high humidity, fog, rain, and low clouds.[41] General Horner considered it so important that he kept a light table next to his desk in order to review the latest data. The capability to provide timely information to the JFACC enabled him to make adjustments to the latest master attack plan.[42]

Civil meteorological satellites were used to supplement DMSP. Unlike the military satellites, many of those owned by civil, i.e., non-DoD, agencies or other governments are bound by international agreement to provide data on a nondiscriminatory basis. This same rule applied during the Gulf War as well. The Commerce Department's National Oceanic and Atmospheric Administration (NOAA) operates two weather satellite systems, NOAA/POES and GOES. The two NOAA/POES (Polar Orbiting Environmental Satellites) in near-polar sun-synchronous orbit each view the earth twice every 24 hours. The satellites transmit unencrypted data down to Air Force Global Weather Central in Omaha, Nebraska, the Fleet Numerical Oceanographic Center in San Diego, California, the National Environmental Data and Information Service (NESDIS, a part of NOAA) in Suitland, Maryland, and deployed tactical receivers worldwide. Only one Geostationary Orbiting Environmental Satellite (GOES-7) was operational over the Western Hemisphere; neither it nor the European Space Agency's METEOSAT-3 that was moved to replace the failed GOES-6 supported

---

[41]Lieutenant Colonel Richard B. H. Lewis, USAF, who served on Glosson's staff during the Gulf War, notes that the eight-hour cycle time was too long. Something less than four hours was needed, in his opinion.

[42]CPGW, pp. 228–229.

Gulf operations. Consequently, other METEOSATs were used, as was the Soviet METEOR polar orbiter, to provide additional weather information to the Coalition forces.[43]

Some consideration was given to denying the Iraqis any information from civil and commercial environmental monitoring satellites, but several factors led to decisions against taking such action. First, U.S. policy on civil and scientific remote sensing has been to provide meteorological data on a nondiscriminatory basis to other nations. Secondly, it was determined that "turning off" the satellites would hurt U.S. and Coalition forces more than keeping them on with the possibility of Iraq receiving the same data. Certain U.S. and Coalition forces (for example, several American carriers) depended upon receiving unencrypted weather data, as they did not have appropriate receivers for DMSP data. While the DMSP "birds" could have been turned off to deny Iraqi access to weather data, it was determined that the Iraqis had multiple receivers for weather data from many other sources. Consequently, any action the U.S. military space community might have taken would likely have been counterproductive.

The Enablers: Remote Sensing

An area of space-related activities considered primarily civil in nature was of great use to military operations in the Gulf. This was the field of multispectral imaging (MSI), otherwise known as remote sensing. While remote sensing can be conducted from a variety of platforms and directed at a variety of targets, in this case we are considering remote sensing of the earth from space, especially of areas considered inaccessible or hostile. Data from remote sensing sources are extensively used in mapping, charting, and geodesy (MC&G).

In Desert Shield and Storm, national systems and two unclassified space systems gathered the bulk of data necessary for the conduct of the air campaign. Our focus is on the latter two systems: Landsat and SPOT. Landsat is a U.S.-owned and operated system that provides 30-meter resolution,[44] while SPOT (Satellite Probatoire d'Observation de la Terre) is a French program that provides 10-meter resolution. The data these systems transmitted were not suitable to be immediately provided to the troops in the field, but had to be

---

[43]See the extensive descriptions of each of these systems in Andrew Wilson (ed.), *Interavia Space Directory 1991–1992*, Surrey, United Kingdom: Jane's Information Group, 1991.

[44]Landsat has historically been managed by the Department of Commerce's NOAA and operated by a private-sector company, Earth Observation Satellite Corporation (EOSAT). However, Public Law 102-555, "Land Remote Sensing Policy Act of 1992" (October 28, 1992), transfers the management of Landsat from Commerce to NASA and the DoD jointly.

manipulated, sometimes with other sets of data, to build composite representations of particular subjects such as geographical regions in order to be operationally useful.

Landsat was used before the war to image the Persian Gulf and therefore identify areas of contention between Iran and Iraq during their conflict and, later, areas of economic interest during the "tanker war." During Desert Shield, Landsat imagery was used to develop engineering plans for the construction of new military airfields. Furthermore, during the war, Landsat imagery would be compared with imagery in the Landsat database to determine spectral changes or disturbances to the ground. This in turn would indicate possible changes in location of Iraqi forces.

SPOT data were heavily exploited by the Air Force and the Marines in preparation for upcoming missions. When combined with other Defense Mapping Agency (DMA) databases, they could be used by a pilot to display attack routes and targets as they would appear at flight and attack altitudes. F-111 pilots used this approach to plan for hitting the Iraqi wellheads that were pumping oil into the Persian Gulf.[45] Prior to the air campaign the Air Force procured 108 SPOT-generated images of downtown Baghdad and other areas; these images were electronically overlaid on digital terrain maps for the rehearsal of missions, which resulted in greater target accuracies during the actual attacks. The digital images were also displayed in the 70 Mission Support Systems IIs (MSS IIs) deployed in the theater.[46] Finally, the oil fires in Kuwait set during the first phase of the Gulf War proved to be highly observable by Landsat and SPOT and helped to determine the extent of environmental damage that resulted.

For Desert Shield and Storm, existing maps of CENTCOM's area of responsibility were anywhere from ten to thirty years old. Table 8.2 illustrates the availability of DMA products to support targeting and BDA prior to Desert Shield. Although a DMA map depot opened in Bahrain on 10 August 1990, it contained only unclassified charts, most of which were outdated. Furthermore, the depot was unauthorized and unable to transport maps and charts to unit locations in the theater.[47] More recent Landsat, SPOT, and to a limited extent, Soviet Soyuzkarta imagery were used by the DMA to build new maps, and to provide information about bathymetric, hydrographic, and terrain categorization in

---

[45]Information provided by USSPACECOM.

[46]John G. Roos, "SPOT Images Helped Allies Hit Targets in Downtown Baghdad," *Armed Forces Journal International,* May 1991, p. 54.

[47]Communication from Major Robert Butler, USAF.

Table 8.2

Availability of DMA Products Before Desert Shield

Type	Percent Coverage	Quality
Land		
1:50,000 topographical maps	50	Most out of date, some inaccurate
City maps	50	Most out of date
Terrain analysis products	50	No digital, out of date
Air		
1:250,000 JOG-AIR	90	Most out of date
Point positioning databases	100	Out of date
TERCOM matrices	0	None available for Iraq
Sea		
Hydro charts	80	In good shape

NOTE: JOG-AIR = Joint Operations Graphic-Air; TERCOM = terrain contour mapping.
SOURCE: RAND working paper by Major Robert Butler, USAF.

support of air, naval, and ground combat operations.[48] By the end of February 1991 the DMA had made up the shortfall in MC&G products, as shown in Table 8.3. (The *CPGW* report has pointed out the importance of remote sensing data to, for example, the Army's 82nd Airborne Division and the Navy and Marines in planning airborne and amphibious operations against Kuwait City.) In Landsat's case, the Earth Observation Satellite Corporation (EOSAT) provided the imaging data required by DMA in anywhere from two days to two or three weeks,[49] as opposed to the usual four to six weeks for data processing, but at a much higher cost.[50]

In contrast to the decision regarding access to Coalition-owned weather satellites, the French government decided to deny Iraq access to SPOT images throughout the war. This had important ramifications for numerous allied mili-

[48]Johnson, Nelson, and Lempert (1993), pp. 17–18.

[49]The process for acquiring Landsat images was as follows: a CINC or a service would request MSI data from DMA, which would then forward the request to EOSAT. If EOSAT had the image available in the Landsat database, it would turn the request around in two to three days. If the data were not available, the Landsat satellite would have to be tasked to image the area. At the time there were two satellites in orbit taking sixteen days to cover the entire earth; this meant that it took eight or sixteen days to acquire the data and then another two to three days for processing and return to DMA. DMA would then need one day to send the image to the requester, or anywhere from four to fourteen days to develop a map from the data. (Information provided by USSPACECOM.)

[50]Timeliness of the data is a critical issue with Landsat, as was quite evident during the war. CBS apparently paid three times the usual price in order to get the data in a timely enough manner for use on its news broadcasts; the DoD apparently decided that timeliness was well worth the money. (Conversations with an EOSAT official.)

Table 8.3

Operational Needs for MC&G Products and DMA Production Totals
as of 24 February 1991

Type of Product	Total Required	Totals Met by DMA
1:50,000 maps	1,191	1,048
City maps	29	22
1:250,000 JOG-AIR	64	51
TERCOM	83	62
Target coordinates	7,972	7,972
PPDB	83	30
Hydro charts	203	198
1:100,000 image maps	147	147
Video PPDB	26	26
Gridded photos	265	265
1:250,000 JOG-RADAR	64	18
Escape and evasion charts	22	22
Digital elevation data	303	293
Firefinder data	387	387

NOTE: MC&G = mapping, charting, and geodesy; JOG = Joint Operations Graphic; TERCOM = terrain contour mapping; PPDB = Point Positioning Data Base.
SOURCE: RAND working paper by Major Robert Butler, USAF.

tary operations as well as for critical U.S. deception efforts. Friedman speculates that the Soviet government may have shown Iraqi foreign minister Tariq Aziz images from its own Cosmos high-resolution satellite to try to end Saddam's intransigence before the start of the allied ground invasion, but it was an apparently futile gesture.[51]

The Enablers: Navigation and Positioning

The exploitation of the Navstar Global Positioning System (GPS) was perhaps the most highlighted and well-received contribution from the military space community to the war. GPS is a space-based radio-navigation system providing precise, worldwide, three-dimensional position, velocity, and timing data that are used for a wide variety of civil and military purposes. At the time of the conflict, 16 satellites out of a planned constellation of 24[52] were available to support air and other military operations in the theater. One squadron of Air Force F-16s (from the 388th TFW at Hill AFB), and many KC-135s and B-52s

---

[51]Friedman (1991), note 3, p. 411.

[52]Twenty-one active satellites and three on-orbit spares are planned.

were equipped with GPS receivers, as were most Marine helicopters, some Navy ships, and the Army's divisions deployed to Saudi Arabia.[53]

Because there were not enough military receivers, U.S. and Coalition forces relied quite heavily on commercial receivers: by March 1991, there were 4,490 commercial and 842 military GPS receivers deployed.[54] Because of the need to use commercially available receivers, the decision was made to turn off Selective Availability (SA), which would restrict nonmilitary access to GPS in times of war;[55] this action contributed to the concern that Iraq might take advantage of the system, but it is unclear whether or not that occurred.

Although the constellation was not yet complete, GPS was critical to ground units navigating the featureless terrain of Iraq and Saudi Arabia. Moreover, GPS was essential for determining accurate firing positions by TLAM launch platforms, for flight guidance for Navy standoff land attack missiles (SLAMs), for providing grid locations for navigation aids and radars, and for many other activities.[56]

COMMUNICATIONS[57]

If the sensors and "enablers" provided information necessary for the conduct of military operations, then communications comprised the means by which the commander relayed that information to his forces. The best decisions made by the JFACC would have come to naught if they were not communicated to

---

[53]"DoD Quickly Buys Commercial GPS Terminals for 'Desert Shield,'" *Aerospace Daily*, August 27, 1990, pp. 330–331.

[54]*CPGW*, p. T-227. It is noteworthy that although the use of GPS was not widespread among the services prior to the war, U.S. troops made extensive use of the commercial receiver, called the small, lightweight GPS receiver unit or SLGR ("Slugger"), to the extent of buying out Trimble Navigation's entire production run of SLGRs and even asking relatives back in CONUS to buy any and all receivers they could find. (Conversations with Trimble Navigation officials.)

[55]The system of Selective Availability requires some explanation. Each GPS satellite broadcasts two signals. One signal, the C/A or clear/acquisition code, which can be received by any GPS receiver, provides accuracy to within 100 meters (330 feet). The second signal, P-code or protected code, usually encrypted and readable only by U.S. military equipment, is supposedly accurate to within 10–20 meters and contains antijam capabilities. In March 1990 the Air Force began to encrypt the GPS signal in preparation for full operational status of the system. However, SA was turned off on August 10, soon after the decision was made to deploy U.S. forces. See Vincent Kiernan, "Air Force Alters GPS Signals to Aid Troops," *Space News*, September 24–30, 1990, p. 3, and Barry Miller, "GPS Proves Its Worth in Operation Desert Storm," *Armed Forces Journal International*, April 1991, pp. 16–20.

[56]*CPGW*, p. 240.

[57]This section relies heavily on Desert Storm–related work done by RAND analysts Leland Joe, Daniel Gonzales, and Katherine Poehlmann, and on earlier analysis of civil/commercial augmentation of military satellites by K. M. Poehlmann, J. J. Milanese, and H. Le. It also makes extensive use of communications analyses provided by the Center for Naval Analyses (CNA).

operational units and if feedback from air operations was not communicated back to the JFACC. As one analyst observed,

> The best modern command and control system provides a central commander with a very current picture of the battle and with the ability to maneuver all of the forces nearly continuously to match the shape of that battle. This requires enormous computer power as well as dense and robust communications.[58]

Moreover, the entire logistics and intelligence systems were based on the availability of long-haul communications to the United States and U.S. commands in Europe (as well as elsewhere). The deployment and logistics miracles described in Chapters Three and Nine would have been impossible without such communications support.

Arriving U.S. forces had to install a major new system to meet their needs. A senior officer on the Joint Staff in Washington remarked, "The services put more electronics communication connectivity into the Gulf in 90 days than we put in Europe in 40 years."[59]

In the aviation dimension, the magnitude of the connectivity task can be seen by looking at the bed-down of the aircraft in theater. If one includes the carrier task forces at sea, the Proven Force wing in Turkey, and the MAC "channels" of aircraft flying to and from the Arabian peninsula, the magnitude of the challenge becomes apparent. Moreover, every aircraft aloft (sometimes as many as 300–400 at a time, excluding helicopters) was its own communications station that had to be served by nets and frequencies. Headquarters, particularly air headquarters and facilities such as the TACC, are a virtual nest of communications lines and nodes. Finally, much of the aviation-related communications also had to be connected to CENTCOM and Coalition headquarters, not to mention back to Washington. No wonder, then, that there was heavy reliance on satellites for long-haul communications and on aircraft such as the AWACS for battlespace communications.

The extent of the reliance on long-haul communications is shown by the following statistic: At the height of Desert Storm, over 95 percent of CENTCOM's long-haul communications were handled by communications satellites, with 72 percent over the military satellite communications (MILSATCOM) network and 24 percent over commercial systems. Airborne systems such as AWACS, JSTARS, Navy E-2s, and ABCCCs (airborne battlefield command and control centers aboard EC-130Es) were deployed and heavily used in both command

---

[58]Friedman (1991), pp. 246–247.

[59]Lieutenant General James S. Cassity, JCS/J-6, January 1991.

and control and communications relay roles, particularly during the early phases of the deployment.

As noted earlier, the C^3I system in the theater had to be built essentially from scratch. As one knowledgeable analyst observed,

> Impressive as the logistics infrastructure in the Gulf was in terms of air bases and seaport facilities, the U.S. defense communications system that had once transited this area of the world was no longer in place. All that remained of U.S. defense communications in the Gulf area, where high frequency radio systems once hopped among such countries as Libya, Ethiopia, and Saudi Arabia, were one shipborne and three tactical satellite terminals, installed in support of the Air Force and the Navy.[60]

This resulted in stresses on all service C^3I systems. Had a larger national emergency occurred at the same time as the Gulf War, a large number of combat communications units and CAFMS (Computer-Aided Force Management System) units would have to have been withdrawn from the theater. Satellite communications systems became overloaded in the early stages of the operation. Delays were experienced in receiving system equipment (e.g., terminals) in the theater for up to two to three weeks after the beginning of the deployment. In order to meet combat requirements, many existing military tactical communications systems, including tactical circuit switches, super high frequency (SHF) satellite terminals, and high-frequency (HF) radio quick reaction packets (QRPs), are heavily constructed, protected, and internally redundant. As a result they are relatively bulky and heavy when compared to commercially available communications gear. These demanding specifications and attendant cost led to insufficient numbers of available equipment for shipment to the Gulf.[61] As a result, commercial communications systems ultimately played a critical role in the desert war. When used with STU-IIIs, they provided quick, secure access from Saudi Arabia to headquarters in CONUS.

While the Air Force and the Army used a variety of SHF, UHF, and HF terminals, the Navy faced a compatibility problem because of its heavy reliance on UHF. This resulted in delays and extensive workarounds in the electronic transmission of message traffic (including the ATO), and remained a problem throughout the war.

One notable workaround was the heavy use of facsimile machines and STU-III secure telephones. This speeded up the process of communicating decisions and requesting information among the different military organizations in

---

[60]Alan D. Campen, "Silent Space Warriors," in Campen (1992), pp. 136–137.
[61]Communication from Fred Frostic of RAND.

theater, and got around the many bottlenecks that occurred because of the sheer size and complexity of the campaign.[62]

Tactical Communications

Communications in support of the control of air attacks against mobile ground forces were constrained by line-of-sight requirements and limited directional capabilities. The aircraft used to control the air attacks included the JSTARS, AWACS, ABCCC, F-16 killer scouts, and Marine OV-10s, F/A-18Ds, and C-130s (airborne DASC). Generally, these aircraft served as command and control and/or surveillance platforms, not as dedicated communications platforms.[63] Much of the communications between these aircraft and the strike aircraft were based on secure voice, datalinks such as the Surveillance and Control Data Link (SCDL), and SATCOM radios. The SCDL was limited by range, line of sight, and the need for code updates to accommodate all users, but it performed better than expected. While some platforms were not initially equipped to pass threat and target data directly to other aircrews, they did have links to such units as the TACC, the AWACS, and Air Support Operations Centers (ASOCs), which could then relay the information appropriately.

Communications among U.S. naval forces as well as allied naval forces remained a problem throughout the war, one that was largely driven by the rapid expansion in the size of naval forces in USCENTCOM's AOR (from fewer than 15 to over 100 ships) and the large number of allied navies involved. Lengthy delays were encountered in message traffic during the deployment stage, but these were gradually corrected before the start of the air campaign.[64] During the first days of Desert Storm, all forms of communication became severely overloaded, and although the time needed to pass the highest-priority messages was reduced, lower-priority messages continued to be inordinately delayed throughout the conflict. This was true not only for the naval forces directly supporting the war, but for U.S. naval forces in other theaters as well. Data and voice circuits also remained heavily overloaded and pointed to the problems inherent in the Navy's communications systems and their ability to support large-scale, joint operations.[65] HF was a problem as well, but workarounds

---

[62]As noted by one analyst from CNA, the negative side to this is the difficulty for postwar analysts to trace the origins of key decisions or day-to-day activities, especially when they were made in telephone conversations and never recorded

[63]Navy S-3Bs were often used in a dedicated communications relay role.

[64]The Navy's own assessment of Desert Shield/Desert Storm provides this example: on 6 September 1990, the mean delay of Flash (highest) precedence messages was 8.6 hours. (Information provided to the authors by CNA.)

[65]CNA reports that the backlogs at the Communications Area Master Stations (CAMS) serving all naval forces grew to 36,000 messages in the Western Pacific and 21,000 in the Mediterranean.

such as software modifications and the addition of Common User Digital Information Exchange System (CUDIXS) suites were implemented, and while they were largely effective in reducing the communications backlog during Desert Shield, the problems resurfaced during Desert Storm. In large part this, as well as compatibility and outage problems, forced naval commanders to use aircraft to carry critical messages such as the ATO.[66]

A common secure voice link was established among COMUSNAVCENT, the battle force commanders in the Red Sea and Persian Gulf, and other naval forces. The use of commercial satellite systems, primarily INMARSAT, relieved the load on this link and assisted in the coordination of activities between COMUSNAVCENT and NAVCENT Riyadh. INMARSAT also supported real-time coordination of the ATO among the Navy JFACC representatives and the Arabian Gulf Battle Force commander (the flagship of the Red Sea Battle Force commander did not get an INMARSAT terminal until late in the war).[67] Furthermore, it proved to be more efficient in passing large data files from CONUS-based naval aviation support units to the theater.[68]

Although tactical communication capabilities were sorely tested and generally up to the demand during the Gulf War, the context was a war in which the enemy (after the initial invasion of Kuwait) never held the initiative. In a maneuver war against a more resourceful enemy, the tactical communication structure employed in the Gulf War probably would have foundered from insufficient capacity, deficient user "discipline," and residual system capabilities. One commander told us: "Communications jamming would have killed us."

Intratheater Communications in Supporting Air and Space Defense

There was an extensive intratheater communications network that underpinned the Coalition's integrated air-defense system (IADS) and its datalinks.

As RAND analysts note:

---

[66]As of this writing, the transmission of the ATO to the carriers by use of S-3 aircraft has been obviated with the wider availability of SHF terminals for the electronic transmission of the ATO. See Tony Capaccio and Eric Rosenberg, "Iraqi Raid Highlighted New Joint Attack Planning," *Defense Week*, 19 January 1993, pp. 1, 11.

[67]The International Maritime Satellite Organization (INMARSAT) is a 64-nation consortium that provides management of a space-based maritime communications system of telephone, telex, data and facsimile services to the shipping, aviation, offshore, and land mobile industries. It also provides the secretariat for the Cospas/Sarsat distress system. The United States is a signatory to the treaty establishing INMARSAT and is represented by COMSAT. The INMARSAT system consists of 21 coastal earth stations. See Wilson (1991), pp. 365–367.

[68]Information provided to the authors by CNA.

A combination of circumstances during Desert Shield led to the rapid deployment of a large number of U.S. air defense systems. This was necessary because of the large number of aircraft involved and the lack of an indigenous IADS.

The core of the U.S. IADS used in Desert Storm was AWACS. The ground component consisted of two Control and Reporting Centers (CRCs) and three Message Processing Centers (MPCs). A web of datalinks connected the airborne AWACS, MPCs, CRCs, and to commanders at the TACC who were responsible for the overall prosecution of the air war.[69]

In its role as combat airspace manager in the KTO, the AWACS was the core of the datalink communications network used in Desert Storm. Three U.S. E-3s provided front-line surveillance from orbit positions just south of the Saudi-Iraqi border. One RSAF E-3 served as a backup surveillance capability, and a fourth U.S. E-3 served as an airborne spare that assumed a front-line position when a U.S. E-3 had to be relieved for refueling. The local air picture was interpreted and analyzed on board each AWACS, thus avoiding the need to send raw data to remote ground processing facilities. Requests for information on the local air situation from the TACC, the Navy's air-defense centers and E-2 aircraft, or elsewhere were transmitted routinely via relays on data communications links.[70]

For specific situations, such as tactical ballistic missile (TBM) attacks, warning of Scud launches was passed over separate voice and computer networks. For voice networks, detailed information was minimized to avoid confusion and misinterpretation at the receiving end. When USCENTCOM received warning, it passed that warning message to Coalition forces, while the National Military Command Center serving the National Command Authority in Washington passed warning information to Israel, and the U.S. European Command (EUCOM) provided warning information to the Turkish government and U.S. forces in Turkey.[71] The five months of leeway before the start of the air campaign was critical to developing the necessary arrangements.

As it turned out, the very short time needed to establish TBM warning became one of the more impressive accomplishments of the war. It is all the more impressive considering that provisions for reacting to Scud attacks did not exist at the time of the Iraqi invasion in August 1990. USSPACECOM noted that the existing space annex to USCENTCOM's Operations Plan (draft USCINCCENT

---

[69]Conversations with RAND's Leland Joe and Daniel Gonzales. The Saudi IADS (Peace Shield) was far from complete when Desert Shield started because of extensive software and integration problems. Previous programs (Peace Pulse and Peace Hawk) had been completed with the Saudi acquisition and installation of ground-based radars and the E-3A.

[70]Navy liaison officers were assigned to each AWACS crew.

[71]Tactical warning functions related to possible attacks against North America continued to be performed in parallel with CENTCOM theater warning throughout the war.

OPLAN 1002–90) did not indicate any level of space-related support in this area other than traditional functions of strategic warning, navigation and positioning, and mapping. Plans had not been formulated to use tactical warning to cue Patriot batteries, or to allow USCENTCOM to receive, process, display, distribute, and react to warning data. This lack of planning was clearly evident in USCENTCOM's Scud alert exercises in December 1990–January 1991 when the command found it took up to 40 minutes to provide warning to its subordinate units.[72]

Long-Haul Communications

Geography proved to be the driving factor in the U.S. military's dependence upon long-haul communications. The size of the theater, the distances between air bases, the long distances between CONUS and the AOR all dictated that satellites be used to communicate during Desert Shield and Desert Storm. In addition, the numbers of U.S. and Coalition forces involved and the volume of data transmitted each day necessitated reliable and timely access. Unfortunately, the communications requirements exceeded the military capabilities, and so commercial systems were called upon for support. Long-haul communications were provided by the Defense Satellite Communications System (DSCS), troposcatter radio, INTELSAT,[73] INMARSAT, UHF MILSATCOM (FLTSAT, LEASAT, and Gapfiller), host country telecommunication services, and HF radio. DSCS provided most of the long-haul communications capacity used by U.S. military forces. Figure 8.4 illustrates the DSCS constellation configuration at the time of the conflict, and the specific satellites supporting U.S. operations. Although the satellites in view of CENTCOM's AOR were capable of handling the military communications traffic for the first month of the deployment, by early September one satellite had become saturated. A request was made of the British government to use a British Skynet IV-B in the area of operations to support DSCS, and this was accomplished soon after. Subsequently, another U.S. satellite, a DSCS II spare, was repositioned and reactivated, becoming operational by mid-December.

As shown in Figure 8.5, four INTELSAT communications satellites provided extensive support during Desert Storm. Although the more advanced space-

---

[72]USSPACECOM report. Currently, with USSPACECOM help, CINC OPLANs are being revised and/or rewritten to include space support annexes with procedures for Scud notification and warning.

[73]The International Telecommunications Satellite Organization is an international consortium of 119 members that operates a space-based system of communications satellites. As of 1991, there were 15 satellites over the Atlantic, Pacific, and Indian Ocean regions providing international telecommunications services to more than 180 countries, territories, and dependencies, and domestic communications services to more than 30 countries. See Wilson (1991), pp. 367–371.

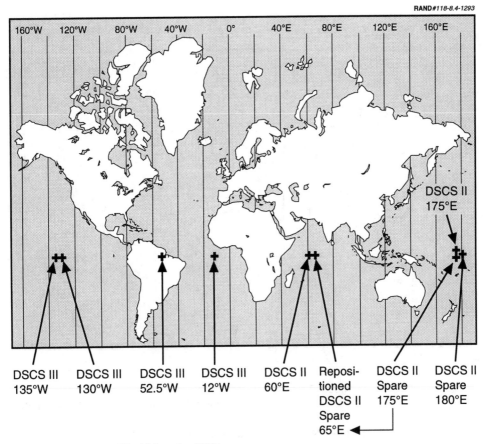

SOURCE: Leland Joe and Daniel Gonzales, RAND.

Figure 8.4—The DSCS Constellation During Desert Shield and Desert Storm

craft have greater capacity than DSCS, their transponders use relatively low power and thus make them vulnerable to jamming. Fifty-five transportable INTELSAT terminals were used by U.S. and Coalition forces to support unclassified systems. There was apparently a shortage of INTELSAT terminals and some Ku-band INTELSAT terminals were modified to operate with INTELSAT C-band transponders. The Defense Communications Agency noted that twelve INTELSAT terminals were used to support the AUTOVON, AUTODIN, and DDN networks.

The Navy made extensive use of INMARSAT satellites to transfer large data files relating to logistics and other support matters because the existing FLTSAT network was overloaded. Had INMARSAT been unavailable, those files would have to have been sent by courier or through the mail. INMARSAT provided real-time telephone, telex, and data communications (up to 9600 baud) for

RAND#118-8.5-1293

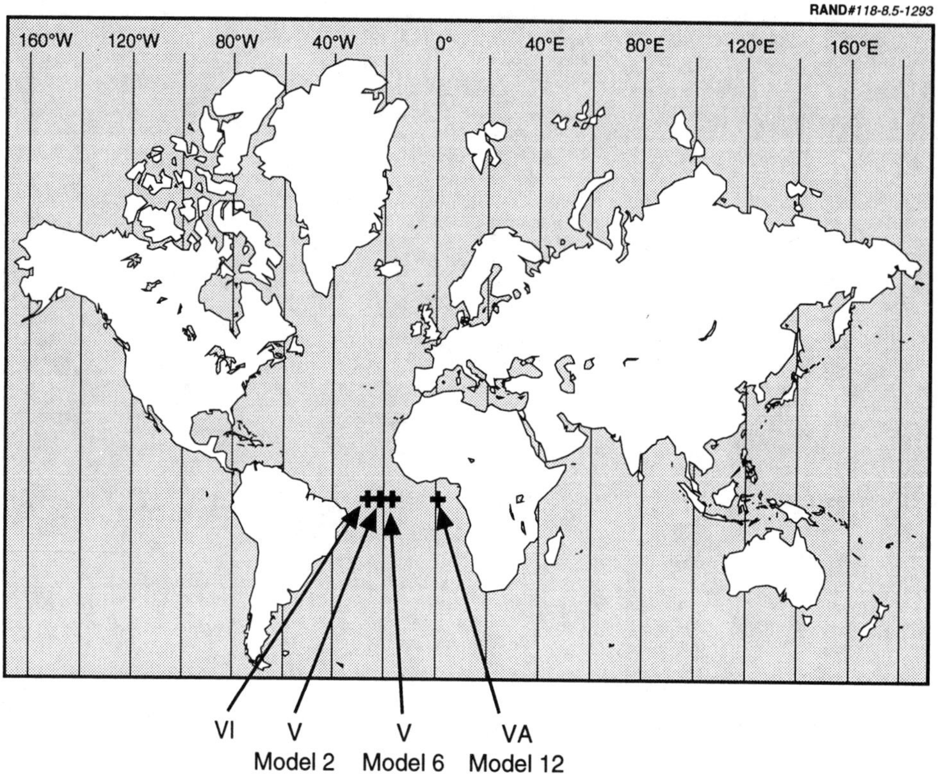

SOURCE: Leland Joe and Daniel Gonzales, RAND.

Figure 8.5—INTELSAT Satellites Used in Desert Storm

ships at sea. Communications between ship and shore were conducted over public-switched telephone and telex communications systems ashore. Ship-to-ship communications were patched via links to FLTSAT and INMARSAT. Fortuitously, the use of INMARSAT by U.S. and Coalition forces did not result in a compatibility problem, as many of the nations involved were signatories. Furthermore, many commercial oil tankers were also equipped with INMARSAT terminals. As CNA noted, "the Naval Representative to JFACC for Persian Gulf forces found INMARSAT to be the most effective means for real-time (voice) coordination with the force commander."[74]

The 2nd Marine Air Wing units attached to the 3rd MAW in the Gulf received some support from two MACSATs (Multiple Access Communications Satellites) beginning on 22 August. The two experimental satellites, known as "lightsats," were built for the Defense Advanced Research Projects Agency (DARPA) and

---

[74]Information provided by CNA.

provided an unclassified store-and-forward capability to transmit spare parts needs and other logistics information to their home base at Cherry Point, North Carolina. MAW priority was to get a separate satellite channel. They used a large amount of information, about twenty to fifty pages of information passed back and forth in four 10-minute periods every day.[75]

In toto, over 90 percent of long-haul communications was carried by communications satellites. Table 8.4 illustrates the complexity of the communications architecture and the agencies involved in processing and approving communications requests, controlling the communications networks, and providing satellite control and engineering. Three DSCS satellites, with an average age of over eight years, were the primary means of long-haul communications and were supported by FLTSAT, NATO, and Skynet satellites. The organization and coordination of these systems and networks extended over months as the deployment was conducted, and necessitated the cooperation of numerous U.S. and foreign governments, agencies, and commercial firms during Desert Shield and Desert Storm.[76]

TARGETING AND MISSION PLANNING

Information technologies greatly aided the targeting and mission planning process. The sheer size of the air tasking order ("a New York phone book by the time it was done") necessitated automated preparation. Personal computers with modems supported by fax machines relayed far greater amounts of information over telephone lines than did the official military message system. The extensive use of PCs, modems, faxes, and other commercially available systems was largely unanticipated, overwhelmed existing communications infrastructures, and became a user-discipline issue in communication content and prioritization. This resulted in data overload, which in turn meant that in many instances data were ignored, misdirected, or misjudged.[77] Furthermore, the more these systems were used, the greater the demand on them for more information.

---

[75]Comment by Colonel Charles Georger, USMC, Deputy Commander, Naval Space Command, Dahlgren, Virginia, in Daniel J. Marcus, "Marines Use Macsats in Mideast," *Space News*, 3–9 September 1990, p. 4; and Campen (1992), pp. 138–139.

[76]Competing or conflicting communications requests among users were adjudicated by the Joint Chiefs of Staff. For example, when Schwarzkopf requested support from DSCS, Army Space Command (USARSPACE) processed the request if it was tactical in nature and Defense Communications Agency (DCA) if it was strategic. DCA coordinated and approved the request if there were no conflicts. Network and payload control were exercised by USARSPACE, but the satellites themselves were controlled by Air Force Space Command (AFSPACECOM). (Information from USSPACECOM.)

[77]Macedonia (1992), pp. 36–37.

Table 8.4

The Military Communications Architecture During Desert Shield and Storm: Agency Authority and Responsibilities

System	Request	Process Request	Coordination	Approve Change	Network Planning	Network Control	Tracking, Telemetry, and Control	Engineering
DSCS	CINC	ARSPACE/DCA	DCA/* JCS	DCA/* JCS	ARSPACE/DCA	ARSPACE	AFSPACE	SSD/DCEC
FLTSAT	CINC	CINC	CINC/* JCS	CINC/* JCS	User NCTAMS	User	AFSPACE	SPAWAR
AFSAT	CINC		SAC/* JCS**	SAC/* JCS**			AFSPACE	SAC
Commercial	CINC	DCA/DECCO	n/a	n/a	Commercial	Commercial	Commercial	Commercial
LEASAT/Gapfiller	CINC	CINC	CINC/* JCS	CINC/* JCS	User NCTAMS	User	Commercial	Commercial
MACSAT	CMD	DARPA	n/a	DARPA	Commercial	Commercial	Commercial	Commercial
Skynet	CINC	ARSPACE	JCS	ARSPACE	British	British	British AFSPACE	British
NATO-3	CINC EUCOM	NATO	NATO JCS	JCS	NATO	NATO	AFSPACE	SSD

*No conflict.

**Conflicts.

SOURCE: Information provided by USSPACECOM.

NOTES: DECCO: Defense Commercial Communications Agency. NCTAMS: Naval Computer and Telecommunications Area Master Station. SSD: Space Systems Division (USAF). DCEC: Defense Communications Engineering Command. SPAWAR: Space Naval Warfare Systems Command. For all other abbreviations, see pp. xix–xxvi.

Interjecting intelligence information into the targeting and mission planning activities in Riyadh was complicated by the physical separation of the component intelligence targeting organization (CENTAF/IN) from the Black Hole, the associated security restrictions and procedures, and the constraints on communications between the organizations. The Black Hole was located in the Royal Saudi Air Force headquarters building, while CENTAF/IN was located in a building belonging to the U.S. Military Training Mission (USMTM) about 200 meters from the RSAF building. The targeting group was placed in an approximately 15 × 30 foot tent in the USMTM facility and, like the Black Hole, had restricted access.[78]

Both the Black Hole and the component intelligence organizations had different communications links back to CONUS-based intelligence agencies, complicating an already difficult problem. Mission planning and targeting activities conducted in the Black Hole were supported by data gathered by various intelligence systems and human intelligence (HUMINT) and analyzed by Checkmate, SPEAR, and other CONUS-based organizations. Checkmate staff interviewed American officers previously stationed in Iraq and officials of European companies that had built the command sites for the Saddam regime, and obtained blueprints for key buildings in Baghdad. While many if not most of Iraq's fixed installations and key targets in the KTO were in the DIA databases, that information was not sufficient for mission planning. Other information, including data on mobile targets, was needed in detail, including photographs and precise target coordinates. While much of this information was available, sometimes it was not passed down to the units that needed and expected it. This outcome often resulted in a level of frustration at the air wing level, and junior officers were sometimes encouraged by senior officers to circumvent the system however they could to get the wing commander the information he needed.[79]

Imagery from overhead sensors was also used extensively. The resolution was good enough to allow Glosson's staff in the Black Hole to identify specific points on targets, such as air conditioning ducts, vents, or air shafts on buildings.[80] However, demands for that imagery carried the penalty of competition with other national priorities in the intelligence collection process. This had an impact on the timeliness of the data and the ability of the intelligence collection system to respond to dynamic changes in tactical targeting priorities. For

---

[78]For a description of the Black Hole and intelligence operations from a naval officer's perspective, see Muir (1991), pp. 85–86.

[79]Hoffman (1993), p. 88; HASC (1993), pp. 26–27.

[80]*Triumph Without Victory*, pp. 231–232.

example, the Army G-2 chief in the theater noted the difficulties in using national assets to assist in the target planning cycle.

> A . . . targeting challenge concerned imagery. In January, we had to rely largely on national imagery for targeting. Team Army in the DIA Joint Intelligence Center did a superb job in supporting our targeting efforts, but there were limitations. Without high resolution imagery—and we could not usually get that kind of support from national assets due to competing national requirements—we could not describe the target in detail (e.g., how deeply armor was dug-in, where it was exposed other than the top, whether it was a T-72 or a T-55). We relied on national imagery, because during the first three or so weeks of the air campaign, Iraqi missile air defense posed a threat to theater imagery aircraft, and they could not fly over targets. This delayed destruction of Iraqi air defense, as I understand it, was due because of the bleed-off of sorties from the KTO to the strategic campaign and SCUD hunting.
>
> These limitations on target development—caused by late changes in target priorities and limitations on intelligence collection assets—made our execution in the first period of the air campaign in the KTO less than we had planned. Later, when theater imagery aircraft flew over targets and provided high resolution photography, the air campaign began to take a devastating toll on enemy units.[81]

However, from the air campaign planners' perspective, the above statement is somewhat misleading: Iraqi air-defense targets were included in the strategic campaign, and the IADS had been rendered functionally inoperable early on.[82] Moreover, in the view of CENTAF planners the real bottleneck was an insufficient number of qualified photo interpreters, not tactical assets.

The Defense Nuclear Agency (DNA) provided Checkmate with both munitions effectiveness assessments and vulnerability analyses of Iraqi underground facilities; the latter were in a format easy to use, and arrived in a timely manner, usually within hours, which supported the dynamics of combat attack planning.[83]

Dissemination of tactically-related intelligence information to the air units was accomplished through two systems, Constant Source and Sentinel Byte, over STU-IIIs and other secure communications. Intelligence updates were also transmitted to wings and squadrons directly.[84] Imagery dissemination suffered from an overabundance of systems (more than a dozen) that were incompatible

---

[81]Brigadier General (P) John F. Stewart, Jr., USA, G-2, 3rd U.S. Army, *Operation Desert Storm, The Military Intelligence Story: A View From the G-2 3rd U.S. Army,* April 1991, pp. 18–19. See also Hoffman (1993), pp. 87–88.

[82]Communications to the authors by Lieutenant General Buster Glosson, USAF, and Major Robert Butler, USAF.

[83]*CPGW*, p. 239.

[84]James R. Clapper, Jr., "Desert War: Crucible for Intelligence Systems," in Campen (1992), p. 82.

with one another. This resulted in time delays in the distribution of critical information. Air planners relied on tactical assets in theater for more timely information, and as we described earlier, developed imaginative ways to get around organizational bottlenecks.

BATTLE DAMAGE ASSESSMENT

While overall the intelligence and space system support to Desert Storm can be considered a qualified success, battle damage assessment was much less so—and in fact was considered by many to be the principal intelligence "failure" of the war. Certain aspects of BDA were necessarily out of CENTCOM's control—the poor weather being the prime example that severely impaired the availability of BDA imagery—but other events, procedures, and processes (such as the dynamics of the ATO, the size of the target list, and the numbers of aircraft involved), as well as the lack of adequate systems, stressed the BDA collection, analysis, and dissemination process.

The lack of an integrated BDA concept of operations (CONOP) for CENTCOM was central. This meant that while some exercises were conducted by DIA, CENTCOM had not adequately exercised its BDA element before the war and thus the BDA process was not fully integrated with the attack planning process. BDA was complicated also by General Schwarzkopf's decision to make ARCENT and MARCENT responsible for assessing battle damage in their own sectors, rather than those responsible for carrying out the air campaign. The rationale for this decision was that ARCENT and MARCENT needed to be able to determine if the air attacks had reduced the Iraqi strength to 50 percent, since they would be conducting major attacks once the ground campaign began. But neither command had a clear idea of how to assess tank kills by aircraft, nor did they have a coordinated approach to conducting BDA. Consequently, many sorties were either miscounted, discounted, or ignored. These problems led to a misreading of Iraqi force strength and perhaps unnecessary adjustments in targeting prioritization and sortie allocations.[85]

In addition to difficulties in collecting information, theater BDA suffered from the conservative approach to damage verification taken by stateside intelligence agencies as measured against General Schwarzkopf's damage criterion of 50 percent destruction of enemy forces by U.S. and Coalition air forces before the start of the ground attack.[86] Complicating this inherent conservatism was the distinction between functional and physical damage in BDA and the impact it had on verification of neutralizing or damaging targets. The assessment rules

---

[85]See Lewis (1993), pp. 12–20; HASC (1993), pp. 27–29.

[86]HASC (1993), pp. 30–31; Coyne (1992a), p. 159.

existing at the time required that more than one source had to verify the same *physical* damage. *Functional* damage information, on the other hand, was rarely available. For example, many times during the Gulf War a postattack videotape would show a weapon hitting a target such as a command and control building, but analysts could not determine exactly how much damage had been inflicted because the building would be left standing. It remained for the photo interpreters to assess the extent of damage inside the building, which might in fact have been gutted. This process took time and would not meet the immediate demands of ATO development deadlines. In addition, satellite imagery for BDA was limited by the orbital characteristics of the satellite. Knowing satellite imagery of Iraq was likely being collected, the Iraqis sometimes attempted to simulate bomb damage in the hope of warding off further attacks.[87]

Dissemination of tactical imagery was poor: wing-level planners were forced to rely on cockpit video, pilot reports, and limited organic intelligence and planning capabilities to support the air campaign planning process and to determine the necessity of restrikes, since few national-level intelligence assets were available to collect BDA.[88] While relying on available wing-level intelligence proved adequate for the job, it was not as "clean" a process as many would have preferred.[89] Furthermore, what BDA collection was available often could not be passed because of the lack of adequate communications. All of these problems point to the absence of an overall architecture for tactical imagery, collection, and dissemination and the lack of an integrated concept of operations.

In Chapter Six we saw how battle damage assessment was conducted for air campaign operations. However, there were a number of larger issues relating to BDA that made it a headache for CENTCOM during the war and that typified the problems associated with information management in general and intelligence in particular. These issues can be summarized as a lack of:

- Knowledge about information-related capabilities and how best to exploit them (i.e., theater commanders understanding the capabilities and limitations of sensors and platforms).

---

[87]*CPGW*, p. 239; Friedman (1991), pp. 186–187.

[88]A dissenting view holds that the wings had a pretty good view of what they did and did not know, based on these same pilot reports and other verbally passed information. For example, the 388th TFW maintained a comprehensive database on its kill boxes that was updated twice daily after each mission. There would be a mass crew debriefing in the morning and in the afternoon, which was used to prepare the next mission's crews for what to expect. Furthermore, after conducting many missions over the same targets and areas, crews eventually became familiar with the territory, a familiarity that was not necessarily reflected in the BDA and mission-planning processes. (Conversation with RAND's Fred Frostic.) Finally, the reason national systems were not available to collect BDA was because BDA was never envisioned as a task for overhead systems, at least below a broad national view. (Communication from a senior Air Force officer.)

[89]Communication from a senior Marine officer.

- Understanding of the processes, procedures, and time involved in the collection, analysis, interpretation, and dissemination of BDA information.

- Commonly agreed upon and standardized rules for conducting BDA among the theater commands, services, and intelligence agencies.

- Timely, tactical poststrike target intelligence other than that transmitted by USAF RF-4Cs, Navy F-14s, VTRs on various tactical aircraft, and Army, Navy, and Marine Corps UAVs.[90] The lack of timely poststrike target intelligence continued to be a problem throughout the war and led to a reliance on fighter-mounted VTRs for timely poststrike tactical BDA.

In sum, many of the BDA problems in Desert Storm arose because an integrated concept of operations did not exist.

INFORMATION ACQUISITION AND MANAGEMENT IN PERSPECTIVE

As we discussed at the beginning of this chapter, Desert Storm was the first modern "information war" in that every aspect of military operations depended to some degree on the acquisition, integration, and management of information by many systems operating in various media and at all echelons. While in most cases the "information community" (for lack of a better term) came through with flying colors, existing problems such as competition among agencies back in CONUS and over scarce resources for different operational priorities in theater were magnified. This led to theater command dissatisfaction with the tactical intelligence support provided, and to postwar calls for ways to provide better support to the tactical commander in the future. While many have recognized this problem for a number of years, the space and intelligence communities are only now beginning to address it from an operational perspective.[91]

---

[90]As Friedman (1991) notes, "The Air Force found itself with far too few RF-4s for strike reconnaissance or BDA. Much of this work was done by seventeen Navy F-14 fighters carrying TARPS pods. They covered all of Kuwait as well as Iraqi targets as assigned (the F-14s could range over most of Iraq). These TARPS aircraft were so important that eventually the S-3 flights to Riyadh were valued at least as much for the TARPS images they brought as for the ATO frags they carried away" (p. 186). CENTAF planners whom we interviewed respond: "B.S., the real problem was a shortage of qualified photo interpreters."

[91]As organizations become familiar with and more dependent upon data provided by airborne and space-based systems, this leads to competition for the same data and a need to determine priorities. Generally, that prioritization is done in CONUS, contributing to the perspective of the theater commander that control over his command's own system or satellite is required to ensure the necessary data will be available when required. As defined in traditional space community idiom, "control" is usually not necessary, as controlling a satellite usually means conducting station-keeping exercises, performing health and status checks of the satellite, etc. Thus, the problem is more one of perception and participation, that is, assuring the combatant commander that he will have timely access to data needed to accomplish his military objectives, and increasing his stake in the process by facilitating user participation in the processing of the data.

Desert Storm saw a variety of means employed to get information to the user. In some cases it was downlinked directly, while in others it went through processing stations located in CONUS or elsewhere and then was transmitted to the theater. Problems occurred when national-level assets were tasked to fulfill higher priorities, leaving the tactical commander without critical intelligence on enemy deployments. This exacerbated pressures from theater commands to ensure that their own intelligence staffs had a hand in processing and disseminating imagery.[92]

Many factors played critical roles in the information acquisition and management process for the air campaign:

- The exploitation of advanced technologies—some of which were available in prototype only—to support theater commanders.

- The innovative use of strategically oriented space-based systems in tactical ways.

- The tactical exploitation of imagery from national systems.

However, the evidence suggests a number of problems as well:

- A failure by the intelligence community to agree on an interpretation of the warning indicators emanating from Iraq, including signs of military buildup along the Kuwaiti border and other evidence (fundamentally, a dispute among agencies).

- Inadequate human intelligence—the result of both a policy focus in the region and the growing dependence of the U.S. intelligence community on advanced technology systems to the detriment of building a sufficient intelligence network in theater. Although the United States has had a long history of relations with many Arab nations in the region, its support of Israel has constrained its ability to build intelligence networks in the Arabic-speaking nations.

- An abundance of systems collecting information, which contributed to data overload and to focusing on the use of imagery to the detriment of other available information.

- A plethora of, and competition among, CONUS-based organizations for the control and dissemination of intelligence products.

- Correspondingly, no overall architecture to coordinate the activities of these agencies, and no one in charge that served the CINC.

---

[92]Stewart (1991), p. 30.

- Limitations on target development due to late changes in targeting priorities and limitations on intelligence-collection assets.

- A misinterpretation of intelligence on the extent of Iraqi Scud and NBC capabilities and their operational procedures, which contributed to an overemphasis on Scud hunting at the expense of other targets.

- An underestimation of the effect of advanced technologies such as personal computers, faxes, and STU-IIIs on mission planning, information transfer, and command and control.

- Inadequate planning and exercises before the conflict to determine operational problems in providing space support to theater commanders, and no (or very inadequate) space and intelligence annexes to the OPLANs and other documents that did exist. One result was insufficient numbers of and incompatibilities among receivers for space system data by the different services, mitigated somewhat but not entirely by the luxury of preparation time prior to the onset of the air campaign.

As important as these problems and shortcomings were, and as obvious as they are in retrospect, we are impressed with the demonstrated ability of sensor, communications, and information assessment and processing planners and operators to overcome most of their difficulties and support theater commanders. Their task was not easy. Their ability to improvise, explore new capabilities, and devise workable alternatives to achieve information superiority over their enemy makes their performance one of several important "war winners," in our estimation.

Chapter Nine

LOGISTICS

> The science of planning and carrying out the movement and maintenance of forces.
>
> —*JCS Pub. 1.1,*
> Organizational Functions of the Joint Chiefs of Staff

In Chapter Three we discussed the movement of the Phase I forces to the theater. In this chapter we will round out the earlier discussion on deployments and then describe how the forces deployed in both phases were supported once they arrived in theater. The latter discussion addresses consumables, including ammunition and petroleum, oil, and lubricants (POL), spares, maintenance of deployed systems, intratheater lift that ties them together, and base building. We will address each in turn.

But first we need to put the logistics effort and consumption requirements in perspective. The Gulf War can be viewed as the equivalent of cramming the Korean or Vietnam conflicts into seven months instead of three or eight years. The amounts of U.S. forces deployed were roughly similar in each conflict. Once the forces were engaged, the support of U.S. forces in the Gulf was excellent when assessed by historical standards. One knowledgeable observer states that

> [aircraft] sortie rates in Desert Storm were ten times as high as in World War II, three times that of Korea, and approximately twice that of Vietnam.[1]

We believe that strategic mobility and sustainability were the essential successes of the Gulf War—without detracting from the deserved accolades given to high-tech weapons, the training of our forces, and a greater degree of joint-

---

[1]General Jasper Welch, USAF (ret.), "Lessons of the Gulf War: Linking Technology and Strategy," summary from *Washington Strategy Seminar,* 14 November 1991, p. 3.

224 A League of Airmen: U.S. Air Power in the Gulf War

ness in command and operations. The indispensable ingredient of victory was getting there—quickly and in force—with the capability to support high-tempo operations. The seeds of that victory were planted by the careful planning and programming of defense resources during the 1980s, the prepositioning of equipment and supplies, the support given to and by the Saudis in building up a militarily usable infrastructure, and the attention given to unit training and readiness after the embarrassments of the 1970s and the early 1980s.

Given what we consider the preeminent role of logistics (including the force deployment), it strikes us as remarkable that few of the official or popular monographs on the Gulf War give the subject much attention.[2] Rather, the attention has been on the strike plan—its development and execution, the performance of specific weapon systems, and implications for future force structure. It is our hope that this chapter will stimulate interest in redressing the imbalance in coverage of the air war.

PHASE II DEPLOYMENTS

The Phase I deployments—those that occurred up through early November 1990—were intended to defend Saudi Arabia. After extended discussions among the Saudis, USCINCCENT, and officials in Washington, the President directed an additional force buildup on 8 November. This buildup was intended to provide the capabilities to go over to the offensive with the objectives of liberating Kuwait and destroying Iraq's principal military capabilities. The effect was to nearly double the size of the forces committed to the security of the Gulf. The DoD report describes the effect in understated language.

> Although it is not difficult to understand the November decision to increase the size of the force in terms of personnel, the fact this decision had significant meaning for the sustainment base is not always clear. Essentially, as initial deployments were made, sustainment stocks were introduced into the theater, first through prepositioned ships, and later from CONUS or stocks in forward bases. As the deployment flow slowed, more lift became available to increase sustainment base shipments. . . . When the decision to deploy additional forces was made, the demands for these stocks increased, and they increased the requirement for the transportation system to bring additional amounts into the region.[3]

---

[2]Exceptions are DoD's *CPGW* report, *GWAPS*, CNA's reconstruction of the Gulf War, and some RAND studies. The more popular (and otherwise excellent) histories of the conflict (e.g., Friedman, Hallion, Coyne) scarcely examine logistics other than the force deployment itself.

[3]*CPGW*, p. F-18.

From a logistician's point of view, the support requirements more than doubled: it is one thing to support a force in a defensive posture, it is quite another to provide the wherewithal to go over to the offensive.[4] Defending may or may not require high-tempo operations and the attendant drain on fuels, munitions, and spares. The offensive is premised on high-tempo operations and in moving support forward to fit the scheme of maneuver.

Table 9.1 suggests some of the dimensions of the Phase II buildup from a lift perspective.

SERVICE AND JOINT LOGISTICS SUPPORT CONCEPTS FOR AIR FORCES[5]

Each service has distinctive deployment and sustainment concepts and plans that strive to match its individual capabilities and requirements. Overarching these service-specific plans and concepts are their joint counterparts. Because logistics is primarily a service responsibility, joint support plans and concepts are not as well developed. However, the systems that implement joint plans and concepts have important interfaces with each of the services. For example, inter- and intratheater lift is largely a joint endeavor (even if provided largely by one service). Providing fuels, munitions, ground transportation, and meals is becoming joint in nature. In this chapter we will attempt to show how individual service plans and concepts operated and how they came to rely on joint systems for critical support. We will then go on to discuss important topics that are central to the logistics support of deployed air forces.

Table 9.1

Phasing of Lift for Operation Desert Shield (short tons)

	Airlift	Sealift (dry cargo)	Sealift (POL)	Total
Phase I	182,500	1,170,000	1,800,000	3,152,500
Phase II	304,000	1,675,000	3,500,000	5,479,000
Total	486,500[a]	2,845,000	5,300,000	8,631,500

SOURCE: Rost, Addams, and Nelson (1991), p. 3.

[a]Lund and Berg (1993) cite a 516,582-ton figure.

---

[4]*CPGW*, p. F-19.

[5]The material presented in this section is largely drawn from app. F of *CPGW* and research conducted by RAND and CNA.

The United States Air Force[6]

The USAF concept of operations for the deployment of air combat units is based on the unit's ability to deploy with its own supply, spares, and maintenance personnel for self-sustainment for the first 30 days of operations. This concept requires that munitions, fuel, and consumable personnel-support items be available in theater or transported rapidly to it. According to the DoD Gulf War report:

> A key aspect of this concept is the War Readiness Spares Kit (WRSK) maintained by deployable aircraft units and prepackaged for rapid movement. These kits are stocked with spare parts, common use items, and hardware according to predicted and known failure rates and contain the necessary parts and supplies to repair the unit's aircraft.[7]

This concept requires that a base, perhaps only a "bare base," is available to receive the squadrons (and their support) that fly in, and that the unit and its base can plug into an established logistics support system within 30 days of deployment.[8] Air Force doctrine requires a logistics staff and Logistics Readiness Center in theater to support the deploying units. Such a system was set up by CENTAF in August 1990. Air Force bases were set up throughout the Gulf region. "Harvest" program prepackaged base development kits were deployed and existing bases brought up to USAF standards, while bare bases (in some cases little more than runways and taxiways) were built largely from the ground up.

Setting up adequate supply support to back up the stocks in deploying WRSKs posed a major challenge. As the DoD report on the war points out:

> WRSK replenishment was dependent on getting the combat supply system transaction files back to the unit's computer support base. Original plans called for the deployment of a mainframe computer with tactical shelter systems (TSS). The TSSs, however, were not deployed. Because computer-to-computer links were not available, combat supply transactions were updated at the computer support base by mailing, hand-carrying floppy diskettes, or modem transmission by phone. This was cumbersome and less than satisfactory.[9]

---

[6]For details of Air Force support concepts for maintaining CENTAF's fighters, see an unpublished RAND working paper by Raymond Pyles and Hyman Shulman, "United States Air Force Fighter Support in Operation Desert Storm."

[7]*CPGW*, p. F-6.

[8]A bare base is one that has only runways, taxiways, and parking areas. Everything else must be provided by the deployers. Considerable Air Force matériel was aboard prepositioning ships based at Diego Garcia. Though not tailored for a specific type unit, as in the case of the Marine prepositioned supplies, the concept is similar.

[9]*CPGW*, p. F-7.

The solution was to set up a single CENTAF chief of supply (fully operational on 5 January 1991) at Langley AFB in Virginia with the necessary data being sent from the Gulf to Langley by satellite.

In spite of initial difficulties, USAF support concepts were validated and the systems worked reasonably well.[10] The experience highlighted a truism of air unit deployments: It is not enough to get the aircraft to the theater and to have bare bases (at a minimum) available to receive them; they must be mated with POL and munitions in theater and a supply umbilical that reaches back to major support bases. What is most remarkable about the USAF logistical support successes is that most peacetime deployment exercises and support systems were principally oriented to the support of deploying forces to bases and support structures in Europe and Northeast Asia. Deployments to other regions were less frequently exercised. However, the justifiable pride in this achievement must be tempered with the knowledge that at no time were any service's theater bases or linkages to the United States placed under attack (except occasionally by inaccurate Iraqi Scuds). Moreover, there was time to learn from logistical mistakes before the air campaign started in mid-January 1991.

Marine Air

The Marines base their planning on the expeditionary mission of their forces. Marine deployments are facilitated by the existence of reception bases but do not depend on an existing base structure in theater.[11] The initial Marine Expeditionary Brigades that deployed to the Gulf were provided with 30 days of support in accordance with Marine deployment concepts. Much of this support was located on the maritime prepositioning ships already in theater.[12] The Marines readily acknowledge that they are not structured for sustained operations and must rely on "joint doctrine and service agreements for such support as intratheater transportation, common-item support, and establishment of extensive base areas and theater-level logistics structures."[13] The Marines (and Army forces) were greatly stressed by the deliberate delay in deploying Army logistics support. The reader will recall that in Chapter Three we discussed General Schwarzkopf's decision to give priority to the deployment of

---

[10]*GWAPS* is critical of the Air Force supply system and plans: "... the Air Force supply system envisioned for the theater had to be completely abandoned—its computer system was inadequate, and the designed telecommunications capability never worked properly" (p. 209).

[11]Much of the justification for the AV-8 Harrier (whose limited capabilities are occasionally derided by the other air services) is based on the fact that it does not require extended runways and can be launched and supported by a wide variety of amphibious ships offshore—in the absence of an overseas base structure.

[12]The Army and Air Force also had supplies on prepositioned ships in theater.

[13]*CPGW*, p. F-11.

combat over support elements in August 1990 when Saudi Arabia was under the perceived threat of Iraqi invasion.

Marine aviation support was much enhanced by the use of specially configured aviation logistics support ships deployed early in Desert Shield. These ships, loaded with spares and with operational intermediate-level support facilities installed, provided the vital link between initial deployment spare stocks and connecting with the more extensive support provided by CONUS bases.[14]

Navy Air

Naval logistics support was (and is) based on a three-echelon concept. Deploying ships carry up to 60–90 days of supplies, including spares, with them. They are backed up by combat logistics force (CLF) ships that provide both consumables and spares and replenish battle force ships at sea as necessary. The CLF ships are backed by long-haul logistics ships and joint intertheater support lift as well as joint and service-specific intratheater lift. Carriers and aviation-capable amphibious and logistics ships arrive on station ready to conduct continuous combat operations. Because they are more dependent on slower-moving sealift, naval air units deploy with larger spares stocks than equivalent Air Force units.

Carriers, while endowed with an important "full up" on arrival operational capability, are less suitable for sustained operations than land-based air units because they must periodically go off line to replenish and undergo other maintenance. We will discuss this point as it applied to Desert Storm later in the chapter.

EXPRESS AIRLIFT[15]

While the regular transportation systems could be relied on to get basic supplies in bulk to the theater, special arrangements were needed for expeditious delivery of critical items, principally spare parts. Because of the unusual operating conditions in the Gulf environment, it was not possible to forecast all spare parts requirements with precision. All it takes is one or two unexpected surges in specific spares requirements to ground an entire weapon system. To provide for the special responsiveness needed, USTRANSCOM set up Desert Express.

---

[14]*CPGW*, p. F-66.

[15]This and the next section draw heavily on *CPGW*, pp. F-32/33; interview with General Hansford T. Johnson (CINC USTRANSCOM) in *Sea Power*, August 1992, p. 8; and Coyne (1992a), p. 139.

Desert Express was built around a dedicated C-141 flying daily from the Gulf to Charleston AFB, South Carolina. The system worked as the functional equivalent of commercial overnight delivery systems in the United States. The result was to reduce response times for priority shipments from two weeks to about three days. Similar systems were operated from Rhein Main AB in the Federal Republic of Germany and from Anderson AFB in Guam. Arrangements were made for intratheater lift schedules to mesh with the arrival of the express flights, so that onward routing of critical items was not delayed in theater.

INTRATHEATER AIRLIFT

It is not enough to drop forces and their support off in the theater. After arrival at a major airport of debarkation (APOD), it is necessary to distribute those forces and support to their bases and lines of logistics support. This in-theater distribution had land, sea, and air components. Overall theater logistics support was under the control of the 22nd Army Support Command.[16] Early in Operation Desert Shield, General Schwarzkopf had designated Army Major General Gus Pagonis as the commander of the theater logistics command. Central control was necessary so that service component commands would not be competing for scarce lift and supplies.[17] General Pagonis, representing the CINC directly, acted as the traffic cop and expediter for all logistics matters in theater. Intratheater airlift was one of the key resources in meeting his responsibilities.

The workhorse of intratheater airlift was the C-130. More than 150 of these aircraft were deployed to the theater. Flying from airlift "hubs," they functioned much as feeder airliners do in domestic commercial aviation. They flew cargo and passengers to bases scattered all over the Arabian peninsula. Some of their destination "airports" were sections of highway in northern Arabia near the front-line troops.

Although intratheater airlift is usually associated with the distribution of supplies in theater, during both Desert Shield and Desert Storm it was also used extensively to move forces to more optimal positions. For example, support for

---

[16]Early in the Desert Shield buildup (18 August), General Schwarzkopf established ARCENT SUPCOM (Provisional) with the three tasks of acting as host nation coordinator, overseeing logistics and supply for the theater at large, and supporting the Army component of USCENTCOM. For a description of the development of this SUPCOM (later 22nd SUPCOM), see Pagonis and Cruickshank (1992), pp. 97–99.

[17]General Michael J. Dugan, USAF (ret.), observes that this rationale for central control in the face of scarcity parallels the rationale for a JFACC to coordinate or control theater air forces.

F-16 squadrons was moved from southern and central Saudi air bases to bases near Dhahran. Some of those movements were completed literally overnight.[18]

The Navy system of intratheater airlift connected with both the MAC long-haul lift channels and with Air Force intratheater channels.[19] Red Sea battle groups were supported by combat logistics force (CLF) "hub" ships with air links to Hurgadha airhead in Egypt and Jiddah, Saudi Arabia. Hurgadha was for all practical purposes a "bare base" insofar as Navy support was concerned. Arabian Sea and Persian Gulf battle groups were supported by logistics hub ships connected to airheads in Bahrain and Fujayrah (UAE). The links from the airheads to the hub ships were in the form of carrier onboard delivery (COD/VOD) aircraft. These aircraft were used at approximately triple the programmed peacetime rate. For Persian Gulf units, Bahrain was the connector to the MAC channel from Norfolk. Fujayrah was the connector to the MAC channel from Cubi Point. The Navy maintained its own air logistics channel between Bahrain and Fujayrah.

The effect of this combined Air Force and Navy lift was the expeditious delivery of high-priority parts for Navy aircraft. CNA data show the time needed to replenish carrier parts stocks from CONUS stocks ranged from five to seven days.

FUELS

One of the most widespread misconceptions of the Gulf War is that because it was fought in a region with most of the world's oil reserves, the availability of fuels was not a problem. The truth was otherwise. Crude oil, even when available in large amounts, must be processed into usable products. In the case of aircraft, the oil must be refined into several grades of jet fuel. Three different grades of jet fuel were used in the Gulf. After the fuel is refined, it must be moved in the requisite quantities to the point where it is needed. Then it must be stored at the site where it is to be pumped into aircraft. During the Gulf War, major difficulties arose at each step of this fuel chain.

The DoD Gulf War report states:

> Host nation contributions were a major factor in the fuels operation's success. All ground fuels, and most jet fuel, except for JP-5 and jet fuel, thermally stable (JPTS), were provided from in the theater.[20]

---

[18]Amy D. Marchand, "Logistics Heroes," *Air Force Magazine*, December 1992, p. 73.

[19]This discussion of Navy intratheater airlift is taken from research directed by CNA's Ronald Nickel.

[20]*CPGW*, p. F-16.

However, large quantities of JP-5 and JPTS had to be lifted into the theater because there was little refining capacity in the Gulf suitable for its production.[21] Table 9.1 suggests that, on a tonnage basis, this lift requirement was greater than all other lift requirements combined. The largest single component of this lift was aviation fuel. Once this fuel was in the theater, it had to be distributed overland.[22] This was accomplished by host nation transport (mainly trucks and pipelines) and controlled by the theater SUPCOM. In some cases, this ground transportation was just barely sufficient, and tactical pipelines and air transportation were used to make up the shortfall.[23] Finally, provision had to be made for fuel servicing of aircraft at the many airfields used. While some of these airfields were fully developed, others consisted of little more than runways and minimal structural improvements. At the developed facilities, commercial airport contractors or host nation military support personnel provided refueling services from existing facilities. At less-developed sites, tank farms and local dispensing systems had to be set up.[24] In many cases, the existing tank farms were not adequate for the high usage rates (driven in part by high sortie rates) of Desert Storm.

Fueling support was greatly simplified by the "single fuel concept" for some forces. This concept

> involves the ability of land-based air and ground forces to operate with a single, common fuel [and] was successfully used by several USAF, USMC, and Army units.[25]

But fueling (particularly airborne tanker) support for Navy aircraft was a problem.

> Although JP-5 is the preferred Navy aviation fuel, it was not practical to designate part of the tanker force to carry JP-5 only to support the Navy, because of the lead time to refuel tankers, the vast numbers of refueling requirements, and the need for mission tasking flexibility. JET A-1, the primary jet fuel available in the theater, provided by Saudi Arabia, was dispensed to the Navy most of the time. JET A-1 is the same basic fuel as the military fuel JP-8. The difference is

---

[21]At one extreme, Friedman (1991) states that "Saudi Arabia had no jet fuel refining capacity of its own. Fuel had to be brought by tanker from Singapore (liquids were by far the largest item in CENTCOM logistics)" (p. 91). At the other extreme, *GWAPS* stated that "except for some specialized jet fuels, Saudi Arabia, Oman, and the United Arab Emirates contributed all the fuel for land, sea, and air operations."

[22]Fuel for Naval forces (including carriers) was transferred from long-haul ("consol") tankers, directly into Navy oilers, and thence to the combatant ships through replenishment at sea (RAS) methods.

[23]*CPGW*, pp. F-16, F-17.

[24]*CPGW*, pp. F-16, F-53.

[25]*CPGW*, p. F-17.

that additives for anti-ice, antistatic, and corrosion have been added to JET A-1 to make JP-8. The flash point for JP-8 is 100 degrees Fahrenheit; the Navy requires a 140 degree F flash point for carrier safety and JP-5 meets that requirement. The reason JP-5 is not the US forces standard fuel is its availability and cost; only two percent of a barrel of crude oil can be refined into JP-5.[26]

MUNITIONS

Unfortunately, most weapons usage data is classified.[27] Therefore, the description of aerial munitions support that follows is necessarily general. All services were bedeviled by inadequate definition of munitions requirements. When combined with long lead times in shipment, major problems can and did develop. To remedy shortages that occurred, both the Navy and the Air Force transferred selected aerial munitions to Marine units in the Gulf, and the Navy transferred some of its stock of Mk-80 series bombs to the Air Force.

Air Force

The key munitions problem was one of geography and tonnage. The 69,000 tons of munitions dropped by USAF aircraft during Desert Storm would have required 2,500 C-141 sorties just to deliver it to theater.[28] Clearly, the munitions could not be moved by air.[29] Slower, higher-volume, sealift modes were required for movements from CONUS to theater, and ground transportation was needed in theater.

Prior to the Desert Shield deployment, some munitions were already prepositioned in depots at Thumrait, Masirah, and Seeb in Oman, Diego Garcia, and elsewhere in the region. In addition, other munitions were stored aboard three maritime prepositioning ships. These facilities and ships contained mostly general-purpose bombs and older-model cluster bombs. Munitions that had been stocked at Incirlik AB in Turkey were available to JTF Proven Force.

---

[26]*CPGW*, p. F-30.

[27]This discussion and the analysis of USAF experience in Desert Storm that follows are drawn almost verbatim from an unpublished RAND working paper by John R. Folkeson.

[28]A C-141B can carry up to 41 tons of cargo. Allowing for 30 percent dunnage (packing and tiedown materials to prevent load shifting during flight), it could carry 28 tons of munitions. But we note that C-141s were usually limited to 20 tons of cargo during the Gulf War deployment because of structural problems.

[29]Some exceptions were made. The highest-volume exceptions were the critical initial munitions moved from CONUS to the theater during the very first few days of Desert Shield. Some one-of-a-kind weapons, like the bomb to penetrate deep bunkers, were also moved by air. Relatively lightweight munitions components (fuses, fins, etc.) were also moved on occasion to meet critical needs.

At the outset of Desert Shield, those prepositioned munitions were dispatched to the initial bed-down bases. Some munitions were also airlifted from CONUS to supplement the prepositioned material. Over time, the additional munitions were sealifted to the port of Jiddah, placed on ground transport there, and delivered to the theater USAF bases to prepare for Desert Storm.

Redeployments, Tactics, and Target Allocation Changes Drove Intratheater Munitions Support Efforts

The *Gulf War Air Power Survey* notes that prepositioned munitions accounted for close to 50 percent of the tonnage dropped during the war.[30] By and large, the USAF had satisfactory levels of munitions and munitions components in the theater. They were sometimes in the wrong place, though. On occasion, unplanned tactics changes caused flurries in demands for some munitions components. For example, the B-52s deployed to the theater in the opening days of the battle with ample Mk-117 bombs, but those bombs had retard tail fins to facilitate safe low-altitude bomb drops. The unit required a special airlift of tail cones so it could convert the bombs to a "slick" configuration that could be dropped accurately from high altitude. In this case, the special support need was due not only to the movement, but to a change in tactics for bomb delivery—from low altitude to high altitude, in light of the potentially dense anti-aircraft and SAM environment over Iraq and Kuwait.

Changes in basing also required munitions movements. For example, after initial attacks had diminished Iraq's threat to the Coalition's air bases, A-10s and F-16s began to operate from forward operating locations, at which munitions had not been prepositioned (to maintain security of plans for such wartime operations).

In one case, the inability to transport bombs early in the war actually dictated the aircraft basing. Because JTF Proven Force was approved just as hostilities commenced, there was no time to disperse the munitions from the storage facilities at Incirlik AB, Turkey, to support air operations from several regional bare bases. As a result, the task force's fighter, special operations, ECM, and other aircraft with nine different MDSs remained concentrated at Incirlik.

Target changes also caused surges in munitions movements. For example, the F-111F had been envisioned as attacking mostly aircraft shelters and other hardened targets with 2,000-lb laser-guided bombs (LGBs). In early February the "tank plinking" concept was demonstrated with the 500-lb LGBs. While seekers were available in quantity at the F-111F base, 500-lb bomb bodies were

---

[30]*GWAPS*, p. 213.

not. Once the basic concept was demonstrated to be effective, the F-111Fs were tasked to attack tanks, and substantial quantities of 500-lb bomb bodies had to be transferred quickly between bases in theater.

The munitions movements required to support reallocation depended on ample surface cargo movement capacity, and excellent ports and transportation (oriented mostly north and south) infrastructure. All those capabilities were available on the Gulf peninsula. Excellent airports and seaports, road structures, and navigable waterways eased the transportation of the large quantities of munitions required for Desert Storm. Without that infrastructure, it would have been difficult to deliver adequate munitions to the theater, let alone redistribute them as the campaign objectives and tactics evolved.

Navy

Naval forces arrived in theater with adequate munitions on board or on the CLF ships. The Navy problem was in getting sufficient quantities of *preferred* munitions to the carriers that needed them. The shortages of some types of laser bomb guidance kits were particularly acute, although there is some evidence this was a problem of distribution (i.e., getting munitions to the right place), not inventory.

Marine Corps

The 3rd Marine Air Wing suffered significant air ordnance shortages—particularly in Mk-20 and Mk-80 series bombs. The problem was, in part, one shared with the Navy: imprecise definition of weapons requirements. Navy requirements models are used to determine Navy and Marine global requirements, not unit requirements in a particular conflict.[31] Another difficulty occurs when the Marine "fair share" of a fleet CINC's ordnance stockpile must be computed.[32] The result of these problems was that during Desert Storm, Marine air units ran short of gravity bombs. The Marines did not run out of bombs, but had an extended ground campaign occurred, stocks of bombs would have been depleted.[33]

Marine air did not have the Navy's advantage of having munitions stocks afloat in the combat logistics force. Its only afloat stocks were those that were

---

[31]Munitions loadouts for Marine assault and assault follow on echelon ships were based on historical expenditure rates.

[32]The Navy programs, buys, and maintains wholesale stocks of Marine aviation ordnance.

[33]*CPGW* (p. F-21) states that MARCENT "did not achieve a satisfactory storage level of air munitions until early February [1991]."

offloaded from the maritime prepositioning ships early in Desert Shield. Thereafter, the Marines were heavily dependent on sealifted stocks arriving from the United States.

SORTIE AND IN-COMMISSION RATES

If the end product of air operations is weapons on target, an important intermediate product is sortie rates of fully mission-capable aircraft. While, as we have seen, weapons on target (as measured by bomb damage assessment) is often difficult to assess, sortie rates and the mission-capable status of aircraft flying the sorties do lend themselves to quantification and some precision.

The key inputs to sortie and in-commission rates are the availability of fuel, weapons, maintenance equipment, spare parts, and trained ground crews. We have dealt already with fuel and munitions. Here we focus on the other factors.

All the services use a three-level aircraft maintenance concept:

- **Unit-level** maintenance: basic servicing such as fueling, arming, and minor repairs and adjustments.

- **Intermediate-level** maintenance: removal, replacement, and repair of major aircraft components.

- **Depot-level** maintenance: industrial repair and refurbishment processes.

In the Gulf War, each squadron deployed with its own unit-level capability, and higher echelons (typically at the wing or group level) provided the necessary intermediate-level maintenance capability. Depot-level maintenance was conducted outside the theater. The CENTAF logistics officer implemented an innovative change to the usual intermediate maintenance repair process. Coordinating with USAFE logistics in Europe, the latter set up "Queen Bee" intermediate maintenance facilities in Europe to take the load off USAF engine repair maintenance crews in theater. This farming out of maintenance to support outside the theater not only reduced in-theater personnel requirements (and associated support), it ensured that the maintenance was conducted at long-established and necessarily more efficient facilities.[34]

Complementing the push of higher-level maintenance to rear areas outside the theater was the setting up of austere forward operating locations to complement existing bases (also a Marine practice). Thus, forward bases were set up at al-Jouf, King Khalid City, and King Fahd International Airport to generate more

---

[34]Marchand (1992), p. 73; *CPGW*, p. F-22. The *CPGW* (p. F-23) states that U.S. Navy facilities in Europe provided similar support for Marine aircraft.

sorties. Instead of returning to their home base after a strike, aircraft would land at forward bases, refuel, rearm, and return to combat. At the end of their "combat day" or when needing maintenance, the aircraft would return to their normal operating bases.

Much of the everyday work in maintenance involves the replacement of components (e.g., electronic black boxes, weapons launchers, engines, hydraulic pumps). The repair of the removed components was either done by intermediate maintenance activities in the field, or on the parent carrier, or by depot and intermediate-level facilities elsewhere.[35] It is here that spare components and parts enter the process. Because many removed components require depot maintenance, spares are needed to fill in.

Air Force units deployed with War Readiness Spares Kits (WRSK) adequate for support of 30 days of operations. The Marines had similar support. Carriers deployed with 60 or more days of spares support. The objective, subsequently, was to fill up the spares pipeline to provide up to 30 days of support in the theater at projected operational tempo levels. The supply of these spares was one of the great (and insufficiently heralded) success stories of air power employment during the Gulf War. This success stemmed from the procurement of adequate spares before the war and the development of storage, accounting, and shipping systems to insure they arrived where they were needed on time. Sortie and in-commission rates rarely achieved in peacetime were attained because the parts were available along with sufficient trained ground personnel to remove, install, and test them. The statistics in Table 9.2 summarize the story.[36]

Alongside the important successes were some failures in the logistics systems. Two were particularly aggravating and experienced by all services. First, there was a major shipping labeling problem. Much of the support was shipped in cargo containers. In most cases those containers had to be opened to ascertain all of their contents. This resulted in shipping delays and many wasted man-hours. Air cargo encountered similar problems. A second failure that could have been serious if the war had lasted longer was the delay in retrograde of defective matériel to the repair depot. Repairing components is a closed cycle, and the defective "carcasses" are a critical input to depots and essential to the output of serviceable spares.

---

[35]Two aviation maintenance ships (TAVBs) were deployed during the war to provide intermediate-level maintenance support for Marine aircraft. Some elements of this capability were offloaded to support fixed-wing aircraft, while intermediate support for helicopters was retained on board. (*CPGW*, p. F-66.)

[36]Care should be exercised in using the figures in Table 9.2. Our intent is to show that all services exceeded their peacetime mission-capable rate targets, not that one service did better or worse than the others. By any measure, these numbers represent an impressive achievement.

Table 9.2

Mission-Capable Rates by Service
(based on averaged daily snapshot data)

	Gulf War	Peacetime Average
Air Force[a]	92%	85%
Navy[b]	90%	85%
Marine Corps[c]	90%	85%

[a]Weighted equally across fighter types. SOURCE: United States Air Force (1991), p. 35.

[b]Limited to aircraft on carriers. SOURCES: United States Navy (1991), p. E-2; CNA data.

[c]Based on aircraft ashore. SOURCE: United States Navy (1991), p. E-2.

BASE BUILDING

Although the base infrastructure in the Gulf region was one of the best in the world for the basing of expeditionary air forces, it was not sufficiently developed in quantity and quality to support the large land-based air forces that would stage into the theater.[37] Coyne cites building the air base at al-Kharj:

> More than 120 AFLC [Air Force Logistics Command] civil engineers, in addition to erecting tents and dining halls, literally helped to build cities in the desert to house thousands of Air Force people coming into the combat zone. To accommodate a new fighter wing at Al Kharj, for example, they helped local engineering people build roads, construct water and sewage facilities, install generators, and string electric lines for a base population of more than 5,000 people.[38]

Most base-building problems centered on providing for personnel support and storage for consumables. Although much of this support was provided by Army logistics commands, Air Force and Marine logisticians performed superbly in establishing and supporting their forces—maintaining good troop morale and providing them the supplies needed to win. Both services proved themselves masters of base building as a component of expeditionary warfare.[39]

---

[37]This discussion focuses on Air Force and Marine air base building. Base building was largely a "nonproblem" for carrier-based air. However, naval air forces did depend on linkages to Navy shore-based airheads and their linkages to the MAC channels that carried high-priority Navy cargo and passengers. Moreover, the Navy did have some shore-based logistics support facilities (and support barges moored close to shore) for warehousing and transferring cargo coming into the theater by sealift. This situation raises two points: carrier air forces are much less (probably an order of magnitude) dependent on in-theater shore facilities than land-based air, but they are not totally independent of shore support if they are to conduct sustained high-tempo operations.

[38]Coyne (1992a), p. 133.

[39]A more detailed description of service base-building efforts is set out in the *CPGW*, pp. F-67, F-68.

LOGISTICS SUPPORT IN PERSPECTIVE[40]

Logistics support of Desert Storm and Desert Shield was a success because it is one of the things the U.S. military does very well *when there is adequate funding support,* as was provided over the decade of the 1980s. Contributing to this success was the fact that there was a small though modern logistics support structure already in place in the Gulf host countries. Some support problems could be solved on the spot (e.g., fuel) or could be ameliorated by capabilities in the host country infrastructure (e.g., transportation, port facilities). Other needed capabilities were readily available in the U.S. resource base. Since many of these capabilities were closely akin to those resident in the U.S. private sector (e.g., construction, transportation), there was scarcely a missed beat in gearing up to support the forces in theater. Fortunately, in this case, there was enough time to work on the kinks before combat operations started.

Although we cannot know what the next war will be like, we have been struck by some emerging implications of the Desert Storm experience. They appeared in more than one Desert Storm situation, and they raised questions about how one might best prepare for future wartime support. We identified four implications: (1) the logistics concept of operations; (2) supporting a downsized force; (3) a tradeoff between transportation, repair, and spares; and (4) a heavy dependence on host nation infrastructure.

Logistics Concept of Operations

First, Desert Storm forcefully reminded us of the inherent unpredictability of wartime demands for logistics support. No matter what we thought we knew about what to expect in the Desert Storm data, it turned out different—explainable after the fact, but different than we predicted.

Six broad sets of factors—changing tactics, new technologies, changing campaign plans and missions, changing performance criteria or tolerances, changing demand processes, and unexpected support constraints—drive those demand variations.

Worse than the statistical variations considered by spares and maintenance requirements models, these factors' uncertainties defy putting names, much less numbers, to them. For example, who knows what new tactic or technology may emerge in the next war? Without even that information, how should the logistician forecast what resources might be needed for support?

---

[40]This discussion is drawn almost verbatim from Pyles and Shulman, op. cit.

We conclude that logisticians cannot rely solely on predicting. Rather, we would emphasize relying more heavily on a wartime concept of operations that provides for enhanced mutual support, transportation, and logistics command and control. This concept of operations would provide a framework for continually adjusting the support process rapidly to match constantly changing operators' needs. As seen in Desert Storm, improved logistics command and control and transportation were the centerpieces of a responsive support system that reallocated aircraft components, whole munitions rounds, and munitions components in response to unplanned operators' needs. Without such command and control, aircraft availability would have been lower, aircraft vulnerability to SAMs would have been higher, night-attack accuracy would have been limited, and mission reassignments across aircraft types would have been constrained.

Supporting a Downsized Wartime Force

The support problem will probably become more complicated for the downsized air forces being conceived and implemented in the post–Desert Storm era. The services will continue to strive to maintain the highest possible technological edge over potential enemies. If fewer forces are maintained, the relative rate of technological innovation will probably not slacken.

Even if fewer new aircraft are introduced, the number of different types and capabilities needed in modern warfare will remain large. The demands of modern warfare are too varied to be met by just one kind of weapon system.

If the force is smaller but retains the same number of aircraft types, there will be fewer of each in the fleet. Then, more of the force in some future contingency will face the support difficulties faced by those aircraft fleets whose aircraft were almost completely deployed in wartime. If more aircraft mission design series have smaller fleet sizes, they will not be able to count so heavily on the nondeployed units' support in future contingencies. Without that large pool of readily available, nondeployed stock, it will be difficult to achieve the high levels of aircraft availability achieved in Desert Storm.

Transportation, Repair, and Spares Tradeoffs

With the emerging capabilities demonstrated by Desert Express, rearward repair, and the Air Force's Combat Supplies Support Activity (CSSA), it may be possible to develop a support system that can compensate for the smaller aircraft type force sizes. In particular, a support system built more directly on the "just-in-time" principles of improved visibility, limited stock, and rapid production and transportation may improve wartime responsiveness to unplanned demands. As a side benefit, it may be less expensive to operate in peacetime as well.

Infrastructure of Host Nation

Finally, we have emphasized how much the well-developed infrastructure of the Arabian peninsula contributed to the land-based air services' ability to prosecute the war. Without the excellent airports and seaports, the extensive air base network, a commercial trucking industry, and an extensive telephone system, the buildup (especially of munitions) would have been much slower, the continuing support would have been less robust, and the logistics constraints would have been more severe. Furthermore, those resources were not threatened seriously by the enemy in Desert Storm.

Many locations in the world do not have such a robust infrastructure. In such regions, one would find it exceedingly difficult to mount a Desert Storm–scale operation with fighter aircraft.

As important, it would be folly to assume that all future contingencies will enjoy the relatively low level of counterattack seen in Desert Storm. While the Scud attacks were intended to achieve mainly political ends in this contingency, future weapons may be more effective, and future enemies' war plans may be better conceived. Even if the enemy does not attack the air bases, attacks against larger, critical rearward logistics facilities could have a telling effect on the air forces' effectiveness.[41]

If attack aircraft are to play a critical role in more austere future contingencies, new support methods or air-delivered weapons must be developed. The current dependence on extensive, uninterdicted lines of communication to deliver large volumes of fuel and munitions to meet the forces' consumption rates could be the Achilles' heel of future fighter forces, especially in regions where the initial logistics infrastructure is limited.

Of course, improved weapons technology might overcome such a limitation. If more reliable, more accurate, more weather-insensitive weapons were available, fewer sorties would be required to eliminate the targets of interest. Then the force would depend less on moving and managing a vast volume of both fuel and general-purpose bombs. Until then, the force depends critically on airports, seaports, and fuel pipelines.

---

[41] Indeed, this interdiction campaign was a key element of the successful air campaign against Iraq's ground army—to shut off resupply and reinforcements and communications for over a month.

Chapter Ten

AIR COMBAT SYSTEM PERFORMANCE

Well, we did not build those bombers to carry crushed rose petals.
—*General Thomas S. Power*

As we have seen in the last chapter, U.S. air combat systems were superbly supported during the Gulf War. Reliability and spare parts support finally caught up to manufacturers' brochures and spare parts inventory targets. But looking beyond in-commission rates, sortie rates, and mean time between failures (MTBF), how effective were air combat systems in performing their missions? It is not enough to get a fully armed and systems-capable aircraft airborne. The right targets must be found, the aircraft must be placed in a position to hit the targets, the targets must be hit, the hits must achieve damage expectations, and the results must be fed back to planners and commanders in a timely manner.

In this book we have made no attempt to conduct the detailed analysis necessary to make the related assessments. Rather, we have attempted to sift through the observations of airmen, planners, commanders, and analysts to draw some general conclusions on system performance. For example, Tomahawk performance has been variously portrayed as having a 90–95 percent mission-capable rate. Yet when one looks more closely, the number of hits per missile fired, while still very high compared to most systems, falls short of that high number. This should in no way be considered a criticism of the Tomahawk weapon system. We can use Tomahawk as an example because the Navy has conducted very careful and detailed studies to determine its combat performance. Most other systems on closer examination have had similar discrep-

---

Most of this system performance assessment is drawn from app. T of *CPGW*, Coyne, (1992a) and numerous RAND working papers. Appendix T of *CPGW* describes system performance, but each system assessment is clearly written by an officer of the owner service. As a result, system successes receive more visibility than the shortcomings. In some cases, the authors seem more intent on making a case for a new system than on describing the operation of the system used in the Gulf.

ancies between the hype contained in initial press reports and the facts of performance as determined by careful analysis. Part of the confusion lies in the measures of performance used and in pressures to rush to judgment before the analysis is complete. The press is not very helpful in this endeavor, as it attempts to obtain instant answers to hardware performance questions, to suspect cover-up if the information is not quickly forthcoming, and to have that suspicion "confirmed" if the early figures are revised when more information is available. The reputations of the Patriot and Tomahawk systems have suffered from having to back off from early glowing performance reports. The F-117A system's performance was impugned by some who charged that it benefited from the protective electronic warfare environment that resulted from support of nearby strikes by nonstealthy aircraft. Some have observed, uncharitably, that all aircraft are stealthy when the enemy is deprived of his radar—conveniently putting aside the fact that some system has to take out the radars.

In examining the performance of individual systems, we emphasize a point made earlier in this book (Chapters Two and Seven) that many if not most of the air systems used were not "new" except to the uninformed. With a few well-publicized exceptions, such as the E-8 JSTARS aircraft, the systems had been in the operating forces for five years or more. In some cases, they had been in the force for over 25 years. Table 10.1 portrays the period from system initial operational capability (IOC) to the start of the Gulf War in early 1991. The fact of the matter is that the Gulf air war was fought for the most part with air systems that were thoroughly "shaken down," serviced by ground personnel who had extended experience with them, supplied by a logistics system that had a full pipeline based on years of parts usage data and adequate buys of spares, and flown by aircrews who had grown up with the airplanes.[1]

How then can we explain the widely held perception of a "revolution" in air warfare technology? Even the widely praised—and then debunked—Patriot system was eight years old.[2] A few new systems—the F-117A, the Tomahawk, and the E-8 JSTARS—garnered disproportionate attention as the press and the public focused on what was novel rather than what comprised most of the force inventory. Precision-guided munitions were "in" and "dumb bombs" were "out." It is our intent in this chapter to look behind the hype and a myopic focus on high-tech to assess what systems performed particularly well and carried the load and identify those that performed less well—or whose publicity outran the facts.

---

[1]One apocryphal story holds that some airmen in the Gulf flew or serviced the same systems that their fathers had a generation earlier.

[2]The hopes for Patriot's success in the anti-TBM role were based on modifications and upgrades to this veteran air-defense system.

Table 10.1

Initial Operational Capability (IOC)

System	IOC[a]	Years in Service as of 1/1/91
A-6 Intruder	1965	25
A-10 Thunderbolt	1976	14
AV-8 Harrier	1984	6
B-52 Stratofortress	1959	31
E-2C Hawkeye	1973	17
E-3 AWACS	1977	13
EA-6B Prowler	1971	19
F-4G Wild Weasel	1978	12
F-14 Tomcat	1972	20
F-15C Eagle	1979	11
F-15E Strike Eagle	1989	1
F-16C Fighting Falcon	1984	6
F-111 Aardvark	1967	23
F-117A Nighthawk	1985	5
F/A-18 Hornet	1983	9
E-8 JSTARS	1997	−7[b]
KC-135 Stratotanker	1957	33
S-3B Viking	1974	16
BGM-109C Tomahawk	1986	4
AGM-86C ALCM	1988	2
A-7E Corsair II	1967	23
Average	1976	14

[a]This is the IOC of the first mission design series aircraft. In most cases, there were later versions. However, most airframe and powerplant and many weapon system design elements were frozen in the initial design.

[b]JSTARS was estimated to be seven years from its IOC in 1990.

Before proceeding to examine individual systems, however, one new dimension to the battlefield that was truly revolutionary should be mentioned: namely, the "force multiplier" effect generated by exploitation of information technologies in an integrated fashion. By this phrase we mean all the various technologies that allowed commanders to see and control the battlefield rapidly, collecting, processing, and fusing enormous amounts of data from a variety of sensors and then transmitting that data in an operationally useful manner. Even personal computers, secure telephone communications, and facsimile machines (very important for imagery transmission) had considerable leverage in air campaign planning and execution, more than their simple numbers-deployed or levels of technology would suggest.

Much of the potential of these new capabilities was not fully realized during the war, as the problems with BDA, ATO transmission, and other instances discussed in Chapter Eight and elsewhere illustrate. Nevertheless, information systems and technologies such as the JSTARS, introduced into the theater while still in development, were crucial to achieving information superiority over the Iraqis and Coalition objectives for the war.

MEASURING AIRCRAFT SYSTEM PERFORMANCE

Aircraft system performance is normally measured using these criteria:[3]

- **Full mission capable (FMC) rates.** This rate measures the percentage of the time that *all* mission systems are in an operational status. It is an extremely demanding criterion, and achieving a 70 percent rate in peacetime for a complex modern weapon system is a major achievement.

- **Mission capable (MC) rates.** This rate measures the percentage of the time that the system can support *at least one* of several aircraft missions. Some aircrews call this bare-bones criterion "wings and engines." Very high MC rates (and those most advertised during and after the Gulf War) were achieved during the conflict.

- **Sortie rates.** This rate measures the number of sorties per day per airframe. For fighter-attack aircraft in combat, this rate is usually between 1 and 1.5 per day over extended periods.

These rates are used liberally in the *CPGW* report and in service testimonials to their own performance during the war. The careful reader will note the more frequent use of MC than FMC rates. As any aircraft maintenance officer would observe, there is a "world of hurt between MC and FMC." Broken and difficult-to-repair-or-replace electronic systems make up most of the difference.[4] Maintenance and supply officers, because they are judged by FMC and MC rates, can (legally) arrange matters to make the numbers look better than they are—particularly when the spotlight of publicity is on their performance. They can move bad parts to a down aircraft ("the hangar queen") and free up good parts for otherwise flyable aircraft—at the cost of extra maintenance person-hours. They can take heroic measures to ensure that an aircraft is in FMC and MC status during any nonflying periods (FMC and MC are often measured throughout the 24-hour day).[5]

---

[3]We do not discuss here "mean time between failures" (MTBF), which usually applies to system components and not the complete aircraft. Low mean time between failures adversely affects the MC and FMC rates to be discussed below. As such, it is an important intermediate measure.

[4]One of the remarkable logistics facts of the war was the air services' success in narrrowing the gap between FMC and MC rates. For the Navy this gap varied from 2 percent to 3 percent.

[5]Pyles and Shulman, op. cit., describe these and other efforts to "meet the schedule" (of flight operations).

There is one more caveat to be kept in mind as one examines MC and FMC data across aircraft types, services, and logistics studies. MC and FMC data can be based on time snapshots (e.g., 1 a.m. daily) or time averaged (the percentage of the time in a 24-hour day that a system is MC or FMC). The latter measurement is more stringent (and better reflects aircraft maintenance and supply performance). But the former may be of more use to operators who are scheduling aircraft for the next day's flight operations. In Table 10.2, we use both measures because of the asymmetric availability of data across services. Accordingly, comparisons across aircraft type or service in the table can be misleading.

The data suggest to us that the services achieved uniformly very high sortie and FMC/MC rates, and that to say one service or aircraft type did better than another is to run the risk of misusing the data for partisan purposes. The data in general do support the logical conclusion that the older systems (e.g., F-111E, A-6) were more difficult to maintain than the newer systems (e.g., F/A-18 and F-16). But there are exceptions in the case of relatively new and complex systems (the F-117 had comparatively lower availability) and relatively old and simple systems (the A-7 and A-10 had high readiness rates).

Table 10.2 presents data that are potentially controversial, in part for the above-cited reasons and in part because one runs the risk of unwarranted selectivity in the presentation. For example, sortie counts can be tailored to exempt or include certain categories to spotlight particular performance attributes. RAND-developed sortie data indicate that 117,131 sorties were scheduled for CENTAF, Proven Force, Navy, Marine, and allied aircraft during the period of Operation Desert Storm. This figure includes some that are not strike or combat sorties narrowly defined (e.g., tactical airlift, aerial refueling). Of these scheduled sorties, 112,235 were actually flown. Of this number flown, 72,158 were for offensive and defensive counterair, suppression of enemy air defense (SEAD), close air support (CAS), interdiction, tactical reconnaissance, electronic combat, forward air control (FAC), and search and rescue (SAR) missions. It is a subset (e.g., allied system performance data are unavailable) of this smaller number that is the focus of the sortie data in Table 10.2.

The sortie rates shown in the table warrant some additional explanation. Some aircraft flew fewer but much longer sorties, in part because they were tanked.[6] Others, because of the vagaries of base location, had little transit time and could be "turned" (around) quickly at their home or forward base. Some aircraft were

---

[6]The duration of the average USAF sortie flown during the war was considerably longer than specified in prewar planning. (Marchand (1992), p. 73.)

Table 10.2

Selected Aircraft Operational and Logistics Data

Component	Aircraft	Sorties Flown[a]	Sortie Rate	FMC	MC
CENTAF[b]	A-10	7,835	1.43	85	88
	B-52	1,624			
	F-4G	2,287	1.08	78	78
	F-15C	4,480	1.14	83	84
	F-15E	2,137	1.07	88	88
	F-16C	10,938	1.22	87	88
	F-111F	2,411	1.43	85	87
	F-117	1,297	0.76	73	78
	EF-111	882	1.11	77	80
Proven Force[b]	F-4G	414	0.74	68	70
	F-15C	890	1.08	71	74
	F-16C	1,677	1.09	83	85
	F-111E	449	0.58	69	71
	EF-111	251	0.81	65	69
NAVCENT[c]	A-6	2,969	1.00	82	
	A-7	797	1.20	95	
	EA-6	1,327	1.00	88	
	F-14	4,128	1.00	82	
	S-3 (strike)	167			
	F/A-18	3,574	1.20	91	
MARCENT[c]	A-6	790			
	AV-8	3,086			
	EA-6	502			
	F/A-18	4,320			
	3rd MAW average[d]			80+	70

[a]NAVCENT sorties are sorties tasked. Sortie data includes OCA, SEAD, CAS, interdiction, DCA, escort.

[b]CENTAF and Proven Force FMC/MC data are *time averaged* and are taken from RAND (Pyles and Shulman). Sortie data are taken from the unpublished working paper by Parker and Emerson of RAND. Sortie *rate* data are from the unpublished working paper by Pyles and Shulman of RAND. Parallel sortie data are taken from Parker and Emerson.

[c]NAVCENT FMC/MC data are from snapshot averages provided by CNA reconstruction analysis. MARCENT sortie data are from RAND (Parker and Emerson) and are for sorties flown. NAVCENT sortie data are also from Parker and Emerson and contain tasked sorties, not flown sorties. Flown sortie data are not available for this format.

[d]Averages from MARCENT after action report briefing.

NOTE: No information was available for empty cells in the table (or is classified).

relatively simple and carried lesser quantities of (and less sophisticated) ordnance and were more quickly armed.[7]

---

[7]For an explanation of the Navy's experience in the Gulf War in trading off sorties for flights of longer duration, see "Kelso Pans Other Services for Their Use of Navy Strike Sortie Statistics," *Aerospace Daily*, February 2, 1993, p. 181.

These differences in data and performance are all understandable, but they require the observer who wants a fundamental understanding of system performance to look behind the figures that are usually cited. Maintenance and supply personnel performed magnificently during the war (as we have outlined in Chapter Nine), and the numbers do them credit, even when one takes into account the pitfalls inherent in the scorekeeping rules.

RAND's Fred Frostic reminds us that the effectiveness of aircraft for air-to-surface missions in Desert Storm was more a function of the weapons they carried (e.g., PGMs of various types) and the characteristics of the avionics and sensors that aided target acquisition and employment than of other aircraft characteristics. This point is important because Iraqi air defenses were neutralized quickly, and survivability, which generally depends on aircraft flight performance, was not the problem that it has been in past wars. Stealth fighters are a special case because they fundamentally changed the parameters of aircraft and weapons employment.

F-117A NIGHTHAWK

This "fighter" (really a strike or attack aircraft) started with a black mark against it as a result of some adverse publicity that arose from its performance (and alleged discrepancies between publicized and actual performance) in the Just Cause operation in Panama in December 1989. However, in Desert Storm, the F-117A was the preferred delivery vehicle for hitting well-defended Iraqi targets, particularly those in and near Baghdad. Since it was mated with laser-guided bombs (GBU-10, 16, 24/27), it performed with deadly precision.

> Over the course of the war, the deployed F-117s flew approximately two percent of the total attack sorties, yet struck about 40 percent of the strategic targets attacked. It was the only aircraft to attack targets in downtown Baghdad and to hit targets in all 12 categories.... No F-117s were lost or damaged.[8]

As good as it was, the F-117 had some important performance limitations that received less attention from the press:

- It had only two bomb stations.

- It was withheld from daytime strikes because of its vulnerability to optically guided ground systems and Iraqi fighters using "eyeball" target acquisition.

---

[8]*CPGW*, p. T-74. United States Air Force (1991, p. 3) notes that it represented only 2.5 percent of the shooters in the theater on the first day, but that it hit 31 percent of the targets. The F-117A enjoyed an 80 percent hit rate for bombs dropped and a 60 percent rate for sorties launched (including aborts). (*Defense Week*, May 10, 1993, p. 19.)

- It was not effective during periods of, or in areas of, poor visibility that restricted use of its laser guidance system.[9]

- It was supported by a slow and tedious mission planning system.[10]

Given the parameters of F-117 employment and the availability of complementary systems (e.g., the Tomahawk), these shortcomings had little adverse effect on the air campaign. The F-117 was one of the few systems whose performance deserved the appellations of "new," "high-tech," and "revolutionary" so lavishly applied to Desert Storm hardware in general. However, it is not clear that substantially more were needed for the Desert Storm air campaign. What made them irreplaceable was their combination of stealth and capability to use laser-guided ordnance. As we have seen in earlier chapters, a shortage of laser-guidance platforms was an important force deficiency.

TOMAHAWK SEA-LAUNCHED CRUISE MISSILE

The Tomahawk system was the F-117A's logical junior partner.[11] It flew at night, during the day, and in bad weather. While not stealthy, because of its size and flight profile, few were shot down. And, naturally, there were no associated aircrew losses. The hit probability for Tomahawk was less than touted by earlier reports based on incomplete data (90 percent or higher was estimated). But the probability was substantially above 50 percent and remarkable by almost any weapons performance standard.[12] The Tomahawk (like the F-117) did not require AWACS, fighter, or electronic jamming support.[13] But unlike the F-117, it did not need tanking support. Provided that a TLAM mission package (software) was available, it could be used against time-urgent targets.

---

[9]During the strikes against Iraqi targets in January 1993, F-117 performance was limited when employed against targets obscured by cloud cover. It shared this weakness with other LGB platforms. (David A. Fulghum, "Pentagon Criticizes Air Strike on Iraq," *Aviation Week & Space Technology*, January 25, 1993, p. 47.)

[10]*CPGW*, p. T-75.

[11]Naval officers interviewed take exception to our according a lesser role to Tomahawk than to the F-117A.

[12]Weapons performance data are tricky and are sometimes used carelessly or otherwise open to misinterpretation. For example, *CPGW* (p. T-201) states that 282 of 288 Tomahawks were launched successfully during ODS. Those numbers do not reflect missiles that were unable to perform the flight profile after a successful launch, were shot down by the Iraqis, or just missed the target. Moreover, by some measures, it is not enough to hit the target—the missile must hit a specific part of the target to be effective. In the January 1993 (two years after Desert Storm) Tomahawk strikes against the Zaafaraniyah nuclear facility, an 82 percent "success rate" was reported for the 45 missiles launched. (David A. Fulghum, "Clashes with Iraq Continue After Week of Heavy Air Strikes," *Aviation Week & Space Technology*, January 25, 1993, pp. 38, 42.)

[13]But note that the F-117A "squawked" its "radar signal generators" when outbound from the target to help the AWACS control aircraft provide for separation from other friendly aircraft. (*U.S. News and World Report*, p. 218.)

The Tomahawk's shortcomings included:

- Limited warhead size (1,000-lb unitary warhead in the TLAM-C and 166 combined-effect bomblets in TLAM-D).

- While more accurate than most munitions, it did not yet have the precision of laser-guided bombs that could be directed to a specific window or airshaft, for example; it could hit part of a building, but not a specific window or duct.

- Considerable time and preplanning were required to prepare the mission packages that defined the route and profile of each missile. As an expedient in some cases, missiles were given the same route and profile, making follow-on missiles more vulnerable to ground fire.

Overall, Tomahawk was one of the major technology success stories of Desert Storm. A contemporary of the F-117, it was its natural partner and should give pause to those who see unnecessary redundancy in systems that perform what appears to be the same mission.

THE F-111 AARDVARK

This aircraft was truly a veteran—not only of warfare, but of the procurement battles of Washington. Born in the 1960s as the Tactical Fighter–Experimental (TFX) of Robert McNamara's whiz kids—a fighter for all seasons and services— it grew into a heavy fighter-bomber that saw service (in different forms) in the Strategic Air Command, as a long-range conventional bomber, and as an electronic warfare platform. It flew the longest fighter-bomber profile in the history of warfare when F-111s based in the UK flew to Libya and back during the El Dorado Canyon strikes of April 1986.

The F-111F's principal tools were its Pave Tack FLIR (forward-looking infrared system) and laser designator capability, its large bomb-carrying capacity, and its long range. During the Gulf War, F-111s flew from Incirlik, Turkey and al-Taif, Saudi Arabia. The F-111F was one of four preferred night-attack systems (the others were the F-117, F-15E, and A-6E) and performed well against Iraqi airfields and shelters, command and control facilities, and a variety of infrastructure and field targets. Its most publicized role was in "tank plinking," already described in Chapters Six and Seven. As important as this role was, it was more a case of tactical innovation than of destroying large numbers of Iraqi tanks. Other systems hit Iraqi tanks without the attendant publicity.

The F-111 proved to be a sturdy and reliable system during the war, and flew some 3,000 combat sorties without a single battle loss and with only one aircraft incurring battle damage.[14] Its limitations centered on its aging systems that required a proportionately greater degree of maintenance and supply support than other aircraft types.

F-15E STRIKE EAGLE

Compared to the 84 F-111s (60 F models and 24 E models) employed in the Gulf War, there were only 48 F-15E Strike Eagles. Based at al-Kharj in Saudi Arabia, these aircraft performed many of the same missions given to the F-111 fleet. With a combat radius similar to the F-111, the aircraft had just become fully operational on the eve of the Gulf War. Equipped with LANTIRN (including targeting) pods, they flew most of their missions (some 2,200) at night. Just as much of the F-111 fleet was making probably its final bow, the F-15E was making its combat debut and provided badly needed capabilities in going after Scud launchers at night and in supplementing the F-111s in attacking a large number of infrastructure and fielded force targets. It, too, conducted nighttime tank plinking along with the F-111s. The F-15E was the darling of both airmen and strike planners for its flexibility and high performance in many dimensions (e.g., speed, range, systems).[15] Several Gulf airmen have stated to the authors that they would have traded off A-10 and F-16 (mostly day-strike) aircraft for more F-15Es. The authors have been unable to ascertain any limitations on its performance—except that more could have been used to good effect, and that additional LANTIRN pods were needed to fully equip the fleet.[16]

A-10 THUNDERBOLT

One hundred forty-four A-10 and OA-10 aircraft were deployed to King Fahd air base in Saudi Arabia for Operation Desert Storm. They arrived in the theater early in the Desert Shield deployment during a period when an Iraqi invasion of Saudi Arabia was a real enough threat.

---

[14]*CPGW*, p. T-70.

[15]In the January 1993 strikes against Iraqi air defense systems, the F-15E was again the star, enjoying a higher hit rate than F-117, F-16, F/A-18, and A-6E aircraft. (Fulghum (1993a), pp. 38, 47.)

[16]No LANTIRN targeting pods were available in theater on 17 January 1990. Twelve were available for F-15Es by 23 January and all were put on Scud alert aircraft. Six more targeting pods were to become available later in the conflict, and these were used for the tank plinking operations described earlier.

The Air Force appears to have a love-hate relationship with this aircraft.[17] Its limitations seem to receive more exposure from Air Force officers than from the officers of the other services and the press. The knocks against the A-10 are that it cannot defend itself against other aircraft, that it has little night capability, that to use its weapons it must subject itself to ground fire, and that its 30mm cannon is dramatic but overrated for its utility and effectiveness. Some Air Force planners have told the authors that A-10s were either not needed in the Gulf War or were moved into the theater too soon. In short, many observers believe that A-10s were not the preferred system for the initial deployments and air campaign.

These knocks probably have their origin in the fact that the A-10 is currently the Air Force's principal close air support aircraft, and that mission is not particularly popular in the Air Force. Moreover, in recent years, the Air Force has pressed hard for a replacement aircraft that was in fact more a tactical fighter than a specialized ground attack aircraft.[18] What is remarkable about criticism of the A-10 is that the system fired some 4,800 Maverick missiles (90 percent of those fired during the war) and that those missiles, along with laser-guided bombs, were the preeminent air-launched antitank weapons. If one believes, as General Schwarzkopf did, that the destruction of enemy tanks was the key to the neutralization of the Iraqi army, it is apparent that criticism of the A-10's performance in the Gulf War has its basis more in Air Force and hardware acquisition preferences than in support of the CINC's objectives.[19]

As we have seen in earlier chapters, the character and duration of the ground campaign was such that little close air support was flown. Only 1,000 of the some 8,000 A-10 sorties flown were tasked for CAS missions. The remainder involved using the aircraft in roles such as interdiction, suppression of enemy air defenses, and Scud hunting. Three A-10 aircraft were lost in combat and 15 were damaged. All but one in the latter category were repaired and returned to combat. When aircraft losses are correlated with sorties flown, it is apparent

---

[17]Hallion (1992), pp. 210–211, provides one of the more balanced assessments we have seen of A-10 shortcomings and successes during the Gulf War.

[18]One can detect the relevant arguments for such aircraft in the Air Force's criticism (*CPGW*, p. T-10) of the A-10 in its Gulf War role:

> The A-10 is susceptible to threats due to the longer exposure time caused by insufficient engine thrust which limits rate of climb, acceleration and maneuver, and cruising speed. . . . The A-10's night attack capability is limited to the use of the Maverick seeker or flares. Neither is viable without a mid- to high-level sanctuary.

It is notable that the A-10 is the only aircraft to receive such a level of criticism in *CPGW*.

[19]Some observers point out that the A-10's good record was based on the fact that it had a Maverick capability, not that it was the best craft for the job. They assert that an F-16 with a Maverick was a better platform. We would respond that this is a "might-have-been." The fact is Maverick-suitable A-10s *were there* and used to good effect (as were a lesser number of Maverick-equipped F-16s).

that the loss experience of the A-10 was better than that of the F-15E and about the same as the F-16.

F-16 FIGHTING FALCON

The F-16 was the most numerous strike aircraft in theater. Some 250 were located at five bases.[20] The F-16 is a multirole aircraft. During Desert Storm, it was most used in ground-attack missions.[21] One squadron of F-16 aircraft was equipped with LANTIRN navigation pods, but because of the limited numbers available none was equipped with LANTIRN targeting pods.[22] Accordingly, the F-16 was the Air Force's principal fighter-bomber user of "dumb bombs." Its role in employing the Maverick missile was small compared to the A-10, although its accuracy was just as high. The principal utility of the F-16 was its flexibility to fly a wide variety of missions and its large numbers. It constituted the Air Force's contribution to the mass of the air attack that was so effective against Iraqi troops in the field.

Some have questioned whether General Horner needed as many F-16s as he was provided.[23] Because they were largely based in UAE initially, they were at some remove from the target set and required extensive tanking. It is difficult to say much about the F-16s' role except that they were always there and in great numbers. In some ways, they performed as a "free safety" in spite of their limitations in conducting night and all-weather strike missions.

F-14 TOMCAT

The Gulf air war was not a Tomcat war.[24] There were 100 in theater spread over five carriers. For a variety of reasons, their performance was overshadowed by the Air Force F-15C fleet. Until late in the war, carrier operating areas were further away from targets than the F-15Cs based at Tabuk, al-Kharj, and Dhahran. Accordingly, F-14s, particularly those flying from Red Sea carriers,

---

[20]The next most numerous were the 170 Navy and Marine F/A-18s, to be described shortly.

[21]F-16s in the Gulf War had no air-to-air kills against Iraq's aircraft. This is a testimonial to the accomplishments of covering CAP provided by other Coalition fighters, rather than a criticism of the F-16. During the January 1993 strikes against Iraqi targets, USAF F-16s claimed two AMRAAM kills against Iraqi aircraft. (Fulghum (1993a), p. 38.)

[22]The USAF eventually had 18 LANTIRN targeting pods in the Gulf, and they were dedicated to the F-15E Strike Eagle squadrons. Hallion (1992), p. 212, points out that only 72 of the 250 F-16s in the Gulf had LANTIRN navigation pods.

[23]This observation has been made by Air Force officers as well as congressional staffers. Note that two squadrons of the National Guard F-16s were deployed to the Gulf during the conflict.

[24]See Eric Rosenberg, "Navy Pilots Help To Do More with Less Money," *Defense Week*, September 16, 1991, p. 1, for a balanced assessment of F-14 performance during the Gulf War.

required a great deal of refueling even though they were among the longer-legged fighter aircraft in the theater. As the air threat was rapidly neutralized and as carriers moved up the Gulf, the number of F-14 escorts for Navy strike packages was reduced.

Aside from its refueling needs, the most damaging limitation of the F-14 fleet was that while it did have an onboard IFF interrogator, it did not have a non-cooperative target recognition system (NCTR).[25] Because of the large number of aircraft airborne at any one time and the attendant danger of fratricide, a criterion for assignment to some important CAP stations was dual phenomenology (IFF and NCTR or visual) for identification of targets. Simply put, the F-14 didn't have state-of-the-art means for differentiating friendly aircraft from hostile and could not by itself take beyond-visual-range (BVR) shots. The Air Force F-15C, tailored for a wide range of air battle scenarios, had the necessary dual capability that the F-14 did not.[26] The F-14 had been optimized for the outer air battle in the maritime environment and could shoot at greater distances with its long-range Phoenix missiles than it could identify what it was shooting at. Thus, the F-14's interceptor capabilities did not fit the Gulf War overland flight environment, and it occupied a lesser role than its Air Force counterpart and those filled by other aircraft in the Navy's carrier air wings.

More useful was the F-14's intelligence-gathering capabilities in its TARPS system. One F-14 squadron in each carrier air wing was TARPS-capable and, along with Air Force RF-4Cs, provided sorely needed fast-reaction tactical reconnaissance capabilities. The F-14s flew over 4,000 sorties for over 14,000 flight hours, more than any other Navy fixed-wing aircraft.

A-6E INTRUDER

This aircraft was flown by Navy and Marine pilots in theater. There were 115 A-6s deployed in the Gulf War scattered among six carriers and the Marine base at Shaikh Isa. They were of the same vintage as the F-111 and had similar capabilities (though the F-111 was much faster). The A-6 has a ground mapping radar, a forward-looking infrared system, and a self-contained laser designator. The A-6 and its electronic partner the EA-6B were the most important (and the

---

[25]F-14 pilots complained that prewar funding priorities deprived them of needed special IFF and NCTR systems and rudimentary bombing capabilities. These complaints are an analog of USAF aircrew complaints about the small number of LANTIRN pods available to them.

[26]Some naval officers believe the rules of engagement that required dual phenomenology were constructed by the Air Force–dominated JFACC staff to ensure preferential (i.e., greater opportunity for air-to-air combat) CAP station assignment to Air Force units. We have found no evidence to support that allegation, although COMNAVCENT did attempt to get the rules of engagement changed to alleviate the restrictions on assignment of Navy fighters to the more desirable CAP stations. (Winnefeld and Johnson, p. 115, and discussions with naval officers on battle group staffs.)

most vulnerable) Navy and Marine aircraft employed in Desert Storm. They brought to the fight the all-important all-weather and laser designator capabilities that were lacking in most of the Coalition fighter inventory.

A-6s were used mostly at night and attacked a wide variety of targets, including Iraqi infrastructure and ground forces. They also performed well in the tank plinking role. They played a key role in defense suppression with their HARM missiles and decoy (TALD) deliveries.[27] About one-third of all strikes required radar-directed deliveries because weather, smoke, or haze prevented FLIR use.

A-6s flew more than 3,700 sorties during Desert Storm, but lost five aircraft to hostile fire. This was the highest loss rate of any U.S. aircraft type and resulted from its slow speed, high cross section, and initial low-altitude delivery tactics. The A-6 was beginning to show its age and did not have the speed enjoyed by its F-111 and F-15E Air Force counterparts.

F/A-18 HORNET

This airplane was the Navy/Marine counterpart of the F-16 (170 in theater compared to 250 F-16s). They were based on five carriers and at Shaikh Isa. Their mission employment paralleled that of their Air Force counterpart. Most of their air-to-ground missions employed iron bombs (Mk-83, Mk-84) or HARM.

The F-16 and F/A-18 are similar in their capabilities. Their differences arise principally in the ordnance and special avionics they carry and the fact that the F-18 has two engines and the F-16 has one. For the air superiority mission their performance is comparable. The F/A-18 has a somewhat better air-to-air radar and during the war carried the AIM-7 (Sparrow) radar-guided missile in addition to the AIM-9M (Sidewinder) infrared-guided missile. In the air-to-surface role, the F/A-18 has slightly longer range and can carry a larger payload. This advantage is reduced when operating from carriers because of the large recovery fuel requirements. The F/A-18 can carry a FLIR pod, and the F-16 carries LANTIRN for night operations and target acquisition. Both can shoot HARM, but not in the range-known mode.

Two-seater F-18Ds made their operational debut during the Gulf War and performed particularly well in the "Fast-FAC" role in guiding strikes to targets in

---

[27]The USAF F-4G Wild Weasels were the only aircraft in that service to fire HARM missiles. A variety of Navy aircraft fired HARM, including the A-6E, EA-6, and F/A-18. Figures comparing SEAD aircraft across services can be misleading. The Air Force had the most dedicated SEAD aircraft: 62 F-4Gs and 18 EF-111s as against the Navy/Marine 35 EA-6Bs. However, the Navy and Marines had over 100 aircraft (other than EA-6Bs) that launched HARM.

designated kill boxes. While on strike missions, two F-18s shot down two Iraqi fighter aircraft.

F-4G WILD WEASEL

The F-4G "Wild Weasel" was the principal USAF SAM-suppression platform used during the Gulf War. It has the best avionics package for lethal defense suppressions. Its closest Navy counterpart was the EA-6B. Both contained missile radar detection systems and the necessary equipment to launch anti-radiation missiles at a wide variety of radars. However, the F-4G, unlike the Navy and Marine aircraft, can determine emitter ranges and thus achieve a higher hit probability. Fifty F-4Gs were based at Bahrain and twelve at Incirlik, Turkey. Most performed direct support missions; that is, they accompanied specific strike packages and launched HARM missiles as necessary to neutralize air defense and SAM fire-control radars.

The F-4G is not a jammer, as are the EA-6 and EF-111. It "duels" with opposing air-defense systems rather than preemptively neutralizing them. Because its airframe and engine technology are obsolescent, it is not fuel-efficient and requires considerable maintenance support.[28] In spite of these shortcomings, the Weasels did a good job in flying over 2,700 sorties while losing only one aircraft. However, all assessments of SEAD performance must be viewed in the context of the scarcity of objective and quantifiable success indicators.

The Air Force practice of using two aircraft in SEAD duties—an EF-111 jammer and an F-4G missile shooter—is probably less efficient than the Navy's single-package EA-6B system. However, it should be noted that Navy SEAD doctrine calls for supplemental HARM shooters (e.g., F/A-18s) to lay down a preemptive strike on potential SAM systems. Air Force SEAD doctrine calls for a more discriminating use of HARM against specific radar emitters at known ranges. The F-4G and EF-111 enjoy a considerable speed advantage over their Navy counterpart and are more suitable for deep strike missions, particularly in cases where enemy air opposition is likely.

B-52 STRATOFORTRESS

The B-52, like the Wild Weasel, is a veteran of the Vietnam War. Its missions were flown from bases in the UK, Diego Garcia, and, in the case of the ALCM

---

[28]On one occasion, five of six Weasels launched on a strike support mission had to return to base because of mechanical difficulties. The urgency of the deployment to their base in Turkey had resulted in the delay of the arrival of their support crews. (*Triumph Without Victory*, p. 254.) This episode supports the point made in Chapter Three that flying even fully armed aircraft into an overseas base does not make them necessarily fully operational.

strikes on the first night, from bases in the United States. It is no stranger to such extended-range bombing missions, having flown them during the Vietnam War from bases in Guam and from CONUS during pre–Gulf War exercises in the Middle East. Ultimately, 68 B-52Gs were employed in Operation Desert Storm. They attacked a wide variety of targets in both Kuwait and Iraq, ranging from chemical and nuclear sites to entrenched Iraqi ground forces. After the fourth day of operations, all B-52 attacks were conducted at high altitudes.[29]

The DoD report on the war summarizes the system's shortcomings:

- Lack of available bases in the theater caused three of the four bomber wings to fly 14- to 16-hour missions routinely and thus limited combat sortie rates.

- The B-52's lack of a precision-guided munitions capability limited target selection to large area targets.

- The B-52's lack of stealth attributes required large force-protection packages to escort or support its attacks against defended targets.[30]

In addition to these shortcomings, there are questions about the accuracy of high-altitude bombing by the B-52 force. Battle damage assessment of strikes against Iraqi ground units suggests the existence of systemic bombing errors.[31] The full contribution of the B-52 force will probably never be known with precision because of its use in area bombing to break the morale of Iraqi front-line ground units. Interviews with Iraqi POWs suggests that the contribution was significant in forcing Iraqi troops to abandon their weapons and look for ways to surrender.[32]

AV-8B HARRIER

The role of the AV-8B, operated by the Marines in the Gulf War, was a curious one. Intended as a short-range CAS platform, it was (like the A-10) used in a war that had little requirement for CAS and more for longer-duration interdiction and deep strike sorties on targets beyond the FSCL. AV-8 sorties were not allocated and tasked by the JFACC, although for coordination and deconfliction purposes they were covered by the ATO. The short range of the AV-8 was not a

---

[29]CPGW, p. T-26.

[30]CPGW, p. T-27.

[31]Hallion (1992), p. 218.

[32]"B-52s Were Only Marginally Successful in Gulf War, Gen. Butler Says," *Aerospace Daily*, January 28, 1993, p. 155.

major disadvantage since they were operated from an expeditionary airfield close to the Kuwaiti border. They did not require tanking during the war. A few were operated from amphibious ships in the northern Gulf.

The AV-8 was employed mostly in daylight operations using a variety of gravity bombs. The AV-8B's shortcomings were based on a lack of suitable munitions more than airframe/engine/system problems. Eighty-six AV-8s were in the theater during Desert Storm, 60 at King Abdul Aziz airfield, and 26 aboard amphibious ships. Advance basing was at Tanajib, 42 miles from the Kuwaiti border.

EF-111 RAVEN

The EF-111 is another veteran that provided excellent service in the Gulf War. Its only previous combat operations had been in Operation El Dorado Canyon in 1986. A 1992 JCS roles and missions report required by the Congress sums up its role as follows:

> [T]he EF-111 is a deep-penetrating, high-speed, long-loiter airframe with all-weather terrain-following capability that is designed for "stand-off" jamming.[33]

In view of the overall shortage of electronic warfare (EW) assets during the Gulf War, these jammer aircraft provided a vitally needed service in spite of their obsolescence and lack of a HARM missile firing capability.

S-3B VIKING

Although designed as an antisubmarine aircraft, the S-3B Viking has become the Navy's jack-of-all-trades. It was used in the Gulf War as a tanker and a strike support aircraft (EW, C^2, and armed reconnaissance missions) as well as in its customary antisubmarine warfare and maritime surveillance roles. On several occasions it was used in a strike role against Iraqi naval targets. In its tanker role, it supplemented A-6 organic tankers and provided in effect an additional refueling point to augment Air Force tankers.[34] Its performance in the Gulf War is perhaps the best example of Navy air wing flexibility.

---

[33]Chairman of the Joint Chiefs of Staff, *Report on the Roles, Missions, and Functions of the Armed Forces of the United States,* February 1993, p. III-28.

[34]The single-point refueling configuration of USAF tankers proved a limitation when large numbers of strike aircraft had to be refueled in a short time. By refueling from large tankers during periods when they were not servicing strike aircraft, the S-3 was, in effect, a hose multiplier. (*CPGW*, p. T-111.)

Chapter Eleven

AIR POWER PERFORMANCE IN THE GULF WAR

> When you are winning a war, almost everything that happens can be claimed to be right and wise.
>
> —*Winston Churchill*

The contribution of air power to the outcome of the Gulf War has been both over- and undersold. Because the Coalition won, there is an opportunity for any institution, special interest, or hardware advocate to claim that they, their product, or their idea provided the "war winner." Because of the central role it occupied in planning and conducting the air campaign, the Air Force is open to the charge that it is drawing too many comfortable conclusions from a unique conflict. Others, whose systems and doctrines played an important though lesser role, have been perhaps too shrill in pointing out the "unique" attributes of the Gulf War. When the strident claims and disclaimers are put aside, the Gulf War remains a test of the performance of air power. By "test" we mean that the bounding conditions were known and controllable, that objectives were specified beforehand, that most variables were under the control of the Coalition once the war began, and that most of the results could be measured against objectives. We will examine this construct in Chapter Twelve when we assess the *role* of air power in the conflict. In this chapter, we turn our attention to the *constituent elements of air power* and assess their performance. We are interested in what was done well and where improvements are needed. We are also interested in what elements of air power performed particularly well under the circumstances of the Gulf deployment and combat operations.

A REVISIONIST VIEW

The conventional wisdom is that the air campaign was decisive because:

- There was an integrated air strategy and plan closely tied to objectives and system capabilities, all based on sound doctrine.[1]

- This strategy employed "decisive mass" and was unencumbered by excessive political direction.

- High-tech weapons (e.g., the stealthy F-117A, the Tomahawk) were available in adequate numbers, and they worked.

- The men and women operating and maintaining these systems were true professionals—well-trained, dedicated, and ready to fight.

- The air weapon was wielded by a single commander.[2]

While acknowledging the major contribution of each of these factors to the Coalition victory, we find the conventional wisdom somewhat glib and incomplete. Air power has performed well even when most of these conditions were not met. Our quarrel with the emphasis and completeness of the conventional wisdom raises the question of what really was the air war winner. Our answer is in three parts. The first is *mobility*—both strategic and operational—in getting air power quickly and in strength to a theater halfway round the world. Once in the theater, that power could strike effectively at long range, and Saddam was powerless to counterattack. Put simply, air power was the first fully usable power on the scene. The Air Force motto of "Global reach, global power" applied to all the air services in this case. The new Navy motto "From the sea" could be amended to "From the sea and the air."

The second part, which receives pro forma nods from the conventional wisdom, is that unglamorous handmaiden of victory, *logistics*. It is not enough to deploy power quickly, reaching globally and powerfully; it must be sustainable after it arrives. Even with the benefit of a robust Saudi (and other GCC) base and support structure in place, the ability of air logisticians to establish a massive support structure on short notice warrants our admiration. The high aircraft sortie and in-commission rates achieved by all services for such a large force over an extended period and over great distances was absolutely unique in the history of warfare. During World War II, Korea, and Vietnam, more time was needed to put the logistics structures in place, and they did not perform as effectively and as efficiently as in the Gulf War.

The final major contribution to the Gulf War victory was the *acquisition and management of information* by and in support of U.S. forces in the theater. While there were major problems—BDA stands out—most of the essential sys-

---

[1]Owens (1992), p. 53.
[2]Record (1993), p. 45.

tem components needed were either available or substitutes could be "jury-rigged." It was the availability of these components and their use by bright and innovative people, rather than in-place full-up systems, that saved the day and provided the Coalition the command and control, logistics, and mobility edge that would decide the conflict.

Without taking away from the glamour and contribution of the planners, operators, and aircrews, our war winner accolades go to the mobility forces of all services (airlift, sealift, aerial tankers, prepositioning managers and operators), to the logisticians who made the systems combat-capable and sustainable, and to information management personnel who provided the underpinnings of the entire war effort. It is an irony—an appropriate irony—of the war that U.S. logistics and other support personnel suffered as many combat and operational accident deaths during the conflict as did the combat forces.[3] It is rare in war that the contribution to victory and the price paid in lives are so commensurate.

FORCE APPLICATION

Putting aside the preeminent role of mobility, logistics, and information management in making the victory possible, what made the operational side work? More to the point, what operational capabilities were most crucial to success? And what common element did these important operational capabilities share?

Rather than try to rank-order these capabilities, we will discuss them in random order. First, we would emphasize the capability to place ordnance precisely on target anywhere in the theater, under any weather conditions, day or night, and against an active enemy. Thus, we believe that the F-117A was the critical weapon early in the conflict. By an accident of the DoD weapons acquisition system, this stealth "fighter" was complemented by the all-weather and day-time capabilities of the Tomahawk cruise missile system.[4] As the air war continued, the laser- and IR-guided weapons of all services provided the most important contribution. But as vital as they are, we do not believe precision-guided weapons can completely replace the mass usually provided by large numbers of "dumb" weapons. We are convinced that there is an important place for weight and continuity of effort separate from precision weapons delivery. Indeed, the *mass* and *variety* of weapons at the Coalition's disposal helped

---

[3]During Desert Shield and Desert Storm, 121 Americans died in combat and 184 in "nonhostile" incidents. Some of the former and most of the latter were support personnel.

[4]Some DoD critics would call this complementarity "overlap" because they hit the same classes of targets. Worse still, many of these critics and some system advocates would see the F-117A and Tomahawk as *competitors,* not *different* skill players on the same team. Unfortunately, Hallion (1992), pp. 250–251, casts his arguments in favor of both systems in such a way as to showcase the comparative advantage of the F-117A.

ensure that the "right" weapons were available when needed. This is not an argument against precision weapons delivery. Rather, it is to assert that there is a role (whether by design or accident) for mass in blanketing imprecisely located area targets.[5] A smart weapon requires an enemy who gives away a precise location (to the weapon or its launch platform). Based on interviews of Iraqi prisoners, it is reasonably clear that it was the weight of the Coalition air effort as much as its precision that broke troop morale in front-line Iraqi units.

It is important also to note that the use of precision-guided munitions changed the nature of "strategic bombing" in this war. In World War II, thousands upon thousands of tons of bombs were dropped on strategic targets, with much less effect than a comparative handful of "smart bombs" achieved in the Gulf. Precision weapons, particularly those delivered by the F-117A and Tomahawk, permitted the Coalition to accomplish strategic attack objectives with relatively few assets, thus facilitating the application of the mass of Coalition air forces against targets in the field.

More importantly, the wholesale destruction of cities and populations was avoided. The success of the Coalition in avoiding collateral damage and casualties was remarkable. Baghdad was not destroyed in a firestorm; to the contrary, it retained much of its day-to-day appearance and activity even during the war. "What struck me most," one observer commented, "was how little damage allied air raids had actually caused to civilian areas, relative to the amount of bombs said to have been dropped. Especially in Baghdad, the bombing was eerily precise."[6] Most basic services were restored within weeks or months of the war's end. In humanitarian terms, this is a significant change in the nature of warfare. However, it is important to note that until the restoration of electricity, water, and other basic services, deaths and illnesses from malnutrition and disease were estimated to increase significantly over expected peacetime levels.[7] Some of this human suffering resulted not from the bombing campaign, however, but from the ongoing maritime and air embargo.

A second essential operational capability does not lie in the quality of the plans and C^3 systems either before or during the conflict. Rather, it was the ability to put together on the fly an air planning and control system from a number of disparate components and make their totality work effectively. This is not an

---

[5]Lewis (1993) goes further and says "infantry battalion targets were not suitable for Coalition air. Target identification and destruction were nearly impossible, because troops were in trenches and widely dispersed." He makes this observation in the context of disagreeing with some Army component target nominations.

[6]Joost Hiltermann, a Dutch sociologist quoted in Record (1993), p. 112.

[7]Ibid., p. 113. See the Harvard Study Team Report, *Public Health in Iraq after the Gulf War,* Cambridge, Massachusetts: Harvard University School of Public Health, May 1991.

argument against plans; it is a suggestion that a capability to plan under unforeseen circumstances is more important than the quality of plans on the shelf.[8]

This ability to innovate and improvise was made possible by a large number of often simple systems (e.g., fax machines, STU-III encrypted voice equipment) and occasionally complex systems (e.g., integrating use of commercial communications links with military communications plans). In spite of the utility of prewar exercises, and we are among their strongest proponents, the fact of the matter is that there was little common experience in the various C^3I structures that were assembled from scratch during the Gulf War. They worked, not just because of prewar plans and exercises, but because of the existence of a variegated set of system components that intelligent people could put together quickly in Tinkertoy fashion to meet the needs of the moment. Examples include the use of space-based sensors in cueing Patriot missile batteries to incoming Scuds, the use of JSTARS to detect possible Scud launchers, and the entire air planning system from the master attack plan through the ATO to control of forces already in the air. Fortunately, the Coalition had the necessary "make ready" time to put systems together on the fly before the start of combat operations.

THE JFACC: A STEP ON THE LONG ROAD TO JOINTNESS

Much, perhaps too much, has been made of the contribution of the Goldwater-Nichols Reform Act of 1986 in contributing to the war's outcome.[9] While we acknowledge the importance of that legislation's role, we believe it has been overblown by critics of the military inclined to criticize military plans, doctrine, and organization and to look for "silver bullet" solutions to complex organizational and doctrinal problems glibly characterized as parochialism or inter-service bickering. Goldwater-Nichols was a useful focusing device that clarified command lines and the theater commander's authority. It set the stage for General Schwarzkopf's establishment of a Joint Force Air Component Commander (JFACC). But at that point the legislation's effect ended. It was left up to the CINC and his component commanders to make it work.

Well before the passage of the Goldwater-Nichols legislation, the services were gradually narrowing the gap to achieve jointness in military planning and operations. But our point is different: Goldwater-Nichols was not the engine of change, and service moves towards jointness remained inadequate. Indeed, we

---

[8]Colleagues Paul K. Davis and Lou Finch make this point in a larger context in their *Defense Planning for the Post–Cold War Era: Giving Meaning to Flexibility, Adaptiveness, and Robustness of Capability*, Santa Monica, California: RAND, MR-322-JS, 1993.

[9]See Hallion (1992), pp. 104, 259–260, for a similar assessment.

contend that Goldwater-Nichols and the trend toward greater jointness masked serious unresolved issues on the employment of air power. It has become an article of the conventional wisdom that the appointment of a single czar for air was a major contributor to victory. We agree—but we would make an additional point: air resources were so plentiful that the Coalition would have won the air campaign without a single czar.

But before going further, we must acknowledge the very real contribution that implementation of the JFACC concept did make. The Gulf War was the first one fought since World War II wherein U.S. air forces were under some form of JFACC control.[10] Air operations were coordinated to prevent mutual interference and controlled to promote effectiveness and efficiency in force application. There were no cases of air-on-air friendly fire. There were no major midair collisions. There was a single air plan conforming with the CINC's direction and prepared by a single command echelon.

But these important accomplishments beg the question of whether Lieutenant General Charles Horner was actually "in command" of the Coalition's air forces, and if not, the type and degree of supervision he exercised. We maintain that, for the most part, Horner exercised "tactical control" of sorties made available by the components for tasking in his daily air tasking order.[11] He coordinated with the components and then put out the air tasking order that ratified the fruits of that coordination. His authority was based on the fact that he controlled airspace in the combat area and could allocate vital support (e.g., tanker and defense suppression).[12] His authority, as JFACC, was never put to the test that would have been imposed by real resource scarcity and a more capable opponent. Our verdict is that the air campaign represented a major step toward the conduct of integrated air operations, but that the JFACC concept was not really put to *the ultimate test posed by a formidable enemy and scarcity of own forces*. More important tests will occur in the future, possibly under circumstances when a resourceful enemy contests our control of the air, when we have fewer air forces than we did in Desert Storm, and when non-USAF components furnish a larger proportion of the total U.S. air assets available.

---

[10]Winnefeld and Johnson (1993), p. 100.

[11]Tactical control was defined in Chapter Five. Note that Horner did not control non-USAF air units (such control would be "operational control"); he controlled those sorties made available to the JFACC by service component commanders.

[12]Air Force officers we interviewed stated that the authority goes beyond "coordination" and was in their view "directive" in nature. Either term is accurate if it includes coordination before issuing directives. Our view is that Horner exercised *control* based on *prior coordination* with the other commands involved.

THE TRIUMPH OF SERVICE DOCTRINE AND PREFERENCES

The Air Force fought a doctrinally satisfying strategic air campaign with assistance from Navy and Marine Corps forces. But Air Force commanders in the field were appropriately sensitive to the need to hit enemy ground forces early in the war. Horner, Glosson, and others saw beyond the limited scope of the Instant Thunder plan developed by the Air Staff in Washington and developed a plan most suitable to the requirements of both the CINC and the sister service components.

Although air power had prepared the battlefield, the Army fought its AirLand Battle with little need for close air support from the other services.[13] Indeed, *during* the ground war, the Army satisfied almost all of its own firepower requirements, while the Air Force conducted its preferred air interdiction campaign against enemy ground forces somewhat removed from the ground front. The Marines adhered to their integrated air-ground concept (MAGTF) and relied mostly on their own firepower, including close air support. The Navy, with no significant air component to the maritime campaign, provided its air sorties for tasking by the JFACC. Some Coalition members imposed their own restrictions on the use of their air. The result of national and service withholds and preferences was that the JFACC acted as broker, coordinator, airspace manager, and air asset provider of last resort, while each service used its air assets pretty much in accordance with the way it preferred to fight.[14] This in no way lessens the accomplishments of joint air operations—the most joint in almost 50 years. It does put that achievement into better focus: jointness in air operations was broad but not very deep. Service doctrines and preferences still ran the show in spite of the progress made.

LAND- AND SEA-BASED AIR

In writing this book we have been urged by service advocates to conduct a detailed land- and sea-based air comparison on the basis of Gulf War experience. Such a comparison becomes an exchange of carefully tailored statistical broadsides that prove little beyond the following:

---

[13]Air Vice Marshal R. A. Mason (RAF) goes farther and states: "Air forces contribution to the 100 hour [ground] battle was relatively small: Bad weather returned and the ground advance was so rapid that no more than on one occasion ground forces overran defensive positions on which they had called down fire but a few minutes previously." (From "The Air War in the Gulf," *Survival*, Vol. 33, No. 3, May/June 1991.) Most airmen would respond that the rapidity of the ground campaign was in large measure the fruits of the air campaign.

[14]RAND's Fred Frostic points out that in some ways the JFACC was "the provider of *first* resort" in that he provided the framework for integrated air operations—the MAP, the ATO, the coordinating instructions, and the system for making changes.

- Artistry in the use of statistics.

- Confirming the unique features or general applicability of the Gulf War experience.

- The wisdom (or folly) of system purchases or deferrals made a decade earlier.

- Demonstrating the marginal utility of some capabilities that would be central in another scenario.

- The difficulty (and dangers) of comparative costing.

Rather than disappear in these analytic potholes, we have chosen to offer a few more general judgments about the roles and performance of land- and sea-based air forces. Clearly, land-based air was the senior partner in Coalition air operations during the Gulf War, in spite of the fact that the largest carrier battle force since World War II had been assembled to support the air campaign. Coyne states that carrier-based air forces provided 16 percent of the sorties flown, dropped 15 percent of the bombs, and accounted for 8 percent of the Iraqi aircraft downed.[15] Coyne's use of the relevant statistics suggests that the Navy's role was very modest indeed. The Navy interprets the statistics differently. Rear Admiral Riley D. Mixson (Deputy Assistant Chief of Naval Operations for Air Warfare) states that "the Navy with 35% of the power projection aircraft flew 35% of the power projection missions. (Power projection includes "strike" support that delivered or was capable of delivering ordnance—HARM, reconnaissance, offensive and defensive combat air patrol, EW, etc.)."[16]

Unlike most contingency operations conducted since World War II, the Gulf theater was not well suited to carrier operations. The enemy coastline, small in any event, was removed from easy blue water access. Until the Arabian Gulf Battle Force moved into the Gulf in strength to conduct combat air operations after 20 January, it was critically dependent on tanking services provided by the Air Force.[17] The Red Sea Battle Force was even further removed from most target areas and could have played no significant role in the war without USAF tanking support.[18]

---

[15]Coyne (1992a), pp. 51, 88, 95.

[16]Mixson (1992), p. 44.

[17]When the air threat had been removed and the mine threat reduced, the carriers moved into the *northern* Gulf on 16 February. At this time, they were closer to targets in the KTO than any Coalition air bases except A-10 and AV-8 advanced staging bases. At that point, tanking requirements for aircraft from the Gulf carriers declined dramatically. (Arabian Gulf Battle Force data.)

[18]According to CNA, the duration of sorties launched from Red Sea carriers was on average over 40 percent greater than sorties launched from Persian Gulf carriers.

Many Navy sorties were used to provide defensive cover for surface and logistics forces in the narrow confines of the Gulf and thus were not available to project power ashore.[19] Navy carrier deck loads were not optimized for the tasking that developed during the course of the Gulf War. Once the Iraqi air force had been defeated and air supremacy achieved, there was little role for the 100 F-14 fighters on five of the six carriers deployed. Air Force F-15Cs and Marine F/A-18s were closer to most combat air patrol (CAP) stations and were used. The venerable A-6 was the Navy's only true all-weather attack platform with the capability to direct laser-guided weapons. However, the Navy's defense suppression capability was impressive and provided an essential capability to support early air operations.

Carrier forces are sometimes criticized for their alleged lack of staying power and their need to go offline every two to four days for refueling and rearming from the afloat combat logistics force. However, during the 42-day Gulf War, carriers were online conducting strike operations for 201 out of a possible total of 252 carrier-days. They averaged 30 *strike* sorties per carrier per day, according to data supplied by CNA.[20] This compares with a planned combat rate of 37 strike sorties per day. Two reasons for the lower-than-planned strike sortie rate is that Navy fighter-bomber aircraft were used extensively in the defense suppression role (e.g., HARM shooters), and that the duration of each sortie was longer than the planning figure.

For the Gulf War, the Navy's impressive capabilities for maritime and coastal warfare were not needed for the most part, except to add to the mass that was vital in causing the collapse of the Iraqi army. It is a quick leap from this conclusion to a judgment that sea-based air is no longer (or rarely) needed in the post–Cold War era. We do not share that judgment and believe that it can lead to dangerous decisions on force structuring and employment. Both the Navy and the Air Force in the past have made pronouncements that were the functional equivalent of "We can win alone." Although Air Force power, in our view, was the central component in the exercise of air power *in the Gulf,* in a future conflict other mixes may be needed.

---

[19]David Perrin of CNA makes a spirited rejoinder to those who assert that the carrier battle group exists largely to defend itself and carries little power projection punch. He believes that Navy critics overlook the contribution of carrier air in enabling access to the theater by sealift. In essence, carrier air provides control of the surface of the sea that carries the sealift that the other services depend on to win. Carriers, other surface forces, and lift are protected by carrier air. See his *A Comparison of Long-Range Bombers and Naval Forces,* Alexandria, Virginia: Center for Naval Analyses, December 1991, p. 55. We would point out that Air Force air superiority fighters provided the same service over land bases and LOCs.

[20]Compare with the 38–58 "power projection" sorties per day cited by Mixson (1992).

HEAVY BOMBERS VERSUS FIGHTER-BOMBERS

For us, the more interesting issue is not sea-based versus land-based air, but theater-based air (land- and sea-based) versus centrally-based air—to use the old terminology, tactical versus strategic air power, or fighter-bombers versus heavy bombers. As in so many either/or arguments, this formulation misses the point: in most circumstances you need both. The issue comes to the fore during arguments about new system acquisition: a new heavy bomber or a new fighter-bomber.

In our judgment, the Gulf War experience made a better case for regionally based long-range fighter-bombers than for centrally based long-range bombers. However, long-range bombers would have been the only U.S. strike platforms that could have hit Iraqi targets between 2 and 5 August 1990.[21] They would have comprised the critical component of any U.S. response to an early Iraqi decision to invade Saudi Arabia.[22] However, it was the rapid buildup of sea- and land-based fighter-bombers in theater that soon took on the critical role of deterring further Iraqi moves. If Horner had had to choose between long-range bombers, "smart" fighter-bombers, and a swarm of "dumb" fighter-bombers, it is our judgment that he would have selected smart fighter-bombers such as the F-15E, A-6E, F-111, and F-117 aircraft. These are all long-range, all-weather systems capable of delivering large quantities of laser-guided munitions.

WHAT WOULD WE CHANGE IN RETROSPECT?

Any discussion along these lines smacks of the most reprehensible form of second-guessing. In our view, there were few egregious errors made during Operations Desert Shield and Desert Storm. Whether faster and decisive deterrent moves could have been made before 2 August 1990 is another matter and outside the scope of this book. Most shortcomings experienced during the war were the result of preconflict choices in force programming and oversights in operational planning. These errors were mostly masked by the lavish applica-

---

[21]Tomahawk missiles were carried aboard some on-station Navy escorts, but did not have on board the necessary software for taking most Iraqi targets under fire. Because only one carrier was within extreme range of Iraqi targets on 5 August and land-based air did not start arriving in theater until 8 August, it is safe to say that long-range bomber forces would have comprised the bulk of initial striking power into mid-August.

[22]However, this is not to say that B-52s dropping gravity bombs would have been particularly effective against fast-moving Iraqi armed columns invading Saudi Arabia. It is at this juncture that arguments for *future* systems (heavy bombers with precision-guided munitions) become entangled with the historic performance of *current* systems.

tion of U.S. mobility and combat capabilities to the problem at hand.[23] Defects in deployment planning, command and control, and battle damage assessment come to mind. We are sympathetic to the many planners and commanders who foresaw the difficulties that would be encountered but were powerless to do anything about them beforehand because of insufficient resources, institutional pressures beyond their control, and the fact that sometimes the needed information simply did not exist. But in our view, combat experience will always point the finger of culpability at precombat planning. There *will* almost always be a gap between the forces (and their capabilities) available for a given conflict and what will ultimately be required. The trick is to minimize the gap, and in our view that gap in the Gulf War was the smallest in U.S. wartime experience in this century.[24]

The Scud Hunt

Although the U.S. military was admirably ready and equipped for Desert Storm, it was not ready to counter the Iraqi Scuds. A spirit of the offensive swamped any similar consideration of an *enemy offensive against the Coalition's center of gravity.* Clearly, planning must encompass possible enemy initiatives, and the necessary tactics and hardware have to be developed. Although the Air Force was sensitive to the need to kill "shoot-and-hide" strategic nuclear systems (e.g., Soviet road-mobile SS-25s), it was not similarly sensitive to the need to kill lesser shoot-and-hide targets. The Navy has been sensitive to the need to kill shoot-and-hide maritime targets (e.g., missile-firing submarines), but not analogous ground targets.

Critics of air power (and the Gulf War) have had a field day in rebutting claims made on the effectiveness of the counter-Scud campaign.[25] Some of the critics' arguments have been confirmed by official sources.[26] If we had it to do over again, we would probably have put even more weight on countering Scuds, starting at H-hour.[27]

---

[23]Some would say "wasteful" or "unnecessary" instead of lavish. Such usage neglects the role of mass in victory and the price paid in lives to gain it. Every parent wants his or her son or daughter in combat to be fully supported.

[24]See the contrast between U.S. preparedness for Operation Desert Storm and the other U.S. wars of the 20th century in James A. Winnefeld, *The Post–Cold War Force-Sizing Debate*, Santa Monica, California: RAND, R-4243-JS, 1993, pp. 20–30.

[25]For an example of this rebuttal, see Mark Crispin Miller, "Operation Desert Storm," *The New York Times*, June 24, 1992, p. 21. Miller's argument was based in part on information provided by an analyst of CENTCOM staff. See also Stuart M. Powell, "Scud War, Round Three," *Air Force Magazine,* October 1992, p. 33.

[26]"DoD Misreported Ability to Hit Iraq's SCUD Launchers," *Defense Daily,* June 26, 1992, p. 5.

[27]Powell, op. cit., p. 33, suggests that the real counter-Scud effort didn't start until four days into the air campaign.

Intelligence/Battle Damage Assessment

In previous conflicts, this subject has been an esoteric "back room" issue largely hidden from public view. In the television—and CNN—age, with the constant demand for instant information and answers, BDA and associated intelligence processes have not so much "come out of the closet" as they have been exposed unceremoniously by the media and unveiled begrudgingly by the military. Good intelligence and BDA were hostages to prewar institutional parochialism (not so much across services as within the larger intelligence community), a failure to field the necessary collection systems (particularly tactical reconnaissance), a "leave it to the spooks" attitude on the part of force plans and operations staffs, and fads that were based on "clean" national technical systems (i.e., spy satellites) as opposed to "dirty" HUMINT (i.e., spies).[28] With these burdens to be borne, there was little room for a beginning-to-end joint BDA architecture. Few prewar BDA and intelligence-collection exercises were held, since the focus was on warning and deployment, not on strike planning. As a result, an ad hoc joint BDA architecture had to be built largely from scratch during the conflict.

Lift Planning

Gulf War lift planning (both sea and air) was hampered by two major deficiencies: (1) the absence of updated TPFDLs and the ability to generate and revise them quickly and if necessary from scratch, and (2) invalid planning factors. In Chapter Three, we discussed both problems at some length. Planning factors can be "cooked" to fit comfortable (e.g., less costly) program planning. The orderly and extended deliberate planning process is not suitable for fast-breaking contingencies or those that lie outside normal planning assumptions.[29] One end of the problem is being solved in the postwar environment by placing all service components of CINC USTRANSCOM under his OPCON in peacetime.[30] The other end of the problem involves developing improved methods for defining lift requirements rapidly now that the defects of the Joint Operation Planning and Execution System (JOPES) are more apparent to suppliers and users of forces.

---

[28]For an official critique of U.S. intelligence preparedness at the national level for the Gulf War, see *CPGW*, p. C-4. A parallel critique of CENTCOM is on pp. C-6 through C-8. A scathing indictment of the BDA system is on pp. C-14 through C-16.

[29]Davis and Finch (1993).

[30]Interview with General Hansford T. Johnson (CINC USTRANSCOM) in *Sea Power*, August 1992, p. 9.

Precision-Guided Munitions Capabilities

All air services were deficient in fielding an adequate precision-guided munitions capability for the Gulf War. The Air Force had 118 aircraft (and pod-mounted systems) capable of launching and guiding laser-guided bombs after almost three decades of development and force programming. It was heavily dependent not only on LANTIRN navigation pods, but also on the even scarcer LANTIRN targeting pods. There simply were not enough to go around. The Navy, for its part, suffered from critical shortages of laser bomb guidance kits. Its LGB-capable aircraft, the vulnerable and venerable A-6E, was husbanded for night missions, thus leaving the Navy without any daylight laser designator platforms. Its capable F/A-18 had IR pods, but no laser guidance pods: it could launch LGBs, but did not have laser illuminators.

This situation was the result of prewar procurement priorities of all air services that put more emphasis on airframes than on weapons and weapons-guidance systems. The platforms were the high-visibility items to be shepherded through congressional budget processes, with the hope that needed follow-on capabilities could be funded later and with less visibility. This gamble came a cropper in the Gulf. Fortunately, enough (just) PGM systems were available. With a smaller force on the programming horizon, the remaining platforms must contain a higher proportion of more capable aircraft.

Moving Naval Air into the Gulf

It had been an article of faith among Navy operational planners for years: the Persian Gulf is poorly suited to carrier operations. It has restricted sea room, shallow and mineable waters, wind patterns that require high launch and recovery speeds, warm water that results in high condenser injection temperatures (limiting top speeds), and—perhaps most importantly—proximity to potentially hostile land areas and associated lack of battle depth and warning of attack. While all these are valid concerns, they would, if honored, have kept most of the Navy out of the Persian Gulf fight. In the event, three and eventually four carriers were moved into the Gulf. However, with two exceptions, the carriers were not moved into the Gulf until mid-January.[31] Consequently, they had few opportunities (during Desert Shield) to coordinate their operations with the growing JFACC control structure in the northern Gulf. Thus when they did move up, they experienced start-up pains in interfacing with the pre-installed command and control structure. Tanking requirements declined and ordnance carriage capacity increased markedly when they moved up. Battle groups must be put in harm's way in the "from the sea" era if they are to

---

[31]Information provided by CNA.

contribute to the total air effort—just as land-based aircraft must be based forward even if they are vulnerable to missile and chemical attack.

Rear Admiral Dan March, the Arabian Gulf Battle Force Commander, in a communication to the authors, takes exception to our evaluation of the initial reluctance to move carriers into the Gulf. He states that planning was well advanced before the war based on putting carriers in the Gulf. He reminds us that both *Independence* and *Midway* made a number of excursions inside the Gulf before the start of combat operations to test the C[3] architecture and operational problems. A major impediment to earlier continuous operations in the Gulf was the pressure applied by the GCC states to limit flight operations there because of airspace limitations and heavy commercial air traffic. Compounding the problem was the fact that most commercial traffic used VHF voice radio, while most USN (and other service) aircraft used UHF voice radio. He goes on to state that the Navy had a carefully orchestrated game plan for carrier positioning throughout the conflict, and as the battlefield preparation phase reached a peak, the carriers moved up to within 100 miles of Kuwait City, closer than all but a few of the Coalition's air bases to the scene of the major ground battles. Admiral March states that initial training was conducted in the Gulf of Oman for two reasons: airspace flexibility and Omani exercise requirements. He acknowledges that there were some within the Navy (and its senior retired officers) who opposed putting carriers in the Gulf, but they did not shape the associated planning and ultimate decisions to deploy the carriers in harm's way.[32]

Lieutenant General Charles Horner corroborates Navy airspace problems. The Saudis, in particular, were reluctant to allow Navy overflights of their territory, stemming from their concern about the reduced accountability of carrier-based flights compared with land-based flights that originated from and returned to bases on Saudi soil.[33]

Tanker and Fuel Compatibility

It is likely that *there were sufficient tankers to support the Gulf air war* (though more could have been used). The problems were more a matter of planning and control, of insufficient offload points (most tankers had only one), and incompatible fuels for Navy aircraft. Of all systems, tankers must be the most flexible and interoperable. DoD must come up with the means for improving the ability of the tanker force to support joint and combined operations.

---

[32]Interview with Rear Admiral Daniel March, 13 May 1993.

[33]CNA Memo 92-0965 of 2 June 1992, recounting an interview with General Horner.

Jointness

As we pointed out in Chapter Five, significant progress was made in improving jointness during Desert Storm. If "we had to do it over again," we would have a prepackaged truly joint JFACC staff (at least in cadre status) ready to deploy. This is one objective that has apparently been realized during the postwar period. A joint JFACC staff set up with an Air Force commander and a Navy deputy directed the Coalition air operations against Iraq in January 1993. ATOs were transmitted electronically to the on-station Navy carrier, and there was compatible software on both ends of the communications link.

On this note of success, we now turn to an examination of the role of air power in the Gulf War, a subject that has been and likely will continue to be a matter of some dispute as the Department of Defense seeks to sort out roles and missions in the post–Cold War era.

Chapter Twelve

AN ASSESSMENT OF AIR POWER'S ROLE

> There is no question that U.S. air power was the single most dominant element of the Allied victory in the Gulf. But to extrapolate from the Gulf experience to argue that air power is the only meaningful component of national power is to set the nation up for failure.[1]

> But the results of our analysis do indicate that the calculus has changed and air power's ability to contribute to the joint battle has increased.[2]

The enduring public images of the Gulf War will center on air power: the in-flight video recording of laser-guided bombs going through ventilator shafts, the "highway of death" wreckage of the Iraqi army retreating from Kuwait, Patriot missiles intercepting Scuds, and the first-night reporting by CNN of the air strike on Baghdad. It was the "clean" war that the American public has always believed to be the right way to fight: it had an enemy leader who was easy to hate, a cause that was just and backed by the international community, an American leadership role in coalition war, a commanding general who cared for his troops and who was blunt and plainspoken, high-technology weapons wielded by clean-cut and well-trained Americans in uniform, the services working together in relative harmony, and perhaps most important, a victory that was easy, quick, and with few casualties. What can the student of air power take away from this impressive performance? Were air power advocates vindicated after the muddles of Korea and Vietnam? Or was air power finally given a role it could perform effectively? Was air power an "enabler" or the war winner? These questions are the focus of this chapter. We will try to sort through the claims of air power advocates, of those who (while not advocates) were pleased

---

[1]Owens (1992), p. 53.

[2]Christopher J. Bowie, Fred Frostic, et al., *The New Calculus: Analyzing Airpower's Changing Role in Joint Theater Campaigns*, Santa Monica, California: RAND, MR-149-AF, 1993.

with air power's performance, and of the skeptics as we attempt to arrive at a fair evaluation of air power's contribution to the victory.

Why are these questions important? The role of air power in the makeup of a smaller American defense establishment in the future poses major issues for the survival of the armed services in their present form. When force structure issues are raised, roles and missions issues are not far behind. But more important than these intra-DoD concerns is the need that the United States be properly armed as it navigates the uncertainties and vicissitudes of the post–Cold War world. We agree with Owens that to take away the wrong lessons from the Gulf War, or to assume that the war is the principal pattern of future conflict, or to dismiss the experience as unique, is to open the door to future disasters.

IS THERE A CONSENSUS VIEW?

Many experts and observers have provided opinions on the role of air power in the Gulf War. They range from the "Douhet was right after all" school to the skeptics who believe that the Gulf War was so unique, or that air power was so misapplied in it, that it holds no major lessons for the future except that every war is different.

To help get our bearings on the conflicting views of air power's role, we have catalogued some of the writings and public statements by important commentators.

The National Leadership

President George Bush: "Lesson number one from the Gulf War is the value of air power."[3]

Secretary of Defense Dick Cheney: "The air campaign was decisive."[4]

"Enemy forces were fielded, for the most part, in terrain ideally suited to armor and air power and largely free of noncombatants."[5]

"On the other hand, air power alone could not have brought the war to so sharp and decisive a conclusion."[6]

---

[3]Quoted in James W. Canan, "Lesson Number One," *Air Force Magazine*, October 1991, p. 26.

[4]"Meet the Press," 14 April 1991, quoted in United States Air Force (1991), p. 52.

[5]*CPGW*, p. vii.

[6]*CPGW*, p. xiv.

"In sum, while air power made a unique and significantly enlarged contribution to the decisive Coalition victory, the combined effects of the air, maritime, and ground offensives—with important contributions from many supporting forces—were key."[7]

Senior Military Officials

Lieutenant General Charles Horner: "[Operation Desert Storm] emphasized the role of air power because of the strategy and the environment—the nature of the war. It did not make air power the only element or the supreme element, but it did emphasize the contribution of air power."[8]

General Colin Powell: "Air power is the decisive arm so far, and I expect it will be the decisive arm into the end of the campaign, even if ground forces and amphibious forces are added to the equation. . . . If anything, I expect air power to be even more decisive in the days and weeks ahead."[9]

General Merrill A. McPeak: "This is the first time in history that a field army has been defeated by air power."[10]

Air Power Advocates

James P. Coyne: "It is impossible to dispute logically that air power was *a* decisive factor in the Gulf War. Furthermore, there are strong grounds for arguing that it was *the* decisive factor."[11]

Richard P. Hallion: "Simply (if boldly) stated, air power won the Gulf War."[12]

Lieutenant Colonel Price T. Bingham: "As a result, perhaps the most important lesson the U.S. military could learn from Desert Storm, is that it needs to change its doctrine to recognize that air power can dominate modern conventional war . . . "[13]

---

[7]*CPGW*, p. xv.

[8]Quoted in Coyne (1992a), p. 178.

[9]Testimony before the Senate Armed Services Committee on February 21, 1991, quoted in Hallion (1992), p. 201.

[10]Quoted in Clodfelter (1991), p. 17.

[11]Coyne (1992a), p. 178.

[12]Hallion (1992), p. 1.

[13]Lieutenant Colonel Price T. Bingham, USAF, "Air Power in Desert Storm: The Need for Doctrinal Change," *Airpower Journal*, Winter 1991, p. 33.

Colonel Dennis M. Drew: "In the Gulf War, the impact of air power . . . was clearly overwhelming and decisive."[14]

Journalists

Harry Smith, CBS News: "The Iraqi military machine folded under the pressure of allied smart bombs and air power."[15]

John D. Morrocco: "While land and naval forces played key roles in the overall strategic plan, air power provided the decisive element."[16]

The Think Tanks, Academics, and Other Know-It-Alls

CSIS Gulf War Study Group: "Naturally, the most convincing confirmation of the revolution in war was seen in the application of air power in the air campaign. The effects of the six-week Coalition air assault on Iraqi forces was devastating."[17]

Rod Alonso et al.: "However, the inescapable conclusion is that air power virtually brought Iraq to its knees, and the air war showed that air power may be enough to win some conflicts."[18]

James F. Dunnigan and Austin Bay: "Desert Storm's air assault was the kind of decisive air war early twentieth-century air-power advocate General Billy Mitchell envisaged. . . . Never in the history of warfare has air power played such a determining role in winning a war."[19]

Kenneth P. Werrell: "Thus, in several ways, air power played a major role in this victory. . . . The air war fatally weakened Iraqi ground forces both physically and psychologically so that they crumbled before the Coalition ground assault."[20]

---

[14]Colonel Dennis M. Drew, USAF, "Desert Storm as Symbol," *Airpower Journal*, Fall 1992, p. 4.

[15]Harry Smith, CBS, 2 August 1991, as quoted in Unites States Air Force (1991), p. 52.

[16]John D. Morrocco, "War Will Reshape Doctrine, But Lessons Are Limited," *Aviation Week & Space Technology*, April 22, 1991, p. 42.

[17]Blackwell, Mazarr, and Snider (1991).

[18]Rod Alonso et al., "The Air War," in Watson et al. (1991), p. 77.

[19]Dunnigan and Bay (1992), p. 145.

[20]Kenneth P. Werrell, "Air War Victorious: The Gulf War vs. Vietnam," *Parameters*, Summer 1992, p. 47.

Jeffrey Record: "There is no question, however, that air power was the fulcrum of the military victory over Iraq."[21]

James Blackwell: "The constant aerial, artillery, and naval gunfire pounding broke the will to fight for more than half of the defending Iraqis."[22]

Mackubin Thomas Owens: "Preliminary indications are that the effectiveness of the bombing campaign was overstated."[23]

Gulf War Air Power Survey: "From the outset, U.S. air power was central to the accomplishment of the United States' and the United Nations' political and military objectives; it enabled the Coalition to deploy its forces and subsequently crippled Iraqi military capabilities, paving the way for Baghdad's defeat on the battlefield.[24]

The Congress

Les Aspin: "Air power: the most significant factor in winning [the Gulf] war."[25]

The Skeptics

Norman Friedman: "The strategic air offensive made little difference to the outcome of the war and almost certainly failed in its objectives.... The interdiction campaign was impressive, but it is not clear that it was necessary.... The air assault to soften up the Iraqi Army was both effective and essential. It did not create the pure 'victory of air power' trumpeted at the time, but it did make a tremendous difference in the ease of the allied victory."[26]

William M. Arkin: "The air war was clean on a strategic level, but irrelevant to the defeat of the Iraqi army."[27]

Caroline F. Ziemke: "One clear lesson of Desert Storm is that while air power provides the technological capability to by-pass the castles, sooner or later you

---

[21]Jeffrey Record, "Why the Air War Worked," *Armed Forces Journal International,* April 1991, p. 44.

[22]James Blackwell, *Thunder in the Desert,* New York: Bantam, 1991, p. 213 (in the chapter, "How the War Was Won").

[23]Owens (1992), p. 54.

[24]*GWAPS,* p. 1.

[25]Chapter heading in HASC (1992), p. 7.

[26]Friedman (1991), p. 447.

[27]Quoted in "Defeat of Iraq Sparks Debate on Which Air Role Was Crucial," *Aviation Week & Space Technology,* January 27, 1992, p. 61.

have to engage the enemy's army on the ground whether with attack aircraft, tanks, artillery, infantry, or bows and arrows."[28]

The Opponent

Saddam Hussein (before the Gulf War): "The United States relies on the Air Force, and the Air Force has never been the decisive factor in the history of war."[29]

*   *   *

Is there a consensus element in these diverse views? The most generally used word to define the air power role is "decisive." Was it a case, as USAF Major General John Corder is alleged to have said, that "the Air Force didn't do it alone. Somebody had to walk in on the ground and plant the flag."[30] Or was more than the Air Force and someone to plant the flag involved? There is general agreement that air power did not win *alone.* The issue turns on the degree of importance or decisiveness of the air power role. Are there more useful ways to frame this point than merely trumpeting the role of one type of forces or one service?

ARGUING AT THE EXTREME

To take the question to the extreme, could any one form of power have won (i.e., achieve the Coalition war aims) without the others? Maritime power, the first to arrive in theater (since it was already there), did not win. As this is written, Iraq is still effectively blockaded over three years after its aggression, and the Saddam Hussein regime is still in power. It is unlikely that maritime power alone could have ejected the Iraqis from Kuwait. Land power, without air and maritime power, probably could not have won either, since Iraqi air and naval forces would likely have denied the Coalition entry of the necessary heavy ground forces.

Air power alone without ground and naval power could not have won either. If there had been no immediate introduction of ground forces, it is likely that Iraqi forces could have seized the principal Saudi oil and air fields during the first

---

[28]Ziemke (1992), p. 17.

[29]*CPGW*, p. xiv.

[30]Coyne (1992a), p. 178.

weeks of August 1990 in spite of attacks by the Coalition air forces on scene.[31] Desert Storm without a Coalition land component would probably find the Iraqis still in Kuwait, even though their army had lost most of its capabilities.

The net effect of this somewhat simple-minded thought process is that comparing the relative contributions of the various forms of military power is like comparing the importance of one hand to the other. The decisive arm of the quarterback is his throwing arm—but to be competitive he needs the other (e.g., to take the ball from the center), and he finds use for his legs as well. The single-service arguments are not particularly relevant to the warfighters, but they are very relevant to those who seek a bigger share of a declining resource pie or pride of place in the command, doctrine, or prestige structures. Thus, they tend to be theological arguments used to gain access to resources or influence. If the theologians of any particular type of military power are to be dismissed, is there a better way to portray the integrated role of the different military arms?

SEQUENTIALLY ENABLING THE APPLICATION OF POWER

One might observe that it was diplomacy and maritime power that enabled the Coalition to establish effective military land and air power on the Arabian peninsula. That the exercise of Coalition maritime power was for the most part uncontested does not make it unimportant—or less than decisive. In one sense, maritime power (and diplomacy) isolated the battlefield before the first shot of Desert Storm was fired. While maritime power was necessary, it was not sufficient.[32] Using the current DoD jargon, maritime power performed an "enabling" function, that is, it made possible the effective application of the other types of military power.

Air power picked up on 17 January 1991 where maritime power left off (or more accurately, continued).[33] With the enemy isolated politically and militarily, it was still necessary to destroy his ability to make war to achieve U.S. national and Coalition objectives.[34] Destroying (or more accurately, neutralizing) those forces was done principally by air power. But it was necessary to use land

---

[31]This point is confirmed by RAND gaming of the opposing forces as they existed up through 15–20 August 1990.

[32]This insufficiency is still being demonstrated today, since the UN blockade remains in place.

[33]Air power, of course, played a major role in deterring an Iraqi move into Saudi Arabia during the Desert Shield phase of the campaign.

[34]It is easy to forget that destroying enemy forces was not the only U.S. objective. Other objectives included neutralizing Iraqi national command authorities and destroying Iraq's ballistic missile and nuclear, biological, and chemical capabilities (*CPGW*, p. 96). These CINC objectives flowed from President Bush's stated objective (inter alia) of providing for the security and stability of Saudi Arabia and the Persian Gulf (*CPGW*, p. 22).

power to eject the enemy from Kuwait and neutralize the remainder of his forces in the field.

We believe Hallion goes too far when he dismisses the ground war as spasmodic and incidental and goes on to say that

> air power can hold territory by denying an enemy the ability to seize it, and by denying an enemy the use of his forces. And, it can seize territory by controlling access to that territory and movement across it.[35]

These statements are admissible only if one redefines "hold" and "seize." We believe Hallion means "deny the enemy the use of his territory." There is an analog in maritime warfare in the difference between sea denial and sea control.

Palmer, though sympathetic to the "air did it all" view, is more circumspect, noting:

> Even before it began, the impending Allied ground campaign more than likely was a factor in Saddam's calculations. Thus, even if he had yielded unconditionally before the start of the ground war, one could not attribute the victory entirely to air power.[36]

We believe the Gulf War was a classic sequential application of the components of a nation's military power during the transition from crisis to war to victory. Maritime power was the principal crisis tool, air power was the principal warfighting tool, and land power provided the capstone necessary to achieve victory. But there is another perspective that needs consideration. Was Douhet "right after all," or was he finally given a chance to make his case? For the answer, we need to look to history.

AIR POWER IN HISTORICAL PERSPECTIVE

Some have argued that Desert Storm was not a vindication of air power as the decisive arm of war, but the culmination of a process of making air power the equal partner of its two elder brothers, land and maritime power. This school holds that the Gulf War demonstrates not some new and possibly superior role for air power, but that air power has come of age. Caroline Ziemke argues that

> the current appraisal of air power's performance in Desert Storm falls firmly in the pattern of past postwar analyses. Both previous postwar assessments (of air

---

[35]Hallion (1992), p. 253.
[36]Palmer (1992a), p. 31.

power in World War II, Korea, and Vietnam) and the current body of post-Desert Storm literature that fall under the general rubric of "Douhet was right after all" share three important and potentially misleading characteristics. First, such assessments generally lack a sense of the historical context in which the air power theorists emerged and thus fail to distinguish the meat of the theory from political hyperbole. Second, those who have, since Desert Storm declared air power either "vindicated" or on the verge of becoming so err in underestimating the contribution of air power to operational successes in the past. It is not, after all, necessary that air forces *alone* win wars for them to be an indispensable and potentially decisive military instrument.[37]

General Horner makes an intellectually consistent point when he states (as we cited in an earlier quote) that Desert Storm "did not make air power the only element or the supreme element, but it did emphasize the contribution of air power."[38] The argument over whether air power provides some new capabilities or whether longstanding capabilities are just now being exploited and recognized is usually focused on *future* roles and missions and acquisition of new systems—in a few words, the Washington game of gaining influence and resources, as opposed to the CINC's "game" of winning *today's* war. Much of the "spin" put on the Gulf War experience is related more to the former than the latter. Air power advocates and some budget cutters see a proportionately greater role for air forces in the future as a "silver bullet" that might cut defense costs.

The attacks on strategic targets at the beginning of the air campaign and the disappointing results of the Scud hunt suggest some of the limits of air power. To hit a target, one must know where it is or be able to find it. While all forms of military power are critically dependent on intelligence (and denying it to the enemy), the air weapon is particularly vulnerable to inadequate intelligence and target information. For example, Iraqi nuclear facilities were a prime target during the air campaign. Yet the Coalition air planners knew of only two targets before the start of the campaign. After the war, we found out that the Iraqi nuclear program was massive and that many important targets were not attacked because we did not know they existed. We agree with the assessment of the *Gulf War Air Power Survey:*

> Overall, the United States did not fully understand the target arrays comprising Iraqi nuclear, biological, chemical, and ballistic missile capabilities before the

---

[37]Ziemke (1992), p. 2.

[38]There are some elements of Ziemke and Horner in Dennis Drew's (1992) observation that "Operation Desert Storm symbolized a fundamental shift in the traditional method of waging mechanized warfare. The stunning performance of coalition air power symbolized both the maturity of air power and its dominant position in late twentieth century warfare" (p. 4).

Gulf war. The Iraqis had, in fact, made those target systems as elusive and resistant to accurate air attack as possible, with some success.[39]

Similar criticisms apply to the Coalition's ability to take out the Iraqi C³ system by air attack. We have already discussed the great difficulties in finding mobile Scud launchers. The point of this discussion is not to criticize the capabilities of air power, but rather to put them in perspective. Control of the ground—by ground forces and/or by political means (e.g., the UN inspections of Iraqi nuclear facilities after the war)—is still essential to winning and exploiting that win.

THE "ALL WARS (AND ESPECIALLY DESERT STORM) ARE UNIQUE" SCHOOL

An extensive literature has grown up about the unique nature of the Gulf War.[40] Every serious discussion of the war starts with a long series of disclaimers about how this war was different from those in the past and, by implication, from those that may occur in the future. These disclaimers are most often advanced by those with interests and attitudes most ready to play down the contribution of air power (or high-tech weapons, or heavy armor, etc.). What is striking is that these disclaimers are usually followed by a "lessons learned" section. Many of those lessons learned do indeed seem nearly unique to the Gulf War.

This emphasis on the unique aspects of Desert Storm logically leads to the question of what was *not* unique—at least insofar as air power is concerned. Our answer is the following:

- The enduring likelihood of insufficient warning needed to defeat aggression immediately at the point of attack.

- The likelihood that potential opponents will have some (possibly considerable) high-tech military capabilities.

- The likelihood that U.S. military actions will be part of a larger Coalition effort.

- The possibility that a future opponent will have chemical and biological weapons and advanced missile systems.

- The high leverage provided by pre-existing theater infrastructure and prepositioned assets.

---

[39]*GWAPS*, p. 79. The *GWAPS* examination of this subject (pp. 78–90) is the best that we have seen.

[40]For example, see *CPGW*, pp. vii–viii; Coyne (1992a), pp. 174–175; Blackwell, Mazarr, and Snider (1991), pp. 1–4; United States Navy (1991), pp. 52–53; and Friedman (1991), pp. 237–240.

- The need to deploy decisive force quickly to remote theaters.

- The need to have usable offensive combat power on arrival.

- The need to sustain those deployed forces for extended periods.

- The need for unity of effort (joint and combined) within likely smaller (than today) force envelopes.

- The need to create battlefield conditions that lead to the rapid destruction of the enemy forces (e.g., fixing mobile forces or flushing concealed or protected forces so they can be destroyed by superior firepower).

- The need to train and exercise the way we intend to fight.

These environmental and force capability characteristics portray the Desert Shield and Storm experience and suggest a continuity with future conflicts that would stress the U.S. military force posture. Air power brings particularly important strengths to situations defined by these conditions.

THE CONTRIBUTION OF AIR POWER TO THE GULF VICTORY

The perspectives and opinions on the air power role that have been outlined in our discussion lead us to suggest a short definition of the role of the various force components, including air power, in the Gulf War.

- Maritime, air, and land power each had a major role in the victory.

- Maritime and political power played the decisive role in isolating the enemy and in enabling the deployment of the decisive mass of Coalition forces in theater.

- Air power played the decisive role in stabilizing the crisis, deterring further aggression, and in the neutralization of enemy forces.

- Land power played the decisive role in the final phases of the defeat of enemy ground forces, taking possession of the battlefield, and forcing the enemy to negotiate an end to the war.

We believe air power was indeed decisive in neutralizing Iraqi forces. The neutralization of such forces was a necessary precondition for a rapid ground campaign with minimal casualties. But this judgment raises the issue of whether the component parts of the air campaign, as it was planned and executed, were each important to the outcome. This evaluation can only be made if one understands the campaign's objectives.

THE OBJECTIVES OF THE AIR CAMPAIGN

Norman Friedman, a long-time critic of the "air can do it all or most of it" view, sees the Gulf air campaign as composed of three functional components:

> There were actually three air campaigns: a classical strategic attack intended to destroy Saddam Hussein's weapons of mass destruction, both existing and embryonic; an interdiction campaign intended to cut off the Iraqi army in Kuwait and southern Iraq; and an assault intended to soften up the Iraqi army for ground assault.[41]

The Department of Defense parsed the campaign differently to include a strategic phase (Phase I), an air supremacy phase (Phase II), an air attack on the Iraq forces in the KTO (Phase III), and finally support of the ground offensive (Phase IV).

The derivative initial objectives of the Phase I strategic air campaign, as approved by the President and the Secretary of Defense, were the following:

- Destroy/neutralize air-defense command and control.

- Destroy nuclear, biological, and chemical storage and production capability.

- Render ineffective national and military command, control, and communications infrastructure.

- Destroy key electrical grids and oil storage facilities.

- Eliminate long-term offensive capability.

- Disrupt and weaken Republican Guard forces.[42]

There was some expectation that these strategic air campaign objectives, if achieved, might persuade the Iraqis to leave Kuwait. By November 1990, however, it became apparent that a follow-on land campaign would be necessary. The objectives of Phases II–IV were to first destroy Iraqi military capabilities in the KTO and then liberate Kuwait. Thus, the effectiveness of the overall air campaign needs to be measured against the totality of its objectives, not just the liberation of Kuwait. Quarreling with the objectives set for Coalition air forces is different from questioning whether they were achieved.

In retrospect, it is easy to conclude that preparing the battlefield with air power was the only *essential* element of the air campaign, since a cease-fire was con-

---

[41]Friedman (1991), pp. 446–447.

[42]Horner (1991), pp. 21–22.

cluded when Iraqi forces were ejected from Kuwait. But this easy conclusion overlooks two important points:

- The objectives of the campaign included neutralization of major Iraqi war-making capabilities, not directly related to the ejection of their forces from Kuwait.

- The strikes on strategic targets had some effect, though difficult to measure, on the effectiveness of Iraqi forces in the KTO. These effects were probably greatest in degraded command and control, interruption of supply lines, and the neutralization of Iraqi air power.

One of the valid criticisms of the strategic air campaign is that it has been over-sold by some of its advocates, not that it was unnecessary or ineffective. Moreover, under somewhat different circumstances (e.g., a more rational leadership in Baghdad) it might have worked without the necessity of a ground campaign. But care is needed even in this judgment because the Iraqis may have left Kuwait under air attack only because they saw that an inevitable ground attack would follow.[43] Under such circumstances the air attack would have been the proximate cause of Iraqi withdrawal, but not sufficient to cause such withdrawal.

Our conclusion on this matter is that the strategic air campaign was necessary given Coalition objectives, and that it had important spillover effects in enabling (to use current Pentagon terminology) the eventual destruction of Iraqi ground forces in Kuwait. If the Coalition objective had been limited to ejecting the Iraqis from Kuwait, a more limited campaign focused on destroying Iraqi ground forces in the KTO might have been appropriate. But such judgments are easily skewed. We need to bear in mind that the Iraqi leadership had been under nearly continuous air attack for five weeks prior to the start of ground operations. This was its only tangible contact with the war. Given the leadership's insensitivity to casualties and military setbacks in the war with Iran, one might argue that the strategic air campaign and the air campaign against Iraqi forces in the KTO were both necessary ingredients to the eventual Iraqi capitulation.

Our bottom line is that air power was decisive in the Gulf War. It was the major factor in achieving Coalition objectives. The danger is that air power advocates will oversell in the Washington arena its major accomplishments, and that its detractors will undersell it (as "unique") for their own doctrinal or other reasons grounded in vested interests. We agree with Mark Clodfelter when he observes that

---

[43]Palmer (1992a), p. 31.

we must avoid creating a new spectre that judges success or failure in future wars according to whether or not the Air Force was the most decisive factor.[44]

But we also agree with General Horner's observation that air power came of age in the Gulf War. It was a war that had a good fit with U.S. Air Force doctrine, just as some prior conflicts had better fits with counterinsurgency doctrine, a maritime strategy, or the constraints of limited war.

The friends of air power cannot afford to rest on the laurels that were won relatively easily (compared to, say, World War II) in the Gulf War. Future conflicts will place different constraints on and provide different opportunities for air power. The next conflict, for example, might require near-immediate application of long-range firepower in regions where bases are not conveniently available. In that case, long-range bombers might be the only readily available weapon—perhaps together with carrier-based air if the targets are on a continental littoral. Or the next conflict might be one with a high insurgency or shoot-and-hide component orthogonal to the strengths of high-tech systems so useful in the Gulf. Or the U.S. air role may be limited to providing combat support to an engaged security partner. This support might take the form of target acquisition, electronic warfare, lift, or tanking, and not involve employment of U.S. "shooters."

There is another danger to the future employment of air power. We might have to fight our way in and wrest air supremacy from an opponent—perhaps under conditions wherein our bases (land and sea) are under attack. We have not faced that problem since World War II. Are our systems and tactics up to the mark? More importantly, do we have the right state of mind, as Kenney had in New Guinea and Geiger had on Guadalcanal in 1942? A state of mind where the need to win pushes out hardware, doctrinal, and who's-in-charge concerns and where we must fight "smart" instead of "big"? This environment will place an even greater premium on fighting as a true league of airmen and not as a collection of service air forces with a veneer of jointness. Mass will not always be on our side, and high-tech might not be there either. In those cases, we will have to fall back on our skills, our teamwork, and our better understanding of both the strengths and limitations of air power.

---

[44]Clodfelter (1991), p. 31. This greater degree of caution, acknowledging that there are important situations when air power cannot do it all, is already in evidence among responsible Air Force officials. See Tony Capaccio, "Military Experts Stressed the Limits of Air Power in the Former Yugoslavia Republics," *Defense Week*, March 1, 1993, pp. 1, 14–15.

STATISTICAL DATA ON DESERT SHIELD AND DESERT STORM

The following figures and tables are drawn from several sources and are intended to supplement the data in other parts of the book on the conduct of air operations during Desert Shield and Desert Storm. The appendix is subdivided into sections on the deployment of forces during Desert Shield; the Iraqi threat; refueling; and operations.

DEPLOYMENT

The airlift for Operation Desert Shield was the largest ever conducted. Figure A.1 shows the flow of cargo and passengers aboard airlift to support the Army and Air Force deployment in Phase I of Desert Shield (through 8 November 1990).[1] Table A.1 provides general statistics on the airlift operation between 8 August and 30 September.

USAF fighter aircraft flew directly to the theater, supported by SAC tankers, to provide air cover for the deploying ground forces and provide an initial measure of deterrence. The arrival of fighters in Phase I is depicted by service in Figure A.2, and in more detail for the Air Force in Figure A.3. Estimates of their air-to-air and antiarmor kill potential are given in Figures A.4 and A.5.

Combat aircraft were not the only types of aircraft deployed to the theater. Table A.2 summarizes the entire range of fixed-wing capabilities provided by all U.S. services and foreign air forces just prior to G-day. Figure A.6 shows the bed-down of forces throughout the CENTCOM AOR.

Finally, Figure A.7 summarizes schematically the gradual buildup in force capabilities from the first day of the mobilization to the beginning of the ground campaign. As more and more units arrived in the theater, the United States and its allies were able to move up the ladder of capabilities from deterrence, to

---

[1] Phase II of Desert Shield began with the President's decision on 8 November to deploy additional forces for possible offensive operations and lasted until 15 January 1991.

minimal defensive counterair, to defense from the air against a ground attack, to a combined air and ground defense, to a combined air and ground offense.

Table A.1

General Statistics on the Airlift Operation, 8 August to 30 September

	C-5	C-141	KC-10	Civil	C-130	Total
Missions	924	1,979	106	502	305	3,816
Sorties	5,000	11,599	471	2,126	1,129	20,325
Flying hours	32,010	72,300	2,933	11,902	4,337	123,482
Passengers	34,248	27,248	214	69,869	3,122	134,701
Cargo	55,266	38,474	3,900	23,926	2,160	123,726

SOURCE: *PAF Assessment.*

Table A.2

Aircraft in Desert Storm on 24 February 1991

Type	USAF	USMC/USN	Foreign	Total
Attack	381	215	129	725
Fighter/attack	234	177	180	591
Fighter	124	84	299	507
Special operations	25	0	0	25
Reconnaissance	45	24	20	89
Electronic warfare	106	38	0	144
C^3 and surveillance	38	96	8	142
Airlift	147	9	61	217
Aerial refueling	304	41	34	379
Total	1,404	684	731	2,819

SOURCE: RAND working paper by T. M. Parker and Donald Emerson, "The Desert Storm Air Campaign: An Overview," p. vii, based on CINCCENT and EUCOM SITREPs and Air Staff background papers.

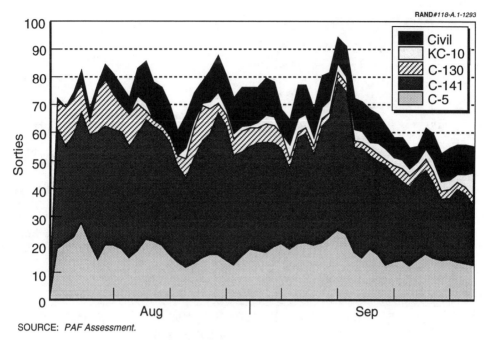

SOURCE: *PAF Assessment.*

Figure A.1—Phase I Airlift Flow

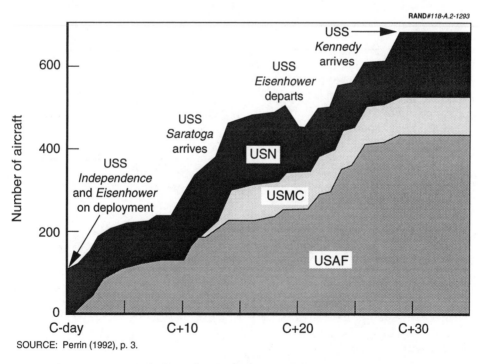

SOURCE: Perrin (1992), p. 3.

Figure A.2—Arrival of Fixed-Wing Fighter and Attack Aircraft in Theater

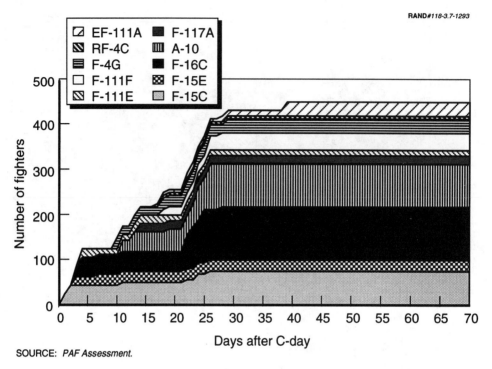

SOURCE: *PAF Assessment.*

Figure A.3—Deployment of USAF Fighters in the Kuwaiti Theater

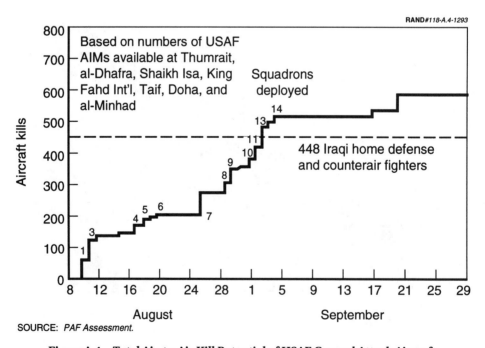

SOURCE: *PAF Assessment.*

Figure A.4—Total Air-to-Air Kill Potential of USAF Ground Attack Aircraft

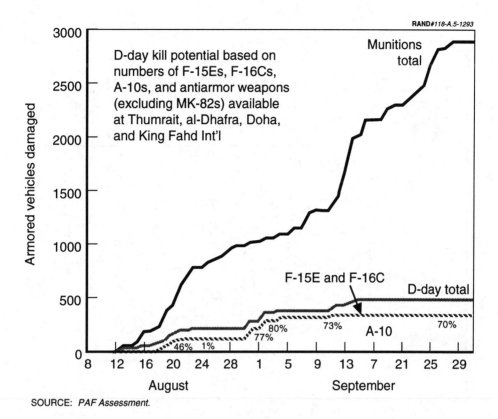

Figure A.5—Total and D-Day USAF Antiarmor Kill Potential

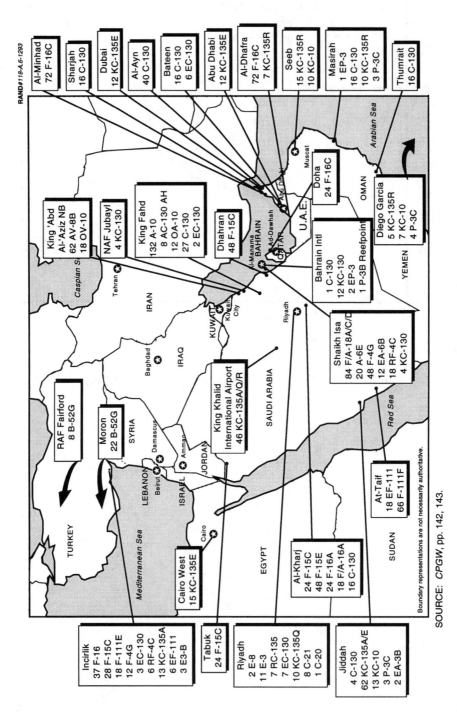

SOURCE: *CPGW*, pp. 142, 143.

Figure A.6—Locations of U.S. Aircraft in the CENTCOM AOR, 24 February 1991

Figure A.7—Buildup of Force Capability

THREAT

The Coalition forces faced what were thought to be large and battle-hardened Iraqi forces. The Iraqi air-defense system (IADS) consisted of a formidable array of surface-to-air missiles and antiaircraft guns (Figure A.8) controlled by a centralized network sector operations center (SOCs) (Figure A.9).

In addition to the Iraqi air-defense threat, Coalition ground forces also faced the Iraqi army, arranged in three operational echelons, as depicted in Figure A.10.

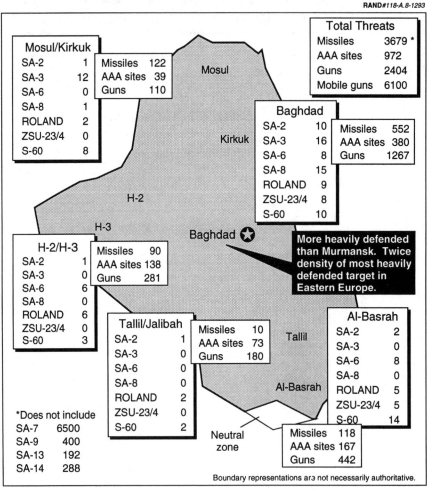

SOURCE: *CPGW*, p. 241.

Figure A.8—Iraqi SAM/AAA Threat, January 1991

RAND #118-A.9-1293

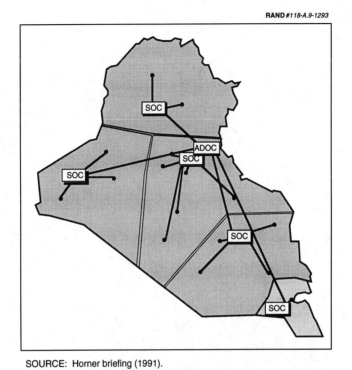

SOURCE: Horner briefing (1991).

Figure A.9—Iraqi IADS Command and Control

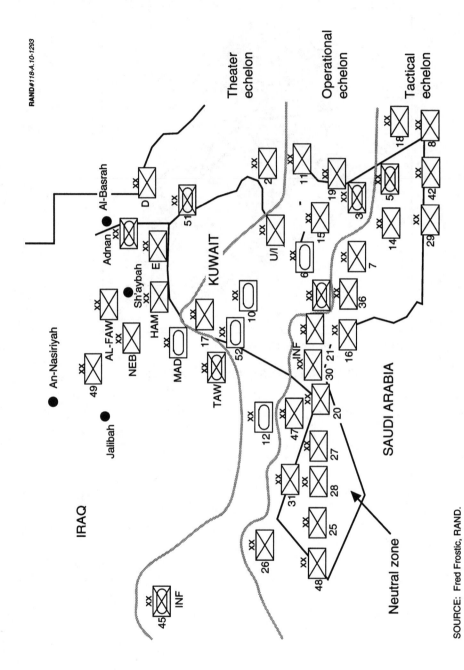

Figure A.10—Disposition of Iraqi Ground Forces in the KTO on G–Day

SOURCE: Fred Frostic, RAND.

SUPPORT OPERATIONS

A huge effort was required to support air operations during Desert Shield and Desert Storm. A principal aspect of this was aerial refueling. Table A.3 provides data on average daily sorties flown, hours logged, aircraft refueled, and millions of gallons of fuel offloaded during Desert Shield and Desert Storm by SAC's KC-10 and KC-135 tankers.

Figure A.11 depicts the air refueling sorties flown each day during Desert Storm, and Figure A.12 the combat and noncombat refueling sorties by user type (Air Force, Navy, Marine Corps, and foreign).

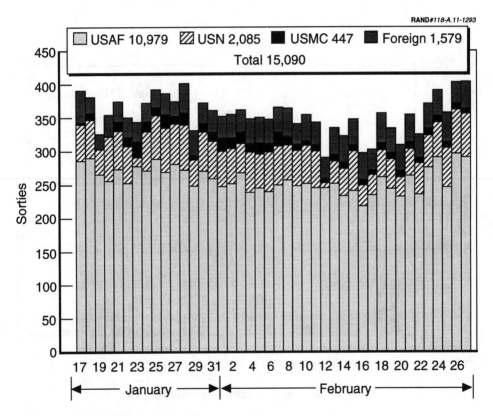

SOURCE: RAND working paper by Major Thomas A. Marshall.

Figure A.11—Air Refueling Sorties Flown During Desert Storm

Table A.3

Average Daily Tanker Statistics

	Desert Shield		Desert Storm	
	KC-10	KC-135	KC-10	KC-135
Sorties flown	2	66	35	215
Hours logged	12	182	240	977
Aircraft refueled	13	175	222	839
Fuel delivered (million gals)	0.2	1.9	4.5	11.0

SOURCE: RAND working paper by Major Thomas A. Marshall.

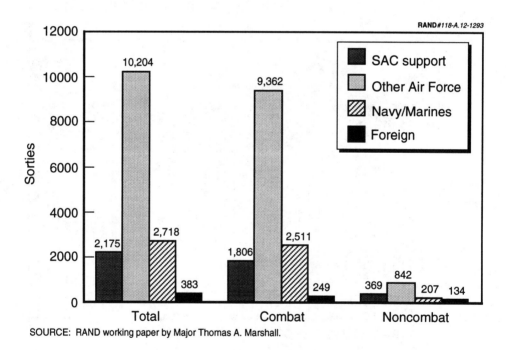

SOURCE: RAND working paper by Major Thomas A. Marshall.

Figure A.12—USAF Air Refueling Sorties by User

OPERATIONS

Obtaining an accurate record of the total number of targets struck and sorties planned in the daily ATOs is a difficult task. Even more difficult is unearthing the number of sorties actually flown. There are differences among sources, but there is enough overall agreement about apportionment of effort among phases of the air campaign, objectives, and missions that the discrepancies are not significant. The statistics presented below are drawn principally from RAND research, supplemented by data from other sources.

We begin with the target set. The air campaign's master target list (MTL) grew with time as new targets were discovered and added. Table A.4 shows the number of targets by category on CENTAF's MTL at D-day, and the number by the end of the war. The additional targets were identified from the daily master attack plan, BDA reports, the JTF Proven Force target list, and other sources. In addition, the final column shows targets defined by CENTAF as "critical," strikes against and damage to which were tracked with so-called Strategic Scorecards.

The sorties planned and flown can be analyzed from a number of different perspectives. We include data here on the number of sorties planned and flown by aircraft type, by mission, by campaign phase, by campaign objective, and by service. First, Table A.5 provides data on counterair, SEAD, attack, and electronic combat sorties scheduled and tasked in the daily ATO (see the note for definitions), and actually flown, for selected fighter and attack aircraft.

Table A.6 shows *scheduled* sorties by mission and service during Desert Storm. Table A.7 provides data on sorties actually *flown* by the same categories. Both tables draw on data collected by RAND analysts. Figure A.13 shows this data graphically for each day of the campaign, from the Navy's official unclassified report. (Note the effects of bad weather in the first week of the campaign.) The two sources differ slightly on total sorties flown (by less than 3 percent) and on total sorties in each mission category, as shown in Table A.8.

Tables A.9 and A.10 provide data on sorties planned and flown arranged by air campaign goal and target category.

The shifting weight of apportionment over time may be seen by the sorties assigned to each of the air campaign's phases up until the start of the ground campaign, as shown in Figure A.14.

The Coalition expended many more sorties than originally foreseen on counter-Scud missions. Figure A.15 depicts the number of sorties flown for each day of the war (including CAPs and sorties against mobile launchers as well as fixed facilities), along with the number of Scud launches.

As discussed in Chapter Six, controversy has surrounded the assessment of the damage to Iraqi forces inflicted by Coalition air power prior to G-day. Table A.11 presents the ARCENT estimates of each Iraqi unit's strengths and losses as of 23 February, the eve of the ground war. Table A.12 shows cumulative losses up through the end of the ground war. Both tables show the effects of ARCENT methodological revisions.

Although the Iraqi air force appeared large and potentially formidable prior to the war, it launched few defensive (and fewer offensive) sorties against Coalition aircraft, and eventually many pilots fled with their aircraft to Iranian territory, as described in Chapter Six. Figures A.16 and A.17 show Iraqi flight activity and flights to Iran. Table A.13 summarizes Iraqi air force losses.

Finally, the Coalition also suffered losses. Table A.14 shows combat aircraft losses by service.

Table A.4

Target Categories and Numbers

Category	CENTAF MTL	RAND Expanded MTL	Critical Targets
Airfields	50	64	31
Breach: fire trenches and minefields	6	34	0
Nuclear, biological, chemical	29	43	38
Command, control, communications	153	202	12
Electric power	26	39	0
Leadership	43	48	26
Military support, production, and storage	95	150	34
Naval	19	36	0
Oil	28	49	0
Republican Guard	35	105	0
Railroads and bridges	93	131	33
Strategic air defenses	78	115	24
SAMs	44	128	0
Scud sites and SRBM support facilities	58	78	43
Total	757	1,222	205

SOURCE: RAND working paper by Parker and Emerson, pp. 8, 9–10.

Table A.5

Desert Storm Scheduled, Tasked, and Flown Counterair, SEAD, Attack, and Electronic Combat Sorties by Aircraft Type

Component	Aircraft	Scheduled	Tasked	Flown
CENTAF	A-10	6,818	9,002	7,835
	B-52	1,686	1,746	1,624
	F-4G	2,395	2,558	2,287
	F-15C	4,448	5,410	4,480
	F-16	11,498	12,089	10,938
	F-111F	2,400	2,768	2,411
	F-117	1,397	1,464	1,297
	EF-111	882	962	882
JTF Proven Force	F-4G	429		414
	F-15C	944		890
	F-16C/WW	1,711		1,677
	F-111E	489		449
	EF-111	273		251
USN	A-6	2,703	2,969	
	A-7	705	797	
	EA-6	1,080	1,327	740
	F-14	3,784	4,128	
	F/A-18	3,163	3,574	
	S-3	156	167	106
USMC	A-6	844	1,004	790
	AV-8B	3,697	4,492	3,086
	EA-6	589	674	502
	F/A-18	5,530	6,853	4,320

SOURCE: RAND working paper by Parker and Emerson, pp. 19–26, based on 507th TACW sortie recaps, JTF Proven Force situation reports, and CNA data.

NOTE: Blank cells indicate unavailable data. "Scheduled": in ATO as published (not including changes, add-ons, and ground alerts). "Tasked": includes ground and airborne alert and ATO add-ons.

Table A.6

Scheduled Sorties by Mission and Service

Mission	CENTAF	JTF-PF	USMC	USN	Foreign	Total
OCA	2,946	829	808	1,796	1,722	8,101
DCA	2,782	318	0	2,491	4,245	9,836
SEAD	2,395	896	949	522	156	4,918
CAS	1,361	0	3,792	0	0	5,153
Interdiction	23,263	1,592	4,738	5,878	5,641	41,112
Tactical reconnaissance	580	131	0	660	235	1,606
Electronic combat	860	260	354	1,121	0	2,595
FAC, SAR, etc.	1,083	4	1,134	0	258	2,479
AEW	293	84	0	1,062	84	1,523
EC-130	427	97	114	0	15	653
Strategic reconnaissance	453	47	0	178	153	831
Aerial refueling	10,775	574	478	2,178	1,705	15,710
Tactical airlift	14,660	0	2	0	4,637	19,299
Training, etc.	167	0	16	2,823	309	3,315
Total	62,045	4,832	12,385	18,709	19,160	117,131

SOURCE: RAND working paper by Parker and Emerson, p. 15, based on 507th TACW cumulative sortie recaps.

NOTES: (1) OCA: offensive counterair (includes fighter escorts and CAPs as well as attack sorties); DCA: defensive counterair (includes fighter sorties over friendly territory); SEAD: suppression of enemy air defenses (sorties against fixed air-defense targets such as radars, IOCs, SAM sites included in interdiction category); CAS: close air support; FAC: forward air control; SAR: search and rescue; AEW: AWACS and USN E-2s.

(2) Air Force officers point out that DCA figures include defensive CAP flown by aircraft from all services. Their point is that the preponderance of Navy DCA was fleet defense. For a Navy rebuttal, see Perrin (1992).

Table A.7

Sorties Flown by Mission and Service

Mission	CENTAF	JTF-PF	USMC	USN	Foreign	Total
OCA	2,999	751	729	1,671	1,463	7,613
DCA	2,916	297	0	2,446	4,349	10,008
SEAD	2,287	778	708	460	66	4,299
CAS	1,461	0	2,932	0	0	4,393
Interdiction	23,282	1,353	4,029	5,582	4,650	38,896
Tactical reconnaissance	723	111	0	655	345	1,834
Electronic combat	859	222	330	1,049	0	2,460
FAC, SAR, etc.	1,329	4	1,063	0	259	2,655
AEW	299	78	0	1,035	85	1,497
EC-130	422	90	110	0	16	638
Strategic reconnaissance	431	42	0	174	150	797
Aerial refueling	13,971	0	7	0	4,477	18,455
Tactical airlift	10,257	500	453	2,093	1,586	15,159
Training, etc.	418	0	43	2,819	251	3,531
Total	61,924	4,226	10,404	17,984	17,697	112,235

SOURCE: RAND working paper by Parker and Emerson, p. 16, based on 507th TACW cumulative sortie recaps.

Table A.8

Navy and RAND Data on Sorties Flown by Mission

	Navy	RAND
OCA	7,544	7,613
DCA	10,793	10,008
Interdiction	38,703	38,896
CAS	4,363	4,393
SEAD	3,652	4,299
Refueling	13,421	15,159
Tactical lift	20,161	18,455
Other support	14,868	13,412
Total	113,505	112,235

Table A.9

Attack Sorties Planned and Flown by Air Campaign Goal

Goal	Sorties Planned	Sorties Flown
1. Isolate and incapacitate the Iraqi regime	1,630	1,245
2. Gain and maintain air supremacy	4,847	3,483
3. Destroy NBC capabilities	1,039	902
4. Eliminate Iraq's offensive military capability	7,678	6,288
5. Render the Iraqi army in the KTO ineffective	37,950	35,712
Total	53,144	47,630

NOTE: Includes 9,000 USMC sorties against ground forces and 500 A-10 sorties (in "Planned" column); does not include SEAD, escort, and CAP flights
(approximately 11,000 planned).

SOURCE: RAND working paper by Parker and Emerson, Tables 16–20 and
23, pp. 28–34.

Table A.10

Sorties Planned and Flown by Air Campaign Goal and Target Category

Air Campaign Objective	Target Categories	Sorties Planned	Sorties Flown
1. Isolate and incapacitate the Iraqi regime	Command, control, communications	1,049	601
	Leadership	340	429
	Electric power	241	215
2. Gain and maintain air supremacy	Strategic air defenses	847	436
	Airfields	3,690	3,047
3. Destroy NBC capabilities	NBC weapons and facilities	1,039	902
4. Eliminate Iraq's offensive military capability	Scuds and SRBM support	3,594	2,767
	Naval bases and forces	362	247
	Oil refining and production	574	518
	Other military support and production	3,538	2,756
5. Render the Iraqi army in the KTO ineffective	Republican Guards	6,987	5,646
	Other ground forces in KTO	28,401	29,354
	Railroads and bridges	1,168	712
Total		51,830	47,630

SOURCE: RAND working paper by Parker and Emerson, p. 34.

Table A.11

KTO Battle Damage Assessment as of 23 February

	Strength			Total Losses			Capital (percent)
	Tanks	APCs	Artillery	Tanks	APCs	Artillery	
ARCENT/NAC AO							
Theater echelon							
Medina	312	177	90	178	55	36	54
Hammurabi	312	177	90	98	14	23	77
Tawakalna	222	249	90	112	73	70	55
Nebuchanezzar	35	0	72	13	2	0	88
Alfaw	35	0	72	0	1	0	100
Adnan	72	0	35	24	0	0	83
Total	988	603	486	425	145	129	66
Operational echelon							
12th Armor	249	177	90	117	36	66	58
17th Armor	249	177	72	82	44	21	70
52nd Armor	249	177	72	136	61	5	59
10th Armor	249	177	72	77	62	59	60
6th Armor	249	177	72	149	116	59	35
53rd Armor Brigade	107	35	18	59	38	19	30
Total	1352	920	396	620	357	229	55
Tactical echelon							
48th Inf	35	0	46	24	17	17	49
25th Inf	35	0	36	11	2	31	41
28th Inf	35	0	72	31	9	71	5
27th Inf	35	0	72	45	18	57	14
26th Inf	35	0	72	14	3	18	70

Table A.11—continued

	Strength			Total Losses			Capital (percent)
	Tanks	APCs	Artillery	Tanks	APCs	Artillery	
31st Inf	35	0	72	13	5	50	41
47th Inf (Light)	140	70	204	53	17	129	52
45th Inf (Light)	37	11	36	17	4	11	62
49th Inf	36	0	72	7	0	0	94
20th Inf	35	0	72	26	1	45	34
16th Inf (Light)	70	70	72	73	45	45	25
36th Inf	35	35	72	46	17	40	35
30th Inf	35	0	72	29	20	90	6
21st Inf	35	0	90	57	3	53	30
Total	633	186	1,060	446	161	657	33
ARCENT/NAC Total	2,973	1,709	1,942	1,491	663	1,015	52
MARCENT AO							
Theater echelon							
51st Mech	177	249	72	5	17	12	93
2nd Inf	142	35	72	1	0	4	98
E Inf	35	35	72	0	0	0	100
D Inf	35	35	72	0	0	1	99
Operational echelon							
1st Mech	177	249	72	15	1	25	92
3rd Armor	249	177	72	37	23	6	87
19th Inf	142	35	72	1	0	8	96
11th Inf	70	107	72	0	0	0	100
15th Inf	35	35	72	4	0	0	97
42nd Inf	35	35	72	2	3	7	92

Table A.11—continued

Tactical echelon	Strength			Total Losses			Capital (percent)
	Tanks	APCs	Artillery	Tanks	APCs	Artillery	
29th Inf	142	35	144	17	9	59	74
8th Inf	142	35	144	30	24	64	63
5th Mech	177	249	72	32	145	42	56
80th Armor Brigade	107	35	18	0	0	6	96
C Inf (Revised)	0	0	0	0	0	0	0
14th Inf	142	35	72	21	35	62	53
18th Inf	142	35	144	24	4	36	80
7th Inf	107	35	144	92	24	127	15
MARCENT Total	19,49	1,416	1,314	281	285	459	78
KTO Total	4,922	3,125	3,256	1,772	948	1,474	63

SOURCE: RAND working paper by Fred Frostic.

Table A.12

Cumulative Iraqi Equipment Losses

	ARCENT				MARCENT				Theater			
	Tanks	APCs	Artillery	Capital (%)	Tanks	APCs	Artillery	Capital (%)	Tanks	APCs	Artillery	Capital (%)
Jan 17	0	0	0	100	0	0	0	100	0	0	0	100
18	9	0	31	99	0	0	0	100	9	0	31	100
19	14	0	47	99	0	2	23	99	14	2	70	99
20	14	0	47	99	0	0	23	100	14	0	70	99
21	14	0	53	99	0	0	23	100	14	0	76	99
22	14	0	53	99	0	2	21	100	14	2	74	99
23	17	6	122	98	0	5	27	99	17	11	149	98
24	26	13	155	97	0	5	31	99	26	18	186	98
25	26	15	157	97	0	5	48	99	26	20	205	98
26	24	20	165	97	0	8	56	99	24	28	221	98
27	63	69	240	94	15	9	65	98	78	78	305	96
28	63	69	240	94	15	9	65	98	78	78	305	96
29	0	0	5	100	1	0	13	100	1	0	18	100
30	189	154	264	91	20	13	42	98	209	167	306	94
31	271	179	281	89	30	13	42	98	301	192	323	93
Feb 1	390	224	293	86	106	33	86	95	496	257	379	90
2	406	225	294	86	136	75	101	93	542	300	395	89
3	475	289	310	84	150	80	107	93	625	369	417	87
4	515	309	344	82	151	80	115	93	666	389	459	87
5	551	359	376	80	0	0	0	100	717	525	522	84
6	598	384	397	79	169	166	151	90	767	550	548	83
7	602	392	407	79	172	167	170	89	774	559	577	83
8	637	421	443	77	78	205	184	90	715	626	627	82
9	718	471	507	74	82	214	184	90	800	685	691	81
10	776	484	551	72	83	208	208	89	859	692	759	79
11	922	531	696	67	99	222	215	89	1,021	753	911	76

Table A.12—continued

	ARCENT				MARCENT				Theater			
	Tanks	APCs	Artillery	Capital (%)	Tanks	APCs	Artillery	Capital (%)	Tanks	APCs	Artillery	Capital (%)
Feb 12	1,010	558	763	65	171	250	340	84	1,181	808	1,103	73
13	1,108	584	816	62	171	250	340	84	1,279	834	1,156	71
14	1,207	563	842	60	190	271	374	82	1,397	834	1,216	69
15	1,178	563	842	61	190	271	378	82	1,368	834	1,220	70
16	1,225	581	868	59	191	271	374	82	1,416	852	1,242	69
17	1,247	587	881	59	198	272	389	82	1,445	859	1,270	68
18	1,279	591	917	58	204	273	408	81	1,483	864	1,325	67
19	1,315	603	948	56	206	274	408	81	1,521	877	1,356	67
20	1,346	607	994	56	215	280	434	80	1,561	887	1,428	66
21	1,389	627	1,005	54	217	281	434	80	1,606	908	1,439	65
22	1,435	644	998	54	252	285	452	79	1,687	929	1,450	64
23	1,491	663	1,015	52	281	285	459	78	1,772	948	1,474	63
24	1,474	695	984	52	391	297	478	75	1,865	992	1,462	62
25	1,470	701	1,007	52	568	308	498	69	2,038	1,009	1,505	59
26	1,559	702	1,007	51	837	735	640	51	2,396	1,437	1,647	51
27	1,598	708	1,009	50	837	735	640	50	2,435	1,443	1,649	50

NOTE: As of the cease-fire at 0800 28 February, 40 of 43 divisions were judged "combat ineffective."
SOURCE: Provided by Lieutenant Colonel Richard B. H. Lewis, USAF.

Table A.13

Iraqi Air Force Attrition (first 30 days)

Air-to-Air		On Ground	
F-1	9	Blinder	1
MiG-29	6	Badger	6
MiG-25	2	Candid	3
MiG-23	9	Colt	1
MiG-21	4	SU-17/22	3
SU-17/22	3	SU-25	1
SU-25	2	MiG-23	1
Unidentified	1		
Subtotal	36	Subtotal	16

Total combat losses	52
Noncombat losses	6
Aircraft to Iran	122
Aircraft estimated destroyed in shelters	141
Total, all losses	221

SOURCE: *Seapower,* April 1991, p. 51.

Table A.14

Coalition Combat Aircraft Losses

Aircraft Type	Number Lost	Service/Country
Tornado	7	6 UK; 1 Italy
A-10	6	USAF
F-16C	5	USAF
AV-8B	5	USMC
A-6	4	USN
OV-10	2	USMC
F-15E	2	USAF
F/A-18	1	USN
F-5	1	Saudi Arabia
AC-130	1	USAF
A-4	1	Kuwait
F-4G	1	USAF
F-14	1	USN
EF-111	1	USAF
Total	38	

SOURCE: Background memorandum prepared for *CPGW* report.

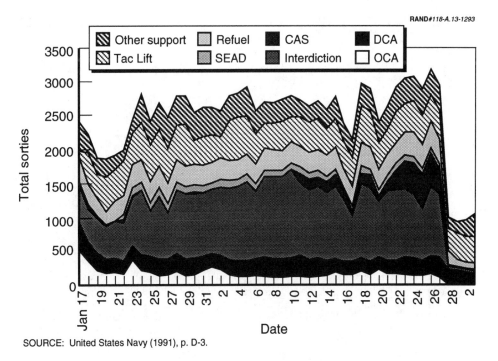

SOURCE: United States Navy (1991), p. D-3.

Figure A.13—Daily Sorties Flown

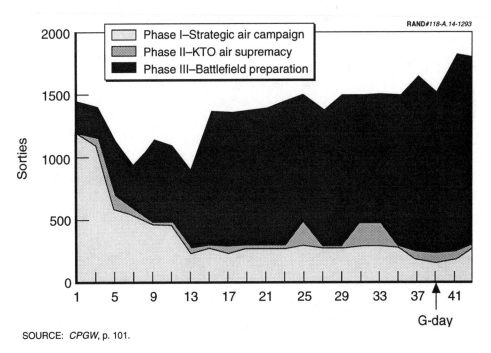

SOURCE: *CPGW*, p. 101.

Figure A.14—Sorties by Air Campaign Phase

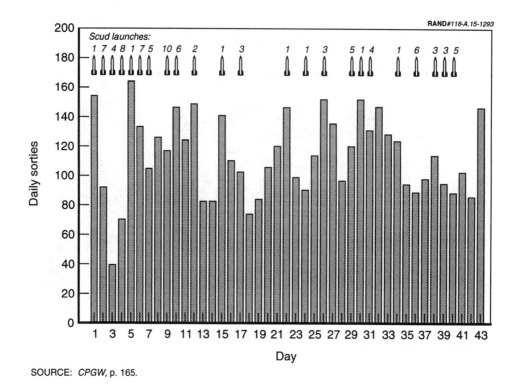

SOURCE: *CPGW*, p. 165.

Figure A.15—Dedicated Counter-Scud Sorties and Scud Launches

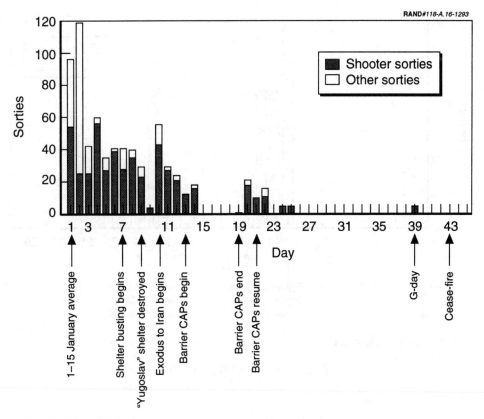

SOURCE: *CPGW*, p. 151.

Figure A.16—Iraqi Flight Activity

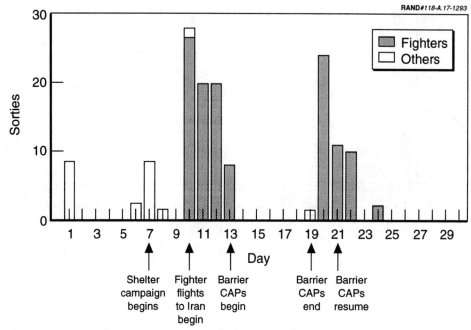

SOURCE: *Seapower,* April 1991, p. 48.

Figure A.17—Iraqi Flights to Iran

BOOKS AND REPORTS

Blackwell, James A., *Thunder in the Desert*, New York: Bantam, 1991.

Blackwell, James A., Michael J. Mazarr, and Don M. Snider, *The Gulf War: Military Lessons Learned*, Washington, D.C.: Center for Strategic and International Studies, July 1991.

Brauner, Marygail, Harry Thie, and Roger Brown, *Assessing the Structure and Mix of Future Active and Reserve Forces: Effectiveness of Total Force Policy During the Persian Gulf Conflict*, Santa Monica, California: RAND, MR-132-OSD, 1992.

Campen, Alan D. (ed.), *The First Information War*, Fairfax, Virginia: AFCEA International Press, October 1992.

Cardwell, Colonel Thomas, *Command Structure for Theater Warfare: The Quest for Unity of Command*, Maxwell AFB, Alabama: Air University Press, September 1984.

Center for Naval Analyses, *Desert Storm Reconstruction Report, Volume I: Summary* (U), Arlington, Virginia: CNA, October 1991.

Center for Naval Analyses, *Desert Storm Reconstruction Report, Volume II: Strike Warfare* (U), Arlington, Virginia: CNA, 1992.

Center for Naval Analyses, *Desert Storm Reconstruction Report, Volume IV: Third Marine Air Wing Operations* (U), Arlington, Virginia: CNA, 1992.

Center for Naval Analyses, *Desert Storm Reconstruction Report, Volume VIII: C³/Space and Electronic Warfare* (U), Arlington, Virginia: CNA, June 1992.

Chenoweth, Mary E., *The Civil Reserve Air Fleet and Operation Desert Shield/Desert Storm*, Santa Monica, California: RAND, MR-298-AF, 1993.

Coyne, James P., *Airpower in the Gulf*, Arlington, Virginia: Air Force Association, 1992a.

Davis, Paul K., and Lou Finch, *Defense Planning for the Post–Cold War Era: Giving Meaning to Flexibility, Adaptiveness, and Robustness of Capability,* Santa Monica, California: RAND, MR-322-JS, 1993.

Dennis, Everett, et al., *The Media at War: The Persian Gulf Conflict: The Press and the Persian Gulf Conflict. A Report of the Gannett Foundation,* New York: Columbia University Press, 1991.

Deputy Chief of Staff, Plans and Operations, *JFACC Primer,* Headquarters United States Air Force, August 1992.

Dunnigan, James F., and Austin Bay, *From Shield to Storm: High-Tech Weapons, Military Strategy, and Coalition Warfare in the Persian Gulf,* New York: William Morrow, 1992.

Fialka, John J., *Hotel Warriors: Covering the Gulf War,* Washington, D.C.: Woodrow Wilson Center Press, 1991.

Friedman, Norman, *Desert Victory: The War for Kuwait,* Annapolis, Maryland: The Naval Institute Press, 1991.

Hallion, Richard P., *Storm over Iraq: Air Power and the Gulf War,* Washington, D.C.: Smithsonian Institution Press, 1992.

Johnson, Dana J., Max Nelson, and Robert J. Lempert, *U.S. Space-Based Remote Sensing: Challenges and Prospects,* Santa Monica, California: RAND, N-3589-AF/A/OSD, 1993.

Kaufmann, William W., and John D. Steinbruner, *Decision for Defense: Prospects for a New Order,* Washington, D.C.:   The Brookings Institution, 1991.

Keaney, Thomas A., and Eliot A. Cohen, *Gulf War Air Power Survey Summary Report,* Washington, D.C.: U.S. Government Printing Office, 1993.

Lambeth, Benjamin S., *Desert Storm and Its Meaning: The View From Moscow,* Santa Monica, California: RAND, R-4164-AF, 1992.

Lewis, Lieutenant Colonel Richard B. H. (USAF), *Desert Storm—JFACC Problems Associated with Battlefield Preparation,* Carlisle Barracks, Pennsylvania: U.S. Army War College, 1993.

Lund, John, Ruth Berg, and Corinne Replogle, *Project AIR FORCE Analysis of the Air War in the Gulf: An Assessment of Strategic Airlift Operational Efficiency,* Santa Monica, California: RAND, R-4269/4-AF, 1993.

Mazarr, Michael J., Don M. Snider, and James A. Blackwell, *Desert Storm: The Gulf War and What We Learned,* Boulder, Colorado: Westview Press, 1993.

Momyer, William W., *Air Power in Three Wars,* Washington, D.C.:   Office of Air Force History, 1978.

Office of the Secretary of Defense (Program Analysis and Evaluation) (OSD (PA&E)), *Capabilities for Limited Contingencies in the Persian Gulf,* June 1979.

Pagonis, William G., with Jeffrey L. Cruikshank, *Moving Mountains: Lessons in Leadership and Logistics from the Gulf War,* Cambridge, Massachusetts: Harvard Business School Press, 1992.

Palmer, Michael A., *Guardians of the Gulf,* New York: The Free Press, 1992a.

———, *On Course to Desert Storm: The United States Navy and the Persian Gulf,* Washington, D.C.: Department of the Navy, Naval Historical Center, 1992b.

Perrin, David A., *A Comparison of Long-Range Bombers and Naval Forces,* Alexandria, Virginia: Center for Naval Analyses, December 1991.

———, *Reflections on the Gulf War: The August Nightmare that Could Happen Next Time,* Alexandria, Virginia: Center for Naval Analyses, May 1992.

Project AIR FORCE, Desert Shield Assessment Team, *Project AIR FORCE Assessment of Operation Desert Shield: Volume I, The Buildup of Combat Power,* Santa Monica, California: RAND, MR-356-AF, 1994.

Project AIR FORCE, Desert Shield Assessment Team, *Project AIR FORCE Assessment of Operation Desert Shield: Volume I, The Buildup of Combat Power* (U), Santa Monica, California: RAND, R-4147-AF, 1992.

Project AIR FORCE, Desert Shield Assessment Team, *Project AIR FORCE Assessment of Operation Desert Shield: Volume II, The Buildup of Combat Power—Technical Appendices* (U), Santa Monica, California: RAND, N-3427-AF, 1992.

Record, Jeffrey, *Hollow Victory: A Contrary View of the Gulf War,* Washington, D.C.: Brassey's, 1993.

Rost, Ronald F., John F. Addams, and John J. Nelson, *Sealift in Operation Desert Shield/Desert Storm: 7 August 1990 to 17 February 1991,* Alexandria, Virginia: Center for Naval Analyses, CRM 91-109, May 1991.

Schwarzkopf, H. Norman, with Peter Petre, *It Doesn't Take a Hero,* New York: Bantam, 1992.

Stewart, Brigadier General (P) John F. (USA), *Operation Desert Storm, The Military Intelligence Story: A View from the G-2 3rd U.S. Army,* April 1991.

Summers, Harry G., Jr, *On Strategy II: A Critical Analysis of the Gulf War,* New York: Dell Press, 1992.

United States Air Force, *Reaching Globally, Reaching Powerfully: The United States Air Force in The Gulf War,* Headquarters, United States Air Force, September 1991.

United States Congress, House Armed Services Committee, *Defense for a New Era: Lessons of the Persian Gulf War*, Washington, D.C.: U.S. Government Printing Office, 30 March 1992.

United States Congress, House Armed Services Committee, *Intelligence Successes and Failures in Operation Desert Shield/Desert Storm*, U.S. House of Representatives, 103rd Congress, 1st Session, August 1993.

United States Department of Defense, *Conduct of the Persian Gulf War; Final Report to Congress Pursuant to Title V of the Persian Gulf Conflict Supplemental Authorization and Personnel Benefits Act of 1991 (Public Law 102-25)*, Washington, D.C.: Department of Defense, April 1992.

United States Navy, Office of the Chief of Naval Operations, *The United States Navy in "Desert Shield," "Desert Storm,"* Headquarters, United States Navy, 15 May 1991.

U.S. News and World Report, *Triumph Without Victory: The Unreported History of the Persian Gulf War*, New York: Random House, 1992.

Warden, John A., *The Air Campaign: Planning for Combat*, Washington, D.C.: National Defense University Press, 1988.

Watson, Bruce W., et al., *Military Lessons of the Gulf War*, London: Greenhill Books, 1991.

Wilson, Andrew (ed.), *Interavia Space Directory 1991–1992*, Surrey, U.K.: Jane's Information Group, 1991.

Winnefeld, James A., and Dana J. Johnson, *Joint Air Operations: Pursuit of Unity in Command and Control, 1942–1991*, Annapolis: Naval Institute Press, 1993.

ARTICLES

Armstong, Douglas G., "The Gulf War's Patched Together Air Intelligence," U.S. Naval Institute *Proceedings*, November 1992.

Clodfelter, Mark, "Of Demons, Storms, and Thunder: A Preliminary Look at Vietnam's Impact on the Persian Gulf Air Campaign," *Airpower Journal*, Winter 1991.

Coyne, James P., "Plan of Attack," *Air Force Magazine*, April 1992b.

Drew, Colonel Dennis M. (USAF, ret.), "Desert Storm as Symbol," *Airpower Journal*, Fall 1992.

Duncan, Robert E., "Responsive Air Support," *Air Force Magazine*, February 1993.

Fulghum, David A., "Clashes with Iraq Continue after Week of Heavy Air Strikes," *Aviation Week & Space Technology,* January 25, 1993a.

——— , "Pentagon Criticizes Air Strike on Iraq," *Aviation Week & Space Technology,* January 25, 1993b.

Gelman, Barton, "Disputes Delay Gulf War History," *The Washington Post,* January 28, 1992.

Hoffman, Daniel M., "A Beltway Warrior Looks at Gulf War Intelligence," U.S. Naval Institute *Proceedings,* January 1993.

Horner, Lieutenant General Charles A. (USAF), "The Air Campaign," *Military Review,* September 1991.

Humphries, Lieutenant Colonel John G., "Operations Law and the Rules of Engagement in Operations Desert Shield and Desert Storm," *Airpower Journal,* Fall 1992.

Macedonia, Major Michael R., (USA), "Information Technology in Desert Storm," *Military Review,* October 1992.

Marchand, Amy D., "Logistics Heroes," *Air Force Magazine,* December 1992.

Mason, Air Vice Marshal R. A. (RAF), "The Air War in the Gulf," *Survival,* Vol. 33, No. 3, May/June 1991.

Mixson, Rear Admiral R. D., "Navy's Version of Carrier Contribution to Desert Shield/Desert Storm," *Armed Forces Journal International,* February 1992.

Muir, Commander Daniel J. (USN), "A View from the Black Hole," U.S. Naval Institute *Proceedings,* October 1991.

Owens, Mackubin Thomas, "Lessons of the Gulf War," *Strategic Review,* Winter 1992.

Palmer, Michael A., "The Storm in the Air: One Plan, Two Air Wars," *Air Power History,* Winter 1992c.

Record, Jeffrey, "Why the Air War Worked," *Armed Forces Journal International,* April 1991.

Ziemke, Caroline F., "Promises Fulfilled? The Prophets of Airpower and Desert Storm," paper presented before the Washington Strategy Seminar series on Airpower and the New Security Environment, January 1992.

BRIEFINGS

Lieutenant Colonel David A. Deptula, USAF, "The Air Campaign: Planning and Execution (rev. 2)," undated, 1991.

Lieutenant General Charles Horner, Briefing to Congress, 1991.

Lieutenant Colonel Rick Lewis, USAF, "Reflections on Desert Storm: The Air Campaign," undated, 1992.

General Merrill McPeak, USAF, "The Air Campaign: Part of the Combined Arms Operation," 15 March 1991.

Captain Steven U. Ramsdell, USN, "Memorandum: Trip Report," 14 May 1991.

INTERVIEWS[1]

Vice Admiral Stan Arthur, USN, Commander Seventh Fleet and COMUSNAV-CENT (after 1 November 1990), 30 November 1992.

Commander Roy Balaconis, USN, Joint Chiefs of Staff, 11 January 1993.

Captain Lyle Bien, USN, Senior NAVCENT representative to JFACC, 21 November 1991.

Colonel John Bioty, USMC, Commander, Marine Air Group 13, 3 September, 3 December 1991, and 2 July 1993.

Lieutenant General Walter Boomer, USMC, Commander I MEF and Commander USMARCENT, 18 November 1991.

Colonel Thomas Cardwell, USAF, HQ Air Force Studies and Analysis, 22 August 1991.

Colonel Robert Coffman, USAF, HQ Air Force, Warfighting Plans and Operations Directorate (Checkmate), 23 August 1991.

Lieutanant Colonel David Deptula, USAF, Chief Planner, CENTAF Special Planning Group (Operation Desert Shield) and Director, Strategic Target Planning Cell (Operation Desert Storm), 28 August 1991.

Lieutenant Colonel Edward Downham, USMC, Staff G-3, 3rd Marine Air Wing, 10 October 1991.

Major General Buster Glosson, Director, CENTAF Special Planning Group, 10 October 1991, 19 July 1993.

Dr. Richard Hallion, Staff Group, Secretary of the Air Force, 5 September 1991.

Colonel Peter Herrly, USA, Joint Doctrine Branch (J-7), Joint Staff, 21 August 1991.

---

[1]The position listed is that held during Operation Desert Shield/Desert Storm. The date of the interview is given at the end of the entry. A number of these interviews were conducted in the course of researching Winnefeld and Johnson (1993).

Lieutenant General Charles A. Horner, USAF, COMUSCENTAF, JFACC, and Commander Ninth Air Force, 26 November 1991.

Major Robert Knutzen, USMC, Operations Officer VMFA 314, 29 October 1991.

Rear Admiral Conrad Lautenbacher, USN, COMUSNAVCENT, Riyadh (after 1 November 1990), 19 September 1991.

Colonel John Lawrie USA, Lieutenant Colonel Paul Dordal, USAF, Captain Greg Johnson, USN, and Major Wilkes, USAF, Joint Operations Directorate (J-3), Joint Staff, 27 August 1991.

Rear Admiral John M. Luecke, Commander (USS *Eisenhower*) Air Wing (Desert Shield), 11 September 1991.

Rear Admiral Daniel March, USN, Commander Arabian Gulf Battle Force, 13 May 1993.

Vice Admiral H. H. Mauz, USN, Commander Seventh Fleet and COMUSNAV-CENT (prior to 1 November 1990), 9 September 1991.

Commander Donald W. McSwain, USN, JFACC Naval Liaison, 23 August 1991.

Rear Admiral Riley Mixson, USN, Commander Red Sea Battle Force, 12 December 1991.

Major Oley Olson, USMC, MARCENT representative to JFACC GAT Cell, 18 November 1991.

Major General J. W. Pearson III, USMC, MARCENT (Rear), 23 December 1991.

Colonel Joe Robben, USMC, MARCENT representative to JFACC, 17 and 30 October 1991.

Dr. Wayne Thompson, HQ AF/Checkmate, 22 August 1991.

Colonel John Warden, USAF, Director Checkmate, 8 October 1991.

James A. Winnefeld, a retired naval aviator, saw active service during the Korean and Vietnam conflicts and has participated in joint air operations in both war and peace. Subsequent to his naval service he was a senior staff member at RAND and directed numerous strategy and command-and-control studies. He and co-author Dana Johnson wrote *Joint Air Operations: Pursuit of Unity in Command and Control, 1942–1991*, published by the Naval Institute Press in 1993. He is now retired from RAND and lives in Annapolis, Maryland.

Preston Niblack is an associate social scientist in RAND's International Policy Department. Since joining RAND in 1986, he has conducted research on issues relating to nuclear weapons policy and international crisis management, and more recently on defense resource management in the post–Cold War drawdown. He was Executive Assistant to RAND's Vice President for Research during 1991. He is currently working on his Ph.D. in public policy at the University of Maryland, and lives in Washington, D.C.

Dana J. Johnson is a national security policy analyst with RAND in space policy issues. Prior to joining RAND in 1988, she was a policy analyst and member of the technical staff for several aerospace companies. She also spent five years at the Department of State as a diplomatic historian. A resident of Alexandria, Virginia, Dr. Johnson holds a Ph.D. in international relations from the University of Southern California.